W9-BHB-094

BRAXTON BRAGG AND CONFEDERATE DEFEAT
Volume I

Braxton Bragg

and Confederate Defeat

VOLUME I

GRADY McWHINEY

The University of Alabama Press

Tuscaloosa and London

Library of Congress Cataloging-in-Publication Data

McWhiney, Grady.
  Braxton Bragg and Confederate defeat / Grady McWhiney.
    p.   cm.
  Vol. 1: Reprint with new pref. and new maps. Originally published:
New York : Columbia University Press, 1969.
  Vol. 2: Judith Lee Hallock.
  Vol. 2 originally presented as thesis (doctoral)—State University
of New York at Stony Brook.
  Includes bibliographical references and indexes.
  ISBN 0-8173-0545-9 (alk. paper)
    1. Bragg, Braxton, 1817-1876.   2. Generals—Confederate States of
America—Biography.   3. Confederate States of America. Army—
Biography.   I. Hallock, Judith Lee, 1940-   . II. Title.
F467.1.B75M3 1991
973.7'13'092—dc20   91-3554
[B]

British Library Cataloguing-in-Publication Data available

To David Donald

CONTENTS

Preface   ix

Acknowledgments   xiii

I A Boy of Fine Parts   1

II Naturally Disputatious   26

III Distinguished for Attention to Minutiae   52

IV A Little More Grape   74

V A Rich Wife   101

VI Obey or Quit   120

VII Give Us All Disciplined Masters   141

VIII War Is Inevitable   157

IX The Highest Administrative Capacity   174

X Dictatorial Measures Are Necessary   204

XI It Is Our Own Fault   228

XII Round into Tennessee   253

XIII By Marching, not by Fighting   272

XIV Many Blame Gen. Bragg   293

XV Fight . . . and Fall Back   337

XVI Send Some One to Relieve Me   374

Selected Bibliography   393

Index   409

MAPS AND ILLUSTRATIONS

Campaigns of Northern Mexico   57
Battle of Monterey, September 19–24, 1846   66
Battle of Buena Vista, February 23, 1847   81
Bragg's Battery at Buena Vista   85
Mrs. Braxton Bragg   116
Braxton Bragg   152
Fort Pickens and Vicinity   158
Corinth, Mississippi, and Vicinity   209
Route of the Confederate Advance on Pittsburg Landing   220
Battle of Shiloh, April 6, 1862   230
Attack on a Confederate Battery, April 7, 1862   248
Bragg's Invasion of Kentucky   269
Roads from Bowling Green to Louisville   287
Location of Forces, October 3, 1862   304
Position of Forces at Perryville, 10 A.M., October 8, 1862   313
Battle of Perryville, October 8, 1862   315
Confederate Attack on Starkweather's Brigade   317
Battle of Murfreesboro, December 31, 1862   351
Confederate Attack on Beatty's Brigade   355
Battle of Murfreesboro, January 2, 1863   368

"Braxton Bragg was as baffling a mixture of high ability and sheer incompetence as the Confederacy could produce," wrote historian Bruce Catton. Other scholars have been even more critical. David H. Donald called Bragg "tense, punctilious, arrogant, a martinet and a dawdler." Clifford Dowdey considered him a "psychotic warrior," who "at the ultimate test of committing an army to battle . . . shrank from the decision." T. Harry Williams believed that Bragg "lacked the determination to carry through his purpose; he did not have the will to overcome the inertia of war." Douglas Southall Freeman, who censured Bragg for failing to win the loyalty of his officers and men, praised Robert E. Lee for "realizing that the volunteer leaders of a revolutionary force could not be given the stern, impersonal treatment that can be meted out to the professional soldier of an established government. How different," concluded Freeman, "might have been the fate of Bragg and perhaps the Confederacy if that officer had learned this lesson from Lee!"[1]

Some of Bragg's contemporaries were even more critical. "Bragg is not fit for a general," a soldier confided to his diary. "If Jeff Davis will just let Bragg alone, I think he will do us more damage than the enemy. . . ." A Georgian wrote: "Napoleon says the art of war consists in knowing how to separate to subsist, and how to unite to fight. The art of Bragg has been to unite to starve, and to separate to be whipped." In a popular canard an old lady

---

[1] Bruce Catton, *U. S. Grant and the American Military Tradition* (Boston, 1954), p. 92; David Donald, ed., *Divided We Fought: A Pictorial History of the War, 1861–1865* (New York, 1952), p. 229; Clifford Dowdey, *The Land They Fought For: The Story of the South as the Confederacy, 1832–65* (New York, 1955), pp. 227, 228; T. Harry Williams, "The Military Leadership of North and South," *Why the North Won the Civil War*, ed. David Donald (Baton Rouge, 1960), p. 34; Douglas Southall Freeman, *R. E. Lee: A Biography* (4 vols., New York, 1934), IV, 183.

said, "I wish General Bragg were dead and in heaven. I think it would be a God send to the Confederacy." "Why, my dear," said her friend, "if the General were near the gates of heaven, and invited in, at the critical moment he would 'fall back.'" An army surgeon's diagnosis: "General Bragg is either stark mad or utterly incompetent. He is ignorant of both the fundamental principles and details of his noble profession. He has lost the confidence of both his men and officers." Mary B. Chesnut, the Confederate diarist, said of Bragg: "I think a general worthless, whose sub-alterns quarrel with him. There is something wrong about the man. Good generals are adored by their soldiers; see Napoleon, Caesar, Stonewall, Lee!"[2]

Several of Bragg's subordinates were certain that something was wrong with their commander. One general swore he would never fight again under Bragg's command; another threatened to resign from the army and challenge Bragg to a duel. General Henry Heth contended that Bragg "lost his head" in the enemy's pres-ence. General Leonidas Polk claimed that after a battle Bragg "let down as usual and allowed the fruits of . . . victory to pass from him by the most criminal incapacity." General Simon B. Buckner told Jefferson Davis: "Mr. President, . . . frankly, General Bragg as a military man, as a commander is wanting in imagination. He cannot foresee what probably may occur. When he has formed his own opinion of what he proposes to do, no advice of all his officers put together can shake him; but when he meets the unexpected, it overwhelms him because he has not been able to foresee, and then he will lean upon the advice of a drummer boy."[3]

[2] Robert Patrick, *Reluctant Rebel: The Secret Diary of Robert Patrick, 1861–1865*, ed. F. Jay Taylor (Baton Rouge, 1959), pp. 80–81; *Richmond Whig*, November 13, 1863; Richmond *Sentinel*, November 10, 1863; Dr. D. W. Yandell to William Preston Johnston, November 8, 1862, Mrs. Mason Barret Collection of Albert Sidney and William Preston Johnston Papers, Tulane University; Mary Boykin Chesnut, *A Diary from Dixie*, ed. Ben Ames Williams (Boston, 1961), p. 316.

[3] Joseph E. Johnston to Jefferson Davis, February 3, 1863, Joseph E. Johnston Papers, Duke University; John B. Gordon, *Reminiscences of the Civil War* (New York, 1904), p. 193; Henry Heth, "Memoirs of Major General Henry Heth,

No one doubted Bragg's ability when the Civil War began. Mexican War hero, retired army lieutenant colonel, Bragg was one of the most distinguished soldiers to join the Confederacy, and for a time one of the most impressive. He rose quickly from brigadier to full general, and in 1862 a congressman informed him: "no General in the army has more of public confidence and admiration. Your praise is on the lips of every man. Mr [Secretary of War Judah P.] Benjamin told me that you were 'the greatest General we had.' President Davis said to me that 'you [were] . . . the only General who had accomplished all you undertook.'"[4]

Bragg, who was neither as outstanding nor as incompetent as scholars and contemporaries suggest, held positions of high responsibility throughout the war. Not an overwhelming success as commander of the Confederacy's principal western army, Bragg nevertheless directed the Army of Tennessee longer than any other general—from June 27, 1862, to November 30, 1863—and after being relieved of army command, he served as President Davis's military adviser. Of all the Confederacy's generals only Robert E. Lee exercised more authority over such an extended period as Bragg.

This volume, which ends at a critical juncture for Bragg and the Confederacy in the spring of 1863, was written more than twenty years ago. In it I emphasize how and why Bragg, as an army commander, contributed to Confederate defeat. My purpose was neither to defend nor to denigrate the man himself, but to untangle many of the exaggerated opinions about him, to present him as his contemporaries saw him and as he saw himself, and to analyze his successes and failures.

The second volume, completing Bragg's life, remained undone

C.S.A.," (typescript) Heth-Seldon Papers, University of Virginia; Leonidas Polk to Jefferson Davis, October 6, 1863, Leonidas Polk Papers, Library of Congress; Arndt M. Stickles, *Simon Bolivar Buckner, Borderland Knight* (Chapel Hill, 1940), p. 236.
   [4] James L. Pugh to Bragg, March 16, 1862, William P. Palmer Collection of Braxton Bragg Papers, Western Reserve Historical Society, Cleveland.

until Judith Lee Hallock took it in hand. I had collected extensive notes, but had written nothing on Bragg since the publication of Volume I in 1969. A few years ago Ms. Hallock, then a graduate student at the State University of New York, Stony Brook, asked my permission to complete Volume II of Bragg as her doctoral dissertation. Delighted, I offered her my notes and my encouragement. I read and commented on the draft chapters, at her request, and I had the pleasure of serving as outside examiner on her dissertation defense. In my opinion, her volume on Bragg is outstanding. It is a pleasure at last to see Volume II finished and Bragg's career completed with so much skill and understanding. I am honored that The University of Alabama Press has reissued Volume I to appear jointly with Judith Lee Hallock's volume.

Forth Worth, Texas, 1991   Grady McWhiney

Many people have helped me with this book. My greatest debt is to David Donald, under whose direction this study was begun some years ago as a doctoral dissertation at Columbia University. His criticism and suggestions as well as his concern and friendship far exceeded what I had any right to expect from even the most conscientious mentor.

Over the years other friends have also given me much aid and encouragement. I am especially grateful to Ari and Olive Hoogenboom, Robert C. Walton, June I. Gow, Charles P. Roland, and Thomas Robson Hay. They read drafts of chapters, directed me to new material, and discussed various problems with me. Parts of this volume were also read by Cody Bernard, Robert D. Cross, Don E. Fehrenbacher, John A. Garraty, Bernard Gronert, John T. Hubbell, Anne Knauerhase, Richard W. Leopold, William E. Leuchtenberg, Robert V. Remini, James I. Robertson, Jr., George T. Romani, Herbert H. Rowen, Lacey Baldwin Smith, John W. Stevenson, W. Patrick Strauss, John Tricamo, and Robert Wiebe. I have gained much from their suggestions and warnings. For sending me valuable material, I am obligated to Richard A. Andrews, Allan C. Ashcraft, Edwin C. Bearss, Richard Beringer, Charles W. F. Bishop, Thomas L. Connelly, Charles L. Dufour, E. B. Long, Jay Luvaas, R. Gerald McMurtry, Bruce Nims, Thomas K. Potter, Jr., Robert L. Reid, William Skelton, Irwin Unger, Kenneth Urquhart, and Bell I. Wiley.

The staffs of the libraries and archives I visited were uniformly courteous and often directed me to sources that I would otherwise have missed. I am particularly indebted to Vernon L. Bedsole, of Louisiana State University; Charlotte Capers, of the Mississippi

Department of Archives; Suzanne Dodson, of the University of British Columbia; Sidney Forman, of the United States Military Academy; Sarah Gray, of Duke University; Robert M. Hamilton, of the University of British Columbia; Milton Kaplan, of the Library of Congress; Georgia MaCrae, of the University of British Columbia; Virginia M. Ott, of Louisiana State University; James W. Patton, of the University of North Carolina; Mattie Russell, of Duke University; Dorothy Shields, of the University of British Columbia; Clement M. Silvestro, of the Chicago Historical Society; and Alene Lowe White, of the Western Reserve Historical Society.

I owe a special acknowledgment to Sue B. McWhiney, my wife and unpaid research assistant, who has contributed incalculably to this volume.

Funds needed for travel, research, and preparation of the manuscript were generously provided by a fellowship and a summer grant from the Southern Fellowships Fund and by summer grants from Northwestern University and the University of British Columbia.

I further acknowledge the kind permission of The Huntington Library, San Marino, California, to quote from the Braxton Bragg, James W. Eldridge, Benjamin S. Ewell, Mansfield Lovell, and Joseph E. Johnston Papers, and to the following publishers to quote from copyrighted materials: to Dodd, Mead & Company, for quotations from *The Diary of Philip Hone*, edited by Allan Nevins; to Doubleday & Company, for quotations from Bruce Catton's *Terrible Swift Sword;* and to Harcourt, Brace & World, for quotations from Carl Sandburg's *The Lincoln Collector.*

Finally, it should be understood that the people whose aid I have acknowledged do not necessarily endorse my finished product, and that I alone am responsible for any errors of fact or interpretation in this book.

G. McW.

BRAXTON BRAGG AND CONFEDERATE DEFEAT

CHAPTER I

A boy of fine parts

1817–1837

IT IS IMPOSSIBLE to describe fully the first twenty years of Braxton Bragg's life—a paucity of sources and the questionable accuracy of others obscures too much—but a fairly detailed outline can be sketched. Two powerful environments influenced Braxton during this formative period: Warrenton, North Carolina, where he was born and spent his first sixteen years, and the United States Military Academy at West Point, New York, where he grew to manhood and studied the art of war.

The Warrenton of Braxton's youth was a pretentious town near the Virginia border with handsome mansions, a race track, nearby resorts, several schools, and a newspaper. Slaves constituted over half the population in this affluent tobacco-growing area of sharp social distinctions, where citizens of wealth and prominence often disdained their humbler neighbors. At one public ball several ladies refused to dance with a butcher's son because he belonged to a lower class.[1]

Socially the Braggs were lesser folk. One story contends that Braxton was born in jail. "Unhappy man, unhappy in his birth," wrote a North Carolina lady, "for he . . . was born in

[1] Guion Griffis Johnson, *Ante-Bellum North Carolina: A Social History* (Chapel Hill, 1937), pp. 63, 157, 182, 188, 247, 289, 306, 307, 425; Lizzie Wilson Montgomery, *Sketches of Old Warrenton, North Carolina* (Raleigh, 1924), pp. 146, 428–29; Stanley L. Falk, "The Warrenton Female Academy of Jacob Mordecai, 1809–1818," *North Carolina Historical Review*, XXXV (1958), 281–98; Rachel Mordecai to Samuel Mordecai, September 24, 1810, Pattie Mordecai Collection, North Carolina State Department of Archives and History, Raleigh.

jail where his mother was imprisoned on a charge of murder and the murder too of a negro. . . ." Another account claims Margaret Crosland Bragg, while pregnant with Braxton, killed a free Negro for impertinence, but never stood trial for murder. She was released from jail in time for Braxton to be born at home on March 21, 1817.[2]

Contrary to what this murder allegation might suggest, the evidence indicates that the Braggs and the Croslands were law-abiding people. One of Margaret's relatives, J. H. Crosland, designed and engraved the first Confederate ten-dollar bill, which featured the artillery battery Braxton commanded during the Mexican War. Braxton's father, Thomas Bragg, had moved from the coast to Warrenton about 1800. A carpenter when he married Margaret on December 20, 1803, Thomas eventually became a moderately successful contractor. He constructed many of the buildings in the county, including some at Jacob Mordecai's famous girls' school, and shortly before Braxton's birth Thomas built one of Warrenton's churches. After a time he also completed a two-story brick home for his family of twelve children, and acquired nearly twenty slaves. In 1832 Senator Willie P. Mangum described Thomas as "a respectable old man" who had "made himself comfortable, brought up a large & very respectable, as well as talented family." [3]

[2] Diary of Mrs. Katharine Ann Devereux Edmondston, February 28, 1864, North Carolina State Department of Archives and History; Margaret Newbold Thorp, "A 'Yankee Teacher' in North Carolina," Richard L. Morton, ed., *North Carolina Historical Review*, XXX (1953), 564–65. The date of Braxton's birth is given by his father in a letter to James Barbour, January 2, 1828, Application Papers of West Point Cadets, 1814–1866, Adjutant General's Office, Old Army Section, War Records Branch, National Archives.

[3] *Confederate Veteran*, XXI (1913), 578; Warren County Marriage Bonds, North Carolina State Department of Archives and History; Montgomery, *Sketches*, pp. 134–35, 271–72; Manly Wade Wellman, *The County of Warren, North Carolina, 1586–1917* (Chapel Hill, 1959),

But Warrenton society never let the Braggs forget their humble origins, and this unquestionably affected Braxton— perhaps more than he realized. He never mentioned his mother in any of the thousands of letters he wrote, though he later spoke fondly of his father. After Braxton reached manhood "he got quite excited" when he spoke of the duties and responsibilities of a mother. Consciously or subconsciously he may have been ashamed of his mother's jail record. He knew too that some of his Warrenton neighbors considered "the Braggs . . . plebeians, as unfit associates for them." In 1848 Congressman David Outlaw wrote his wife: "It will be awful if the people of Warrenton should fail to make proper preparations to receive properly Col. Bragg, who I am certain must in his heart despise those who were formerly disposed to sneer at his family. . . ." [4]

If Braxton hated his snobbish neighbors, he also admired their success, for Thomas Bragg taught his boys to be ambitious. He believed that prestige and success came only to those who made the best use of their opportunities; to reach a place of importance required both determination and ability. Thomas knew his sons needed a good education to overcome their family background. He enrolled Braxton at the age of seven in the Warrenton Male Academy, one of the state's best

---

p. 90; Thomas M. Owen, *History of Alabama and Dictionary of Alabama Biography* (4 vols., Chicago, 1921), III, 200; Pulaski Cowper, "Thomas Bragg [Jr.]," *Lives of Distinguished North Carolinians*, collected by W. J. Peele (Raleigh, 1898), pp. 306, 312; Fourth Census of the United States, 1820, Population Schedules, North Carolina, National Archives; Willie P. Mangum to Lewis Cass, July 28, 1832, Application Papers. According to Mangum, Thomas Bragg "began life as a mechanic."

[4] Elise Ellis to Sarah J. D. Butler, February 13, 1849, Thomas Butler and Family Papers, Butler Family Papers (F), Louisiana State University; David Outlaw to His Wife, August 1, 4, 1848, David Outlaw Papers, Southern Historical Collection, University of North Carolina, Chapel Hill.

schools. That same year Braxton's oldest brother, John, was graduated from the University of North Carolina, and Thomas Jr. was at Captain Partridge's Military Academy in Middleton, Connecticut. Both John and Thomas Jr. became prominent lawyers and politicians. John later moved to Mobile, Alabama, and served his adopted state as a congressman and judge; Thomas Jr. remained in North Carolina and became governor of the state and attorney general of the Confederacy. Little is known about Braxton's less distinguished brothers: Alexander, an architect; Dunbar, a Texas merchant; and William, the youngest, who was killed in the Civil War.[5]

School was never a problem for Braxton. At the Warrenton Male Academy, where he studied for nine years, his instructors considered him an excellent student. In 1828 a teacher described Braxton as "a youth of attentive habits & tractable & docile disposition." Either his disposition changed as he matured or his teacher erred, for in manhood pliancy was not one of Braxton's attributes. In 1832 the school principal stated that Braxton excelled in Latin and that his knowledge of mathematics was "more extensive than is usual with young men of his age."[6]

There is no indication that Braxton took more than a passing interest in the highly competitive games played in Warrenton. Sports like hunting, long bullets (similar to modern football), and fives (played somewhat like handball), stressed endurance and courage; a few years before Braxton's birth a Warrenton boy had died during a game of fives after fainting twice and refusing to quit because it might seem cowardly. Braxton never made recreation a habit, possibly because he was so ambitious and sports took time from serious pursuits. His only

[5] Montgomery, *Sketches*, p. 428; Owen, *History of Alabama*, III, 200; Cowper, "Thomas Bragg [Jr.]," p. 306.

[6] Statement of M. D. Donnellan, January 3, 1828, Application Papers; Thomas Vaiden to Lewis Cass, February ?, 1832, *ibid.*

physical pastime appears to have been the genteel yet practical
art of riding. A reporter later described him as "a superb
horseman." [7]

When Braxton was ten years old his father chose the boy's
career. Thomas Bragg decided to send Braxton to the United
States Military Academy at West Point. It must have seemed
an ideal place to Thomas, who had spent much on his older
boys' educations and no longer had enough money for Braxton's college fees. Tuition was free at West Point; moreover,
graduates automatically became officers in the United States
Army, a relatively secure if less than lucrative profession.
Later, if army life became tiresome, a West Point graduate
could resign his commission and obtain a good civilian job.
The upsurgent country needed all the engineers West Point
could train. To an ambitious old carpenter, the opportunity
for his boy to study engineering free and to become an officer
—a person of some social position—must have made the military academy irresistible. Thomas's preoccupation was how to
get Braxton an appointment.

No West Pointer could have improved upon Thomas
Bragg's strategy. He immediately sought the support of important North Carolina politicians and wrote directly to Secretary
of War James Barbour. For a time no one made Thomas any
promises, partly because Braxton was still too young to be a
cadet. But a few years later John Bragg, who had been elected
to the state legislature, cornered United States Senator Willie
P. Mangum and got his pledge of support. "I learn that Braxton is a boy of fine parts," Mangum wrote Secretary of War
Lewis Cass. "The energy, marked with so much delicacy &
modesty, with which Mr. Jno. Bragg pressed his brother's
wishes upon me last year as well as this winter; has given to
the subject . . . more than ordinary interest." Congressman

[7] Johnson, *Ante-Bellum North Carolina*, pp. 63, 157, 182, 188, 247, 289,
306, 307, 425; Montgomery, *Sketches*, pp. 146, 428–29; Richmond *Daily
Dispatch*, October 2, 1861.

M. T. Hawkins, Judge John Hall of the North Carolina Supreme Court, and former Congressman Daniel Turner also supported Braxton, but Mangum's assistance appears to have been decisive. Shortly after his sixteenth birthday Braxton learned that he had been appointed to the military academy, provided he could pass the entrance examination.[8]

The academy, despite its magnificent site, was neither architecturally nor academically impressive in 1833. The admission examination, about which Braxton may have had some apprehensions, turned out to be surprisingly easy. He had only to prove he was over four feet nine inches in height and free of disease or infirmity; to show he could read, write, and count; and to present letters attesting to his morality. Except during the summer, cadets were expected to study and sleep three or four to a twelve-foot square room, in two stone dormitories. Their beds were mattresses placed on the floor; later, after Braxton left West Point, cadets were issued bedsteads. Classes met in a two-story academic building and in the library. Other structures included a moldering mess hall, a chapel, a hotel, and the superintendent's house, occupied by Major R. E. De Russy. Just before Braxton arrived in the early summer, the Board of Visitors—distinguished men appointed by the Secretary of War to supervise final examinations—had reported the West Point buildings badly constructed and insufficient to accommodate the cadets. Furthermore, the curriculum was scanty and the library inadequate.[9]

[8] Cowper, "Thomas Bragg [Jr.]," p. 312; Thomas Bragg to James Barbour, January 2, 1828, Application Papers; M. T. Hawkins, John Hall, and Daniel Turner to Lewis Cass, March 7, 1832, *ibid.*; Willie P. Mangum to Cass, July 28, 1832, *ibid.*; John Bragg to Mangum, March 4, 1832, *The Papers of Willie Person Mangum*, Henry Thomas Shanks, ed. (5 vols., Raleigh, 1950–1956), I, 504–6; Braxton Bragg to Cass, March 24, 1833, Application Papers. Montgomery (*Sketches*, p. 429) says Braxton received his appointment from Congressman M. T. Hawkins. Perhaps so, but Mangum seems to have been primarily responsible.

[9] *Register of the Officers and Cadets of the U. S. Military Academy, 1833* (New York, 1833), pp. 30–34; *The Centennial of the United States*

The most onerous part of life at West Point, Braxton soon learned, was the severe discipline imposed upon the cadets. There were rules to cover everything. Violations meant demerits; two hundred of them in any one year meant dismissal from the academy. Cadets received demerits for such trivial offenses as the failure to roll a mattress a certain way or to arrange equipment in a prescribed manner. Cadets could be expelled if they insulted a sentinel, were absent at night, behaved improperly in church, possessed liquor, played cards or games of chance, or were connected in any way with a duel. Withal, cadets were forbidden to use tobacco, to cook in their rooms, to keep a horse or dog, to receive goods or money from home, or even to visit a latrine at night without permission from a sentry. "We are kept tremendously strict, I assure you," wrote a student. "I was visiting last Wednesday evening, and they arrested me for it, and did not release me until this evening, and in addition to that they obliged me to perform an extra tour of Sunday guard duty." [10]

Initiation into West Point life began at nearby Camp Rensselaer where Braxton and the other new cadets spent the summer learning to march, to handle weapons properly, to stand guard, and even to dance. "It is rather dry business dancing without ladies," complained a cadet. But the routine, less rigorous than it would be during the winter, gave the newcomers a chance to adjust. "Since we have been in Camp," wrote one of Braxton's contemporaries, "we have had a very

Military Academy at West Point . . . 1802–1902 (2 vols., Washington, 1904), II, 94; Sidney Forman, *West Point: A History of the United States Military Academy* (New York, 1950), pp. 59, 91–92; *Regulations of the U. S. Military Academy, at West Point* (New York, 1832), pp. 7, 25; Asbury Dickins and John W. Forney, eds., *American State Papers* (38 vols., Washington, 1832–1861), *Military Affairs*, VII, 1–108.

[10] *Regulations*, pp. 7, 28–40; Forman, *West Point*, p. 92; *Official Register of the Officers and Cadets of the U. S. Military Academy . . . 1834* (New York, 1834), p. 16; Hazard Stevens, *The Life of Isaac Ingalls Stevens* (2 vols., Boston, 1900), I, 30.

easy time—nothing to do but go on guard two or three times per week, attend roll-calls and Dress Parades." [11]

On Independence Day the entire cadet corps paraded for General Winfield Scott, the honored guest, and then enjoyed a banquet. "A great many elegant toasts were drank," reported a cadet. "We had claret and champagne but not a drop of it touched my lips, and may God grant that it never will." [12] Braxton probably drank some, though later he became somewhat prudish about liquor.

By August the new boys had begun to look and act much more like soldiers. "We have been in camp 74 days and I can say with truth that I never enjoyed better health in my life and never was so strong and vigorous," admitted one lad. "All the cadets enjoy first rate health and are very strong and active. We can endure now with the greatest of ease what once would have seemed an intolerable hardship." Three hours of drill, a dress parade, and eight roll calls every day, plus guard duty and camp policing twice a week had toughened them. "We are obliged to scrub considerably in order to keep our things . . . bright, as great attention is paid to neatness," explained a cadet. "At dress parade we are obliged to have on clean pantaloons, clean shoes, belts, etc. and have our guns, plates, scales etc. in good order; we then go through the manual and are obliged to be very careful." Most cadets hated guard—two hours on and four off duty alternately for twenty-four hours—because guards rarely slept even during their rest periods. Years after Braxton left West Point, a cadet explained why: "We all sleep on the ground in front of the guard tents

[11] Order No. 66, June 16, 1833, Post Orders (1833–1837), United States Military Academy Archives; *Regulations*, pp. 13–14; Stevens, *Life of Isaac Stevens*, I, 36–38; Forman, *West Point*, p. 95; Isaac I. Stevens to William Stevens, July 6, 1836, Isaac Ingalls Stevens Papers, University of Washington (microfilm copy, University of British Columbia).

[12] Order No. 80, July 4, 1833, Post Orders; William Fraser to His Brother, July 9, 1833, William Fraser Papers, United States Military Academy.

wrapped up in our blankets with belts and cart[r]idge box on. I have been both times on the first relief which comes off at ten and goes on at two A.M. again, but during these four hours you are disturbed several times, once by the next relief and then the officer comes and turns out the guard and inspects us, to see if our gloves are on, coats buttoned, belts properly adjusted. You can see that there is not much rest to be had." [13]

By fall most of Braxton's eighty-four classmates, including future generals Joseph Hooker, John C. Pemberton, Jubal A. Early, John Sedgwick, William H. T. Walker, William W. Mackall, and St. John R. Liddell, probably would have admitted that summer camp had not been too bad. "We have got somewhat use[d] to military life and like it pretty well," acknowledged one cadet. "In fact the time passed in camp is our vacation and I really believe we see more pleasure and certainly much more benefit than if we were idling away our time at home." Boys from diverse backgrounds and sections of the country had learned to know and respect each other. A boy from Massachusetts boasted: "During the encampment we often went out foraging, as it is called, and got the Professor's apples. We also steal corn and roast it. Although we run some risk, yet some of the cadets generally went every night and there was no one found out. In the winter the cadets get bread, butter and sugar from the table and cook for themselves and make candy, etc. We are rather . . . wild, yet I do not believe there is a finer set of fellows on earth, and I never saw an assemblage of students, where there were less envy, rancour and animosity than there is here." [14]

Even so, some conflict occurred after the corps broke camp in September. The forced cultural exchange and close quarters

[13] Isaac I. Stevens to Aaron Cummings, Jr., August 30, 1835, Stevens Papers; Stephen E. Ambrose, ed., "West Point in the Fifties: The Letters of Henry A. du Pont," *Civil War History*, X (1964), 296–97.

[14] Isaac I. Stevens to Aaron Cummings, Jr., August 30, 1835, Stevens Papers.

of barracks life caused more than a few fights, and even one or two duels, despite regulations. "There have been two duels fought . . . since I have been here," wrote a boy in 1835. "In each case the combatants were westerners. If they had been found out they, together with their seconds, would have been dismissed." St. John R. Liddell of Mississippi, who would serve under Braxton in the 1860s, was expelled when he wounded another cadet in a duel. After Liddell left West Point a classmate wrote him: "Perry has nearly recovered (I believe), he *Limps* considerably yet from the wound which he received in his *seat of honor*. You will receive in a few days a letter signed by the whole corps save seven or eight *Damned Yankees* . . . commending your conduct &c." [15]

Braxton fought no duels, though a classmate remembered him as "a reckless and daring fellow, who was always ready for any sort of a racket." Tall and grim-visaged, Braxton "prided himself on being the ugliest man in the corps," and expressed "his opinions on all occasions and all subjects" in a most tactless manner. This was his way; he would always be outspoken, never able to conceal or moderate his views. As a consequence, some cadets thought him "uncouth, brusque and rude"; others, who could see more than his crusty veneer, considered him "a genial, generous, brave and clever companion." Joseph Hooker remembered Braxton as "bright and engaging," a cadet admired for his "manliness, independence and unbending integrity." [16]

During his first academic year Braxton had little time to roister. "We study hard, eat hearty, sleep sound, and play

[15] Stevens to His Father, December 20, 1835, *ibid.;* Ripley A. Arnold to St. John R. Liddell, February 19, March 2, 21, 1835, Moses, St. John R. Liddell and Family Papers, Louisiana State University. See also Moses Liddell to St. John R. Liddell, March 26, 1835, *ibid.*

[16] "Recollections of Cadet Life," *Army and Navy Journal*, XXXIX (June 14, 1902), 1027; *Eighth Annual Reunion of the Association of the Graduates of the United States Military Academy . . . 1877* (New York, 1877), p. 28.

little," wrote a cadet. "In camp every one was wide awake for a scrape, or for any kind of fun. But in barracks, we are as sober and steady as quakers. We go to the section room with long and serious faces, I assure you. We know that by study and severe application alone, we can keep our places." Braxton's class studied only mathematics, French, and the duties of a private soldier. The men awakened at dawn to attend roll call, then cleaned their rooms and weapons and studied mathematics until breakfast at seven. "We have meat every morning with bread and butter," explained a cadet. "I use no butter but always eat very heartily of the meat and I never was so strong and healthy in my life." Before their first class at eight, cadets had to attend guard mount and class parade. From eight until eleven they recited in mathematics class; Braxton attended a special section because of his high score on the mathematics orientation examination. From eleven until one all first-year men studied French. After dinner Braxton's class participated in supervised games until two, then recited in French until four. From four until sunset they were busy with military exercises and dress parade; fifteen minutes after supper they retired to their quarters to study mathematics until nine-thirty. At ten they went to bed. This inflexible program molded the study habits of even the most reluctant student.[17]

Instruction usually was by rote from foreign and American textbooks. Braxton's class studied Legendre's *Plain and Spherical (Analytical) Trigonometry;* Legendre's *Treatise on Geometry;* an English translation of Bourdon's *Algebra;* Professor Charles Davies's *Treatise on Descriptive Geometry; Histoire de Gil Blas;* and two books by West Point's First Teacher of French, Claudius Berard—*French Grammar* and *Leçons Françaises.* "The principle [sic] object of this [French]

[17] Isaac I. Stevens to Hannah P. Stevens, September 6, 1835, Stevens Papers; Stevens to Susan B. Stevens, February 23, 1836, *ibid.; Regulations,* p. 13, folded pages I and A; Order No. 119, October 2, 1833, Post Orders.

course," admitted the Board of Visitors in 1833, "is to enable the Cadets to consult the best French authors on Military Science." At every lesson, explained a cadet, "we get about half page of exercises and are obliged to get them so that we can write any sentence our Prof. gives us upon the black-board without referring to the books." A typical daily French lesson consisted of eight pages of translation. Cadet Isaac I. Stevens considered "Mr. Berard . . . a very good linguist and the most thorough teacher I ever was under. He is very particular about our pronunciation and corrects us very frequently. I think by June I shall be able to pronounce French pretty well and read it fluently. . . ."[18]

Braxton too made steady progress in his studies. When the year's final grades were posted in June, he ranked fifteenth in a class of eighty-five students. Out of a total of 242 students in all classes Braxton stood twenty-sixth in conduct. He had acquired just nine demerits. Only five new cadets had better conduct records, and two future Confederate generals had far worse: John C. Pemberton with seventy-two demerits and Jubal A. Early with 142. Both had been arrested during the year; Pemberton for throwing bread in the mess hall and Early for disobedience of orders at drill.[19]

If Braxton congratulated himself on his conduct he was premature. Arrested for negligence as a sentinel in the summer of 1834, he had to perform an extra tour of guard duty. In the fall

[18] *Regulations*, folded p. I; *Register of Officers and Cadets, 1833*, p. 27; Isaac I. Stevens to Susan B. Stevens, February 23, 1836, Stevens Papers. A somewhat biased Englishman wrote in 1833: "The cadets are confined to their halls of study for about ten hours per day! They seemed to be very well prepared with their exercises, but had a yellow, unhealthy look, stooped, some wore spectacles . . . it was really painful to see young men under such a rigorous system." Anon., "Notes on the Army of the United States," *Military and Naval Magazine of the United States,* I (1833), 104.

[19] *Official Register, 1834*, pp. 11-13, 17-19 (both conduct and grades were considered in determining class standing); Battalion Order No. 101, November 27, 1833, Post Orders; Battalion Order No. 19, March 19, 1834, *ibid.*

he began to take greater risks: he often made forbidden visits to Benny Haven's tavern, a traditional cadet rendezvous. Several times he and some friends were almost caught as they slipped back into barracks. If discovered, they probably would have been expelled.[20] This danger alone doubtless convinced them that their trips to Benny Haven's were worthwhile.

Although Braxton failed to receive promotion to cadet corporal, his escapades had no evident effect upon his second year's academic work. He remained one of the best mathematics and French students in his class, and he did equally well in his new subjects of drawing, artillery, and the duties of a corporal. At the end of the academic year he placed eleventh in his then diminished class of seventy-three. Only the twenty-four demerits he received for careless conduct prevented him from ranking even higher.[21]

Good grades and his brother's influence got Braxton a summer furlough in 1835. John Bragg, whose name was on Vice-President Martin Van Buren's list of the twenty-seven most important Democrats in North Carolina, was a member of West Point's Board of Visitors in 1835. Doubtless academy officials considered it appropriate for Cadet Bragg to accompany his brother to North Carolina after the spring examinations, but John's political influence was not the sole reason for Braxton's leave. Cadets with satisfactory records frequently got a furlough at the end of their second year at West Point.[22]

[20] Battalion Order No. 64, July 24, 1834, *ibid.;* "Recollections of Cadet Life," p. 1027. "As no watch is kept over the cadets at night," claimed an English visitor, "some leave their rooms and repair to haunts of dissipation among the hills, known only to themselves, where they meet women of loose character, eat pork and molasses, drink, and chew tobacco. . . ." "Notes on the Army of the United States," p. 104.
[21] *Regulations*, p. 13; *Official Register of the Officers and Cadets of the U. S. Military Academy . . . 1835* (New York, 1835), pp. 10-19. Twelve of Braxton's classmates failed the spring examinations and had to resign or repeat their second-year studies.
[22] Special Order No. 113, June 12, 1835, Post Orders; *Official Register, 1835,* p. 2; Elizabeth Gregory McPherson, ed., "Unpublished Letters from North Carolinians to Van Buren," *North Carolina Historical Re-*

Braxton, dressed in his gray uniform and highly polished leather cap with its eight-inch black plume, must have attracted attention even in sophisticated Warrenton. He may have paraded about just to show those who had snubbed the Braggs that yet another member of the family was on his way to a respectable position. He probably visited some of his former teachers at the Warrenton Male Academy, and surely he spent some time nearby in the law office of his brothers John and Thomas, who were partners. At least once Braxton may have forgotten that he was training to be an officer and a gentleman. An editor, Charles Plummer Green, one of John's political enemies, came to Warrenton during the summer to buy some clothes. John saw him; a fight started. A newspaper reported that John, "accompanied by his brother and several friends," attacked Green "with a bludgeon, bringing the editor to the floor." Green arose with a pistol in his hand; he wounded a bystander, and John knocked the editor down again. Green then drew a dirk, cut "one of his assailants through the throat," and stabbed another. "Green himself came out of the fight with severe cuts about the head and a fractured arm." [23] Though unnamed in the newspaper story, Braxton may have been present during the encounter; if so, he almost surely supported his brother. Any other action would have been inconsistent with Braxton's later behavior.

Perhaps his summer leave encouraged Braxton to be more reckless after he returned to West Point. Nothing unusual happened immediately. He probably enjoyed the fall ball, though it cost him and the other cadets $8.00 each. "The Corps," wrote a cadet, "sent invitations to a large number of gentlemen and ladies in all parts of the country; it [the ball]

view, XV (1938), 65n; Special Order No. 35 and No. 45, June 30 and August 10, 1834, Post Orders; Stevens, _Life of Isaac Stevens_, I, 36, 39.

[23] _Regulations_, pp. 23–24; Wellman, _The County of Warren_, p. 110; Raleigh _Star_, August 6, 1835, cited in Johnson, _Ante-Bellum North Carolina_, p. 790.

lasted until about 2 o'clock in the morning; the mess hall, 90 by 30 feet, was splendidly fitted up for the occasion and was crowded to excess. Our band consisting of 20 musicians were present and there were wines, cakes, ice creams, etc. in the greatest profusion. There were also rockets, fire balls etc. . . . and we had a fine time." [24] After classes began Braxton continued to do well in his studies: landscape and topographical drawing, natural philosophy (physics), chemistry, artillery, and the duties of a sergeant. But in March 1836 he and four other cadets—Marcellus C. M. Hammond, Francis Woodbridge, Alexander B. Dyer, and Robert T. Jones—were arrested and confined to quarters. They had been caught playing cards, a serious offense which could cause their dismissal from the academy. Braxton could only wait anxiously while others determined his fate.

At this point the corps intervened. Card games, though forbidden, were not unusual at West Point. Most cadets knew they were guilty of various rule violations and lucky to have escaped detection. To save their schoolmates from expulsion, the entire student body promised to abstain from cards if the Secretary of War would pardon Braxton and the others. The Secretary of War, impressed by this offer, allowed Braxton and his fellow players to return to duty.[25]

Their near dismissal may have taught Braxton and his friends a lesson. None of them got into any more serious trouble before they graduated. Braxton managed to keep his grades and class standing high, and at the end of the academic year he ranked seventh in his class in scholarship as well as in conduct.[26]

His good grades seem to have been based almost exclusively

[24] Isaac I. Stevens to Aaron Cummings, Jr., August 30, 1835, Stevens Papers.
[25] *Regulations*, p. 13 and folded p. I; Battalion Order No. 23 and No. 34, March 19 and April 3, 1836, Post Orders.
[26] *Official Register of the U. S. Military Academy . . . 1836* (New York, 1836), pp. 9–11, 21–24.

upon his ability to recite textbook assignments. He "acquired knowledge easily, and never forgot it," recalled a classmate. But there is no indication that Braxton ever looked at a book beyond what his instructors assigned. Not once in four years did he check out any of the library's 8,000 volumes. Though he could never be considered a scholar, Braxton later in life read some works on military subjects. Doubtless he also learned from his West Point contemporaries who did read books. Joseph Hooker liked biographies, but additionally he read Smith's *Wealth of Nations* and the *North American Review*. Jubal Early's interest was history; John Bratt's was philosophy. John Gunnison of Braxton's class, and P. G. T. Beauregard, one class behind Braxton, shared an interest in military campaigns: Gunnison read Napier's *War in the Peninsula;* Beauregard read *Campagnes de Bonaparte* and Beauchamp's *Champagne de 1814–15.*[27]

The summer and fall of his last year at West Point passed smoothly with Braxton perhaps unaware that he was learning lessons which would shape all his future military actions. He studied the duties of an orderly sergeant and a commissioned officer, advanced artillery, rhetoric, ethics, political science, and use of the sword, but none of these subjects influenced him as profoundly as Professor Dennis H. Mahan's course in civil and military engineering, which included instruction in the science of war. Mahan, who had studied warfare in France and admired Napoleon, was the primary molder of military theory in America from 1832 to the Civil War. He wrote six books; his first two were a treatise on field fortifications and a volume on civil engineering, which appeared while Braxton was at West Point. Mahan's most influential work—*An Ele-*

27 *Eighth Annual Reunion of the* . . . *Graduates of the* . . . *Military Academy,* p. 28; Circulation Records, 1831–1841, United States Military Academy Library. Future generals Jubal A. Early, Joseph Hooker, William J. Hardee, Henry W. Halleck, and P. G. T. Beauregard, all of whom were at West Point with Braxton, often checked books out of the library.

*mentary Treatise on Advanced-Guard, Out-Post, and Detach-
ment Service of Troops, and the Manner of Posting and Handling Them in Presence of an Enemy*—was first published in
1847. It was a summary of his lectures.[28]

A cadet recalled that Mahan's lectures "were restricted almost entirely to short descriptions of campaigns and battles
with criticisms upon the tactical positions involved," yet the
professor frequently gave professional and personal advice to
West Pointers. As early as 1834 he admonished them not to
think they had "sprung full fledged from a nest of Phoenixes."
They should act "like ordinary people, to court society in
general" because there they would "find the greatest amount
and variety of that floating capital—ideas common to the mass
—called common sense,—and because, the best of all maxims is
the anti exclusive maxim,—'Homo sum nil humani &c.' A for-
getfulness of this is the first and great fault of our graduates,"
insisted Mahan. "They think they must look wisdom, talk wisdom, and forget, that the essential is to think wisdom, and act
like your fellow mortals." On the other hand, a young officer
should not be too reserved; he must furnish himself "with
what Chesterfield calls small change, and let it rattle in his
pocket." Mahan advised students: first, "to keep always awake
when with others,—to accustom the eyes and ears to that sensibility, that neither the slightest whisper nor the quickest
glance shall ever escape them"; second, to study their profession, but "not to neglect the lighter accomplishments," for he
had "found that the man who talks well on subjects which are
generally understood receives credit for being properly con-
versant with the one which he pretends to have chiefly
studied"; and third, to frequent as much as possible "the society of those whose position has given them the best oppor-

[28] *Regulations*, p. 14; *Centennial of the Academy*, II, 94–95; *Official
Register of the U. S. Military Academy . . . 1837* (New York, 1837), pp.
3–4. For a sketch of Mahan and his influence upon American military
thought, see Russell F. Weigley, *Towards an American Army: Military
Thought from Washington to Marshall* (New York, 1962), pp. 38–53.

tunities for acquiring the world's best ways." Be perceptive, warned Mahan, "for a man, who would succeed in this world, must be able, after the third spoon full of his soup, to give a pretty accurate guess at the outward claims, at least, of every one at [his] table." [29]

Mahan's students listened most attentively when he preached two themes: the necessity of a professional army, and the superiority of offensive over defensive warfare. Amateurs had no place in a sound army, said Mahan: "An active, intelligent officer, with an imagination fertile in the expedients of his profession, will seldom be at a loss as to his best course when the occasion offers; to one without these qualities, opportunities present themselves in vain." [30] Only offensive-minded professionals with a broad knowledge of warfare could win future conflicts. Mahan taught his students that boldness in an officer was as essential as military skill. Fortifications might help exhaust an enemy, but they were useless if they encouraged passive defense. Forts should be springboards for assaults. "Carrying the war into the heart of the enemy's country," he insisted, "is the surest plan of making him share its burdens and foiling his plans." [31] Disciplined forces led by professionals should be aggressive. "If the main-body falters in its attack, or gives any sign of want of resolution," Mahan counseled, "the reserve should advance at once through the intervals, and make a vigorous charge with the bayonet." He favored "successive cavalry charges" to check infantry and

[29] *Centennial of the Academy*, I, 279; Dennis H. Mahan to "Dear Sir," April 5, 1834, David B. Harris Papers, Duke University.

[30] Dennis H. Mahan, *An Elementary Treatise on Advanced-Guard* . . . (New Orleans, 1861), p. 143. For a somewhat different interpretation of Mahan's theories of war, see Stephen E. Ambrose, *Duty, Honor, Country: A History of West Point* (Baltimore, 1966), pp. 99–102, and Edward Hagerman, "From Jomini to Dennis Hart Mahan: The Evolution of Trench Warfare and the American Civil War," *Civil War History*, XIII (1967), 197–220.

[31] Mahan, *An Elementary Treatise on Advanced-Guard* (New York, 1864), pp. 198–199, 202.

artillery, and advocated that artillery take an active role in assaults. Moreover, he was certain that a "charge by column, when the enemy is within fifty paces, will prove effective, if resolutely made." Mahan believed Napoleon had proved the advantages of offensive warfare. "To him," Mahan announced, "we owe those grand features of the art, by which an enemy is broken and utterly dispersed by one and the same blow." [32]

Yet Mahan, who always carried an umbrella, was too cautious to teach an unqualified offensive dogma. "Great prudence must be shown in advancing," he warned, "as the troops engaged are liable at any moment to an attack on their flank." [33] He also recognized the value of economy, mobility, security, information, and deception. He opposed the waste of either men or material. "*To do the greatest damage to our enemy with the least exposure to ourselves,*" he stressed, "is the military axiom lost sight of by ignorance to the true ends of victory." [34] Some positions were "more favorable to the defensive than the offensive," and he advised that "barricades should not be attacked in front, except for very grave reasons, as, if skilfully defended, they can only be carried at great cost of life." Security was so important that no less than a third of an army should be assigned to outpost duty. "Our purpose, in all cases," lectured Mahan, "should be to keep the enemy in a state of uncertainty as to our actual force and movements, and this can be effected only by keeping constantly between him and our main-body a force of sufficient strength to offer an obstinate resistance, if necessary, to every attempt he may openly make to gain information. . . ." Mahan considered the collecting and arranging of military information one of the most vital duties an officer could perform. "With clear and specific information before him, one-half of a general's difficul-

[32] *Ibid.* (New Orleans, 1861), pp. 13, 45, 11; *ibid.* (New York, 1864), p. 30.

[33] *Ibid.* (New Orleans, 1861), p. 43.

[34] *Ibid.* (New York, 1864), pp. 30–31.

ties in planning his measures, are dissipated," argued Mahan. But success depended upon how a commander used information. Mahan, who believed "every means should . . . be employed to deceive the enemy," contended that to "keep an enemy in ignorance of the state of our forces and the character of our position is one of the most indispensable duties of war. It is in this way that we oblige him to take every possible precaution in advancing; forcing him to feel his way step by step, and to avoid risking his own safety in hazarding those bold and rapid movements which, when made against a feeble or an unprepared enemy, lead to the most brilliant results." [35]

Mahan's students trimmed and oversimplified their master's lessons. Enamoured with professionalism and offensives, they ignored many of his warnings and qualifications and much of his discussion of other principles. Their commitment to professionalism and to the offensive doctrine soon became orthodoxy in the regular army, although both concepts were foreign to the American tradition of citizen soldiers and defensive strategy and tactics. Curiously, this quiet revolution in military thought went almost unnoticed outside the army. Only a few citizens complained that Mahan's "aristocratic and anti-republican" doctrines "utterly and forever excluded [amateur soldiers] from holding any office of honor, trust, or emolument in the [United States] military service." Without real protest from any quarter, Braxton and his contemporaries elevated the offensive to an inviolate canon of American military policy.[36]

They found, or believed they found, support for the offensive dogma in the works of Napoleon and Antoine Henri Jomini, besides Mahan the ante bellum West Pointer's most revered authorities on the art of war.[37] Napoleon had said: "It

[35] *Ibid.* (New Orleans, 1861), pp. 37, 112, 50, 74, 46, 49.

[36] John A. Logan, *The Volunteer Soldier of America* (Chicago, 1887), pp. 225–26; Weigley, *Towards an American Army*, pp. 64–67, 72–73, 75, 85, 95, 140, 194–95, 224.

[37] On the military concepts and influence of Napoleon and Jomini, see David Donald, *Lincoln Reconsidered: Essays on the Civil War Era* (New York, 1956), pp. 82–102; T. Harry Williams, "The Military

is axiomatic in the art of war that the side which remains behind its fortified lines is always defeated." Jomini was more cautious. He insisted a weaker army should adopt a "defensive-offensive" policy: a defensive attitude frequently modified by offensive feints and forays against the enemy. But when opponents are equal in strength he considered the offensive "almost always advantageous," because "the art of war consists in throwing the masses upon the decisive points, [and] to do this it will be necessary to take the initiative. The attacking party knows what he is doing and what he desires to do; he leads his masses to the point where he desires to strike. He who awaits the attack is everywhere anticipated; the enemy falls with large force upon fractions of his force." [38]

In books written before the Civil War, three of Mahan's students—William J. Hardee, West Point class of 1838, Henry W. Halleck, class of 1839, and George B. McClellan, class of 1846—emphasized the advantage of offensive over defensive operations.[39]

Braxton wrote no books, but he absorbed the dogma of

Leadership of North and South," *Why the North Won the Civil War*, Donald, ed., pp. 23–47; Bruce Catton, "The Generalship of Ulysses S. Grant," *Grant, Lee, Lincoln and the Radicals: Essays on Civil War Leadership*, Grady McWhiney, ed. (Evanston, 1964), pp. 3–30; Charles P. Roland, "The Generalship of Robert E. Lee," *ibid.*, pp. 31–69; Archer Jones, "Jomini and Napoleon as Civil War Mentors," paper read at the Thirty-first Annual Meeting of the Southern Historical Association, November 18, 1965; Crane Brinton, Gordon A. Craig and Felix Gilbert, "Jomini," *Makers of Modern Strategy: Military Thought from Machiavelli to Hitler*, Edward Meade Earle, ed. (Princeton, 1944), pp. 77–92; Michael Howard, "Jomini and the Classical Tradition in Military Thought," *The Theory and Practice of War: Essays Presented to Captain B. H. Liddell Hart*, Michael Howard, ed. (London, 1965), pp. 5–20.
[38] J. Christopher Herold, ed., *The Mind of Napoleon: A Selection from His Written and Spoken Words* (New York, 1955), p. 217; Antoine Henri Jomini, *Summary of the Art of War*, trans. G. H. Mendell and W. P. Craighill (Philadelphia, 1879), pp. 72–74.
[39] Weigley, *Towards an American Army*, pp. 55–78; Nathaniel Cheairs Hughes, Jr., *General William J. Hardee, Old Reliable* (Baton Rouge, 1965), pp. 41–50.

professionalism and the offensive. Some twenty-five years after he had sat in Mahan's class, Braxton explained how he intended to meet the enemy: "I shall promptly assail him in the open field with my whole available force, if he does not exceed me more than four to one." [40] Other Mahan students remained equally devoted to the offensive doctrine even after the test of battle. P. G. T. Beauregard, who graduated from West Point in 1838, insisted after the Civil War that the South's only hope of victory "lay in a short, quick war of decisive blows," an "enterprising offensive." [41] James Longstreet, class of 1842, wrote just before his bloody and unsuccessful attack upon Federal fortifications at Knoxville, Tennessee, in late 1863: "I am entirely convinced that our only safety is in making the assault upon the enemy's position." [42] Braxton's classmate William H. T. Walker complained in 1861 that "this sitting down and waiting to be whipped . . . is to me the most disgusting. If it be my fate to lose my life in the [Confederate] cause . . . in Heavens name let me die like a soldier with sword in hand boldly leading my men on a fair and open field." [43] In 1862 William T. Sherman, West Point class of 1840, announced: "Should any officer high or low . . . be ignorant of his tactics, regulations, or . . . of the principles of the Art of War (Mahan and Jomini), it would be a lasting disgrace." Though after the Civil War Sherman admitted that usually "whichever party attacked got the worst of it," he nevertheless argued that "intrenching certainly does have the effect of making new troops timid," and he warned that "the general must watch closely to see that his men do not neglect an opportunity to

[40] Bragg to Mansfield Lovell, January 8, 1862, Mansfield Lovell Collection, Henry E. Huntington Library.

[41] G. T. Beauregard, "The First Battle of Bull Run," *Battles and Leaders of the Civil War*, Robert U. Johnson and Clarence C. Buel, eds. (4 vols., New York, 1956), I, 221–22.

[42] James Longstreet to Lafayette McLaws, November 28, 1863, Lafayette McLaws Papers, Duke University.

[43] William H. T. Walker to His Wife, July 12, 1861, William Henry Talbot Walker Papers, Duke University.

drop . . . precautionary defenses, and act promptly on the 'offensive' at every chance." [44] Ulysses S. Grant, who sat through Mahan's lectures in 1843, never read any of Jomini's works, but he had some respect for Napoleon. "I never admired the character of the first Napoleon; but I recognize his great genius," Grant wrote after the Civil War. "The art of war is simple enough," claimed Grant, who favored a totally unsophisticated offensive doctrine. "Find out where your enemy is. Get at him as soon as you can. Strike at him as hard as you can and as often as you can, and keep moving on." [45]

This concept of offensive warfare had become fixed in the minds of Braxton and most of the men who would lead Civil War armies before they left West Point. By the end of January 1837 Braxton had learned enough from Mahan's lectures to rank fourth in the engineering and science of war class. In both ethics and artillery, he ranked eighth, but he still remained a cadet private.[46]

A month later, however, Braxton became a cadet captain. How he obtained this rank lessened some of the honor usually attached to it. Several cadet officers objected to the appointment of a sergeant and resigned their positions in protest. The Superintendent rejected their resignations, but he removed them from command and appointed new officers, among whom were Braxton and his friends Dyer and Jones. Braxton and Dyer became captains and Jones a lieutenant in Braxton's company. Jones declined promotion, however, and John Sedgwick received the appointment instead. John Pemberton also declined promotion; he had been appointed cadet captain despite his arrest a few months before for having a jug of whis-

---

[44] *OR*, XVII (pt. 2), 119; William T. Sherman, *Memoirs of General William T. Sherman* (2 vols. in one, Bloomington, 1957), II, 56, 396–97.

[45] Ulysses S. Grant, *Personal Memoirs of U. S. Grant* (2 vols., New York, 1885), II, 547; quoted in Williams, "The Military Leadership of North and South," p. 43.

[46] First Class Rolls According to Merit in Engineering, Ethics, and Artillery, January 14, 17 and 20, 1837, Post Orders.

key. Like Braxton, Pemberton had been saved from expulsion by the promise of the corps to forego liquor until after graduation.[47] Braxton probably enjoyed the prestige of his new rank, but the additional duties took time he might have devoted to academic subjects.

Even so, he was graduated near the top of his class. He ranked second in tactics, fifth in engineering and the science of war, sixth in ethics, and seventh in artillery. Ironically, only four of his classmates had better conduct records. He finished fifth in general merit, a rather impressive achievement for a boy who was never a committed scholar. Joseph Hooker recalled that Braxton had "developed in physical and intellectual strength and character" each year at West Point, and that his final class rank "was considered highly honorable . . . as his preparation had been limited, and he had won his standing on the academic rolls without having been considered a laborious student." [48]

His education, of course, was incomplete. "You are probably aware of the great defects in our course of study," a cadet wrote the year Braxton left West Point. "It is not calculated generally to strengthen and improve the mind as much as a four year course of study should. Some of the faculties are developed in a high degree whilst others are almost entirely neglected—its effect is, if the expression can be used, to cast the mind in a rough strong mould, without embellishing and polishing it in the least. Its effect is also (perhaps no more than any regular course of study) to confine our attention to particular pursuits and make us neglect all that general information which is so essential to a man of liberal education and in

[47] Order No. 19 and No. 23, February 7 and 14, 1837, Post Orders; Battalion Order No. 122, November 20, 1836, *ibid.*

[48] *Official Register of Officers and Cadets of the U.S. Military Academy . . . 1837* (New York, 1837), pp. 6–8, 21–24; First Class Rolls in General Merit, Engineering, Tactics, Ethics, and Artillery, June 8, 12 and 20, 1837, Post Orders; *Eighth Annual Reunion of the Graduates*, p. 28.

fact absolutely indispensable for anyone who engages in the active pursuits of life." [49]

Yet, if Braxton left West Point in June 1837 proud of himself, there was suitable cause. He had completed his military apprenticeship with distinction, and his classmates considered him "equal, if not superior, to any member of their class." [50] He could go home to await assignment confident that his superior officers adjudged him a young man of considerable promise. He had justified his father's ambition for him.

[49] Isaac I. Stevens to N. W. Harper, November 5, 1837, Stevens Papers.
[50] Order No. 75, June 14, 1837, Post Orders; *Eighth Annual Reunion of the Graduates*, p. 28.

CHAPTER II

Naturally disputatious

1837–1845

AMBITIOUS young officers always hoped for war. To them peace meant boredom and such slow promotion that they might remain lieutenants after twenty years' service. War, on the other hand, meant excitement and opportunity. There was some personal danger, of course, but with a bit of luck a man might live to win glory and promotion. He might, in fact, rise several grades in a few months if more than the usual number of field officers died in action.

As fate would have it, a war awaited Braxton Bragg. Appointed a second lieutenant in the Third Artillery in July 1837, he was ordered to Florida, where for nearly two years the army had been fighting Seminole Indians who refused to move west. The regiment, desperately short of men and officers, welcomed Bragg and eight other new second lieutenants, including Jubal A. Early and Alexander B. Dyer. "Many of the companies . . . are mere skeletons," complained an officer just before Bragg arrived. "Some of them will be without . . . officers, and will be reduced to from eight to fifteen men in . . . a few weeks." The Third Artillery had an authorized complement of forty-eight officers and 497 enlisted men, but the regiment actually consisted of twenty-six officers and 278 enlisted men. "I have now five companies under my command, and only three officers to take charge of them," wrote Lieutenant Colonel William Gates, acting commander of the Third Artillery. "Frequently, the quartermaster, commissary, and adjutant command two companies." [1]

[1] Bragg to Roger Jones, July 27, 1837, Letters Received, Adjutant

If Bragg expected army service to be pleasant he soon changed his mind. The Florida war was a guerilla action unlike anything his West Point training had prepared him for. He rarely saw a hostile Indian, and he won no military honors. His first assignments, as assistant commissary officer and later as regimental adjutant, taught him much about army routine, but nothing about combat.[2]

Soon he learned something significant and worrisome about himself: his body was weak and susceptible to disease. To Bragg the climate proved more dangerous than the Seminoles, for behind the bright proscenium of sun, blue ocean, and sand Florida was a murky land of insects and fevers. At times illness struck soldiers and civilians alike. "During the past winter and spring my family has suffered greatly from sickness," complained an officer in 1837, "and . . . they are still not restored to health, nor likely to be until a change of residence takes place." But knowledge that others ailed was no consolation to Bragg. By the spring of 1838 he was too sick to remain on duty, and was sent home to recover.[3] This was the first hint that he might not be physically strong enough for the demands of war.

General's Office, Old Army Section, War Records Branch, National Archives. Hereafter cited as Letters Received or Sent, AGO. In 1837 American forces in Florida consisted of ten companies of the Second Dragoons; the First, Second, Third, and Fourth Artillery (thirty-five companies); thirty-two regular infantry companies; and fifty-nine companies of volunteers—a total of 8,900 regular and volunteer troops. Dickins and Forney, eds., *American State Papers, Military Affairs*, VII, 125–465, 591, 596, 841, 847, 920, 933. On the Seminole campaigns see John T. Sprague, *The Origins, Progress, and Conclusion of the Florida War* . . . (New York, 1848), *passim*; James W. Silver, *Edmund Pendleton Gaines: Frontier General* (Baton Rouge, 1949), pp. 167–90.

[2] Bragg served as regimental adjutant from November 19, 1837, to March 8, 1838. Charles Kitchell Gardner, *A Dictionary of All Officers . . . in the Army* . . . (New York, 1860), p. 81; Colonel William H. Powell, *List of Officers of the Army* . . . (New York, 1900), p. 207.

[3] John M. Washington to Thomas S. Jesup, May 11, 1837, Zachary Taylor Papers, Library of Congress; Bragg to Jones, May 12, 1838, Letters Received, AGO.

Illness hampered Bragg all his life; it was as much a part of him as ambition, worry, dissatisfaction, and contentiousness. His various sicknesses, which became more pronounced as his responsibilities increased, seem to have been partly psychosomatic, for they frequently occurred when he was despondent or frustrated. Too ambitious to be satisfied with himself or with others, he sought perfection, and was disappointed when he failed to find or achieve it. Authoritarian himself, he neverthelesş resented his superiors' authority. Yet Bragg won and held the friendship and admiration of some of the army's best minds despite his cantankerousness. He represented an unusual combination of potentially dangerous eccentricities and high ability.

In 1838 he and others could put all the blame for his poor health on the Florida climate. While Bragg recuperated in Warrenton, he learned that his regiment had been ordered to escort some captured Indians to the West, and he wrote Adjutant General Roger Jones: ". . . my physician forbids my returning to Florida so soon tho' he thinks a trip to the mountains of the Cherokee might prove beneficial." Bragg made the westward journey, but by the end of the year he was back in Florida and once again became ill. This time he was given three months' leave.[4]

Besides his health problems, Bragg worried about his rank. He had been promoted to first lieutenant on July 7, 1838, two days after Congress authorized the addition of one company to each artillery regiment and a reduction in the number of second lieutenants in each company from two to one, but Bragg never received official notice of his promotion. He had seen his name listed as a first lieutenant in the *Official Army Register* of September 1838, but he wrote Secretary of War Joel R. Poinsett, "I have not been commissioned as such or

[4] Bragg to Jones, May 12, 1838, November 4, 1839, December 29, 1839, Letters Received, AGO; Special Order No. 150, Headquarters, Army of the South, November 20, 1839, *ibid.*

officially informed of it." Bragg even claimed to be uncertain about his commission as second lieutenant. "I was informed by you in July 1837," he lectured Poinsett, "that the President . . . had on the 1st of July appointed me a Second Lieutenant in the 3rd Regt Artillery, and if the Senate should advise and consent thereto, I should be commissioned accordingly; and as I have not yet received a commission I am led to suppose my appointment was rejected by the Senate. I have to request that I may be informed of the Senate's action if any has been had in my case." [5]

When his furlough expired in March 1840 Bragg went to Washington and convinced Adjutant General Jones he was still too sick for duty in Florida. Months later Jones wrote: "On my personal observation of the impaired state of your health, I thought it most proper to offer you temporary service at the north." [6]

Sent to Philadelphia to await assignment, Bragg grew impatient when neither orders nor answers to his letters came. "I am at present doing nothing here," he wrote Jones. "I therefore request that I . . . be assigned some duty as early as convenient." Despite his irritation, Jones must have admired such enthusiasm, for he ordered Bragg to recruiting service in New York City. [7]

Bragg spent the spring and summer as a recruiter. There is no record of how he liked the job or whether he performed it well, but he probably used the standard ploys of the period. Recruiters usually encouraged young men of good character to join the army by promising those who could pass the surgeon's inspection good quarters, an ample and wholesome diet, an abundant supply of clothing, and the best medical care. Prospective recruits were told that in a single enlistment of five years they could save from four to seven hundred dollars.

[5] Bragg to Joel R. Poinsett, May 30, 1839, ibid.
[6] Jones to Bragg, October 7, 1840 (copy), Letters Sent, AGO.
[7] Bragg to Jones, April 10, 1840, Letters Received, AGO.

Such promises convinced few native Americans, who generally held the regular army in low esteem; most of the recruits were immigrant Irish or other foreigners.[8]

More than most officers, Bragg lacked the successful recruiter's personality, and though he obviously preferred light duties, his wishes were ignored. In October 1840 he was ordered back to Florida, despite his request in September for an assignment more suitable to his "broken constitution." When Jones refused this request, Bragg started an acerbic exchange of letters with the adjutant general. Jones had promised him a more desirable station, Bragg insisted; if he had known Jones's true intentions he would "have applied for a leave of absence for my health and could have furnished . . . one, two, three or more surgeon's certificates of my inability to perform duty at all in Florida or here during the winter." Bragg also complained that Jones had treated him unfairly, and had denied him even the usual furlough given West Point graduates. At least, Bragg insisted, he should be allowed to go back to Florida by land. He had made "arrangements in regard to private business" which would cause him "great inconvenience and trouble and probably some loss" if forced to go by sea as ordered. Years later William T. Sherman claimed that Bragg based his request to return to Florida by land on his father's illness, but no such letter has been found in the adjutant general's files.[9]

8 [George Ballentine], *Autobiography of an English Soldier in the United States Army* . . . (New York, 1854), pp. 13–14, 18, 22, 25, 34–35, 39. Conditions in the army were not as recruiters described them. Rations mainly consisted of bread and salt pork; troops slept two to a bed, frequently without mattresses; and were compelled to act as servants for officers. In 1845 George Ballentine's company contained sixty men: two Englishmen, four Scotchmen, seven Germans, sixteen Americans, and thirty-one Irishmen. See also Leonard D. White, *The Jacksonians: A Study in Administrative History, 1829–1861* (New York, 1954), p. 202–5.

9 Bragg to Jones, September 27, 1840, Letters Received, AGO; William T. Sherman, "Old Shady, With a Moral," *North American Review,* CXLVII (1888), 364.

Jones replied that he had given Bragg no assurance of assignment in the North, or of "any detached duty, after the lapse of the sickly season and the approach of Winter." If Bragg was still ill, Jones suggested he apply for leave; if not, he must board ship and escort a group of Third Artillery recruits to Florida.[10]

This settled it: Bragg sailed with the recruits. The trip was tiresome, but at least he shared the monotony with a new friend—a young Virginian named George H. Thomas, one of the recent West Point graduates assigned to the Third Artillery.[11]

Bragg remained relatively healthy during the next three years he spent at various Florida frontier posts, but each month he seemed to grow more contentious. Doubtless he still fumed over being sent back to Florida against his wishes. Yet another explanation of his peevishness seems equally tenable: he tended to overwork. Soon he took charge of Company E, Third Artillery, and a few months later commanded Fort Marion, near St. Augustine. As a commander, Bragg devoted all his time and energy to his duties. He was strict, solicitous of his men's welfare, and apt to quarrel with his superiors.[12] When Adjutant General Jones failed to answer a query promptly, Bragg complained: "About five weeks since I addressed you a communication on an official subject, an answer to which involves the correct discharge of my duties as an officer, and up to this time you have not condescended to notice me." Nor, Bragg insisted, was this the first time his requests for information had been treated "with *silent contempt*." Why, he demanded, was Jones "adopting so extraordinary a course towards a junior [officer] who has no redress for the insults thus offered him except in violation of that

[10] Jones to Bragg, October 7, 1840 (copy), Letters Sent, AGO.

[11] Freeman Cleaves, *Rock of Chickamauga: The Life of General George H. Thomas* (Norman, Okla., 1948), p. 16.

[12] Bragg to Jones, December 12, 1840, January 1, 1841, Letters Received, AGO.

official respect which the law requires him to maintain towards his superiors?" [13]

When General Winfield Scott, the commanding general of the army, saw this letter he probably took an instant dislike to Bragg. On the back of the communication Scott wrote: "The within is deemed an improper letter to go on file. Let it be returned." [14]

After a copy had been made, the original letter was returned with a crushing rebuke from Jones, who warned that Bragg was doing "himself much injustice, as well as this office in allowing himself to imagine that his communications had been slighted." [15]

Jones's admonishment appears to have made no impression on Bragg; less than two weeks later he complained to the adjutant general about the deplorable condition of army buildings at his post. Jones knew "that the quarters here have been examined several times and estimates made for funds to repair or rebuild," wrote Bragg. "This has been done twice within my knowledge, yet not the slightest notice has been taken of these reports—no estimate made even for appropriation." Leaky roofs, rotten walls, and falling plaster endangered the health and safety of the entire company. The quarters were so rickety that Bragg was "daily under apprehension of some serious accident." One of his men had just died of fever, he informed Jones, and unless something was done to improve living conditions "the scenes of death I passed through here last year are again to be met and combated." Bragg added that if General Scott had any compassion he would allow the com-

13 Bragg to Jones, May 5, 1842 (copy), *ibid.*

14 *Ibid.* Scott's impatience with impertinent young officers is substantiated by numerous examples. See Erasmus D. Keyes, *Fifty Years' Observation of Men and Events, Civil and Military* (New York, 1884), chapters 1–9.

15 Endorsement on Bragg to Jones, June 1, 1842 (copy), Letters Received, AGO. See also Jones to Bragg, June 13, 1842, Letters Sent, AGO.

pany to rent quarters until their barracks had been repaired.[16]

When not harassing his superiors, Bragg wrangled with the army paymaster over money owed deserters and posed several difficult questions about pay: Would a man convicted of desertion but not sentenced to any forfeiture of pay receive pay for the time he was a deserter? What pay and adjustment should be made in case a deserter were pardoned? Should a deserter's pay begin after he served his sentence, or after he made up the time lost by desertion? There is no indication that Bragg requested this information for use in a particular case. His questions appear to have been purely rhetorical, perhaps meant only to confound the paymaster and the adjutant general.[17]

Such caviling soon earned Bragg an unenviable reputation. Ulysses S. Grant remembered Bragg as "a remarkably intelligent and well-informed man, professionally and otherwise," who had an "irascible temper, and was naturally disputatious." Despite his high moral character and correct habits, "he was in frequent trouble. As a subordinate he was always on the lookout to catch his commanding officer infringing his prerogatives; as a post commander he was equally vigilant to detect the slightest neglect, even of the most trivial order." Grant recalled a popular story about Bragg, who at the time was both company commander and company quartermaster. "As commander of the company he made a requisition upon the quartermaster—himself—for something he wanted. As quartermaster he declined to fill the requisition, and endorsed on the back of it his reasons for so doing. As company commander he responded to this, urging that his requisition called for nothing but what he was entitled to, and that it was the duty of the quartermaster to fill it. As quartermaster he still persisted that he was right." Unable to resolve the dilemma, Bragg referred the whole matter to the post commander, who exclaimed: "My God, Mr. Bragg, you have quarreled with

[16] Bragg to Jones, June 24, 1842, Letters Received, AGO.
[17] Bragg to Jones, November 3, 1842, *ibid.*

every officer in the army, and now you are quarreling with yourself." [18]

After the Third Artillery moved to Fort Moultrie, South Carolina, in 1843, Bragg got into additional disputes. Several officers objected to his outspoken opinions and his obdurate determination to protect what he considered his rights. Soon enmity flamed between Bragg and his regimental commander, Lieutenant Colonel William Gates, Captain Martin Burke, an eccentric who avoided civilians, and Captain Erasmus D. Keyes, an ardent admirer of General Scott.[19]

Bragg particularly disliked Gates, whom he considered a man of weak character and inferior education. Consequently, Bragg only spoke to Gates on official business. When they met in the officers' club one day, Gates asked Bragg to join him for a glass of wine. Bragg replied: "Colonel Gates, if you order me to drink a glass of wine with you, I shall have to do it." [20]

In Bragg's opinion Keyes was a "sly, insinuating sycophant who will wring the very blood from your fingers in shaking hands today, and in six hours after will steal your reputation behind your back." Keys considered Bragg very ambitious, "but being of a saturnine disposition and morbid temperament, his ambition was of the vitriolic kind. He could see nothing bad in the South and little good in the North, although he was disposed to smile on his satellites and sycophants whencesoever they came. He was intelligent," Keyes admitted, "and the exact performance of all his military duties added force to his pernicious influence. As I was not disposed to concede to his intolerant sectionalism, nor to be influenced by his dictatorial utterances, our social relations could not long remain harmonious." [21]

---

[18] Grant, *Personal Memoirs*, II, 86–87.   [19] Keyes, *Observation*, p. 185.
[20] Bragg to William T. Sherman, March 1, 1848, William T. Sherman Papers, Library of Congress; Don Carlos Seitz, *Braxton Bragg, General of the Confederacy* (Columbia, S. C., 1924), p. 4.
[21] Bragg to James Duncan, August 12, 1844, James Duncan Papers, United States Military Academy; Keyes, *Observation*, p. 178.

Despite all his polemics, Bragg does not seem to have been an "intolerant sectionalist" at this time. His closest army friends included James Duncan, of the Second Artillery; George H. Thomas and John F. Reynolds, who were lieutenants in Bragg's company; and William Tecumseh (Cump) Sherman. Of this group, only Thomas was a Southerner. In fact, D.H. Hill, a North Carolinian who joined Bragg's battery in 1845, recalled that of his three messmates Thomas was "the strongest and most pronounced Southerner." Bragg and Sherman were particularly close, and remained friends for the rest of their lives. Cump Sherman was a plain, straightforward Midwesterner; like Bragg, he was ambitious, conservative, and always attentive to duty. In 1888 Sherman wrote: "I think I knew Bragg as well as any living man, appreciated his good qualities, and had charity for his weaknesses. His heart was never in the Rebel cause." Sherman acknowledged that Bragg was "austere, severe, stern," but he also was a man of "great integrity" and not an intolerant sectionalist, as Keyes claimed.[22]

As his friends admitted, Bragg had a temper and an easily aroused sense of honor. When a Charlestonian called North Carolina a strip of land between two states at an Independence Day celebration, Bragg challenged him to a duel. Ultimately Bragg withdrew his challenge, but only after Sherman and Reynolds got the Charlestonian to apologize.[23]

Perhaps Bragg considered these local enemies insufficient, for he soon attacked the entire army administration in the *Southern Literary Messenger*. In a series of nine articles, published in 1844 and 1845 under the title "Notes on Our Army,"

[22] Bragg to John Reynolds, Sr., July 23, 1842, cited in Edward J. Nichols, *Toward Gettysburg: A Biography of General John F. Reynolds* (University Park, Pa., 1958), p. 15; Daniel H. Hill, "Chickamauga— The Great Battle of the West," *Battles and Leaders*, III, 639; Lloyd Lewis, *Sherman: Fighting Prophet* (New York, 1932), *passim*; Sherman, "Old Shady, With a Moral," p. 365. Sherman modestly claimed that Thomas was Bragg's best friend.

[23] Sherman, "Old Shady, With a Moral," pp. 364–65.

Bragg signed himself "A Subaltern." Anonymity was necessary because the articles clearly violated military protocol. Even so, he had jeopardized his career. Public criticism of high army officials, especially by a junior officer, was unusual and dangerous. To cautious men, Bragg must have seemed daft.

In his first article he insisted that his only objective was the "correction of abuses which have gradually crept into our service"; indeed, he may have thought that this was his only motive. If so, he deluded himself when he claimed to be "free from all political and party prejudices, uninfluenced by any private animosity, or personal dislikes." [24] His political sympathies were strongly Democratic,[25] and his earlier letters indicate that he resented the way he had been treated by the army's administrators. Consciously or unconsciously, Bragg's articles were directed at his enemies.

The recurrent theme of these caustic essays was the necessity of army reform. Bragg criticized every branch of the service, but he saved his harshest prose for General Scott. Bragg called Scott a "vain, petty, conniving man," who had used patronage to consolidate his military and political power. When Scott's actions brought objections from General Edmund Pendleton Gaines, Scott had started an "indelicate, ungenerous, and unprovoked attack" on his old enemy, whom Bragg described as Scott's "senior in years, his equal in rank, and certainly not his inferior in those qualities which ennoble the man and elevate the soldier."

Furthermore, Bragg charged that since Scott became commander of the army the staff had been increased 700 per cent. During the same period the army proper had been increased only 28 per cent. When Scott wanted to reward a man, he gave him an easy staff job in Washington or in one of the large eastern cities. "Where," asked Bragg, "is there any Army on

[24] A Subaltern, "Notes on Our Army," *Southern Literary Messenger*, X (1844), 86–88.
[25] Bragg to Duncan, August 12, December 6, 1844, Duncan Papers.

the face of the globe having more General and field officers by one half in its *staff* than it has in the line?" Glutted with idlers and favorites, the American staff used one fifth of the money allotted to the entire army; the British staff used only one twenty-eighth. "These results show one of two things," explained Bragg; "either that our Staff is unnecessarily large and expensive, or that it requires six times the expense to get the same Staff duties performed in our service that it does in the British." Bragg emphasized that all staff officers drew extra pay and allowances, and the commissary department was full of "mere drivers of mules, and slayers of bullocks clothed with the military rank . . . of colonel"; small wonder American staff expenses had increased 1,500 per cent since 1821.[26]

Regardless of his aim, Bragg offered more than mere criticism. He suggested two important ways to improve the army. First, he advised that the many separate staff bureaus be unified under one chief. Second, he proposed that staff assignments be rotated so that all officers could learn staff duties. In addition to these major suggestions, Bragg favored several other changes: the integration of the topographical and military engineers, the equalization of base pay for line and staff officers of equal rank, and the replacement of junior officers in the quartermaster department with civilian workers.[27]

Bragg's first two proposals were substantial contributions to the military thought of the period. No modern general staff *in USA* existed in 1844; each administrative bureau operated more or less independently under the Secretary of War. Bragg saw that this cumbersome bureau system lacked "unity of interest, unity of feeling, unity of purpose, and unity of action." [28] It

---

[26] A Subaltern, "Notes on Our Army," pp. 155–57. For an earlier and somewhat similar criticism of army organization, see Mentor, "To the Commanding General of the Army," *Military and Naval Magazine of the United States*, IV (1834), 179–85.

[27] A Subaltern, "Notes on Our Army," pp. 246–51, 283–87, 372–88, 750–53; XI (1845), 39–47, 104–9.

[28] *Ibid.*, p. 39.

encouraged narrow self-interest and service rivalry. So did the absence of a rotation policy. This inflexible arrangement fixed men in bureaucratic concrete. It created specialists, but without any certainty that these specialists were the best men for their jobs. An officer with unusual talent for staff work might never get a staff assignment simply because he had been placed in a line company immediately upon graduation from West Point.

Bragg's plea for army reforms went unheeded. No significant staff changes were made until 1903, when Congress adopted a program suggested by Secretary of War Elihu Root. At the heart of this new system was what Bragg had proposed nearly sixty years before—the establishment of an integrated bureau organization headed by a chief of staff and the abolition of permanent staff assignments.[29]

The articles Bragg wrote for the *Messenger* were only his initial contribution to a general feud between Generals Scott and Gaines and their supporters. On March 1, 1844, Bragg received thirty days' leave and joined his friend James Duncan in Washington. Duncan had been sent to the city to represent the interests of his regiment, the Second Artillery. The First Artillery had also sent a representative, but the Fourth Artillery refused to send anyone to Washington, and relied instead on General Scott to protect its interests. Later Bragg denied that he was an official representative of his regiment, but he may have been. The officers of the Second and Third Artillery favored Gaines, while those of the First and Fourth Artillery supported Scott.[30]

Whatever their primary purpose, neither Bragg nor Duncan

[29] T. Harry Williams, *Americans at War: The Development of the American Military System* (Collier ed., New York, 1962), pp. 38–39, 115–16.

[30] Document K, Braxton Bragg Court-Martial (April 2, 1844), National Archives; Leslie Chase to James Duncan, February 20, 1844, Duncan Papers; *Congressional Globe*, 28 Cong., 1 sess. (1844), XIII, 462; *House Executive Document*, 28 Cong., 1 sess., No. 211, pp. 1–8; New York *Daily Plebian*, May 10, 1844.

neglected the Washington ladies. A few months later, Bragg wrote Duncan: "Our lady friends are all well and desire to be remembered. If I had time Mrs. H. would get me into a scrape with Dick Johnson's niece, just arrived from Ky. to attend the Baltimore [Democratic] convention with her Pa; [she is] young, handsome, rich, and, I should judge from appearances, *anxious*." [31]

While the officers courted the girls, congressmen courted the officers. Representative James G. Clinton, a New York Democrat and chairman of the House Committee on Public Expenditures, was most interested in Bragg's charges against General Scott's administration of the army. On March 18, after a number of informal talks with Bragg and Duncan, Clinton decided they should testify before his committee. Two days later, Bragg and Duncan were questioned informally by William H. Hammett of Mississippi, a member of the House Committee on Retrenchment, and by James A. Black of South Carolina, chairman of the subdivision of the retrenchment committee which was investigating the army. Black subsequently introduced an army reform bill that contained some of Bragg's proposals, but the bill failed to pass.[32]

Because these congressmen were so receptive to his arguments, Bragg got into unexpected difficulty. Shortly after three o'clock on the afternoon of March 20, as he was dining, a messenger from the War Department handed him a letter from the adjutant general. It read: "On the supposition that you are in this city . . . in connection with measures before Congress or expected to be brought forward in that honorable body, the General in Chief [orders] . . . you forthwith to return to your post or duties, unless, indeed you should be under the summons of a Committee of Congress, or under examination by some such Committee." [33]

[31] Bragg to Duncan, May 18, 1844, Duncan Papers.
[32] Testimony of James G. Clinton and William H. Hammett, Bragg Court-Martial; *Congressional Globe*, 28 Cong., 1 sess. (1844), XIII, 461.
[33] Testimony of James Duncan and Document C, Bragg Court-Martial.

Bragg and Duncan, who had received a similar letter, could not agree on what they should do. Duncan believed the letter, though vague, was intended as an order. Bragg considered it only a question to be answered. In any case, he argued, neither he nor Duncan could leave Washington immediately. Their clothes were being laundered and would not be returned until the next afternoon. Furthermore, they had promised to appear before Congressman Clinton's committee. Duncan, despite his pledge to Clinton, decided to leave; he wrote Adjutant General Jones that he was not under examination by a committee of Congress and that he would "proceed forthwith" to his post "as required by your letter." [34]

Bragg replied in his typically contentious style. He wrote: "In reply to your letter . . . calling for certain *supposed* facts connected with my presence in this city, I have the honor to enclose you a copy of an order granting me a leave of absence, which has not yet expired. . . . I take great pleasure in stating that I shall never fail, either here or elsewhere, to sustain, to the utmost of my abilities, what I conceive to be the interests of my regiment and grade, and I must acknowledge the honor done me in supposing I am the delegated organ of either. As I am in doubt as to the intention of your letter, please inform me whether I am to consider it as an order to rejoin my post." Before sending this letter, Bragg showed it to Duncan and asked if he thought "it was an improper communication or one that could be construed into anything disrespectful." Duncan said that in his "opinion it was not." [35]

Still uncertain after mailing their letters to Jones, Bragg and Duncan decided to discuss their problem with Congressman Clinton. He assured them that they had nothing to fear; that it made no difference whether Jones's letter was an order. He then took a subpoena from his pocket, handed it to Bragg, and said: "There is a paper which in time of peace will override

[34] Testimony of Duncan, *ibid*.
[35] Document H and testimony of Duncan, *ibid*.

any military order." The next morning, Clinton promised
Bragg and Duncan, he would write a letter to Jones which
would "exonerate them from any disobedience of military
orders." At this point, Bragg began to have doubts about what
he had done and suggested that perhaps he should return to his
post. Clinton told him that if either he or Duncan left Washington, now that the subpoenas had been served, they would
be brought back at public expense and tried for contempt of
the House of Representatives. Both men decided to stay.[36]

General Scott was unimpressed by Clinton's letter which
explained that Bragg and Duncan could not leave Washington
immediately because they had to testify before the public
expenditure committee. On March 26, the day Bragg was
released by the committee, Scott had him arrested and sent to
Fort Monroe, Virginia, to await trial for disobedience to
orders and disrespect toward his superior officers.[37]

When Clinton heard what had happened he rushed to
Bragg's defense. He got the House of Representatives to adopt
a resolution demanding that Secretary of War William
Wilkins explain why Bragg had been arrested. Wilkins replied
that Scott had ordered Bragg's arrest and trial because information "casually came to his knowledge" that Bragg was
insolent and disobedient. The charges against him, Scott said,
"have been fully sustained and corroborated by the conduct
and letter of . . . Bragg himself." Congressman John Quincy
Adams, who backed Scott, noted in his diary on March 30:
"The whole proceeding is characteristic of the malignant
stolidity of James G. Clinton, and of the base subserviency of
the majority of the House to the venomous passions of the
meanest of their party hacks." [38]

[36] Testimony of Clinton, *ibid*.
[37] Document L, testimony of Roger Jones, and Charges, *ibid*.
[38] *Congressional Globe*, 28 Cong., 1 sess. (1844), XIII, 446–47, 462;
Charles Francis Adams, ed., *Memoirs of John Quincy Adams . . . Portions of His Diary From 1795 to 1848* (12 vols., Philadelphia, 1874–1877),
XI, 545.

At his trial, which began on April 2, Bragg conducted his own defense. His brother Thomas and Clinton counseled him, but Bragg questioned all witnesses. The defense's case rested mainly upon the testimony of Duncan and Clinton, though Bragg also called Hammett, Scott, and Jones to the stand.

From the outset Bragg tried unsuccessfully to turn the court-martial into a trial of Scott. The prosecutor, Lieutenant S. G. Ridgley of the Fourth Artillery, objected to all references to Scott, and the court, composed mainly of officers from the same regiment, sustained his objections. Indeed, the court warned Bragg about his derogatory references to Scott. "I can assure you I did not spare the 'Vain and arrogant Chief,' " Bragg wrote Duncan, who had returned to his post after testifying. "In fact, I was so hard on him that Ridgley replied . . . and the Court, true to its master, made him write out his remarks for the record. They were . . . highly eulogistic of Scott." Under cross-examination, Jones admitted that Bragg "was not informed that any exception had been taken to his letter of the 20th March" before his arrest, and Jones added: "It may be due to Mr. Bragg to state that after . . . his arrival at Fort Monroe, he [wrote me] . . . stating that had he supposed that the letter would have been regarded as disrespectful . . . he would have withdrawn it." [39]

Bragg believed he had won, but he was worried. He wrote that if he were being judged by any other officers in the army except those from the Fourth Artillery, he would be "confident of an honorable acquittal, but as it is I have my fears and though I try I cannot expel them." [40]

His fears proved to be justified. He was found guilty of disrespect toward his superiors, and his only consolation was a comparatively light sentence: a reprimand in general orders, suspension from rank and command for two months, and

[39] Bragg to Duncan, April 22, 1844, Duncan Papers; Testimony of Winfield Scott and Roger Jones, Bragg Court-Martial.
[40] Bragg to Duncan, April 22, 1844, Duncan Papers.

forfeiture of one half his pay and allowances for the same period. President John Tyler approved the sentence, and Secretary of War Wilkins reprimanded Bragg in a general order. Wilkins wrote: "Lieutenant Bragg seems to be unmindful of what is due to the service and himself, as evinced even by the tone and scope of a portion of his *defense*. The disrespectful tenor of his remarks in reference to the Major General commanding the Army of the United States is not justified by the facts, and is highly disapproved. The Lieutenant is admonished to correct his error, lest its too frequent indulgence may become a confirmed and dangerous habit." [41]

Impertinence had already become a "dangerous habit." Indignant over the outcome of his trial, Bragg ignored the Secretary of War's advice. Instead, he hurried to Washington to appeal his sentence. "I have hoped every day, in fact, every hour to be able to give you the gratifying intelligence that I had succeeded in obtaining justice," he wrote Duncan. When Bragg confronted the Secretary of War, Wilkins actually claimed he had signed the rebuke without reading it. Bragg railed: "Such a piece of rascality has never before been practiced since I have been in the service, and never will be again. They have enough of it for this time and regret that they ever got into it." [42]

Bragg failed to get his sentence reversed; nevertheless, he believed his trial had benefitted rather than blemished his reputation. "I ought to have known of course that defeat was certain," he admitted to Duncan, "but with that unconquerable thirst for action, which actually pursues me, I feel that I can never rest without some excitement, and I am not so sure but that I have even bettered myself by the scrape; my friends all think so, at least, and the *dear people* applaud my course wherever they speak of it, and I find it is generally

[41] Sentence and General Orders, No. 21, April 27, 1844, Bragg Court-Martial.
[42] Bragg to Duncan, May 18, 1844, Duncan Papers.

known." Even his brother John, who had advised Bragg to resign his commission, reconsidered after a talk with officers in New Orleans and Mobile. They were all against Scott.[43]

General Gaines also came to Bragg's defense. Before the trial ended, he had called on Clinton to thank him "for the active and valuable assistance he rendered" Bragg, whom Gaines called his "special favorite." Furthermore, Gaines promised a position in his own division to Bragg to remove him from Scott's power. "What think you of that my dear fellow?" Bragg asked Duncan. "A post of honor for disobedience of orders, and contempt & disrespect to my Com[man]d[ing] officer. This is a strange world." Gaines also praised Bragg in letters to John Bragg and to Clinton. "Yesterday," Clinton wrote Duncan on June 3, "I received a letter from Genl. Gaines," which called Scott " 'a vain glorious dabbler in politics,' " who wanted to " 'establish a *Prison discipline* in the army.' " Gaines particularly deplored Scott's " 'iniquitous attempt to crush that talented young officer Lt. Bragg.' " [44]

Besides Gaines, another high ranking officer seems to have sided with Bragg. General Thomas S. Jesup is reported to have said he would like to know Bragg; " 'if he would only correct a few errors he has unintentionally committed about the Quartermaster Department, I should say *Amen* to all his views.' " [45]

Such support only confirmed Bragg's belief that he had been justified in his challenge of authority. "I feel deeply indebted to the officers . . . who have stood by me so firmly and are still undismayed," he wrote. "I fear no such man as Scott before the Army and shall be happy to compare 'notes' with him at any time." And Bragg exulted "that Scott was dissatisfied and chagrined . . . to find [his daughter] Miss Virginia,

[43] Bragg to Duncan, June 16, 1844, *ibid.*
[44] Bragg to Duncan, April 22, June 16, 1844, *ibid.;* Clinton to Duncan, June 3, 1844, *ibid.*
[45] Bragg to Duncan, May 18, 1844, *ibid.*

the beautiful, gay and accomplished had betaken herself to a convent, and that Gaines had succeeded in getting his Maj. Gen'ls. command restored. Were I as able and ingenious as old Amos Kendall," bantered Bragg, "I might write a tract on 'Providential Dispensation,' but the guilty conscience must prey on him [Scott] severely enough without my adding fuel to the fire." [46]

Despite his words, Bragg found silence unbearable. The June issue of the *Southern Literary Messenger* carried a letter from officers at an unnamed fort which was critical of Bragg's articles. Benjamin B. Minor, editor of the magazine, defended Bragg as "a fearless writer" and boasted that the articles had "already attracted the attention of several distinguished members of both houses of Congress, who are willing and anxious to ferret out and correct the many grievous abuses which have crept into the Army, . . . and which 'A Subaltern' so independently rebukes and exposes." The officers objected to the tone of the articles, but Minor explained: "The tone of a writer is an inherent part of his style and a nice discriminator of tones would strip of its essence the style of some of the greatest worthies of English literature. Pope, Swift and a host of others did not pause to weigh their words, when they were enlisted warmly in a favorite cause." Minor promised that the articles would continue. Bragg claimed the critical letter was signed by his old enemies from the Third Artillery—Gates, Burke, and Keyes. "Oh Christ, but I'll peal 'em," Bragg promised Duncan. [47]

In his reply to Gates and the other officers, printed in the August issue of the *Messenger*, Bragg used curious logic. Disregarding his own violation of army protocol, he insisted the officers who had criticized him in print had "gone beyond

[46] Bragg to Duncan, April 22, May 18, 1844, *ibid.* Kendall, a talented journalist, wrote many of Andrew Jackson's messages.

[47] Benjamin B. Minor, "Editor's Table," *Southern Literary Messenger*, X (1844), 387–88; Bragg to Duncan, June 18, 1844, Duncan Papers.

the prescribed limits of their duties, as laid down in the regulations for government of the Army. . . . They can not thus clothe the act of individuals with an official robe; the attempt will be justly appreciated by all who understand the regulations of our service." [48]

The August issue of the *Messenger* also carried an anonymous article which criticized Bragg's essay on the ordnance department.[49] To Duncan, Bragg wrote: "You have seen by the last Messenger what a hornets nest is aroused and how I am to be stung to death." His anonymous attacker had written a "pretty good" article, Bragg admitted, "but he is unfortunate in not being supported by the truth. However, the whole affair is beneath my notice, and I shall not say a word in reply." [50]

Perhaps Bragg failed to reply because he was already engaged in other disputes at Fort Moultrie. When he returned to duty there his friends gave him a "most cordial and hearty reception," which convinced him that he had not "suffered in the estimation of the Army or the country by the recent abortive attempt of the 'Vain & arrogant' to crush me." Gates and Burke were silent, and Keyes, Bragg's "only real & active enemy . . . in these parts," had joined Scott's staff, "having received the reward due for faithful service," wrote Bragg. His friends told him Keyes had been Scott's spy. "He had left when I returned," Bragg explained, "but I learn he did not deny having written to Washington . . . giving all the details of my going on. But says he: I never for a moment dreamed it was to be used *officially*." [51] With Keyes gone Bragg turned on his other enemies. He continued to write for the *Messenger;* he offended the Whig officers at Fort Moultrie by his

[48] A Subaltern, "Our Army Again," *Southern Literary Messenger,* X (1844), 512.

[49] Fair Play, "Reply to 'A Subaltern,'" *ibid.,* 509–10. "Fair Play" appears to have been Lieutenant Colonel George Talcott, who became chief of ordnance in 1848 and was dismissed in 1851.

[50] Bragg to Duncan, August 12, 1844, Duncan Papers.   [51] *Ibid.*

Democratic partisanship; and he started a heated harangue with Colonel Gates over quarters.

Bragg was an ardent Democrat. His articles in the *Messenger* exhorted Senator Thomas Hart Benton and other important Democrats to make army reforms; his main supporters in Washington were Democratic politicians. After his court-martial, Bragg lingered five days in Baltimore at the Democratic convention and left enthusiastic over the nomination of James K. Polk for the presidency. People rallied to Polk "like wild-fire, and I am really gaining confidence," Bragg had written from North Carolina in June. "We shall carry every state south of the Potomac except this . . . and here . . . it is doubtful!" But by August Bragg conceded that the Democrats would lose in North Carolina. "I can scarcely realize that a Bragg can live in the Federal atmosphere of N. Ca.," wrote Bragg, "and I am half inclined to believe one brother, Thos., suffers severely from that cause." His brother John, "as good a Democrat as ever you could want," had moved to Alabama partly because the political climate in North Carolina was unfavorable to his party. Nevertheless, Bragg believed "the people will see through the clouds which cover them 'ere long, and the [Democratic] torrent will then sweep all before it." He thought it strange that many officers in his regiment were solid Whigs, and he tried unsuccessfully to convert them. "I confess my inability to understand it," he wrote Duncan. "Men otherwise astute & shrewd will talk . . . and if needs be, fight against their own interests." [52]

Polk's election delighted Bragg. He called it "this glorious triumph of the democracy; this triumph of principle." He advised Duncan that New York voters deserved much of the credit for saving "the country from four years of misrule, and probably from final ruin, for I cannot conceive any other

[52] Bragg to Duncan, June 16, August 12, December 6, 1844, *ibid.*; John Bragg to William B. Randolph, August 29, 1843, William B. Randolph Papers, Library of Congress.

result to such measures as are proposed by the leaders of the Whig party." [53]

His brothers' influence doubtless helped make Bragg a loyal Democrat. But there is another reason for his enthusiastic attachment to the Democratic party. General Scott was a Whig. In Bragg's mind, this was reason enough for any sensible man to be a Democrat.

Soon after Bragg returned to Fort Moultrie the discord between him and Gates erupted into an open quarrel. Bragg considered the rooms assigned to him almost "uninhabitable owing to the heat and the quantities of insects which a want of circulation of air accumulated." In August, he asked the post quartermaster, Captain Abraham C. Myers, to assign him other quarters. Myers claimed none was available, but that Captain Burke had applied for quarters in a house, formerly rented for Keyes, outside the post. If more officers arrived at the fort, Myers promised Bragg, the house would again be rented; Burke would move in, and Bragg could occupy Burke's old quarters inside the post. Bragg, who knew that George Thomas was due back in October, officially applied to Myers for new quarters. Myers refused the request on the grounds that vacant quarters were unavailable. Yet less than two weeks later Thomas arrived, the house was rented, and assigned to Lieutenant William H. Churchill, who had recently married.[54]

Bragg was furious at the disregard of his rights. On November 22 he reminded Gates that Article 967 of *Army Regulations* specifically gave Bragg the right to choose quarters over his junior in rank, Churchill. A lively exchange of letters followed. Gates insisted that Bragg must keep his same quarters; Bragg threatened to appeal Gates's decision to

[53] Bragg to Duncan, December 6, 1844, Duncan Papers. In New York, James K. Polk received 5,000 votes more than the Whig candidate, Henry Clay.

[54] Testimony of Henry B. Judd and Abraham C. Myers, Bragg Court of Inquiry (January 15, 1845), National Archives.

General John E. Wool, commander of the Eastern Division. Gates lost his temper, returned Bragg's first letter, and accused him of "indulging in a freedom of writing that is offensive from a junior to a senior, and of undertaking to dictate by a reference to the regulations what is my duty." Bragg's response to Gates's accusation was to ask for a court of inquiry, but Gates refused to forward the request to General Wool. Instead, Gates charged Bragg with trying "to make a serious matter of a trifle," and informed him that his "pen is not so serviceable to the public in this matter as he supposes." When Bragg renewed his request for a court of inquiry, Gates begged him "not to urge the matter," but "to let it rest where it is." Bragg refused; Gates reluctantly forwarded the request, and on December 20 General Wool ordered a court of inquiry "to examine into the nature of the accusations or imputations made" against Bragg "by his commanding officer Lieut. Col. Wm. Gates." [55]

Bragg, certain the court would exonerate him, assembled an impressive number of documents to prove his case, and confidently called his witnesses. Myers testified that Colonel Gates ordered the house now occupied by Churchill assigned first to Burke and then to Thomas. Burke said he withdrew his request for the house when he learned that Churchill was to be married.[56] Thomas insisted no agreement had been made between him and Churchill to exchange quarters; Churchill, who outranked Thomas, merely moved into the house. Bragg next examined Lieutenant Joseph Stewart, who testified that he had been allowed to change quarters in October, the same month Bragg had made a similar request. Stewart said he wanted to move because his quarters were "unfit for winter . . . as there was no fire place and the rooms were very open." To conclude his case Bragg questioned Lieutenants Henry B.

[55] Documents A through K, and Eastern Division Headquarters Order No. 12, December 20, 1844, *ibid.*

[56] Document L, Testimony of Myers and Martin Burke, *ibid.*

Judd and William T. Sherman. Both testified that Bragg's rooms were "inferior to most of the quarters within the fort," and that Bragg had complained frequently about how uncomfortable they were.[57]

The court vindicated Bragg. It decided his rank entitled him to select "the quarters hired on the arrival of Lieut. Thomas, after Capt. Burke had waived his right of choice." Moreover, "Bragg had a perfect right to appeal" when Gates denied him his prerogative. In the court's opinion, Bragg's first letter to Gates "was objectionable in tone, and language," but some of the remarks Gates made in reply were "uncalled for, and calculated to irritate the feelings of Lieut. Bragg."[58]

General Wool approved the court's decision and publicly reprimanded Gates for "an error in judgment . . . a deviation from that strictly impartial course which should be followed by every military commander." Wool saw no "reasons for hiring additional quarters outside the fort, on the arrival of Lieut. Thomas, when . . . there were two rooms vacant." But after outside quarters had been rented, Bragg should have been given his right of choice. "Had Lieut. Col. Gates done what was plainly his duty in this respect," censured Wool, "he might have avoided all difficulty, and the consequently unmilitary, and undignified correspondence in which he is made to appear a suppliant to a junior." The entire affair had lowered Gates's "dignity and impaired his usefulnes as a commander."

Though Gates was the main target for criticism, some of Wool's strictures were reserved for Bragg, who should have been more courteous. Wool maintained that the "language and tone" of Bragg's "letter to Col. Gates was, as the Court justly remarks, objectionable. A simple statement of fact was all that was necessary." Wool concluded his reproof with an order to reassign all quarters on the basis of rank.[59]

[57] Testimony of George H. Thomas, Joseph Stewart, Judd, and William T. Sherman, *ibid.*
[58] Verdict, *ibid.*
[59] Eastern Division Headquarters Order No. 4, February 3, 1845, *ibid.*

If the sum of such arguments seem somehow smaller than the whole issue, they nevertheless established Bragg's distinction as the most cantankerous man in the army. He had been court-martialed and convicted; he had been censured by the Secretary of War, the Adjutant General, and the Commander of the Eastern Division. No other junior officer could boast of so many high ranking enemies. Both the Commander of the Third Artillery and the Commanding General of the United States Army hated Bragg. His future in his regiment and in the army seemed most uncertain.

Ironically, he received the greatest boost to his career only a few months after the quarters controversy. On June 18, 1845, Bragg requested a three-months' leave of absence. That same day he and his company were ordered to join General Zachary Taylor's army for the defense of Texas against Mexico.[60] Taylor received only a few artillery companies for his little force, and it is uncertain why Bragg's battery was selected. Later, Bragg would claim he went with Taylor "against Scott's objections." [61] Possibly, but it seems unlikely. Scott controlled most troop assignments; perhaps he wanted Bragg as far away from Washington as possible. It is also conceivable that Scott considered Bragg a courageous officer who would fight as fiercely as he argued.

[60] Bragg to Jones, June 18, 1845, Letters Received, AGO; Jones to Bragg, and Jones to William Gates, June 18, 1845 (copies), Letters Sent, AGO.

[61] Bragg to Duncan, January 13, 1848, Duncan Papers.

CHAPTER III

Distinguished for attention to minutiae

1845–1846

W<small>HEN</small> <small>BRAGG</small> joined General Taylor's Army in New Orleans on July 19, 1845, preparations were under way to meet an expected Mexican invasion of Texas. Men moved about the congested wharves loading piles of crates into ships, and every day companies arrived from distant posts. But only part of the army's supplies and equipment had been assembled when Bragg landed, and he was especially concerned about his own shortages. A battery of light artillery virtually never had the full number of men and implements allowed—a captain, four lieutenants, eight noncommissioned officers, about seventy privates, and from four to six horse-drawn guns, carriages, and caissons—though it rarely lacked as much equipment as did Bragg's. None of the four new brass guns, the horses, or the ammunition Adjutant General Jones had promised were in New Orleans when Taylor decided to embark. Nevertheless, Bragg's artillerymen, without guns, sailed south on July 23 to help check the Mexicans.[1]

[1] Jones to Bragg, June 18, 1845 (copy), Letters Sent, AGO; Fayette Robinson, *An Account of the Organization of the Army of the United States . . .* (2 vols., Philadelphia, 1848), II, 174; W. S. Henry, *Campaign Sketches of the War With Mexico* (New York, 1847), p. 12. The most detailed account of Mexican War military operations is Justin Smith, *The War With Mexico* (2 vols., New York, 1919). Among the most useful of the recent work on the war are Robert S. Henry, *The Story of the Mexican War* (Indianapolis, 1950), Otis Singletary, *The Mexican War* (Chicago, 1960), and Edward J. Nichols, *Zach Taylor's Little Army* (New York, 1963). On Taylor see: Holman Hamilton, *Zachary Taylor, Soldier of the Republic* (Indianapolis, 1941), and Brainerd Dyer, *Zachary Taylor* (Baton Rouge, 1946).

The army landed at Corpus Christi, near the mouth of the Nueces River, where Taylor established a camp. Orders from President James K. Polk held the force north of the disputed territory between the Nueces and the Rio Grande in hopes that negotiations with Mexico might yet prevent war. Fortunately for the poorly equipped Americans, no Mexican troops met them on the beach. For a time there was little to do but fish and wait. A newspaperman reported: "The cool nights invite weariness to repose, disturbed neither by the promenading flea, nor the buzzing mosquito." [2]

Bragg and his lieutenants—Thomas, Reynolds, and D. H. Hill—settled into the camp routine. As they dined together in the battery mess probably none of them imagined that one day they would be generals, and on opposite sides; Reynolds and Thomas, Union commanders in the Civil War; Bragg and Hill, Confederate. Hill, a brevet second lieutenant, had recently transferred from the First Artillery. Bragg explained years later that he had supported the request for transfer because he sympathized with Hill's "inability to coalesce with the fast material in the 1st." Before the army left Corpus Christi, Hill was promoted to full second lieutenant and reassigned to the Fourth Artillery at Fort Monroe, Virginia, where he denounced in the *Southern Quarterly Review* the "ignorance and imbecility of the War Department" as responsible for shortages of equipment and supplies at Corpus Christi. The tone of his article was so scathing that one historian incorrectly believed Bragg wrote it.[3]

Soon reinforcements and equipment began to arrive. Bragg got his guns and horses; additionally, his friend James Duncan and Major Samuel Ringgold landed with their batteries.

[2] Smith, *War With Mexico*, I, 142–43; Nichols, *Zach Taylor's Little Army*, p. 22.

[3] Braxton Bragg, "Memorandum" [June, 1864], Palmer Collection; Hill, "Chickamauga—The Great Battle of the West," p. 639; Hal Bridges, *Lee's Maverick General: Daniel Harvey Hill* (New York, 1961), pp. 19–20; Smith, *War With Mexico*, I, 452–53.

Ringgold's was the army's only battery of "flying artillery." In previous American wars oxen driven by hired civilians had pulled artillery into battle. A brief attempt to substitute horses for oxen had been abandoned shortly after 1800, but Napoleon's European success with horse-drawn guns finally revived enthusiasm for light artillery in America. In 1839 the War Department decided to make a timid experiment. "Your company will be mounted as horse artillery, and consequently the men should *not* be carried on the guns and carriages, but . . . each man [will] be mounted separately," Adjutant General Jones had informed Ringgold. Soon Ringgold's battery dazzled observers with its speed and precision, but in 1845 it was still the only battery in the army in which every man was mounted. The other batteries were called light artillery, which in the military terminology of the period meant that all the men rode horses, but actually the cannoneers walked; they mounted the limbers and caissons only for rapid movement.[4]

Whether artillerymen rode or walked mattered little to General Taylor. He had an infantryman's prejudice against artillery, which in his opinion had never done much in battle. Moreover, means of transport seemed academic at the moment because the army was stuck. As the months passed without action or orders to move, discipline deteriorated, desertions increased, and soldiers spent much time in the gambling dens, bars, and brothels that sprang up around the camp. Boredom laced with liquor caused arguments, and often men trained for combat against each other.

The most celebrated quarrel, between Colonels David E. Twiggs and William J. Worth over rank, shed no blood, but it divided the army. Worth claimed his brevet rank of brigadier general entitled him to be second-in-command of the army. Brevet ranks were inexpensive ways to promote officers for

[4] Robinson, *Organization of the Army*, II, 177; William E. Birkhimer, *Historical Sketch of the Organization, Administration, Material and Tactics of the Artillery* . . . (Washington, 1884), pp. 55-57.

heroic service; a man might be a brevet major but draw only the pay of a captain, his actual rank. Twiggs argued that he deserved the post because in actual rank he was Worth's senior. When General Scott, to whom the question was referred, decided in favor of Worth, Bragg joined 157 other officers in a protest to Congress. At first, Taylor defied Scott's order and named Twiggs second-in-command; later, Taylor surprised the entire camp by reversing his decision.[5]

Quarrels broke the monotony, at least, and helped divert men's thoughts from the sickness that raged through the camp. After a few months nearly a third of the army was ill with diarrhea or fever. Cold weather and rain lengthened the sick list, and even such hardy fellows as John Reynolds of Bragg's battery stopped sleeping on the ground. A surgeon complained that the Americans were the world's worst lodged troops when Taylor refused to replace the sleazy canvas tents. Surprisingly, Bragg remained well, but one of the three or four slaves he brought with him was killed by lightning and another was badly injured during one of the frequent storms. Despite skimpy rations, brackish water, and leaky tents, most of the men survived.[6]

Opinion varied on the condition of the army and its readiness for combat. All the senior officers were over fifty years old. Taylor, who was sixty-one, was popular with the troops partly because he ignored conventional military routine and dress. "He looks more like an old farmer going to market with eggs to sell than anything I can . . . think of," admitted an officer. Another wrote: "Taylor is short and very heavy with pronounced face lines and gray hair, wears an old oil cap, a dusty green coat, a frightful pair of trousers and on horseback

[5] Smith, *War With Mexico*, I, 144; Milo M. Quaife, ed., *The Diary of James K. Polk* (4 vols., Chicago, 1910), I, 284–85; W. A. Croffut, ed., *Fifty Years in Camp and Field: Diary of . . . Ethan Allen Hitchcock* . . . (New York, 1909), pp. 204–6.

[6] Henry, *Campaign Sketches*, p. 32; Smith, *War With Mexico*, I, 143; Nichols, *Zach Taylor's Little Army*, pp. 24–25.

looks like a toad." Worth, at fifty-two, was a heavy drinker who often lost his temper. Twiggs, a bull-voiced old soldier of fifty-six, took large doses of castor oil just before battle because he thought this would allow a bullet to pass through him without injury to his intestines. Colonel William Whistler, the army's patriarch, had passed his sixty-sixth birthday. Each of these ancients was ready to fight as most American commanders had fought in the War of 1812: courageously but without technical skill. "Neither General Taylor nor [any other high ranking officer] . . . could form . . . [the army] into line," sneered Captain Ethan Allen Hitchcock, a West Point graduate. "As for manoeuvering, not one of them can move [the army] . . . a step." Yet Lieutenant George G. Meade reported constant "drill and parades . . . ears . . . filled all day with drumming and fifeing," and Captain William S. Henry thought "a more efficient army, for its size, was never brought into the field." [7]

Bragg, of course, drilled his men regularly. He agreed with a reporter who observed "that very few soldiers are fit for the light artillery arms—that it requires picked men, bold and expert horsemen—and these only become good light artillerymen after long practice in riding, driving, managing, and attending their horses, and in using the sabre." For hours each day Bragg wheeled his guns from column to line formation, changed direction at top speed, limbered, and unlimbered. Lieutenant Cadmus M. Wilcox of the Fourth Infantry thought the battery's movements were almost perfect. The men and horses responded instantly as Bragg, a tall, thin man with "large black eyes and heavy brows," gave commands in "a nervous, tremulous voice." What impressed Wilcox most was

[7] Quoted in Hamilton, *Zachary Taylor*, p. 230; Lloyd Lewis, *Captain Sam Grant* (Boston, 1950), p. 175; Nichols, *Zach Taylor's Little Army*, p. 39; Croffut, ed., *Fifty Years in Camp and Field*, pp. 198–99; George Meade, *The Life and Letters of George Gordon Meade* (2 vols., New York, 1913), I, 35; Henry, *Campaign Sketches*, p. 40.

CAMPAIGNS OF NORTHERN MEXICO

Bragg's "industry, attention to duty, and strict regard for discipline." [8]

When news came that peace negotiations with Mexico had failed, Bragg was ready. Taylor, ordered by the President to

[8] Quoted in Nichols, *Zach Taylor's Little Army*, p. 37; Cadmus Marcellus Wilcox, *History of the Mexican War*, Mary Rachel Wilcox, ed. (Washington, 1892), p. 118.

move south, sent supply ships ahead to establish a depot at Point Isabel, near the mouth of the Rio Grande, and marched his 3,500 men away from Corpus Christi in March 1846. Impatiently, Bragg watched the first units start: Twiggs's dragoons and Ringgold's battery led the way, followed by Worth's First Brigade and Duncan's battery. As they rode out of camp, Bragg doubtless concurred with the soldier who remarked that Duncan "was a man the Mexicans would need to watch." [9] The third column, Colonel James S. McIntosh's Second Brigade, left on March 10, and Colonel Whistler's Third Brigade and Bragg's battery followed the next day.

It was a dreary march, hot one day and cold the next. On March 14 men and animals almost perished for lack of water until Bragg, riding out from the column, discovered a safe source. Poorly disciplined infantrymen broke ranks to chase wild hogs or mustangs, or to applaud the pratfalls of camp followers from unruly mules. The few women brave enough to accompany the army south of Corpus Christi were mostly amazons like Mrs. Sarah Bourdett, a six-foot burly washerwoman called "the Great Western." The wife of an enlisted man, she had worked as a laundress and kept a mess for young officers at Corpus Christi. When the army moved she refused to remain behind; "her boys must have somebody to take care of them," she insisted. Astride her donkey she often led the column, and when a small Mexican force tried to bluff the Americans at the Colorado River, she announced her willingness to "*wade* the river and whip every scoundrel that dare show himself." Many soldiers admired her pluck, but it was Bragg who first praised her to newspapermen. Among other qualities, he "mentioned her gallant conduct and noble bearing." She stayed with the army throughout the campaign in northern Mexico, kept a mess, and exhibited her characteristic "rough-and-ready good-nature." [10]

[9] Quoted in Lewis, *Captain Sam Grant*, pp. 132–33.
[10] Henry, *Campaign Sketches*, pp. 52–55; "The Heroine of Fort

By March 28 the army had reached the Rio Grande. While the soldiers began to construct Fort Texas, off-duty officers hunted antelope, peccary, and wild cattle. Captain George A. McCall of the Third Infantry, who killed a large bull, gave Bragg its tail and "a good steak." So far the Americans had encountered no real opposition. Across the river Mexican troops merely paraded through the streets of Matamoros behind frenetically noisy bands, while curious citizens hovered on housetops to watch the Yankees. In a few days Mexican girls began to swim naked in the river, and a flock of Americans deserted. "We have lost about 30 men from . . . desertion to the enemy," wrote an officer on April 4. "Several slaves belonging to officers have left their masters and gone over to Matamoros. Capt. Gatlin and Lieuts. Bragg and Gantt have each lost a boy. If we are located on this border we shall have to employ white servants." [11]

More serious than a few desertions was a report that Mexican forces had crossed the Rio Grande. Taylor sent Captain Seth Thornton with some dragoons to investigate. On April 25 Thornton rode into an ambush, got some of his men killed, and himself and the rest of his command captured.[12] The war had begun. Taylor, anxious for his supply depot at Point Isabel, hastened to the coast on May 1 with all but five hundred of his men. To defend Fort Texas he left the Seventh Infantry, Bragg's battery, four eighteen-pound guns, the sick, the malingerers, and "the Great Western."

The fort, which covered eight hundred yards, had an earthen wall nine and one-half feet high, a parapet fifteen feet

Brown," New York *Spirit of the Times*, July 25, 1846; *New Orleans Weekly Delta*, April 5, 1847.

[11] George A. McCall, *Letters From the Frontiers* . . . (Philadelphia, 1868), pp. 440–41; Rhoda van Bibber Tanner Doubleday, ed., *Journals of . . . Brevet Major Philip Norbourne Barbour* . . . (New York, 1936), p. 28.

[12] Smith, *War With Mexico*, I, 149–50; Henry, *Story of the Mexican War*, pp. 47, 327; Doubleday, ed., *Journals of Major Barbour*, pp. 45–48.

thick, and was fronted by a ditch eight feet deep and from fifteen to twenty-two feet wide. Hopefully, Bragg's six-pounders and the eighteen-pound guns would provide the necessary defensive firepower to check any Mexican advance, but only 150 rounds of ammunition per gun were at hand. The magazine, fashioned of pork barrels filled with sand, was seven tiers thick, and covered with over ten feet of sand. Though the fort was strong at certain points, it was too large for five hundred men to defend against a vigorous assault. One wall, the drawbridge, and the interior defenses were unfinished. Nevertheless, Taylor believed the fort to be "in a good state of defense," and he expected the Americans to keep the Mexicans out until he returned. The fort's commander was Jacob Brown, a veteran of thirty-one years' service who had risen from private to major, noted for his "habits of exact discipline and strict accountability." [13]

The siege of Fort Texas—an artillery duel between the Mexicans and the Americans—began two days after Taylor left. A newspaperman reported: "On the morning of the 3rd at daylight the Mexicans opened their batteries on our fort, or rather our grand entrenchments; from that moment it was right hot work until after 12 o'clock, when both parties had to cease until their guns would cool." While the guns cooled, the American officers drank a brandy toddy. It was an exciting introduction to war for Bragg and his fellow lieutenants. Rapid and accurate fire by the American artillerymen prevented an enemy assault, but by May 6 Bragg had lost four horses and the Mexicans had surrounded the fort. They threatened to kill any man who failed to surrender immediately. A council of officers met to consider the Mexican ultimatum; Major Brown was mortally wounded, and the Americans were

[13] Henry, *Campaign Sketches*, p. 86; Doubleday, ed., *Journals of Major Barbour*, pp. 49–51; Smith, *War With Mexico*, I, 163, 467–568; Robinson, *Organization of the Army*, II, 49–50.

disturbingly short of ammunition. Even so, the officers voted unanimously to continue their defense; they were confident Taylor would return in time to relieve the fort. On May 9 their anxiety vanished; Taylor's force, which had won victories at Palo Alto on the eighth and at Resaca de la Palma on the ninth, arrived and the Mexicans retreated across the Rio Grande. Tired but happy men greeted the relief columns. "The defenders of the fort have suffered every thing," wrote an infantry officer; "they have been harassed night and day, and all looked haggard from the want of sleep." Though the Mexicans had fired some 2,700 shells into Fort Texas, only fifteen Americans had been killed or wounded. Yet an officer who had been with Taylor admitted: "I would have rather fought twenty battles than have passed the bombardment." [14]

For days after these battles the army luxuriated in its success. Fort Texas, renamed Fort Brown in memory of its dead commander, resounded with victory celebrations as the Americans consumed gallons of liquor and honored their heroes. Ringgold had been killed at Palo Alto, but all the other light artillery commanders were alive to enjoy their new prestige and promotions: Duncan from captain to brevet lieutenant colonel; Bragg and Randolph Ridgely, who had assumed command of Ringgold's battery, from lieutenants to brevet captains. Ridgely, a classmate of Bragg at West Point, had barely managed to graduate, but a volunteer considered him "a splendid officer, and the bravest and most reckless man, that I ever saw." [15]

[14] Nichols, *Zach Taylor's Little Army*, pp. 68, 81–82; Smith, *War With Mexico*, I, 176, 468; George H. Thomas to "Captain," September 21, 1859 (microfilm copy), George H. Thomas Papers, New York Public Library; Lewis, *Captain Sam Grant*, p. 152; Hubert Howe Bancroft, *History of Mexico* (6 vols., San Francisco, 1883–1888), V, 364–65; Henry, *Campaign Sketches*, pp. 103–4.

[15] Doubleday, ed., *Journals of Major Barbour*, p. 70; Smith, *War With Mexico*, I, 164–79, 465–69; First Class Rolls at West Point in Engineering, Ethics, and Artillery, June 8, 12, 1837, Post Orders; Dickins and

These young artillery commanders deserved promotion, for they directed the army's "secret" weapons—the "flying guns" which had broken Mexican infantry and cavalry columns in the initial battles and would do so repeatedly throughout the war. The light batteries actually gave the Americans a decisive advantage over the Mexicans, and clearly proved how superior training and technological improvement could upset traditional tactics. During the first half of the nineteenth century military tactics were designed to compensate for the inaccuracy and short range of the basic infantry weapon, the smoothbore musket. Troops fought in tight formations and fired in volleys because a soldier might fire a smoothbore at a man all day from a distance of a few hundred yards and never hit him. The usual battle alignment was two or three lines of infantry, armed with smoothbores and long bayonets, and supported in the rear by artillery and on the flanks by cavalry. After the infantrymen had fired a volley, they advanced, elbow to elbow, at a trot. The defenders, who had time to fire only one or two volleys before the attackers reached their line, either repulsed the assault or retreated to reform and counterattack. Success in battle usually depended upon strict discipline and precise movements. If the infantrymen on either side broke ranks, enemy cavalry dashed in from the flanks to slash at the retreaters with sabers. Artillery might provide the necessary firepower to stop an infantry attack, but only if the guns were well placed.[16] Before 1846 artillery had been relatively immobile in North American battles; consequently, commanders always tried to attack where there were few guns.

Forney, eds., *American State Papers, Military Affairs*, VII, 933; Benjamin F. Cheatham to His Sister, October 6, 1846, Benjamin Franklin Cheatham Papers, Tennessee State Library, Nashville.

[16] Grant, *Personal Memoirs*, I, 95; Mahan, *An Elementary Treatise on Advanced-Guard* (New Orleans, 1861), pp. 9–25; Winfield Scott, *Infantry Tactics* (New York, 1861), *passim*.

Mexican generals tried to attack American weak points, only to suffer surprisingly heavy losses. The horse-drawn American guns, fewer but lighter than the relatively immobile Mexican pieces, moved quickly along the battleline to threatened points and repeatedly checked infantry or cavalry assaults with scattershot. "How magnificently has the Horse Artillery proved its efficiency," wrote Captain William S. Henry of the Fourth Infantry. "After witnessing its destructive effects on the field [at Palo Alto and Resaca de la Palma] . . . the most skeptical must be convinced it is an arm that throws any amount of strength into an army, and actually makes up in its dreadful efficiency for want of numbers." Taylor himself admitted that "The affair of the 8th [at Palo Alto] was for the most part one of artillery in which ours proved vastly superior. . . ." [17]

Neither the artillerymen nor any other troops saw action again for several months after the first battles. Following the occupation of Matamoros on May 18 Bragg spent much of his time directing the defense of Captain Seth Thornton, whose ambush and capture had been the immediate cause of war. Thornton, who had been arrested and charged with cowardice after his release by the Mexicans, selected as his lawyers Bragg and Major Philip Barbour of the Third Infantry. Perhaps Thornton picked Bragg because he was acquainted with courts-martial. At the trial, which lasted a week and was followed closely by the newspapermen who were with the army, Bragg presented an elaborate defense. "It was a strong one," reported Barbour. In any event, it was effective, for the court acquitted Thornton.[18]

[17] Henry, *Campaign Sketches*, p. 129; Zachary Taylor to "My dear Sir," June 18, 1846, Zachary Taylor Papers, Library of Congress.

[18] *New Orleans Daily Delta*, October 16, 1846; Doubleday, ed., *Journals of Major Barbour*, pp. 88–89; Henry, *Story of the Mexican War*, p. 327. Some months later Bragg volunteered to serve as counsel for Lieutenant Samuel D. Sturgis who had been arrested for losing some men to the Mexicans near Victoria. Sturgis was acquitted and "came out of the affair with more credit than any one concerned with it." Dabney Hern-

Bragg turned from law to war again in early August when the army, augmented by volunteer units and supplies, started for Monterey, some 250 miles southwest of Matamoros. Instead of taking the most direct route over arid land, Taylor decided to go up the Rio Grande to Camargo and then follow the fertile San Juan Valley south to Monterey. Bragg's battery, together with Lieutenant Colonel John Garland and four companies of infantry, marched away from Matamoros in rain and ankle-deep mud on August 5 as fife and drum played "The Girl I Left Behind Me." It took them eight days to cover the 128 miles to Camargo. When the rain stopped the heat became so intense even some veterans straggled.[19]

Throughout the march Bragg maintained strict discipline, and he used the army's short stop in Camargo to practice combat formations. "We paused in our walk to witness the morning drill of Captain Bragg's excellent company of artillery," wrote Major Luther Giddings of the First Ohio Volunteers. "The horses, as well as men, seemed to understand their business perfectly . . . they whirled the guns and caissons over the plain with wonderful rapidity and ease." Giddings believed that light field batteries were "the most formidable auxiliaries that science has ever given to war," and he reported that "Bragg, a skillful and courageous officer, is . . . distinguished for his attention to the minutiae of his profession; a merit to be esteemed no less than heroic daring, when it is remembered what disasters may result in critical moments from the most trifling casualties." [20]

Bragg's battery was primed for battle when it arrived at the American camp three miles northeast of Monterey on Septem-

<hr />

don Maury, *Recollections of a Virginian in the Mexican, Indian, and Civil Wars* (New York, 1894), p. 31.

[19] Henry, *Campaign Sketches*, pp. 132-52.

[20] [Luther Giddings], *Sketches of the Campaign in Northern Mexico in Eighteen Hundred Forty-Six and Seven* (New York, 1853), p. 76.

ber 19. So was Taylor, who intended to take the city. Monterey was protected by strong forts, an army larger than Taylor's, mountains on three sides, and looked impregnable. The Americans numbered slightly more than 6,000 men, divided into two divisions of regulars and two divisions of volunteers. Their artillery consisted of four field batteries, a pair of twenty-four-pound howitzers, and a ten-pound mortar. Taylor assigned the light guns to the regular divisions: Twiggs got Bragg's and Ridgely's batteries; Worth got Duncan's and William W. Mackall's, which recently had joined Taylor's army.[21]

On September 20, after an incomplete reconnaissance, Taylor sent Worth's Division of 2,000 men to flank the forts at the western edge of the city and close the highway to Saltillo. This division of his army just before battle must have shocked the West Pointers, for it seemed to violate the rule they had learned about concentration of forces when facing the enemy. "No detachment should be made on the eve of battle," Napoleon had written. "The first principle of war is never to give battle except with all the troops that can be collected on the field of operations."[22] To Mahan's students this meant all forces should be massed to meet the enemy. If Taylor had heard of such a rule, it made no difference to him. Contemptuous of both military theory and Mexican generalship, he based his battle plan upon raw courage—his own and his troops'.

To divert attention from Worth's movements, Taylor placed Bragg's and Ridgely's batteries along with several infantry regiments on the plain before Monterey in full view of

---

[21] Samuel G. French, *Two Wars: An Autobiography* (Nashville, 1901), p. 60; Smith, *War With Mexico*, I, 492–93; George W. Cullum, *Biographical Register of the Officers and Graduates of the U.S. Military Academy* . . . (2 vols., New York, 1868), I, 569–70.

[22] Napoleon, *Commentaires de Napoleon Premier* (6 vols., Paris, 1867), II, 56; III, 295.

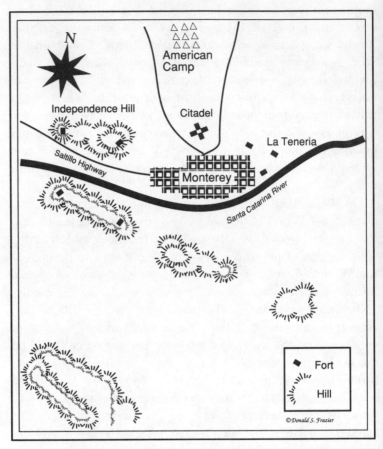

BATTLE OF MONTEREY, September 19-24, 1846

the Mexicans. "We presented quite an imposing appearance," wrote one of the infantry officers. Taylor and his staff rode out, the Mexicans fired a few shots that did no damage, and after dark all the troops except Bragg's battery and the Third Infantry retired. Bragg remained on the plain until nine that night to cover the placement of the army's "big guns," the ten-inch mortar and the two howitzers, near the citadel, which guarded the northern approaches to the city.[23]

The next morning, while Worth's Division cut the Mexican supply line and blocked retreat from the city by occupying the road to Saltillo, Taylor's troops attacked Monterey's eastern defenses. Twiggs's Division, led by Lieutenant Colonel Garland because Twiggs had taken an overdose of medicine the night before, moved first. In his rather vague instructions, Taylor told Garland "if you . . . can take any of them little Forts down there with the bay'net you better do it." Garland thought he could; he ordered his infantry and Bragg's and Ridgely's batteries into Monterey through a crossfire from the citadel and the forts at the city's eastern edge. As the infantry advanced, Taylor noticed some Mexican cavalry on his flank. He reported: "Captain Bragg, who was at hand, immediately galloped with his battery to a suitable position, from which a few discharges effectually dispersed the enemy." Those inside the city were more difficult to dislodge. With more courage than discretion the Americans charged down barricaded streets and into a pointblank Mexican fire which halted the advance. "Being in utter ignorance of our locality," wrote an officer, "we had to stand and take it . . . there was no resisting the deadly concealed fire, which appeared to come from every direction." Twiggs recalled: "Captain B. Bragg's battery accompanied the command under a destructive fire, which killed and disabled several of his men and horses." [24]

When Garland ordered the division to withdraw, Bragg did so with difficulty. His gunners, temporarily blinded by dust diffused as Mexican shells hit adobe and stone buildings, had been unable to fire a shot.[25] To retreat, Bragg had to unlimber

[23] Henry, *Campaign Sketches*, pp. 192–93; Smith, *War With Mexico*, I, 238–42.

[24] *House Document*, 29 Cong., 2 sess., No. 4, pp. 86, 100; Lewis, *Captain Sam Grant*, p. 175; Smith, *War With Mexico*, I, 250–51; Henry, *Campaign Sketches*, pp. 194–95.

[25] French, *Two Wars*, p. 62; Henry, *Campaign Sketches*, p. 195; John

his gun carriages and reverse them; there was no room to turn
about in the narrow streets. Before the battery reached the
city's outskirts, two of its horses had been killed. Bragg halted
his men and ordered Lieutenants John F. Reynolds and Samuel
G. French to cut the harnesses and push the dead animals off
the road. By the time this had been done, two more horses had
been hit. They were released, wrote French, "and with their
entrails dragging . . . commenced eating grass." An officer
who passed Bragg's battery at this point pronounced it "a
perfect wreck." He wrote: "a number of artillerymen, and
more than a dozen . . . horses, were down in the same spot
. . . the ground about the guns [was] slippery with . . .
foam and blood," but Bragg and his men, still "exposed . . .
to a galling fire, were deliberately . . . stripping the harness
from the dead and disabled animals, determined that not a
buckle or strap should be lost upon the field." [26]

Bragg began to make repairs as soon as his battery got beyond the range of the Mexican guns. His heavy losses [27]
troubled him, for he knew that his ability to fight—indeed the
success of the campaign—depended upon sufficient men,
horses, and equipment. Since he could count on no replace-
ments,[28] he resolved to salvage everything possible; therefore,
he sent French back to the outskirts of Monterey to retrieve
any equipment left with the dead horses. French went reluctantly. On the way he met General Taylor who told him to

---

R. Kenly, *Memoirs of a Maryland Volunteer* . . . (Philadelphia, 1873),
pp. 111, 113–14.

[26] *House Document*, 29 Cong., 2 sess., No. 4, p. 101; Samuel C. Reid,
Jr., *The Scouting Expedition of McCollouch's Texas Rangers* . . .
(Philadelphia, 1848), p. 172; French, *Two Wars*, p. 62; Giddings,
Sketches, pp. 168–69.

[27] Reid (*Scouting Expeditions*, p. 172) states that Bragg lost two men
and four horses killed, and four men and seven horses wounded. But
Giddings (*Sketches*, p. 168) mentions "a dozen . . . horses . . . down."

[28] Bragg wrote Duncan (April 4, 1847, Duncan Papers): "We cannot
get men, not a recruit having been sent . . . since we came into the
field."

forget about lost equipment. French had some anxious moments on his ride back to camp as he dodged shells, and he "never forgave Bragg for the picayune order." [29]

At the time, however, French had little opportunity to consider his grievance because shortly after his mission the battery returned to action. General William O. Butler's Volunteer Division, which had pressed the attack after Garland's men withdrew, needed help, so Taylor again sent Garland forward. For the second time that day Bragg led his battery into Monterey. He did his best to support the infantry, but the narrow streets prevented him from bringing more than one gun into action. With it he raked the street with grape shot, broke a charge by Mexican lancers, and impressed American infantrymen by exposing himself to enemy fire while coolly directing his gunner.[30]

Just before dark Taylor recalled his forces. He had won no decision in the confused and bloody battle at the eastern edge of the city, but Fort Teneria, a major bastion, was in American hands. Garland's infantry stayed behind to hold the captured forts while the rest of the troops under Taylor's direct control retired to their main camp for food and ammunition.

The next day Taylor's men merely held their ground. A heavy enemy fire raked exposed positions, but the Mexicans launched no counterattacks. Taylor reported: "The guard left in [the captured points] . . . the preceding night, except Captain Ridgely's company, was relieved at midday by General [John A.] Quitman's brigade. Captain Bragg's battery was thrown under cover in front of the town, to repel any demonstration of cavalry in that quarter." [31]

Fortunately for the Americans, General Worth had achieved a number of tactical successes which more than

[29] French, *Two Wars*, p. 62.

[30] Smith, *War With Mexico*, I, 252–54; Henry, *Campaign Sketches*, p. 200; T. B. Thorpe, *Our Army at Monterey* (Philadelphia, 1847), p. 53.

[31] *House Document*, 29 Cong., 2 sess., No. 4, pp. 86–87.

compensated for Taylor's limited gains. By nightfall on September 21 Worth had captured all but one of the forts that protected the rear and western flank of Monterey. The following day, while Taylor's men remained inactive, Worth took the works on Independence Hill, and trapped the Mexican army in the city. That night, as the enemy concentrated near the central plaza, the Americans shivered through a second night of rain and prepared for another assault.[32]

Taylor's entire army advanced at daybreak on September 23. Bragg's battery crossed the plain within range of the citadel's guns and rushed into Monterey at full gallop. "The fighting was very severe, but nothing compared to that on the 21st," wrote an officer of the Third Infantry, "except at one street running directly from the Cathedral." There the Mexicans, protected by a barricade and stone houses, poured a "*shower of bullets*" down the street and stopped the American advance. The Third Infantry was still pinned down when Bragg arrived to support them. He immediately moved one of his guns into the open and fired "up the street [but] with very little effect, as the weight of the metal was entirely too light." Nevertheless, Bragg's action allowed the infantry to maneuver. An officer recalled that when the gun was pointed at the Mexicans, they "would fall behind their barricade, and at that time we could cross without a certainty of being shot." The artillerymen suffered heavy losses; among the men killed was Bragg's first sergeant who "was shot through the heart while aiming his gun." [33]

When ammunition ran low in the afternoon Taylor broke off the engagement. Orders to withdraw came none too soon for Bragg. The action in Monterey had been a field artilleryman's nightmare; aside from a body of lancers, which he easily

[32] Smith, *War With Mexico*, I, 254-55, 243-46; Henry, *Campaign Sketches*, pp. 200-1.

[33] *House Document*, 29 Cong., 2 sess., No. 4, pp. 87, 101; Henry, *Campaign Sketches*, pp. 206-7.

dispersed, Bragg had been unable to find a good target. He and the other artillery officers believed Taylor had misused the light guns where they could neither find targets nor maneuver. A volunteer officer agreed. "In this engagement, the artillery-men, or cavalry, neither had an opportunity of doing much, because the artillery we had was too light to damage the strong walls," Captain Benjamin F. Cheatham of the Third Tennessee Volunteer Infantry explained to his sister. "I consider that old Taylor committed one of the greatest blunders that ever a General was guilty of in coming here to attack one of the strongest fortified towns in Mexico, with nothing in the world but small artillery for open field fighting . . . ." [34]

Before Bragg's battery could withdraw from Monterey, Reynolds had to call on volunteers to help dislodge a gun carriage from the narrow street, and several additional artillerymen were killed. When a horse driver fell dead from his saddle, Bragg ordered a halt and directed French "to dismount and take off the man's sword." "I did so," recalled French, "and took from his pocket a knife, for I thought I might be sent back if I did not save that too." But Bragg refused to take the knife because "it was not public property." French explained: "I write down these little things, for they give instances of the observance of details, characteristic of this officer, not obtained from history." [35]

This was the last time Bragg or any other American had to worry about salvaging "public property" from Monterey, for the next day, as Taylor prepared another assault, Mexican officers rode into the American lines under a flag of truce to seek surrender terms. At first Taylor demanded unconditional surrender, but when the Mexicans demurred he allowed a joint commission to negotiate the capitulation. Under the terms

[34] Smith, *War With Mexico*, I, 256; Benjamin F. Cheatham to His Sister, October 6, 1846, Cheatham Papers.
[35] Nichols, *Zach Taylor's Little Army*, pp. 163–65; Henry, *Campaign Sketches*, p. 208; French, *Two Wars*, pp. 63–64.

agreed upon the Mexicans withdrew from the city with all their arms and equipment, and an armistice of eight weeks followed.[36]

In the subsequent battle reports the artillerymen were acclaimed for their conduct. Taylor wrote: "Captains Bragg and Ridgely served with their batteries during the operation under my own observation, and in part under my immediate orders, and exhibited distinguished skill and gallantry." Twiggs insisted that Bragg, Ridgely, "and their subalterns . . . deserve the highest praise for their skill and good conduct under the heaviest fire." [37]

Unfortunately, no amount of commendation could offset the false lesson Bragg learned at Monterey. "You will perceive that our loss has been severe," Taylor admitted to a friend, "but when the superior numbers of the enemy, and his strongly fortified position are taken into consideration, I think we may congratulate ourselves that it was not greater. A great destruction of life must, at best, generally attend an attack upon an enemy in a fortified position." Taylor was right; he had been lucky indeed to capture a stronghold by assault with relatively light losses of approximately eight hundred casualties.[38] But impressionable young officers like Bragg missed the point. They discounted the hazards of such assaults, and even

[36] Smith, *War With Mexico*, I, 258-61; Hamilton, *Zachary Taylor*, pp. 214-15; Singletary, *The Mexican War*, pp. 41-42.

[37] *House Document*, 29 Cong., 2 sess., No. 4, pp. 89, 101.

[38] Zachary Taylor to Nathaniel Young, October 27, 1846, Taylor Papers; Hamilton, *Zachary Taylor*, pp. 215-16. Captain Benjamin F. Cheatham of the Third Tennessee Volunteer Infantry believed his regiment "had the misfortune . . . to suffer more than any other two Regiments." "We took into the field three hundred and forty men, and had killed and wounded one hundred and four," he informed his sister. "So you see that we had killed and wounded nearly one third of our force, which is a thing almost unheard of. The Mexicans say that we are the first people that they ever saw run up into the cannon's mouth, they wanted to know where we came from, and what kind of people we were." Cheatham to His Sister, October 6, 16, 1846, Cheatham Papers.

minimized Taylor's misuse of artillery. What seemed important to them was Taylor's success; he had proved that a determined attack could overcome the strongest defense. After Monterey, if not before, Taylor became Bragg's military ideal and mentor.[39]

[39] Bragg's admiration for Taylor is expressed in several letters. See, for example, Bragg to Duncan, January 13, 1848, Duncan Papers; Bragg to French, October 13, 1847, Samuel G. French Papers, United States Military Academy.

CHAPTER IV

A little more grape

1846–1848

WHILE THE AMERICAN troops rested at Monterey during the armistice, Bragg received official notice of his promotion to captain and his assignment to a new command. For months Congressman George S. Houston of Alabama, probably at the insistence of Bragg's brother John, had demanded that Bragg be given command of the fully equipped light battery, formerly commanded by Ringgold, and since his death by Ridgely. Just after the fall of Monterey the War Department acquiesced. Responding to another prod by Houston, Adjutant General Jones wrote: "on 25th Sept. an order was issued transferring Capt. Bragg to Light Company C, 3rd Artillery, the Company commanded by the late Maj. Ringgold." [1]

Bragg's right to command Company C was challenged, not by Ridgely, who was killed when his horse fell on him before the news of Bragg's assignment reached Monterey, but by Captain Thomas W. Sherman, who informed the War Department that he deserved the appointment. General Scott refused to decide the issue; rather, he authorized Taylor to transfer Bragg and Sherman out of his army if such action seemed "essential to the good of the service." Taylor opposed the tranfer of either man; he needed and hoped to retain them both, but he definitely intended to keep Bragg. "It is vitally important, for the good of the service, that a permanent and

---

[1] Roger Jones to Zachary Taylor, October 8, 1846 (copy), Letters Sent, AGO; George S. Houston to Secretary of War William L. Marcy, and Jones's endorsement, December 28, 1846, Letters Received, AGO.

efficient captain, experienced in the field service of artillery
. . . be attached to Company C, which is greatly in want of
administrative care and management," Taylor informed Scott.
"I deem Captain Bragg eminently qualified in all respects for
this command . . . the battery which he leaves has by his care
been brought into such good condition, and is withal so well
officered, that it may suffer a change of commanders without
material injury." Taylor's strong letter settled the question.
Bragg assumed command of Company C and Sherman got
Bragg's old battery.[2]

To his new command Bragg brought his usual high standards of drill, discipline, and efficiency. Company C, though
still the best-equipped battery in the army, had lost heavily in
horses and material during the recent campaign. To recoup
these losses, Bragg swept the area around Monterey for
leather, metal, and horses. When he could find any of these
items he bought them with Company money. His attitude was
wholly pragmatic; so much so, in fact, that he purchased
animals which belonged to other American units. The bereft
colonel of a Tennessee volunteer cavalry regiment complained
acidly to General Gideon J. Pillow: "I am under the disagreeable necessity of reporting to you the fact that some five soldiers in the cavalry regiment have sold their horses to Capt.
Bragg of the 3rd Artillery." When Bragg could not buy horses
he borrowed them. An officer, who had loaned his animal to
the artillery while temporarily detached from the army, wrote
from Camargo in October 1846: "I shall [go to Monterey
tomorrow] . . . to get my horse, who is with Bragg's battery.
This is my favorite horse Champion." Several days later the
officer announced: "I have received my horse Champion; he is
in fine condition and full of spirit."[3]

[2] Jones to Taylor, October 8, 1846, and Taylor to Jones, November 8,
1846, *House Executive Document*, 30 Cong., 1 sess., No. 60, pp. 475, 435;
McCall, *Letters From the Frontiers*, p. 466.

[3] J.E. Thomas to Gideon J. Pillow, January 13, 1847, Mexican War

Despite the loss of Champion, Bragg soon had Company C in excellent repair. An officer who joined the company shortly after Bragg took command considered it "in the highest state of efficiency, discipline, and drill of any organization, of any arm, that I have ever seen." Six horse teams pulled the battery's four guns, each "served by a detachment of twelve men mounted . . . on high-mettled and well-trained horses . . . over the plain of exercise like a whirlwind." [4]

When the truce ended Bragg was ready for action. Taylor, who had opposed the War Department's suggestion that he move directly toward Mexico City from Monterey because he believed his supply line would be too exposed, now proposed an alternative movement. He wanted to establish a large supply base at the port of Vera Cruz and then to advance west on the Mexican capital. When the government approved this plan, Taylor left the bulk of his army behind and marched to Victoria, 150 miles southeast of Monterey, to make a reconnaissance in force. With him went Bragg's battery, Twiggs's Division, and several regiments of volunteers. While in Victoria, on January 14, 1847, Taylor received a letter from General Scott, who was on his way to capture Vera Cruz and to conquer Mexico. "I am not coming, my dear General, to supersede you in the immediate command on the line of operations rendered illustrious by you and your gallant army," wrote Scott. "But, my dear General, I shall be obliged to take from you most of the gallant officers and men (regulars & volunteers) whom you have so long and so nobly commanded. I am afraid that I shall, by imperious necessity . . . reduce you, for the time, to stand on the defensive. This will be infinitely painful to you, and for that reason distressing to me.

Record Group 94, Adjutant General's Office, Old Army Section, War Records Branch, National Archives; McCall, *Letters From the Frontiers,* p. 466.

[4] Birkhimer, *Historical Sketch,* p. 62.

But I rely upon your patriotism to submit to the temporary sacrifice with cheerfulness." [5]

Taylor, who had presaged such developments, was apoplectic. He believed the President had hampered the war from the outset. Moreover, Taylor knew the administration had condemned him for the liberal terms granted the Mexicans at Monterey, though he had no conception of the depth of Polk's dislike. On November 14, 1846, the President had written in his diary: "The Cabinet fully discussed the conduct of General Taylor and were agreed that he was unfit for the chief command, that he had not mind enough for the station, that he was a bitter political partisan, and had no sympathies with the administration. . . ." Taylor had counted on his own popularity and on General Scott for protection against Polk, but now the beleaguered general suspected a plot. To his brother Taylor complained: "The course which [Scott pursues] . . . cannot be misunderstood, it is to break me down, a plan concocted by Scott, Marcy & Worth; which was to strip me of my command or the greater part of those that could be relied on, under the expectation that I would either leave the country in disgust, or be driven from it by the enemy, in either case they & their creatures would make the most of it. . . ." [6]

Bragg shared his chieftain's views. He was too emotionally committed to do otherwise. In his ambivalent attitude toward authority, superiors were either heroes with whom Bragg could identify or villains and fools. He denounced Scott and the administration, and called Scott's proposed campaign a " 'd—d expedition' [which] has carried off everything." Why capture Vera Cruz? Bragg asked Duncan, who had already

[5] Smith, *War With Mexico*, I, 355–56; Dyer, *Taylor*, pp. 212–25; Nichols, *Zach Taylor's Little Army*, pp. 181–82; Winfield Scott to Zachary Taylor, November 25, 1846, Zachary Taylor Papers.

[6] Dyer, *Taylor*, pp. 207–26; Quaife, ed., *Polk Diary*, II, 119, 229–36; Zachary Taylor to Joseph P. Taylor, January 14, 1847, Zachary Taylor Papers.

been transferred to Scott's army; "after you have it I don't see its use. I agree with you and always have that this is the only route by which to attack the country." Bragg happily reported that Taylor no longer intended to remain on the defensive in northern Mexico: "He has received new lights on the subject. . . . I heard him most emphatically express his opinions, and candidly confess that he had changed his mind completely." [7]

Taylor definitely wanted to launch an offensive. "I believe they [the troops] are ready to meet the enemy at any moment, no matter as to numbers," he wrote. "I shall in a day or two have near 5,000 men . . . the greater portion of them will be volunteers yet I have no fears but we will give a satisfactory account. . . . I have just received [a letter] from Genl Scott . . . he advises me to fall back . . . in reply to the same I have informed him I would do no such thing without orders to that effect from proper authority." [8]

Hatred of Scott overcame reason in both Taylor and Bragg. To advance deeper into Mexico with only five thousand soldiers, mostly inexperienced volunteers, was rash indeed. The only veteran regulars that remained from Taylor's old army were four companies of dragoons and Bragg's and Thomas Sherman's undermanned batteries, which had been virtually stripped of experienced men. Instead of its full complement of five officers and seventy enlisted men, Bragg's company consisted of three officers and thirty men, nearly all of them raw recruits. To supplement his veterans Taylor had merely General John E. Wool and Major John M. Washington's untried eight-gun battery; these were the only regulars the government allowed Taylor to retain from a division which arrived in December. Nor was the country over which Taylor pro-

[7] Robert Anderson, *An Artillery Officer in the Mexican War, 1846-7: Letters of Robert Anderson, Captain, 3rd Artillery, U.S.A.* (New York, 1911), p. 49; Bragg to Duncan, April 4, 1847, Duncan Papers.

[8] Zachary Taylor to Joseph P. Taylor, February 8, 1847, Zachary Taylor Papers.

posed to advance favorable for invaders. A volunteer who had just arrived wrote on January 20: "Mexico, so far as we have seen it, is by no means an inviting country. High, *bare*, and rugged mountains, and dry, and (consequently) barren plains, constitute the leading features of the country everywhere. Not a foot of land is attempted to be cultivated which is not susceptible of irrigation. No rain has fallen since we entered Mexico, and we are told that *none is expected*, here, till May or June." [9]

Regardless of handicaps Taylor left Monterey in early February looking for a fight. He marched seventy miles to Saltillo, where he left a detachment, then recklessly proceeded eighteen miles farther south to Agua Nueva. Here reports on the approach of a large Mexican army cooled Taylor's offensive ardor, and on February 21 the Americans retreated. General Wool, Taylor's second-in-command, stopped with the bulk of the army to establish a defense line near the hacienda of Buena Vista, while Taylor and a small escort—which included Bragg's battery—hurried to Saltillo, some five miles closer to Monterey. [10]

At Saltillo Taylor divided Bragg's battery. One gun, under Captain William H. Shover, was detached for the defense of the town; another, under Lieutenant Charles L. Kilburn, was sent to guard the army's supply wagons. Bragg, without officers and with only two guns under his control, went along with Colonel William R. McKee's regiment of Kentucky volunteers to hold the extreme right of the Buena Vista defense line. [11]

[9] *Senate Executive Document*, 30 Cong., 1 sess., No. 1, p. 203; Smith, *War With Mexico*, I, 555–56; Dyer, *Taylor*, p. 229; W. H. Bissell to Gustav Koerner, January 20, 1847, *Transactions of the Illinois State Historical Society, 1907* (Springfield, 1908), p. 234.

[10] Joseph P. Taylor to Winfield Scott, February 12, 1847, Zachary Taylor Papers; Maurice G. Fulton, ed., *Diary & Letters of Josiah Gregg: Excursions in Mexico & California, 1847–1850* (Norman, 1944), p. 35; Smith, *War With Mexico*, I, 383–85.

[11] *Senate Executive Document*, 30 Cong., 1 sess., No. 1, p. 200.

When Bragg reached his assigned position on the afternoon of February 22, he unlimbered his two guns, threw up a "slight breastwork," and waited. From his location on the American right flank, he could view the entire defense position, which extended some three miles east across the Saltillo road to a mountain pass. Bragg's battery and McKee's Kentuckians were separated from the other American units by a series of almost impassable gullies, ten and twenty feet deep, which ran southwest from Buena Vista. Beyond these gullies Bragg could see part of Washington's battery and two regiments of volunteers guarding the road to Saltillo. Farther east were other regiments, T. W. Sherman's battery, dragoons, and the rest of Washington's battery. Near the base of the mountains, far to the east, Bragg could barely distinguish Arkansas and Kentucky cavalry regiments. The American line was thin, and Bragg kept "a vigilant watch" during the night. Sleep was impossible for most men anyway. Early in the evening martial music filtering up from the enemy's camp nearby kept them awake; later, it rained and turned cold.[12]

The battle opened the next morning on the extreme left of the American line. "From my position," wrote Bragg, "I could clearly observe the enemy's movements, and perceived that unless I recrossed the ravine, I should be excluded from the action. . . ." He secured permission to move from Taylor's chief engineer, who was in the vicinity, and started toward the fighting. Before he had gone far, Bragg noticed a heavy cloud of dust in the direction of Saltillo. Alarmed that this might indicate Mexican cavalry in the American rear, he hastened to investigate only to discover that Taylor and his escort had raised the dust as they hurried to the front.

From this point, Bragg followed the action to the left-center of the American line, halted near a squadron of the First Dragoons, and opened fire with what he called "marked effect on masses of the enemy's infantry. . . . Here I remained,"

[12] *Ibid.*; Smith, *War With Mexico*, I, 385-88.

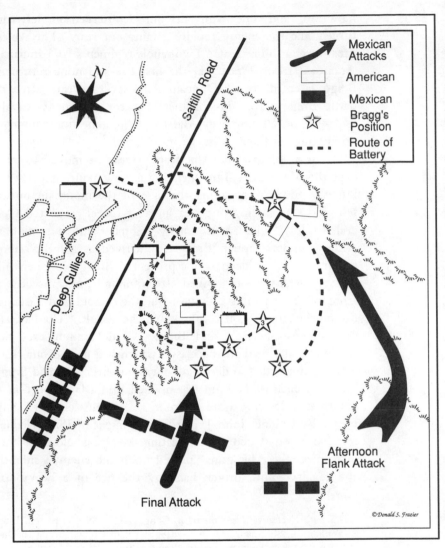

Legend:
- Mexican Attacks
- American
- Mexican
- Bragg's Position
- Route of Battery

N

Saltillo Road

Deep Gullies

5

2

3

4

6

Afternoon Flank Attack

Final Attack

©Donald S. Frazier

BATTLE OF BUENA VISTA, February 23, 1847

he wrote, "and kept up my fire until I observed our left flank turned, and the enemy rapidly gaining our rear." The Americans were in full retreat. "Two whole regiments [of] Indiana & Arkansas [troops] ran [at] the first fire and none returned," Bragg later informed Duncan. And several years after the battle Bragg wrote his brother that the Kentucky cavalry under Colonel Humphrey Marshall "did some fine running & no fighting [at Buena Vista]." [13]

When Bragg saw the Americans retreat, he moved to intercept the Mexicans. "The enemy was now pouring masses of infantry and cavalry along the base of the mountain on our left, and was gaining our rear in great force," reported General Taylor. "The 2d Kentucky regiment and a section of artillery under Captain Bragg . . . arrived at a most opportune moment." A deep ravine prevented Bragg's or Sherman's battery, which soon arrived, from unlimbering directly in front of the enemy's columns, but their rapid and sustained fire on the attacker's flank disrupted the assault. "The batteries of Captains Sherman and Bragg . . . did much execution . . . particularly upon the masses which had gained our rear," Taylor admitted. "So destructive was our fire," claimed Bragg, "that the enemy's column was divided, and a large portion of it retreated, leaving those in front . . . totally cut off." Supported by Colonel John J. Hardin's regiment of Illinois volunteers, Bragg pursued the retreating Mexicans close to their own lines where his guns "played upon the enemy's infantry and cavalry" until driven back by the fire of a heavy battery.[14]

[13] *Senate Executive Document*, 30 Cong., 1 sess., No. 1, p. 200; Bragg to William T. Sherman, March 1, 1848, Sherman Papers; Bragg to Duncan, April 4, 1847, Duncan Papers; Bragg to John Bragg, March 25, 1852, John Bragg Papers, Southern Historical Collection, University of North Carolina.

[14] *Senate Executive Document*, 30 Cong., 1 sess., No. 1, pp. 134, 200-2; James Henry Carleton, *The Battle of Buena Vista* (New York, 1848), pp. 68-69.

Temporarily Bragg was out of action. As he explained in his report: "My ammunition, by this time, was exhausted from my limberboxes; my old cannoneers could not leave their guns; and my recruits—for the first time under fire—I found unequal to the task of replenishing my supply." He halted the battery under the cover of a ravine and personally supervised the transfer of ammunition to the forward boxes.

While he replenished his ammunition, Bragg had heard heavy firing; the Mexicans, heavily reinforced, had renewed their attack on the American left flank. As Bragg returned to action he could see that only Sherman, with one gun, and Colonel Jefferson Davis's red-shirted Mississippi regiment stood between the enemy and the rear of the American army. The outnumbered Mississippians had just been overwhelmed and were in retreat as Bragg arrived. "I am happy to believe," he wrote, "that my rapid . . . fire, opened just at this time, held the enemy in check until Colonel Davis could gain a position, and assume a stand." General Wool reported: "This was the hottest as well as the most critical part of the action; and at the moment when our troops were about giving way . . . the batteries of Captains Sherman and Bragg . . . by a well directed fire checked and drove back with great loss the enemy who had come close upon the muzzles of their pieces." With his three guns—Kilburn had recently rejoined the battery with his gun—Bragg pounded the Mexicans, and as they withdrew he advanced several hundred yards. "From this point I several times fell back, and as often advanced," he wrote, "regulating my movements by those of the enemy, my support being weak and uncertain." Wool ordered cavalry forward at Bragg's request to support the artillery. When the Americans counterattacked Bragg advanced to within canister range of the Mexican masses, confident that he could "inflict a loss upon the enemy from which he could not possibly recover."

But at this juncture an unusual event prevented the enemy's

annihilation. As Bragg's unrelenting fire, which "frequently threw whole columns into disorder," panicked the Mexican troops, several of their officers galloped into the American lines and asked, in the name of the Mexican commander, what peace terms Taylor would accept. General Wool, the senior American officer in the area, had no idea, but the question so confounded him that he halted the action to discuss the matter. The Mexicans that Bragg thought were trapped escaped as the American barrage ceased, but only when the enemy opened fire as Wool rode toward them with a white flag did the general realize he had been tricked.[15]

The American left flank now seemed secure, but Bragg feared the Mexicans would next attack the center of the defense line. Consequently, he moved in that direction. It was now past noon. The battery had been in action since early morning, the men were tired, and the horses, Bragg recalled, "were so exhausted . . . that a walk was all that could be forced from them by both whip and spur." Several deep ravines blocked his path, so Bragg took a circuitous route. Before he reached the front, however, he heard "an awful roar of musketry." Certain that Taylor needed more guns, Bragg left some of his "heaviest carriages [and] caissons, and pushed on with such as could move most rapidly."

It was fortunate that he did, for as Taylor admitted: "The moment was most critical. Captain O'Brien . . . was finally obliged to leave his guns on the field—his infantry support being entirely routed." Mexican forces advanced unopposed as Bragg's exhausted battery reached the front. While his gunners unlimbered and loaded with canister, Bragg asked Taylor, who was nearby, for infantry support. None was available; the battery alone stood between the Mexicans and victory. "Now, for the first time," recalled Bragg, "I felt the imminent peril in which we stood." He returned to his guns,

[15] Senate Executive Document, 30 Cong., 1 sess., No. 1, pp. 200-2, 149; Smith, War With Mexico, I, 389-93.

BRAGG'S BATTERY AT BUENA VISTA
Library of Congress

steadied his men with a few words, and directed his gunners to fire as rapidly as they could load. Colonel Jefferson Davis, some distance away, "saw the enemy's infantry advancing in three lines upon Captain Bragg's battery; which though entirely unsupported, resolutely held its position." Bragg withheld his fire until the Mexicans were but a few yards away. "The first discharge of canister caused the enemy to hesitate," reported Taylor, "the second and third drove him back in disorder, and saved the day." [16]

The battered American defense line had held. "At the close of the day," recalled Bragg, "we had not more than 2000 men on the field, the rest had fled." [17] Later he revised his estimate:

[16] *Senate Executive Document*, 30 Cong., 1 sess., No. 1, pp. 202, 136, 194.
[17] Bragg to Duncan, April 4, 1847, Duncan Papers.

"When the day closed we could not have mustered 2500 men," Bragg wrote Cump Sherman. Numbers were unimportant; what mattered was that Taylor's men had stopped the Mexicans. Both armies were exhausted, but Bragg was too tense to relax. That night he remained at the front with guards posted and horses in harness. The anticipated Mexican attack never came. At daylight the Americans discovered that the enemy had deserted the field. Taylor wanted to pursue and harass the Mexicans, but "on examin[in]g the state of the men & horses, found that five days marching, incipient watching in addition to 16 hours hard fighting had exhausted the first & broken the latter, that it was next to impossible to accomplish anything of importance without rest, I abandoned my intention." [18]

Afterwards Bragg called Buena Vista "an awful fight" which the Americans had been fortunate to win. "Nothing under Heaven . . . saved us . . . but the prestige of old Zach," insisted Bragg. "Wool was whipped . . . when Gen'l Taylor reached the ground." Wool had ordered Washington's battery to retreat, but Taylor countermanded the order and thus saved the army. Taylor, Bragg told a reporter, "did what no other general ever did—he rallied the beaten forces, a large portion of whom had never stood under fire before, and brought them back upon the field." "This [rout of the volunteers] is all denied now with solemnity and indignation, but it's still true," Bragg wrote Sherman. "Old Z. has said so, and officers who heard the order still repeat it—among them Henry Whiting [of the] 4th Art[iller]y. Indeed, Cump, to go to the merits of the case, no man . . . deserved so little credit at Buena Vista as Genl Wool." [19]

Generally, historians have been less critical than Bragg of

[18] *Senate Executive Document*, 30 Cong., 1 sess., No. 1, pp. 202–3; Smith, *War With Mexico*, I, 395; Zachary Taylor to Joseph P. Taylor, March 27, 1847, Zachary Taylor Papers.
[19] Bragg to Duncan, April 4, 1847, January 13, 1848, Duncan Papers; *Morning Courier & New York Inquirer*, October 28, 1848; Bragg to Sherman, March 1, 1848, Sherman Papers.

Wool's generalship at Buena Vista, yet most of the officers who were present agreed with Bragg's judgment. George Thomas wrote Jefferson Davis in 1858: "I do not believe there is a single officer whose mind is unprejudiced of all those who participated in the battle who does not give full credit to General Taylor for the selection of the ground and the general plan of arranging the army for the reception of the enemy. . . . Without wishing to disparage General Wool's talents as a commander it is my belief that he had lost the battle before General Taylor reached the field. . . ."[20]

Only volunteer troops, Bragg believed, matched Wool's incompetence. "For the details of the military operations . . . on this line," Bragg wrote Sherman, "I refer you to Genl Taylor's despatches. They are generously full so far as good conduct went, but rather silent on the subject of volunteers running &c &c." If the Americans had had "any one of our old regular Infantry regiments," contended Bragg, "we would have carried the enemy's artillery and destroyed his army." With two thousand regulars, he believed, the entire Mexican army could have been captured. In these views, Bragg echoed Taylor, who boasted: "Had they [Scott, Polk & Marcy] left me 1000, or even 500 regulars I feel satisfied the Mexican Army would have been completely broken down, & the whole of its artillery, & baggage captured or destroyed. . . ." But an army of volunteers had been unequal to the task. Three entire regiments scattered at the first shot, and only nine men out of five companies of the Baltimore Volunteer Battalion "remained on the field at night," claimed Bragg. "With the exception of the Miss. regiment under Col Davis, a graduate [of West Point], you may say *ditto* of almost all who were here. The extolled Texans in every instance where not sustained and urged on by regular troops . . . retreated—frequently in shameful confusion—from equal or inferior numbers." Only

[20] George H. Thomas to Jefferson Davis, August 1, 1858 (copy), Thomas Papers.

"when the plundering, murdering & ravishing commenced" were the Texans always present. "It is a fact," asserted Bragg, "that the wounded in the hospitals were trampled to death by refugees endeavoring to hide and pass for sick and wounded. And yet, that was a volunteer victory!! If any action in the whole war, Cump, proves the inefficiency of Vols. that is the one." [21]

Bragg's harsh opinions of volunteers, which most young regular army officers shared, were neither unusual nor unjustified. Regular officers naturally resented the high rank given many of the politicians and citizen soldiers who commanded volunteer units. Moreover, some volunteers had behaved shamefully in Mexico. To Mahan's students, these amateur warriors seemed untrustworthy; no one could tell what they might do in camp or in combat. They were too unpredictable, too undisciplined.

Most regular officers were less vociferous than Bragg, though they shared his contempt for volunteers and agreed with him on the merits of rigid discipline. Their criticism was more circumspect. "I perfectly agree with you as to the injurious effects the battle of Buena Vista will have on the stability of the Regular Army, being for the most part fought by the Volunteers, altho, its success was mainly due to the few regular artillery we had with us," Taylor wrote in a private letter. He also admitted: "It is true one of the Indiana Regts. did give way, & most of them could not be again brought back to face the enemy, & no doubt a good many from other corps done fully as bad, & perhaps a few from all, but the least said about the matter the better, which course I advised all concerned to pursue; but unfortunately my advice was not adopted. . . ." [22]

21 Bragg to Duncan, April 4, 1847, Duncan Papers; Zachary Taylor to Joseph P. Taylor, March 27, 1847, Zachary Taylor Papers; Bragg to Sherman, March 1, 1848, Sherman Papers.

22 Zachary Taylor to Joseph P. Taylor, April 25, 1847, Zachary Taylor Papers.

Bragg, of course, had always been frank and critical. Toler-
ance of those he disliked was impossible. He passed moral
judgments quickly and constantly sought to justify his own
and his heroes' prejudices. He rarely saw more than one side
to any question. Things were either right or wrong; people
were either good or bad, friends or enemies. Bragg invariably
denounced his enemies openly and in the most sarcastic
manner; he learned neither tact nor restraint in Mexico.[23]

Discretion seemed too pale a virtue after Buena Vista.
Neither the march from Monterey nor the stand against the
Mexicans had been discreet. Boldness, bravery, and independent action had characterized the campaign. These were the
traits both Bragg and his military ideal, Taylor, had demonstrated at Buena Vista; these were also the military characteristics, sanctioned by Napoleon and Mahan, Bragg admired most
at the outbreak of the Civil War.

Bragg learned little from Taylor, whose strategy and tactics
were essentially reckless attacks or stubborn defenses, or from
the war itself. What Bragg appears to have missed, the real
lesson of Buena Vista, was the great advantage defenders with
sufficient mobile firepower enjoyed over attackers. This failure
to understand what had happened and how it could be applied
in later battles is both significant and curious. It is significant
because of Bragg's command responsibilities in the Civil War;
it is curious because a close examination of the Buena Vista
battlefield convinced Bragg that artillery had accounted for
"nine-tenths of the [enemy's] killed and wounded." He proudly
informed Duncan that "old Zach accords the whole credit of
the day to the artillery ."[24]

Taylor was even more specific; he officially reported: "Captain Bragg . . . saved the day." Later, General Joseph Hooker
would call Taylor's statement "the highest praise . . . ever

[23] French, *Two Wars*, p. 76; Nichols, *Zach Taylor's Little Army*, pp.
185–86.
[24] Bragg to Duncan, April 4, 1847, Duncan Papers.

awarded an officer of . . . [Bragg's] rank . . . on the battle-field." [25]

No doubt Bragg deserved Taylor's praise. He had been fortunate enough to be in the right place at the propitious moment, but he had helped make his own luck. From the outset he had followed the fight and sought to put his guns where they would do the most damage to the Mexicans. He, in turn, commended his subordinate officers and men, who had "fully sustained the distinguished reputation" they had already established. They were well drilled and disciplined because Bragg had given that meticulous attention to detail Samuel French thought ridiculous but Major Luther Giddings correctly considered "a merit to be esteemed no less than heroic daring." Though Bragg's firepower at Buena Vista was hampered by inept recruits and by the detachment of two of his guns, his battery nevertheless established an unparalleled record for muzzle-loading cannon—each gun fired an average of 250 rounds of ammunition. [26]

Almost immediately Taylor and Bragg became the subjects of an apocryphal anecdote. During the final Mexican attack, so the story went, Taylor rode up to Bragg's battery and said, "A little more grape, Captain Bragg!" Inspired by these words, Bragg and his men fired with redoubled vigor and repulsed the enemy. [27]

Romantic Americans believed this widely circulated story, which probably originated in the *New Orleans Daily Delta*.

[25] *Senate Executive Document*, 30 Cong., 1 sess., No. 1, p. 136; *Society of the Army of the Cumberland, Fifth Re-Union, Detroit, 1871* (Cincinnati, 1872), pp. 16–17.

[26] French, *Two Wars*, p. 62; Giddings, *Sketches*, p. 76; *Senate Executive Document*, 30 Cong., 1 sess., No. 1, pp. 202–3; Smith, *War With Mexico*, I, 558. There is an unconfirmed report that the cannon fire at Buena Vista permanently injured Bragg's hearing. *Confederate Veteran*, XIX (1911), 292.

[27] *The General Taylor Almanac, for the Year of our Lord 1848* . . . (Philadelphia, 1848), p. 31.

"At one time during the battle," claimed the *Delta* on March 31, 1847, "Capt. Bragg expressed some apprehension to Gen. Taylor in relation to the position of his battery, and asked what he was to do. 'Give them more grape, Bragg—more grape,' says old Rough and Ready, 'and that will secure their safety.' Bragg tried the prescription and found it to have the best effect." [28]

Various accounts of the alleged incident appeared. General S. E. Chamberlain said Taylor merely told Bragg: "Double-shot your guns and give 'em hell!" [29] Marcellus C. M. Hammond, who had played cards with Bragg at West Point, claimed Taylor responded to Bragg's request for support: "'There is none, but Major [W. W. S.] Bliss [of Taylor's staff] and myself. Stand to your guns and give them (the Mexicans) H---!'" The "little more grape" statement, wrote Hammond, was a "good catch phrase, but not true. We give," he insisted, "the exact, or nearly exact words spoken, as we heard them from one of the best authorities." [30]

Major Bliss denied that Taylor said anything to Bragg. On December 29, 1848, Captain Ethan Allen Hitchcock wrote in his diary: "Bliss tells me that the stories of the General in connection with Bragg are all false. He never said 'A little more grape, Captain Bragg,' nor did he say 'Major Bliss and I will support you.'" A few months later Bliss told a reporter: "General Taylor was not and ought not to have been within speaking distance of Captain Bragg during the fire. Besides, Bragg knew how much to put in his guns—and, moreover, there was no grape used at all!" [31]

If Taylor said anything quotable in those anxious moments

[28] *New Orleans Daily Delta*, March 31, 1847.

[29] Quoted in Smith, *War With Mexico*, I, 559.

[30] [Marcellus C. M. Hammond], "Battle of Buena Vista," *Southern Quarterly Review*, new series, III (1851), 179.

[31] Croffut, ed., *Fifty Years in Camp and Field*, p. 329; *New York Herald*, March 25, 1849.

at Buena Vista, it probably was "Give them hell!" These are the words Bragg recalled.[32] Certainly they were more typical of the rough old general's speech than "A little more grape." As an unknown writer explained in a letter to the editor of the *New York Herald* in 1859: "While every one acquainted with General Taylor and his emphatic style of language knew from the beginning that he never said any such thing, yet the fable has . . . gone without public correction . . . an amazing illustration of the truth of history, when dressed up by newspaper correspondents, school book makers and platform . . . orators." This same writer quoted one of Bragg's relatives who claimed he knew exactly what Taylor said. When Bragg arrived at the front he saw an " 'aide-de-camp . . . [and] asked him to go and tell "the old man" how he was situated and ask what was to be done about it. General Taylor received this message in the crisis of the battle when the result was doubtful . . . . The entire force was engaged; there were no reserves; reenforcement was out of the question. When the aide delivered the message, General Taylor's only reply was "Tell him to give 'em hell, God damn 'em." This was exactly what the old man said and was immediately reported as such by the aide-de-camp to Braxton and Braxton told me.' " The recounter admitted that "this version of the anecdote is not so quotable . . . as the recorded one, but it has, besides being true, the further advantage of photographing how human nature really expresses itself in the ardor of battle; of illustrating the desperate heroism to which Bragg showed himself to be more than equal and of displaying General Taylor as . . . he really was in contrast with what civilians might suppose him to have been from such out of place phraseological dandyisms as 'a little more grape.' " [33]

[32] David Urquhart, "Bragg's Advance and Retreat," *Battles and Leaders*, III, 605. Colonel Urquhart was a member of Bragg's staff during the Civil War.
[33] *New York Herald*, August 7, 1859.

Yet the "little more grape" myth persisted, and as memories faded and conditions changed new variations of the incident evolved. After Bragg joined the Confederacy, Thomas Ewing, an Ohio politican, claimed "Genl Taylor told him that at the Battle of Buena Vista Bragg was in full run with his battery, and about to throw his guns into a ravine and follow them himself when he, Taylor, rode up to him, stopped him, and ordered him instantly to put his guns in battery. Bragg remonstrated saying they would all be captured but Taylor compelled him, and thus saved the day."[34] This uncollaborated statement appears contrary to what is known about Bragg's actions, and is refuted by Taylor's official report.[35]

Immediately after Buena Vista Taylor recommended Bragg for promotion to brevet lieutenant colonel, and made Bragg's battery part of Taylor's bodyguard. These splendid distinctions evidenced the general's revised opinion of light artillery as well as his high regard for Bragg. Taylor had still doubted the value of horse-drawn guns before Buena Vista, but afterwards he "yielded all his prejudices and gave in to our demonstration upon the field," wrote Bragg. "He even acknowledges his previous errors." More important, Taylor ordered the batteries refitted, and several months later Bragg announced: "I have a new and complete battery of the latest model."[36]

The Americans, too debilitated to chase the enemy,[37] had returned to Monterey soon after Buena Vista and settled into the drab routine of occupation duty. Bragg welcomed six new guns, seventy recruits, and a complete set of horses, but he most urgently needed officers. Ill throughout the summer and

[34] Theodore Calvin Pease and James G. Randall, eds., *The Diary of Orville Hickman Browning* (2 vols., Springfield, Ill., 1925), I, 616.
[35] *Senate Executive Document*, 30 Cong., 1 sess., No. 1, p. 136.
[36] Bragg to Duncan, April 4, 1847, January 13, 1848, Duncan Papers.
[37] Smith, *War With Mexico*, I, 396, 399. Bragg reported no casualties in his company, though Taylor's army lost 673 men at Buena Vista. Taylor failed to pursue the Mexicans because he feared his communication line could not be maintained.

fall, he had suffered what he called "two severe attacks." [38] Probably these resulted from nervous strain, for Bragg complained of migraine headaches, boils, and "dyspepsia" throughout his later life, especially when he overworked or worried. In November 1847 he wrote Adjutant General Jones: "The laborious duties which I have performed for the last twelve months, during which I have never had but two subalterns, and frequently but one for duty, when I require four, have in a great degree impaired my health and rendered me incapable of that constant and active exaction necessary to keep a Light Battery, especially of Horse Artillery, in complete order." [39]

Unfortunately, Bragg had lost the services of both Shover and Kilburn. Shortly after Buena Vista Shover had been assigned an independent command. His replacement, Francis J. Thomas, was "the worst officer in the reg[imen]t," insisted Bragg. Kilburn, "a capital sub[altern] & noble fellow," had to perform most of Thomas's duties as well as his own. By September Kilburn was in such "desperate health," so "reduced and exhausted by long and anxious strain," Bragg sent him to the hospital. [40]

As a temporary replacement for Kilburn, Taylor assigned George Thomas to Bragg's battery. Bragg immediately petitioned to keep him permanently. "It has been the wish of Captain Thomas and myself to effect this arrangement ever since my promotion to the [command of the] company," Bragg wrote General Jones, "and I hope that his distinguished services as an officer of Light Artillery will be considered as entitling him to a choice." Bragg also appealed to his old enemy, Colonel William Gates. [41]

[38] Bragg to Samuel G. French, October 13, 1847, French Papers.

[39] Bragg to Jones, November 22, 1847, Letters Received, AGO.

[40] Bragg to French, October 13, 1847, French Papers; Bragg to Duncan, January 13, 1848, Duncan Papers.

[41] Bragg to Jones, November 22, 1847, Letters Received, AGO; Bragg to William Gates, November 22, 1847, Braxton Bragg Papers, Duke University.

When the War Department refused his request to keep
Thomas, Bragg blamed "the 'perfidious Scott.' Though I have
been apparently beyond the influence of this man, he has
found opportunities to annoy & injure me. He has left me
without officers for more than a year. . . ." To Bragg it
seemed obvious why he had been without subalterns. "I knew
that . . . my being in favor with Gen'l Taylor, whose hon-
esty cannot be appreciated by S[cott] . . . would give him
additional cause to abuse me," Bragg complained. "But, thank
God! Duncan, we have had opportunities, and we have improved them. . . ." [42]

Though Bragg's charge that Scott willfully deprived him of
officers sounds dubious, it may have been true. In September
1847 Adjutant General Jones endorsed one of Bragg's letters:
"The subject of officers for Major Bragg's company was presented to Major General Scott, and no further action at this
time should be taken." Scott appears to have ignored Bragg's
request. True, he was in the field and busy with his own
campaign against Mexico City, but he found time to assign
officers to other units in Taylor's army. [43]

Anger tempted Bragg to plot against Scott. "When all is
over, what say you to a union of our strength against the vain-
glorious? We can crush him," Bragg boasted. It is uncertain
just what role Bragg envisioned for himself, but he seems to
have guessed that Scott and Taylor would be presidential
prospects after the war. Apparently Bragg thought he and
Duncan could discredit Scott with the voters. "Taylor's word
is of higher value than Scott's oath," asserted Bragg, "and the
contrast between him and old Zach will kill him with the
people, & there he dies as a politicano." [44]

Bragg's vexation increased after Taylor relinquished army

[42] Bragg to Duncan, January 13, 1848, Duncan Papers.
[43] Bragg to Jones, September 2, 1847, Letters Received, AGO; Bragg
to French, October 13, 1847, French Papers.
[44] Bragg to Duncan, January 13, 1848, Duncan Papers.

command to Wool and returned to the United States. "This
will leave myself, Thomas & Reynolds of the old 'Army of
Occupation' which left New Orleans," lamented Bragg. "No
one is pleased at exchanging [Taylor] for Wool, as but few
have any confidence in him and none respect him. We shall
have a stampede every week and probably fall back on the Rio
Grande some day." There were rumors that General William
O. Butler might assume command, although he was a volunteer. Even so, many regular officers preferred him to Wool.
"In the way of stampedes [Butler] . . . will equal any one,
but in his intercourse he cannot be so destitute of principle and
justice [as Wool]," concluded Bragg. "Butler's faults would be
of the head. Wool's are known to originate from that and the
heart." [45]

With Taylor gone morale sagged. "God only knows what is
to become of us here," wrote Bragg, whose main duty was the
protection of wagon trains which brought supplies to Monterey. "The country here is still infested with robbers &
murderers," he complained, "but for want of a proper force
we can do nothing." [46]

The licentious spent their time with bottles, cards, and
women. The brazen conduct of some officers shocked Bragg.
Lieutenant John Pope, later a Civil War general, and another
officer were "accused of kidnapping two Mexican women, one
14 yrs old . . . for carnal purposes." Bragg wrote: "One
thing is certain, the women live with them now, and ride thru
the city with them in defiance of decency in an open carriage
furnished by the Q[uarter] M[aster] Dept." [47]

Bragg considered Wool responsible for the deterioration of
the army. He "is . . . the weakest and most contemptible
apology for a great man I have had the misfortune to meet,"
Bragg informed Sherman. "He is equally as weak a man as

[45] Bragg to French, October 13, 1847, French Papers.
[46] Bragg to Duncan, January 13, 1848, April 4, 1847, Duncan Papers.
[47] Bragg to French, October 13, 1847, French Papers.

[Colonel William] Gates, with a little more education which has only seemed to increase his dishonesty. A sample.`He sustains from the revenues of the city a dirty, filthy little 4 x 5 newspaper in Monterey, printed by soldiers on extra duty, devoted solely and entirely to puffing 'Genl Wool—the real Hero of Buena Vista'. . . ." To Duncan, Bragg lamented that with Wool in command, "we have but little to excite pride or emulation, professionally." [48]

Nevertheless, Bragg refused to let his battery deteriorate. Despite the laxity of other units and his own illness, he continued to drill his men. In October 1847 he reported his battery "in better condition than it has been since I joined it." A few months later, after he had assumed command of the camp outside Monterey, he wrote: "I have my own battery & Rucker's squadron [of the] 1 [st] Drag[oons], a very handsome com[man]d, for my rank, and in splendid condition." Wool, who preferred to remain in the city, allowed Bragg complete administrative control over the camp. "As a result," Bragg admitted, "I am somewhat obnoxious to a few. . . . Having prohibited drunkenness on duty by officers & tried them for it, I am now desired to be [military] Gov[ernor] of Monterey, but refuse as it will bring me too near Wool." [49]

The rigid discipline Bragg imposed upon the camp won him the respect of most professional soldiers. Years later General Lovell H. Rousseau would testify that "all the officers who knew Bragg . . . thought he was perhaps the best disciplinarian in the United States Army. . . . That is the universal opinion as far as I have heard," said Rousseau, "and I have conversed with a great many of the old Regular Army officers." [50]

But his severity almost cost Bragg his life. In October 1847

[48] Bragg to William T. Sherman, March 1, 1848, Sherman Papers; Bragg to Duncan, January 13, 1848, Duncan Papers.
[49] Bragg to French, October 13, 1847, French Papers; Bragg to Duncan, January 13, 1848, Duncan Papers.
[50] OR, XVI (pt. 1), 438.

reports reached the United States that "Some fiend in human shape . . . made a terrible illustration of a 'little more grape Captain Bragg,' for he placed under the bed of the gallant soldier an eight inch bomb shell, with a train leading off by which it was ignited. The explosion was terrific, but fortunately the captain received no injury. Two of the missiles went through his bed without touching him." This account could offer no reason why anyone would want to harm Bragg, "except that some of his men think he is too severe in his discipline. This is the second attempt upon his life." Bragg believed a private in his company, a self-confessed "fugitive from the laws of Ohio," had made the assassination attempt. "The same reasons that satisfy me," wrote Bragg, "might not convince a court, and therefore I do not charge him with it." Several years later Lieutenant George H. Derby apprehended an army deserter, Samuel R. Church, who claimed he exploded the shell under Bragg's bed.[51]

Many people knew Bragg was a martinet; few realized that he was equally devoted to the welfare of his men. From them he demanded instant obedience and courage under fire. They feared but respected him too, for he was as ready to protect their interests as to punish those who shirked their duty. When the War Department ordered every soldier assigned to a field artillery company to purchase an extra uniform, Bragg protested. "This is a great hardship to the soldier," he informed Adjutant General Jones. If the government wanted a sartorial change for artillerymen, Bragg argued, the government should pay for the clothing. Moreover, Bragg could be compassionate. In at least one case he even aided the rehabilitation of a deserter. "Private Robert Allen," wrote Bragg, "has been with my company since the date of his apprehension . . . has served out his sentence, and become one of the most

[51] *Niles' National Register*, sixth series, XXIII (1847), 88; Bragg to W. W. S. Bliss, October 20, 1847, Palmer Collection of Bragg Papers; George R. Stewart, *John Phoenix, Esq., . . . A Life of Captain George H. Derby, U. S. A.* (New York, 1937), p. 87.

expert and valuable men of my command. I should much prefer keeping him instead of receiving a recruit." [52]

While Bragg worried about uniforms and discipline Mexico City fell to General Scott's army. This great victory along with rumors of peace troubled Bragg. He feared President Polk would weaken the army and the Mexicans would renew hostilities. Even worse, Scott's success might win him the presidency. Before news that war was over reached Monterey, Bragg wrote: "I pray to God & hope . . . that the war may last till Mr Polk goes out of office. For the Lord save us if he reduces the army." [53]

To be sure, Bragg begrudged Scott's army the last major battle, but he was ready for peace. His poor health and his long stay in Texas and Mexico had exhausted him; he felt much older than his thirty-one years. "Three years, my dear fellow, tells on a middle aged man," he wrote Sherman in March 1848. "I have some consolation in a handsome command, and enjoy life about as well as a man can without society," continued Bragg, yet he was bone-tired and he disliked Mexico. "I give you no description of this country," he commented, "it is not worth the paper & ink." [54]

In June 1848 Bragg received sixty days leave, much less than he had expected and only a fraction of what he thought he deserved. No matter; it was enough to get him out of Mexico, and he was sure that once he reached the United States he could get an extension. After all, he was no longer the quarrelsome lieutenant with an uncertain future who had joined Taylor's army in New Orleans three years before. He was as flammable as ever, of course, but now he was a brevet lieutenant colonel [55] and a distinguished veteran of the campaigns of northern Mexico, whose bravery and skill had won him three

---

[52] Bragg to Jones, March 2, May 29, 1848, Letters Received, AGO.
[53] Bragg to Sherman, March 1, 1848, Sherman Papers.   [54] *Ibid.*
[55] Bragg received his commission as brevet lieutenant colonel at Brazos Island, Texas, on June 22, 1848, as he was returning to the United States. Bragg to Jones, June 30, 1848, Letters Received, AGO.

brevet promotions—no other officer in the army had received more. Years later General Joseph Hooker would say that Bragg, George Thomas, and Don Carlos Buell were the "three young officers . . . who were foremost in the estimation of the army" at the close of the Mexican War. Even Adjutant General Jones, with whom Bragg had feuded for years, wrote in 1849: "Col. Bragg is one of our best artillery officers." Naturally, Bragg savored this reputation he had won on the battlefield. Fate, he wrote, "sent me originally to Gen'l Taylor . . . and as a consequence made me all that I am." [56]

[56] *Society of the Army of the Cumberland, Re-Union, 1871*, p. 16; Jones's endorsement on Bragg to Jones, March 7, 1849, Letters Received, AGO; Bragg to Duncan, January 13, 1848, Duncan Papers.

CHAPTER V

A rich wife

1848–1849

Bragg returned to the United States a national hero.
As the man who had stopped the Mexicans at Buena Vista with
"a little more grape," he had taken the public's fancy. Everybody treated him as though he alone had won the war. There
were even undercurrents that he might be endorsed by one of
the major political parties as a candidate for public office in
1848.[1] Though this seems to have been only a rumor, the army
did name a military post in his honor, not the modern base at
Fort Bragg, North Carolina, established much later, but an
earlier Fort Bragg on the northern coast of California.[2]

The first of a number of public dinners and celebrations
awaited Bragg in New Orleans. When he arrived on June 6,
1848, aboard the U.S.S. *Fashion*, the city welcomed him and
the other veterans with a levee at the St. Charles Hotel. A few
days later in Mobile, where Bragg visited his brother John, the
citizens feted him with a parade and a barbecue. Orators told
how he had saved Taylor's army in words likely to raise even
the most modest man's ego, and praise continued to be lavished
upon him as he traveled overland from Mobile to Warrenton.
He stopped in several places, but was compelled to decline
many more invitations than he accepted.[3]

[1] Mobile *Daily Tribune*, September 29, 1876.
[2] *House Executive Document*, 35 Cong., 2 sess., No. 93, p. 23. Abandoned by the army during the Civil War, Fort Bragg, California, continued as a lumbering town.
[3] Bragg to Roger Jones, June 30, 1848, Letters Received, AGO; New
Orleans *Daily Picayune*, June 27, July 7, 26, 1848; *Morning Courier &
New York Enquirer*, July 31, 1848.

More approbation greeted him in Warrenton. Seated conspicuously on a platform with his father and brother Thomas, Bragg again heard himself panoplied in language usually reserved for political aspirants. "What a libel are the proceedings of the people of Warren upon their former conduct," wrote Congressman David Outlaw. "Col. Bragg having, no thanks to them, won for himself a brilliant reputation, is now the object of the most fulsome adulation. Those who formerly sneered at the Braggs as plebeians, as unfit associates for them, they are glad to honor. With what scorn must Col. Bragg, in his secret heart regard them." Whatever his true feelings, Bragg graciously thanked the citizens of Warrenton for honoring him. He said he was unable "to express . . . [his] gratitude," but was proud that "the hearts of . . . [his] fellow countrymen throb in unison." He mentioned "the fair hands of their lovely daughters," and his love for his father, "a venerable parent of more than threescore years and ten, whose snowy locks . . . indicate that his race is almost run." When presented with a sword, Bragg promised it would be ready "whenever my country shall require its use, as pure and bright as when first entrusted to my humble protection." [4]

After the festivities in Warrenton, Bragg hurried to Washington to seek redress. His battery had not been allowed to accompany him back from Mexico; instead, it had been sent to New Mexico. Bragg considered this an insult to his men as well as a "personal indignity." Straightway, he told Secretary of War Marcy that his battery had been ordered to New Mexico simply because it was available. This was unfair, Bragg contended, because his command had been on field duty as long as any of the army's eight permanent batteries. His men were "naturally and justly dissatisfied at being required to perform more than a double share of field and frontier service." He had

[4] David Outlaw to His Wife, August 1, 1848, Outlaw Papers; *Warrenton Reporter*, August 12, 1848, cited in Greensboro *Alabama Beacon*, September 9, 1848; Montgomery, *Old Warrenton*, pp. 429–30.

expected all of his men "worth keeping" to reenlist "had justice been done them," but because of their new assignment "all . . . left us, but one," and a year spent in "perfecting the command" had been wasted.

Nor was the assignment of his company to New Mexico a mere expedient, argued Bragg, for John M. Washington's battery, which was "better suited to the peculiar service, was sixty miles nearer and had to be passed . . . on the route, and had been in but one engagement." As for himself, Bragg complained he had "been much longer on field service than any Captain of Light Artillery. And yet," he told Marcy, "I am the only one selected to remain." Bragg professed amazement that such injustice had originated in the War Department; nevertheless, he was "satisfied that it was known, and intentionally committed elsewhere." Of course this was a strong hint that Scott was responsible. Bragg claimed that Washington had curried favor with certain high ranking officers. Had not Washington been "assigned by his *brevet rank, to command me,* whilst by such rank I am his senior?" asked Bragg. He could not serve "under an officer who is my junior according to the rank he is assigned to exercise. It is a reflection I cannot rest under." Moreover, Bragg had served "during the whole war without a day's relief, and . . . enjoyed but one month's leave" in his previous eight years' service. Yet the War Department had granted him only two months' leave of absence. It would take him two months to reach his company, he told Marcy, "were I to start today." [5]

Marcy "unhesitatingly acknowledged the injustice of the order," Bragg claimed, and "promptly offered me detached service, with a view of buying me off and allowing my command to suffer. This was promptly refused. . . ." Bragg did accept Marcy's offer to extend his leave, and he privately

[5] Bragg to Marcellus C. M. Hammond, August 15, 1848, James H. Hammond Papers, Library of Congress; Bragg to William L. Marcy, August 12, 1848, Letters Received, AGO.

admitted to a friend that if he could not "do better the detached service will be accepted . . . for I cannot live out of the army, until I get a rich wife, but I shall fight to the last for my poor men who nobly stood by me when Marcy and all others had abandoned us to our fate at Buena Vista." Before their interview ended, Marcy asked Bragg to write out his complaints and to call again later.[6]

Before he visited Marcy again, Bragg gained the support of the North Carolina congressmen. "A strong remonstrance from my old state delegation goes in this morning to the President," he wrote on August 15.[7]

Bragg also rewarded himself with a trip to New York City, where on September 7 he attended a dinner. Philip Hone, who presided, described the occasion in his diary: "I remained in town to attend a dinner at the Astor House, given to Lieut. Col. Braxton Bragg, better known on the records of fame as 'Captain Bragg,' the gallant supporter of Gen. Taylor at the Battle of Buena Vista, where he commanded a battery of flying artillery which contributed, by a ready supply of 'more grape,' to the brilliant success of the day." There was no escape from the grape story. Hone considered Bragg "like all brave men, modest and unassuming, not too 'rough' and ever 'ready.' He was much gratified by the handsome compliment of which he was the honored recipient, and gave us during the evening many amusing anecdotes of the brave old general, and instructive details of the events of the campaign in which he was engaged." Proudly, Hone reported, "It was one of the Stetson and Coleman's very best round-table entertainments. I performed to the best of my ability . . . the duty of calling out the guests, and made a speech to each in succession to which a ready response was given." [8]

Back in Washington after his New York sojourn, Bragg paid

[6] Bragg to Hammond, August 15, 1848, Hammond Papers.   [7] *Ibid.*
[8] *National Intelligencer*, September 12, 1848; Allan Nevins, ed., *The Diary of Philip Hone, 1828–1851* (2 vols., New York, 1927), II, 853–54.

another visit to the War Department. Marcy, who seemed "particularly kind and cordial," agreed to recall Bragg's battery from New Mexico, and to place Bragg, after his leave expired, temporarily on detached duty in New Orleans until his battery reached Fort Leavenworth. Apparently Marcy also promised further favors, for several months later Bragg wrote Congressman Daniel M. Barringer of North Carolina: "Sometime next summer or fall I expect to remove to Newport, R. I. Present my kindest regards to the friends around you who were so kind as to assist me in effecting this object." [9]

Once Secretary Marcy granted his military demands, Bragg shifted his immediate attention to politics. The Washington political climate disturbed him. Sectionalism seemed to pervade every issue, with the South under heavy verbal attack. "The disgraceful scenes now being enacted in Congress . . . are the theme of universal condemnation," he wrote. Even his old favorite Thomas Hart Benton had turned against the South. "Old Bullion Benton is believed to be crazy. The votes given by himself & [Sam] Houston against the South are viewed as bids for the Presidency to secure northern votes." Bragg believed "the South must take a stand and maintain it." He opposed further compromise. If conflict resulted from the South's firm stand then, "as [Willie P.] Mangum [of North Carolina] told them yesterday in the Senate, Old Zach will be there with Capt Bragg and a full supply of grape." [10]

Two months later, when Bragg reached Mobile after a leisurely trip south, he again expressed concern over the increase of sectional bitterness. He had found more political excitement in Charleston, South Carolina, than he had ever seen in any part of the country. This together with other developments convinced him "that everything is soon to turn on *section*. No

[9] Bragg to Hammond, October 20, 1848, Hammond Papers; Bragg to Jones, March 7, 1849, Letters Received, AGO; Bragg to Daniel M. Barringer, February 24, 1849, Daniel Moreau Barringer Papers, Southern Historical Collection, University of North Carolina.
[10] Bragg to Hammond, August 11, 1848, Hammond Papers.

Whig or Democrat is to be returned to Congress from the North who is not against us in toto," he wrote. The Democratic nominee for President, Lewis Cass of Michigan, Bragg dismissed as devoid of "candor & boldness." [11]

Bragg still considered himself a Democrat, but during the Mexican War he had become disenchanted with the party leaders, especially "his Majesty," President Polk. In fact, Bragg had written Sherman in March 1848: "I am no longer a modern democrat—Cump! (Throw up your hat)." For President, Bragg favored his hero General Zachary Taylor, the Whig nominee. "Genl. Taylor must be elected," Bragg announced in October 1848. With Taylor in the White House, Bragg hoped, the sectional dispute would end: "We must settle the [sectional] question amicably, *if* we can, at the next session [of Congress]. The consequences of a failure look to me too serious for speculation." [12]

Bragg considered the condition of the army just as alarming as the political situation. In Washington he had seen a large number of "loafers," officers who had never "done any service" and "avoided all duty" except the collection of their pay. This and what he viewed as other reprehensible practices had to be changed, and he and his friends, the young heroes of the Mexican War, would have to lead the reform movement. He could not count on the older officers, for they were too satisfied. Bragg believed the army must be purged of "old fogies who did nothing in the field [during the Mexican War], without consulting with and relying upon . . . young men. Now they are attempting to get clear of them." A good example was "Old Twiggs ('The hero of all the letters and none of the battles'—correct edition)" who was "courting a pretty young

11 *Morning Courier & New York Enquirer*, October 28, 1848; Bragg to Hammond, October 20, 1848, Hammond Papers.

12 Bragg to Sherman, March 1, 1848, Sherman Papers; Bragg to Hammond, October 20, 1848, Hammond Papers.

girl" in Mobile. "He avoids me as if he feared contagion," wrote Bragg.[13]

In a speech at Mobile, Bragg praised the "rank & file" of the army and struck a *"blow at fogies."* He insisted the enlisted men and the company officers deserved "most [of the] credit [for the American victory in Mexico] tho' it has been bestowed on those whom accident, not merit, placed over them." [14]

Bragg used all his influence for army reform. He sought political support for the appointment of his friend George Thomas as chief of artillery at West Point, and Bragg reminded James Duncan, the new inspector general of the army, that "your present position will enable you to do more [for our cause] than any other [man] in the army, and we shall expect much from you." Lest Duncan forget the common enemy, Bragg added a note of caution: "The days of fogyism are on the wane, but the ball must be kept in motion." [15]

All this plotting brought about no immediate reforms and Bragg soon returned to the public responsibilities of a hero. When his leave ended in January 1849, he went to New Orleans to become a temporary member of General Edmund Pendleton Gaines's staff. Gaines "is crazy," wrote Bragg, "[but New Orleans] will be a fine loafing place for me until my Company gets back [from New Mexico]. There will be nothing to do but look at the sugar and girls." He might have added that there would still be many functions to attend. On January 22 he was the guest of the Mobile bar, and two months later he and Senator Henry Clay dedicated a new military hospital at Jackson Barracks, Louisiana. Several days before, Bragg had been the honored guest at a private party in New Orleans. A newspaper reported: "At supper were some

---

[13] Bragg to Hammond, October 20, 1848, Hammond Papers.

[14] Bragg to James Y. Mason, November 17, 1848, Bragg Papers, Duke University.

[15] *Ibid.;* Bragg to Duncan, January 29, 1849, Duncan Papers.

very fine green grapes to which the Colonel for some time paid assidious court." After he stopped eating the grapes, "a lady who sat near him . . . raising the salver on which the favorite fruit was and gracefully presenting it to the gallant Colonel, she said: 'A little more grape, Capt. B!' " [16]

Doubtless Bragg had become a bit tired of being a celebrity. He "traveled as quietly as possible" to escape notice, but was recognized and "almost overrun by civilities" nearly everywhere he went. Of one such occasion, he reported: "The day was very bad, or I should have been run off by the ladies anxious to see the curiosity. I had no *cage* along, and was consequently unprotected." At times like these, Bragg confessed, he wished some lady, "deserving a clever fellow for a husband, would marry me at once and put a stop to my wild roving about this credulous country." [17]

Little did Bragg realize when he accepted an invitation in January to visit Thibodaux, a town of less than a thousand population some forty miles west of New Orleans, that his "wild roving" was nearly over. Thibodaux, center of a rich sugar producing area where Creole and American culture met but did not always mingle, was the local social center for some of the richest families in Louisiana. [18]

Nearby, at Evergreen Plantation, lived twenty-three-year-old Eliza Brooks Ellis, who called herself Elise. A friend remembered her as "a beautiful girl," and a reporter agreed. "I knew this lady many years ago," he wrote in 1862, "and few women were handsomer or more eloquent with the tongue." Intelligent, poised, and witty, she was also rich. The eldest child of the late Richard Gaillard Ellis and Mary Jane Towson Ellis, Elise had become heiress in 1844, along with seven other

[16] New York *Herald*, February 14, 1849; Bragg to Duncan, January 29, 1849, Duncan Papers; *New Orleans Weekly Delta*, March 5, 1849.

[17] Bragg to Hammond, October 20, 1848, Hammond Papers.

[18] Louisiana Historical Records Survey, *Inventory of the Parish Archives of Louisiana No. 29, Lafourche Parish (Thibodaux)* (Baton Rouge, 1942), p. 5.

children, to an estate valued at $308,723. Moreover, her kins-
men included General Nathaniel Towson, Bishop Phillips
Brooks, the Gaillards of South Carolina, the Farars, the
Duncans, the Mercers, the Minors, and the Butlers of Louisiana and Mississippi. Born in Natchez, Mississippi, where her
great-grandfather Ellis had moved from Virginia in the 1760s,
Elise had spent most of her mature years on her father's sugar
plantations.[19]

Since her father's death in 1844, she had been unhappy.
"Does it not seem strange that we should be such a miserable
family and yet have every worldly advantage?" she asked in
1845. Frequently, she was as " 'low as the hung up lute.' My
only employments," she complained in 1846, "are mastering
French verbs and combatting with the mosquitoes." Elise
had few visitors and this made her wish she "lived in a country
that had some attractions to induce persons to visit it; but
mosquitoes, mud and rain are great drawbacks to any place."
Occasionally she looked forward to trips and visits from her
cousins when they rode horses and enjoyed chess and piquet.
"I have beaten Cousin Pierce [Butler] at a game of piquet," she
informed her Cousin Anna; "pray do not let him have any
peace on the subject; he boasts so much of his skill." But she
often preferred to be alone. For some reason she did not get
along well with her mother, and their quarrels became known
to the neighbors. "I could not have the heart to visit after every
one in the neighbourhood has heard such accounts of our
conduct," she confessed to her cousin, "and you know what a
time I have at home." [20]

[19] *Confederate Veteran*, IV (1896), 102; Richmond *Daily Dispatch*,
December 27, 1862; Richard G. Ellis Estate, 1844–1858 (bound ledger
kept by Richard E. Butler, Executor), Thomas W. Butler Papers, Louisiana State University; Pierce Butler, *The Unhurried Years: Memoirs of
the Old Natchez Region* (Baton Rouge, 1948), pp. 1–15; Charlotte
Beatty Diary, July 1, 14, October 24, 1843, Southern Historical Collection, University of North Carolina.
[20] Elise Ellis to Anna E. Butler, January 30, 1845, January 16, Septem-

Occasionally, when family quarrels or loneliness palled, Elise speculated on death. "I have always hoped my death would be by consumption," she wrote Anna Butler in 1845; "you know when once his strong grasp is laid on you, there is no resisting it, and you sink so slowly and gradually. Time is given you to prepare for eternity, and the pain that wracks your body, purifies your mind by serious and solemn warnings to get ready for the grave." [21]

Usually, Elise let good humor prevail over her morbidity. "You have left several mementoes behind you," she wrote Anna in 1847, "among others a pair of drawers, were they full of what they usually contain, they would be very welcome to remain here pour jamais." Her young friends considered Elise "the most fickle of human beings" and a bit of a flirt. "Cousin Pierce calls Anna and myself coquet[te]s," she admitted to her Cousin Sarah Butler. Apparently Elise had a guilty conscience after eyeing one of her friend's suitors, for she warned Sarah to "continue as you have begun, and beware of flirting—it is like a constitutional disease, it grows upon one—it is like smoking, when you once acquire a fondness for it, you are obliged to continue it; notwithstanding what effect it has on the system of morals—it is like drinking, one indulgence leads on to another, with you becoming an habitual drunkard, or an experienced coquette. . . ." [22]

Nor was Elise above gossip. "Strange rumors are afloat about la nouvelle mariee Mrs. Urquhart," she wrote, "he left her shortly after their marriage to attend his *club* in the City—on dit, they occupy separate apartments, because he smokes before leaving his bed—don't you think ladies should be more

ber 5, 1846, Anna E. Butler Correspondence, Butler Family Papers (G), Louisiana State University.

[21] Elise to Anna Butler, January 30, 1845, Anna E. Butler Correspondence.

[22] Elise to Anna Butler, January 5, 1847, *ibid.*; Elise to Sarah J.D. Butler, May 5, July 27, 1848, Thomas Butler and Family Papers, Butler Family Papers (F), Louisiana State University.

violent than ever against the use of the Indian weed?" [23]

On one of her infrequent trips Elise had become interested in army men. While in "dear delightful Pascagoula," Mississippi, in August 1848 she noticed some soldiers encamped near her hotel. She "could see their white tents gleaming in the sunshine and their banner . . . waving in the sea breeze. Oh Beautiful sight! how could it fail to arouse every patriotic feeling in our breasts?" she asked Sarah. Indeed, Elise had been "introduced to a number of agreeable officers." One lieutenant's "morning costume was so exceedingly becoming, consisting of white pants, white jacket with buttons, and the most bewitching hat, turned up so picturesquely at the sides," that she had tried repeatedly "to twist [her brother] Towson's hat in the same manner." Not even the scolding she received for dancing "with a handsome lieutenant who was teaching [her] to waltz a' l'espagnole" weakened her fascination. [24]

This infatuation with the military continued. When Elise "received an invitation to a ball headed, 'a little more grape Captain Bragg,'" she "was bent on going," even though "a powerful mustard plaster" had removed so much skin from her face she could not "laugh without displaying a thousand *wrinkles*." She wrote Sarah: "Oh mon dieu, mon dieu! I am like to die with laughter . . . at the very recollection." The ball was held in the new Thibodaux school house, "with damp walls, just ready for the first coat of plastering, no fires, and a bitter cold night. As the Colonel was to be exhibited to the public at five dollars a ticket, the Creoles got up an opposition ball, engaged the music, lights, et cetera. The *Bragg ball*, was therefore most thinly attended." [25]

Before the festivities began, a deputy arrived from the Creole ball "to invite the *ladies and the Colonel* over." A local

[23] Elise to Sarah Butler, August 28, 1848, Thomas Butler and Family Papers.
[24] Elise to Sarah Butler, August 8, 1848, *ibid.*
[25] Elise to Sarah Butler, January 19, 1849, *ibid.*

doctor, without waiting for the deputy to finish his message, seized him "by the hair" and "the poor man disappeared like magic down the steps his head thumping on each one. . . ." Soon, "a second deputation of some *forty armed* men came to demand satisfaction, for the insult offered their deputy." Elise was "terribly frightened" when the men went outside, although many words and no blows were exchanged. What pleased her most was the conduct of the guest of honor, who "acted most nobly, just what you would expect from so perfect a gentleman—he took no notice of the whole affair, remaining quietly seated by the ladies."

As tempers cooled and the ball resumed, Elise became even more impressed with Bragg. She was surprised when he asked her to dance the "first set with him" for she "had understood him to say he did not dance . . . but he danced with perfect ease." Moreover, he continued to dance with her. It was obviously more than politeness that caused him to pay her so much attention. Others observed this too, because soon after the ball a New Orleans newspaper printed a letter signed "Q, in a corner," which described Bragg as "the lion of the occasion," and mentioned that he had been "wounded in the heart." [26]

After the dancing and the supper which followed, everyone toasted Bragg. But Elise remembered only two toasts: one offered by a man with "a strong lisp," who hoped Bragg would be "as successful in attacking ladies hearts, as he was the Mexicans," and a toast by a Dr. Williams "delivered in the most drunken manner imaginable—'may the grapes—ah— planted in Colonel Bragg's vineyard, ah—produce better wine—ah—than that we are—ah, ah—now drinking'—'good' exclaimed [a] Mr. Cole, 'you mean the *little Braggs*.' " Elise was sure she had never heard "anything so shockingly vulgar. Imagine the Colonel's feelings," she wrote. "They *graped* him so unmercifully," that Bragg finally turned to Elise and "ex-

[26] *Ibid.; New Orleans Weekly Delta*, February 19, 1849.

claimed in a whisper, 'I fear my grapes will get sour, if I remain here much longer.' " [27]

Bragg, accompanied by a prominent resident of Thibodaux, John C. Beatty, rode out to dine with Elise the morning after the ball. She "was in despair about entertaining him," because the weather "was indeed horrible." But she had no difficulty. He "was quite the life of us," she wrote her cousin, "exceedingly playful in retort, and very agreeable. But alas! he has gone!" [28]

Elise need not have worried; Bragg returned to Thibodaux in less than a month. She saw one of his friends at a party "and my heart assured me *he was not alone*," she wrote. "I was not disappointed; the 'gallant Bragg' was with him dressed in military undress." When Elise asked what had brought him such a distance "*solely* to attend a party to which . . . he had no invitation," Bragg teasingly answered that he had promised to show a certain Miss Kees his uniform. Elise laughed, and wrote her cousin: "Really, officers are the most accommodating men in existence."

Bragg spent most of the evening with Elise, and rode out to Evergreen the next morning alone. After they had exhausted such subjects as the weather, his impressions of New Orleans, and his temporary duties as General Gaines's adjutant general, Bragg warmed to his favorite topic of conversation with ladies —"women's significance." Elise wrote: "The Colonel told me . . . he had . . . a book called 'Women's Mission,' which he would be obliged to me if I would read." This may have been Bragg's idea of a pre-engagement manual. Elise recalled that "he got quite excited with the topic, spoke of the power which Mothers possessed, and ended by saying, 'It is a situation which every lady should prepare herself for, as she *may*

[27] Elise to Sarah Butler, January 19, 1849, Thomas Butler and Family Papers.
[28] Louisiana Records Survey, *Lafourche Parish*, p. 5; Elise to Sarah Butler, January 19, 1849, Thomas Butler and Family Papers.

be called upon to exercise its responsibilities.' " Elise remembered the toast to Bragg's success "in *attacking* ladies hearts" at the January ball, and she had to exert "the utmost" effort "to keep from bursting into a loud laugh. Had you or Anna been present," she wrote Sarah, "I should have disgraced myself." Bragg kept talking and lost all track of time. "When dinner was ready," wrote Elise, "the Colonel said nothing of leaving to Ma's great despair; t'was the same case at tea, and when we were on the point of wishing him 'good night,' he drew out his watch, found it had run down at *ten* in the morning (hadn't noticed the *sun set*) and paid his parting adieux in some haste." [29]

The Colonel was in love. Fortunately, he had few military duties, and could visit Elise regularly at Evergreen. One weekend in April he proposed and was accepted. "I am actually *engaged,* & unless I change my mind, going *to be married!*" Elise wrote Sarah. How did it happen? "Why, t'was brought about by one whose motto like Caesar's is 'Veni Vidi Vici,' " exclaimed Elise. "Of course it was no use for me to resist, I could not do anything, the willful woman, the capricious Elise is quite humbled, & converted into a gentle loving being, how much can be affected by '*a little more grape*.' " [30]

Bragg, with his usual impatience, wanted to be married right away. He had secured a leave of absence until July 1, and hoped Elise would accompany him to Fort Leavenworth as his bride. Elise preferred a fall wedding, but complained that Bragg "will not listen to such arrangement, & allows me until *June*." She believed he was afraid to trust her; "he has heard that I am famed for not knowing my own mind." [31]

Indeed, the more Elise thought about being an officer's wife, the more she was "opposed to trying it." She wrote: "Do dear

[29] Elise to Sarah Butler, February 13, 1849, *ibid.*
[30] Elise to Sarah Butler, April 17, 1849, *ibid.*
[31] Bragg to Elise, May 23 [1849], Braxton Bragg Papers, Henry E. Huntington Library, San Marino, California; Elise to Sarah Butler, April 17, 1849, Thomas Butler and Family Papers.

Sallie, take the map, and see where your poor Cousin has to go, way up among the wild Indians, in a miserable log Fort with nothing to eat, and nothing to amuse, but the dances of the savages. Oh me! I shall certainly die—I, whose dreams of love have always been in the very lap of luxury, in beautiful palaces by silvery lakes."

More important, Elise wondered if she really loved Bragg. She admired his character. "He is *truth itself*," she wrote, "firm, unbending with principles most exalted, & with a holy horror of *flirting, waltzing*, & the *Polka*." But she was not sure she loved him.[32]

Bragg too had his doubts about Elise's decision. "I am fearful . . . that upon an insufficient knowledge of my profession and its disadvantages, the many sacrifices you are making have been but hastily considered," he wrote. "Relations, friends, society, and most of the comforts of life are to be abandoned—a sudden transition is to be made from the very hot-house of social pleasures to the bleak & chilling atmosphere of a frontier life, and for what? Why simply the *love* of *Braxton Bragg*."[33]

There was no question about his own feelings for Elise. He wrote her from New Orleans on May 12: "Read I cannot, and quiet meditation at this time is inconsistent with my impetuous temperament." He had received letters of congratulations from many friends, and John Bragg and his wife, who planned a summer vacation in the North, had invited Braxton and Elise to join them. "For your sake," Bragg wrote Elise, "I wish it would be so, and my own pleasure would be unbounded in visiting old scenes & friends with such a bride. But I fear it will be inconsistent with other demands upon our time and means."[34]

[32] Elise to Sarah Butler, April 17, 1849, Thomas Butler and Family Papers.
[33] Bragg to Elise, May 23 [1849], Bragg Papers, Huntington Library.
[34] Bragg to Elise, May 12 [1849], Braxton Bragg Papers, Rosenberg Library, Galveston, Texas.

MRS. BRAXTON BRAGG
Confederate Veteran

Elise teased Bragg about how their engagement had distracted him. "You wrote that you found it impossible to read, meditate or turn your attention to anything serious," she bantered. "One could account for such a prostration of the faculties by accusing Cupid of having done the mischief, but you know you laugh at such idle folly as *love* and maintain that *reason* alone controls your feelings. Will you give me then my dear sir, a logical explanation of your being so very distrait?" [35]

By the time Elise had selected her bridesmaids and "wedding paraphernalia" she had convinced herself she loved Bragg and wanted to live at Fort Leavenworth. "I do not I assure you regret that Fort Leavenworth is to be your present station," she wrote on May 23. "I prefer it now to an eastern post, as we

[35] Elise to Bragg, May 23, 1849, *ibid*.

shall be more to ourselves, and I can turn my undivided attention to the acquirement of such very necessary knowledge in
the art of housekeeping. Would to Heaven that half of that
time which I have passed in idle amusement and gayety had
been employed in learning such things as would really be of
use to me." [36]

Somehow Bragg managed to control his excitement enough
to make wedding plans. He asked Bishop James H. Otey of
Natchez to perform the ceremony. At first the bishop agreed.
He was a close friend of Elise's family and had directed the
Warrenton Male Academy when Bragg attended. But a family
matter made it impossible for Otey to officiate at the wedding
and he expressed his "great regret" to his "estimable & amiable
young friend Miss E." and to Bragg.[37]

Bragg had more luck with James Duncan, whom he selected
as his best man, though for a while it seemed he too would be
unavailable. Duncan was on an inspection trip to Fort Leavenworth when the invitation reached him. "I am to be married
. . . just one month [from] today," Bragg wrote, "and you
[must] sustain me on the occasion. My intended is very
anxious for your presence, and joins me in wishing you may be
able to get to us in time." In addition, Bragg nervously asked
his friend to learn everything "on all subjects interesting to a
newly married man . . . and be prepared to report." Bragg
was not as naive as his request sounded. What he really wanted
to know was the likelihood of obtaining a house, servants, and
furniture at Fort Leavenworth. He feared he would have to
take both servants and furniture with him. "Will you ascertain
for me as far as practicable?" he asked Duncan. "Is there any

[36] Elise to Sarah Butler, April 28, 1849, Thomas Butler and Family
Papers; Mary Ker to Mrs. Mary Liddell, May 6, 1849, Moses, St. John R.
Liddell and Family Papers; Elise to Bragg, May 23, 1849, Bragg Papers,
Rosenberg Library.
[37] James H. Otey to Bragg, May 22, 1849, Bragg Papers, Rosenberg
Library.

place near where I can live until my own home can be fitted up? These are strange favors to ask you, but I know of no one to do it for me." [38]

To Bragg's appeal, Duncan replied, "I have telegraphed you at Mobile and New Orleans both, to say that I shall be with you in time." He had been tempted to inform Bragg: " 'I'll *join* you if possible on the 1st of June, if not I'll see you *joined* on the 7th.' This is just the despatch under like circumstances you would have sent to me, and now that it is too late, I am a little sorry I didn't pay you in your own coin, as I may not have so good a chance again." [39]

Duncan arrived in time for the wedding which took place on June 7, 1849. It was an unpretentious affair performed at Elise's home, Evergreen, by the Reverend John Sandel, the local Episcopal minister. Nevertheless, several national and local newspapers carried stories on the wedding and Bragg. [40] "I caused the important event to be announced in the Picayune of Sunday and the Crescent of Monday," Duncan wrote Bragg, "copies of the former I caused to be sent you from the office, of the latter I send myself—thinking you might wish to astonish some of your distant friends by enlightening them as to your change of condition." [41]

Marriage delighted Bragg for he and Elise suited each other. During their honeymoon at Evergreen they discovered just how similar they were in taste and temperament. They even looked akin, though such observations scarcely seem consistent with reports of the bride's beauty. Nevertheless, shortly after their marriage Elise wrote Bragg of a lady who "asked if we were not related, from the *striking* resemblance between us. See, Cousin Eliza [Butler] is not alone in holding such an opin-

[38] Bragg to Duncan, May 8, 1849, Duncan Papers.
[39] Duncan to Bragg, May 22, 1849, Bragg Papers, Rosenberg Library.
[40] New Orleans *Daily Picayune*, June 10, 1849; *National Intelligencer*, June 19, 1849; New York *Herald*, June 20, 1849; *Wetumpka* [Alabama] *Daily State Guard*, June 18, 1849; *Confederate Veteran*, IV (1896), 102.
[41] Duncan to Bragg, June 13, 1849, Bragg Papers, Rosenberg Library.

ion, & we have not been married sufficiently long, to have *grown alike*." [42]

Only one Ellis still considered Bragg standoffish and formidable. Elise's sister Margaret wrote him a year after his marriage: "I expect you think this nonsense ridiculous, but somehow or other I do not feel the same fear in writing to you, which I always felt in conversing with you." With Elise, of course, Bragg was less reserved. A few weeks after her wedding, she wrote Sarah: "You say you are satisfied you left me happy. I ought to be so. You know I censured Col. Bragg for being too cold & reserved a lover. I little knew the depth of affection that was concealed under such an exterior—he is an ardent & devoted husband & fonder of displaying his affection in a thousand little tendernesses than even myself. The fact is," Elise admitted, "we are a silly (to a *third person*) new married couple, & it is fortunate you did not remain longer, or you would have been sickened with matrimony." [43]

[42] Elise to Bragg [Winter, c. 1850], Mrs. Braxton Bragg Papers, University of Texas.

[43] Margaret Ellis to Bragg, June 2, 1850, Bragg Papers, Rosenberg Library; Elise to Sarah Butler, June 29, 1849, Thomas Butler and Family Papers.

CHAPTER VI

Obey or quit

1 8 4 9 – 1 8 5 6

L ESS THAN A MONTH after Bragg's marriage, on July
3, James Duncan died in Mobile. In his last letter to Bragg,
Duncan wrote: "I think I shall go over to Mobile tomorrow.
. . . I need not remind you that you are . . . at liberty to
command me in any way I can be useful to you . . . I claim
as a right that you shall call on me." [1] Doubtless Bragg
mourned for this old friend, with whom he had shared so
much, but he left no record of his grief.

Perhaps his new responsibilities blunted his sorrow, for he
worried throughout his honeymoon about how Elise would
react to army life. Fort Leavenworth, where he was scheduled
to report for duty, was hardly the place to take a bride. At
best, it was a rough frontier post. His concern for Elise, along
with other considerations, caused him to request another assignment when a cholera epidemic in St. Louis delayed their
departure for Fort Leavenworth. He argued that the President
had promised to assign units with extensive field service to
comfortable stations in the East. Consequently, "I should infer
my company could not be kept on the frontier," Bragg wrote
Adjutant General Jones. "But I should be pleased to know
something definite as my private arrangements are now of
some importance." His most persuasive argument was that his
battery, which was traveling overland from New Mexico,
could not be refitted properly and quickly at Fort Leavenworth. He had discussed this problem with General Twiggs,

1 Duncan to Bragg, June 13, 1849, Bragg Papers, Rosenberg Library;
Cullum, *Biographical Register*, I, 570.

who had succeeded General Gaines in New Orleans, and
Twiggs agreed that it would be better to organize and instruct
the battery at Jefferson Barracks, near St. Louis. Fort Leavenworth lacked adequate "grounds for battery exercises," and it
would be easier to equip and train a battery at Jefferson Barracks.[2]

Bragg got part of what he wanted. The War Department
ignored his request for assignment to a comfortable eastern
station, but new orders directed him to refit and instruct his
battery at Jefferson Barracks. He and Elise arrived there on
September 10, 1849, and Bragg wrote: "I have this day assumed the command of this post, finding on my arrival no
officer senior to me."[3] Soon the regular post commander returned, and Bragg began to restore his battery to the condition
it was in when he left Mexico. But the renovation of the
battery, hampered by various problems and shortages, took
nearly three years.

They were years layered with frustration and happiness.
Jefferson Barracks was one of the army's most attractive bases,
but neither Bragg nor Elise liked the Missouri climate. "I do
not think the winters this far north can boast much over those
of Louisiana," she wrote; "the rotation of snow-storms, thaws
& freezes, are an equivalent of our rains; & we have more
genial sunshiny days." Bragg was less restrained in his criticism. "The great father of waters is first frozen, then it thaws
and overflows the whole country for 1400 miles, and finally
dries up by way of variety," he deplored. "The great kingdom
of Illinois, too, in wet seasons is one *vast sea*—not of water, but
black mud. Under the circumstances we get a mail semi-
occasionally."[4]

Nevertheless, life was relatively pleasant for the Braggs at

[2] Bragg to Roger Jones, July 24, 1849, Letters Received, AGO.
[3] Bragg to Jones, September 10, 1849, *ibid.*
[4] Elise to Bragg [December] 14-19 [1851?], Mrs. Braxton Bragg Papers,
University of Texas; Bragg to John Bragg, February 10, 1852, John
Bragg Papers.

Jefferson Barracks. He enjoyed the prestige and authority due his brevet rank, and Elise adjusted quickly to life at an army post. When the weather allowed, they rode about the country-side, visited, or shopped in nearby St. Louis. They joined in the local social life, and made some strong friendships. After they had been transferred to another post, the wife of General Kirkham wrote Elise: "You have waited a long time for an answer to your kind letter, and if I did not know your kind, good heart, would find a ready excuse for me, I should feel like a culprit. I cannot tell you how much the Colonel and yourself have been missed this winter and I can truly say Jefferson Barracks no longer seems like a home to me. I seldom go to your old quarters, as I am so forcibly reminded of what I have lost by my friends removal." Mrs. Kirkham insisted her little girl said, "Mamma, tell Mrs. Bragg I wish she could come back here again and live, and if I could only see him . . . the Colonel might kiss me as much as he chooses." [5]

Elise was as childishly demonstrative with her husband. "All [the family] send . . . much love . . . and a few kisses to brother," wrote her sister Mag; "I fear if I do not say a few you will bother him too much, for you are always glad to find some excuse for kissing him." Another preoccupation of Elise and Bragg was reading, which he often did aloud. Once when he was away she mentioned a novel "about quiet home virtues. It would have been so much more interesting had you have read it to me," she lamented. "I think it will bear a second perusal. It is said 'nothing so tedious as a twice told tale'—I differ from the adage, if it is told by lips that we love." [6]

The Braggs had ample opportunity for these pleasant diversions for they occupied comfortable quarters at Jefferson Bar-

[5] Elise to Bragg [June] 12, 1853, Mrs. Bragg Papers, University of Texas; Lewis, *Sherman*, pp. 85–86; Mrs. Kate Kirkham to Elise, March 15, 1854, Bragg Papers, Rosenberg Library.

[6] Margaret Ellis to Elise [c. 1850], Bragg Papers, Rosenberg Library; Elise to Bragg [December] 14–19 [1851?], Mrs. Bragg Papers, University of Texas.

racks and had plenty of servants. Elise brought four slaves
from Evergreen to do the chores. The women—Jane and
Charlotte—ran the household, though Elise supervised their
work. Charlotte, who appears to have been somewhat sickly,
slept in Elise's room when Bragg was away and kept "up a
bright fire all night." Elise considered Jane "invaluable; untiring in her endeavours to please & so good natured." But the
male slaves, Demos and Dick, proved unsuited for any jobs
besides driver and groom. To tend to his cow and vegetable
garden, Bragg had to secure the services of a soldier named
Garth, whom Elise insisted on calling Gatt.[7]

Elise and her sister Mary Seraphine (Puss), who frequently
visited the Braggs, had only one objection to Gatt—he talked
too much. "One day last week we went into the country
marketing," wrote Elise. "We carried our books along determined that Gatt should not be garrulous. But the poor fellow
was so good natured & tried so hard to drive bargains with his
'German friends,' that we could not help being amused & permitting him to talk. We . . . returned with plenty of eggs &
some chickens." [8]

The Braggs ate well, though not sumptuously. At times they
served champagne, strawberries, and ice cream to their guests.
More often they treated visitors to simpler fare, as when Elise
invited a captain "to eat some curd & cream with us." [9]

One of their most frequent visitors was Mrs. Mary F. Love,
who lived next door. Elise thought Mrs. Love as shortsighted
as most women—"they generally rush heedlessly into matrimony like moths into a candle"—but she liked her nonetheless.
"I am more pleased with her every time I see her," wrote
Elise; "I think her a sweet artless creature. She asked me *how* I
managed about housekeeping, everything was so new, so
strange to her, she really felt quite bewildered; & then naively

[7] Elise to Bragg [Winter, c. 1850], [June] 12, 1853, *ibid.*; Bragg to Elise,
June 9, 1853, Braxton Bragg Papers, Duke University.
[8] Elise to Bragg, June 1, 1853, Mrs. Bragg Papers, University of Texas.
[9] Elise to Bragg [June] 12, 1853, *ibid.*

remarked with a blush, 'she had not yet got accustomed to her husband.' I laughingly told her, I had the advantage, as I had remained at home two months after my marriage—with nothing to do, but to get accustomed *to mine*." [10]

Another regular caller was a local minister, a Mr. McCarty, whom Elise characterized as "a bad preacher . . . [but] an agreeable talker." She described one of his calls as "a *visitation* instead of a visit." He rushed past "Charlotte before she could show him to the parlor," found Elise in the dining room, and regaled her for hours on "the difference of navigation on eastern & western streams [and] . . . drunkenness [which] . . . he looks upon . . . in the light I do—as a *vice* . . . making its unfortunate victim more an object of *pity* than *contempt*. When he painted the horrors too often resulting from it," Elise wrote Bragg, "I felt my heart swell—with thankfulness & sweet delight, to think how perfectly free from evil, you are Dearest." After McCarty exhausted his initial topics, he turned to politics. But he must have realized he had stayed too long, for when Elise started to order candles lit he leaped from his chair and "seized [Bragg's] . . . hat . . . with which he would have decamped" had not his hostess noticed the mistake. After he had taken an erratic path through the snow, Elise enjoyed a "heady laugh . . . *not at the man* for he is too excellent, but his excentricities." [11]

Elise usually had little to laugh about when Bragg was away from the post. "Just a week today Love, since you left," she wrote when he was on an inspection trip. "It has been a long, long one to me; & I can only sigh, when I think how much time remains to be passed without you. . . . I wish there were some means of transporting *kisses*, a lover's post office especially for them. Unfortunately there is no tangibility in the abstract kiss. Whatever its *effects* may be, it is born & dies in

10 Mary F. Love to Elise, May 24, 1852, Bragg Papers, Rosenberg Library; Elise to Bragg [June] 12, 1853, [Winter, c. 1850], Mrs. Bragg Papers, University of Texas.
11 Elise to Bragg [December] 14-19 [1851?], *ibid*.

the same breath. How many you will owe me on your return, beyond all power of computation." Another time she wrote: "I need not tell you how much, how *very* much I miss you. . . . I have spoken of the *days, the nights* are far more lonely, save when consciousness is buried in sleep. I miss the beloved companion from my side, & *the* pillow for my head." [12]

Bragg also missed Elise when he was away from home. While at Fort Leavenworth on court duty in 1853 he admitted: "I am lost without you, dear wife. . . ." On the date of their fourth wedding anniversary, "the 7th [of June] (the memorable 7th)," he assured her, "I took a . . . glass of champagne to ourselves, sparkling & bright, as the original occasion required. God grant us many returns of the day, and as happy ones as the past." He comforted Elise, and explained that they were fortunate to be together as much as they were. "You are right dear B. B. in saying how much we both have for which to be truly grateful to a kind Providence," she wrote. "I have more for I have a kind loving husband who patiently bears with my faults & many murmurs." [13]

Usually, Elise restricted her social activities while Bragg was away from the post, and this doubtless added to her loneliness. She suffered "the same familiar objects" daily. "The greatest excitement in our household," she wrote in 1853, "was caused by the *swarming of the bees* from the old hive." After declining an invitation to a ball, she explained to her husband: "I should feel but little interest in attending one . . . *without you,* the music, lights & gayety, would be a mockery." Instead, she preferred to remain at home with her books or knitting. "I worked at your slippers nearly all the forenoon," she informed Bragg; "how pleasant to work for one you love! Every stitch

[12] Elise to Bragg [Winter, c. 1850], [December] 14–19 [1851?], June 1, 12, 1853, *ibid.*
[13] Bragg to Elise, June 9, 1853, Bragg Papers, Duke University; Elise to Bragg [June] 12, 1853, Mrs. Bragg Papers, University of Texas.

is associated with a thought, so that your slippers will be filled with 'sweet memories.' " [14]

But Elise was no recluse. She visited or gossiped with her friends and even once ventured out on a sleigh ride. "I had hoped that all *new pleasures* were to be participated in with you," she avowed to Bragg, but she could not resist when "shortly after breakfast I heard the tinkling of bells, & a sleigh with twelve horses . . . dashed to the door, Capt. Love & Mr. Willcox, jumped out, & invited me to join the other ladies in a ride." It was a pleasant day, and the snow looked so beautiful, Elise "thought an *upset* in a bed so soft & white could scarcely be a misfortune. No sooner thought than done—on turning down by the church . . . over we went. I was up & shaking off the flakes before I recovered from my surprise," she recalled. "As usual I believe, there was much laughter & no bruises."

Even so, when someone suggested they continue to St. Louis, Elise objected. "I had become heartily tired by this time," she wrote, "my curiosity had been *fully* gratified, & not having the exuberant spirits of the other ladies, I wanted to return to my quiet fireside." Hers was the only dissenting voice, and she might have been carried along withal, had not a neighbor returning in his buggy from St. Louis offered her a ride. When the sleigh riders returned to the post after sunset, Elise invited them over for a "glass of egg nogg, which [she] . . . had prepared to atone for [her] . . . French leave of them." She admitted: "A year or two ago, I might have enjoyed such a trip; but I have since discarded the imp called *fun*, for a calmer & far sweeter happiness." [15]

One pastime Elise continued to enjoy was shopping. "We managed to take several excursions without you," she informed Bragg in 1853. "Saturday week, Puss and I under es-

[14] Elise to Bragg, June 1, 1853, [December] 14–19 [1851?], [Winter, c. 1850], Mrs. Bragg Papers, University of Texas.
[15] *Ibid.*

cort of Demos & Dick, went to town. It was quite astonishing
to hear how correctly I gave directions about the different
stores & streets. We . . . did a good deal of shopping, as you
will find by the decreased size of your purse." [16]
Elise affected a helplessness in money and other matters
which her husband encouraged, and she rationalized her de-
pendency upon him. "It seems the world is the same in a
garrison, & out of it," she wrote. "Citizens & officers selfish,
save where their individual interests are concerned. I have such
a dislike to asking a *favour*, I scarcely know what would become of me if thrown on my own resources. I trust I shall
never be put to the trial." She refused to worry about bills;
instead, she wrote Bragg, "I have been sorely puzzled over the
accounts, & have put them away for B. B." [17]
Her unwillingness to budget stemmed partly from the relative affluence in which she grew up and partly from her belief
that of "all the world can give [the most desirable are] youth,
talents, beauty [and], boundless wealth." [18]
Despite her commitment to self-indulgent values, Elise controlled her jealousy when Bragg received a letter from another
woman. Often Elise had opened his mail, but this time she
restrained herself. "I felt somewhat tempted to break open
[the letter]," she admitted to him, "it was from Baltimore
folded in what is called 'a lover's style,' directed in a lady's
hand, tho' I can't say I much admire her calligraphy. Am I not
a wise daughter of Eve's, or a *trusting wife?*" [19]
She had every reason to trust Bragg, for there is no indication that he ever cared for another woman. He apparently
remained in love with Elise throughout his life. Furthermore,
neither flirtation nor infidelity would have been consistent
with his standard of personal conduct and rigid self-discipline.
Even if Bragg had been a philanderer, he would have had

[16] Elise to Bragg [June] 12, 1853, *ibid.*
[17] Elise to Bragg [December] 14–19 [1851?], [June] 12, 1853, *ibid.*
[18] Elise to Bragg [December] 14–19 [1851?], *ibid.*   [19] *Ibid.*

little time for any woman besides Elise at Jefferson Barracks. He was too busy rejuvenating his battery with long hours of drill and instruction. One of his main problems was how to get enough men and material to keep his command together. In May 1850 he complained to the War Department: "Lieut. F. J. Thomas, is the Chief of the Commissary Department in New Mexico, and is not permitted to join me. Some other 1st. Lieutenant or a Brevet Second [lieutenant] will be necessary." In September 1850 Bragg's old friend Cump Sherman arrived to assume his duties as a lieutenant in the battery. "New horses had just been purchased for the battery and we were preparing for work," recalled Sherman, when he was commissioned a captain in the Commissary Department and transferred.[20]

Bragg believed the War Department was determined to frustrate his efforts. In January 1851 he again asked the government for a brevet second lieutenant. "One of my 1st Lieutenants has been under orders [to report here] since the 2d. [of] November, last," wrote Bragg, "but has not yet joined [me]. My Second Lieut. is on leave, and will probably be absent for several months. I have but two instructed non-commissioned officers, sergeants, one of whom has been sick for four months." A clerk in the War Department scribbled across the bottom of Bragg's request: "Except in cases where the Captain is indefinitely absent, Brevet 2d Lieutenants cannot be attached to Light Artillery companies." [21]

Enlisted men, Bragg soon discovered, were as difficult to obtain as officers. Eight months after he arrived at Jefferson Barracks he had only twenty-two men present, and most of these were scheduled to be discharged in a few months. Thirty-three of his men remained on duty in New Mexico. "As long as they are borne on my rolls I can make no progress in getting up a new Battery," Bragg complained. He asked for "at least

[20] Bragg to Jones, May 28, 1850, Letters Received, AGO; Sherman, *Memoirs*, I, 87–92.
[21] Bragg to Jones, January 9, 1851, Letters Received, AGO.

OBEY OR QUIT 129

forty choice recruits . . . drawn from the cavalry depot." [22]

The recruits sent were scarcely choice. Most of them were too small for artillery service and unable to ride a horse. "As a whole," wrote Bragg, "I consider them very inferior." Nor, apparently did their quality improve. "We are kept quite close prisoners by the recruits," Elise wrote in 1853. "They swarm in every direction, dirty, undisciplined; though considering Rifles are among them they keep quiet." [23]

Bragg's problems, though no worse than those of most unit commanders, probably rankled him more than similar difficulties would other officers because he was so scrupulous. He fumed when the War Department neglected to provide the extra copies of the tactical manuals he needed to "unite theoretical with practical instruction." His wrath can only be imagined when the government sent gun primers of the wrong size. He had ordered the right primers months before and could not fire his guns without them.[24]

Mistakes and shortages were irritating enough, but Bragg had even more serious complaints against the government. He believed peacetime economy measures, badly administered, were destroying his command. In 1851 his company was reorganized as a battery of foot artillery instead of horse artillery.[25] Bragg protested and in September 1852 asked Secretary of War Charles M. Conrad to restore his company "to its former organization of Horse Artillery. . . . Much of the necessary armament and equipment is still on hand," wrote Bragg, "and the present is the most favorable season on the

[22] Bragg to Jones, May 28, 1850, *ibid.*

[23] Bragg to Jones, November 3, 1850, *ibid.;* Elise to Bragg, June 1, 1853, Mrs. Bragg Papers, University of Texas.

[24] Bragg to Jones, July 17, 1850, Letters Received, AGO; Bragg to "Colonel of Ordnance," July 18, 1852, Braxton Bragg Papers, Southern Historical Collection, University of North Carolina.

[25] General Orders, No. 18, Adjutant General's Office, March 31, 1851, Old Army Section, War Records Branch, National Archives. It will be recalled that foot artillery gunners rode on the ammunition chests, while those of the horse artillery were mounted.

score of economy, for the purchase of the few additional horses necessary. The reasons for keeping up the instruction in *Horse Artillery* are too obvious, and were too strongly illustrated in our last war to require recapitulation."

The reasons were not obvious to Conrad, a Louisiana Whig appointed to the War Department by President Fillmore, who endorsed Bragg's letter: "In ordinary marches, for service with bodies of troops composed of cavalry & either of the other arms, or for maneuvering on the field of battle, the foot artillery will be found to be quite as efficient as the horse, and is much less expensive." [26]

The rejection of his request convinced Bragg that Conrad was a menace. To his brother John, who had recently been elected to Congress from Alabama, Bragg wrote: "The head of the Army is a dishonest man and a maneuvering politician. He is doing all he can, covertly, to injure Mr. Fillmore's administration . . . and to that end shamefully neglects the Army." A number of high ranking officers were as irresponsible as Conrad, asserted Bragg; "Washington . . . has become . . . the scene of as much intrigue & double dealing by the Army and its officers, as it has been for years by politicians." [27]

Furthermore, Bragg considered most of the members of Congress totally ignorant and hopelessly corrupt. "How delighted you must be with the honors of your position," he chided John. "Not only a looker on but participant in the Bear dance. But then the road to fame must be rough sometimes, and an ambitious man forgets the little annoyances in consideration of the end. How long are you willing to serve in the House & face the climate of Washington for the handle of Honorable to your name?" Bragg believed John could "not by any possibility be able to benefit the country thro' such loafers as compose the House of Reps." As an example of the stupidity

[26] Bragg to Charles M. Conrad, September 15, 1852, Letters Received, AGO.
[27] Bragg to John Bragg, March 25, 1852, John Bragg Papers.

of congressmen, Bragg called John's attention to "an ignorant exposé . . . on the subject of military matters" made recently by General Joseph Lane. "Lane was the prince of loafers & blackguards in Mexico," Bragg charged. Not only was Lane a liar, "he was a regular marauder & murderer—[he] robbed Santa Anna's private house & brought home a quantity of his effects, such as horse equipage, clothing & even a number of his wife's dresses, & jewelry. He is a man you cannot believe under oath," contended Bragg. "Yet I see he is one of the Democratic candidates for the Presidency." Humphrey Marshall of Kentucky was another congressman whom Bragg considered "a great humbug and a superficial tho' fluent fool." In Mexico Marshall's "regiment did some fine running & no fighting, as all mounted volunteers ever will do." [28]

What especially upset Bragg was a bill introduced by General James Shields, Chairman of the Senate Military Committee. The bill proposed to unify all artillery, which Shields considered "the most inefficient and worst managed military service in the world," under a chief who would then "eliminate from the present artillery force a sufficient number of officers and companies to constitute a competent corps . . . and employ the residue as cavalry or as infantry companies for the defense of the frontier." [29] Bragg considered the bill "a great evil" even though it would unify the artillery. "How Shields came to be so used," Bragg wrote John, "I cannot see unless he was drunk, which by the man, is very probable." It was really General Scott's bill, contended Bragg. "Scott has been striving for ten years to accomplish this object, has had several insidious bills before Congress admitting such a construction, but this is the first time he has found a democrat so weak as to yield." [30]

[28] *Ibid.* Santa Anna was Mexico's president and principal general during the Mexican War.
[29] Shields's bill is printed in Birkhimer, *Historical Sketch,* pp. 376–77.
[30] Bragg to John Bragg, June 28, 1852, John Bragg Papers.

When John asked what legislation was needed to improve the army, Bragg responded with a number of recommendations. First, he suggested that all superannuated or disabled officers be retired. Such a proposal "has been before Congress for ten years," he wrote "and has several times passed the Senate, and last year it was killed in the House by [Robert] Toombs [of Georgia] because it was pressed to the exclusion of some hobby he wished to ride." To be effective, such a bill should compel "all officers *to serve in* their appropriate duties or retire." Bragg believed a well-written law would make the army 50 per cent more efficient and cost the country nothing. The disabled officers would be retired on half pay and the money saved could be used to increase the pay of officers on duty. "Now," he complained, "the disabled draw full pay and stay at home, or encumber any command with which they serve." If Congress refused to increase the pay of active officers, Bragg insisted, "we had rather get clear of the imbecility any way, and we will do the duty without the pay, as we do now."

Second, Bragg thought the artillery should be reorganized, but not as Shields's bill proposed. Instead of a reduced corps, Bragg wanted the artillery expanded and merged with the Ordnance Corps, "as in the French and English" armies. "I do not intend to take an active part in this matter," he wrote, "for I cannot be benefitted personally, and I have only received kicks heretofore for endeavoring to do the same thing for the benefit of others. But to save the Artillery at large something prompt and decisive is necessary."

Third, he suggested that officers be paid regular salaries. "We are paid in a way neither you nor any other member of Congress can understand," wrote Bragg, "and to prevent this & secure uniformity & abolish abuses we ought to be paid as the Navy [a graduated amount according to rank and duties]. . . ." He proposed as a yearly scale: major generals $5,000; brigadiers $3,000; colonels $2,500; lieutenant colonels $2,000;

majors $1,700; captains $1,400; first lieutenants $1,000; and second lieutenants $800. In addition all officers should be allowed one ration a day so that they could subsist when in the field and unable to buy food. Mounted officers should receive extra allowances because they "have to keep *private* horses & equipment for public duties." Bragg believed any bill would be ineffective unless it made "a general sweep of *all special laws and provisos* by which individuals are receiving double pay for feasting members of Congress a few times. Beware of bills for the relief of Adjt. General R[oger] Jones," warned Bragg. "He gets a few thousands from every new Congress."

Fourth, Bragg favored the revision of laws relating to the general organization and administration of the army. In his opinion the army had deteriorated since "Scott became 'General-in-chief' (as he styles himself)." Favoritism prevailed in every staff department. "We have staff enough for 30,000 men," Bragg asserted. Moreover, the $60,000 a year spent on the Corps of Topographical Engineers, which he claimed did nothing but survey boundaries and improve rivers and harbors, should not be charged to the army. He believed the Department of Interior should take over the topographical engineers. "But if you southern men wish to check internal improvements by the general government," he informed John, "abolish *it* [the topographical engineers] and your blow will be effectual." Another drain upon the army, Bragg insisted, was money spent on bands: "We have about 300 men in the Army in Musical Bands whose sole occupation is to amuse the ladies & solace the tedium of superan[n]uated commanders of regiments & pvts." He insisted that the "field music allowed companies is all that is required, and these 300 men, half a regiment, had better lay aside their fiddles & horns and take up muskets."

Of all his proposals, Bragg considered the first "the most important for the *efficiency of the Army*." The second, he thought "necessary for the preservation of the Artillery"; the

fourth "essential for the harmony and concert of action necessary in any military expedition." [31]

Bragg was always critical, but his proposals cannot be dismissed as merely chronic complaints of a malcontent. True, his
suggestions were neither more original nor less self-interested
than those he had published in 1844. Yet some of them were
economically sound ideas which would have improved the
army's efficiency. Eight years before he had attacked, among
other things, Scott's administration of the army, the size of the
staff, the organization of the artillery, the topographical engineers, the way officers were paid, and the administration of
military justice. His experiences in Mexico had convinced him
that old officers hindered the army, and that the artillery
needed to be merged with the ordnance department. Many
officers favored these and other army reforms, but few expressed their opinions as openly and as persistently as Bragg.

His discontent with the system was caused partly by his
commitment to professionalism, and partly by his own personality. He believed the army must be efficiently organized,
composed of rigidly disciplined regular troops, and led by
young and able professional officers. He also seemed to favor a
military establishment free from political interference, but this
was not precisely so. Distrustful of all authority except his
own and that with which he agreed, Bragg only wanted to
prevent cooperation between those inside and outside the
army who favored policies different from his. He was quite
willing to use John's political power for army reform.

Bragg's proposals impressed John. He expected Franklin
Pierce to be elected President in November 1852 and hoped
that a Democratic administration would make army reform
easier. Bragg had no doubt that Pierce would win the election—
"The party . . . seems to unite, and in that case he must be

[31] Bragg to John Bragg, February 10, 1852, *ibid.* Captain W. S. Henry
(*Campaign Sketches*, pp. 129-31) also considered the retirement of
disabled officers essential.

elected," reasoned Bragg—but he feared Congress would continue to ignore proposals to improve the army as it had for the past few years. "And Congress is not alone in this shameful neglect of duties," argued Bragg. "All departments of the government . . . are as bad. The Secretary of War and Genl Scott have most shamefully abandoned their duties, and have done nothing for months past but issue a few electioneering orders. The discipline, instruction and moral character of the Army are lower than at any time in my recollection." What could Pierce do? He was no reformer. "I did not know *Pierce* in Mexico," Bragg informed John, "but his reputation was *very low*. He drank, gambled & generally kept low company, was destitute of tone & independence of character." Bragg guessed that "Old Miss Nancy King [vice presidential candidate William R. King of Alabama] must be sore at occupying a seat below him. But we go for 'principles not men'!!" [32]

Pierce won the election and, much to Bragg's surprise, supported army reforms. Secretary of War Jefferson Davis, who had served with Bragg in Mexico, organized four new regiments, raised the army's pay, retired some of the older officers, and adopted several new weapons. Davis's pet projects were increasing the number of troops guarding the frontier, and directing surveys for railroads to the Pacific coast.[33] He did nothing to restore the horse artillery or to curb Scott's power.

[32] Bragg to John Bragg, June 28, 1852, John Bragg Papers. For additional criticism of Pierce, see *Philadelphia North American and U. S. Gazette*, September 25, 1852; Captain George McLane to J. F. McHilton, September 16, 1852, unidentified newspaper clipping, Franklin Pierce Papers, Library of Congress.

[33] Roy F. Nichols, *Franklin Pierce: Young Hickory of the Granite Hills* (Philadelphia, 1931), pp. 272, 295, 490. Besides Nichols, a number of twentieth-century writers consider Davis an outstanding Secretary of War who did much to improve the army. See, for example, Allan Nevins, *Ordeal of the Union* (2 vols., New York, 1947), II, 50; and the most recent biography of Davis by Hudson Strode, *Jefferson Davis: American Patriot, 1808–1861* (New York, 1955), pp. 260–80. Strode says (p. 260), "Davis renovated and rejuvenated the whole army." Bragg disagreed.

Consequently, the reforms of the new administration only partially appeased Bragg. He lost his strongest ally in Washington when John went home at the end of 1853 disgusted with politics and refused to be a candidate for Congress again,[34] but Bragg still hoped to save the horse artillery. In 1853 he appealed to Secretary Davis's military experience. Unless some of the horse artillery companies were restored, contended Bragg, "practical knowledge of that branch of the service will soon be extinct. I therefore submit for . . . consideration . . . an application for the restoration of my battery to 'Horse Artillery'. . . . Facts and arguments on the advantage of that branch . . . would be unnecessarily addressed to one whose experience on the march and in action has amply furnished both." [35]

Davis was no more sympathetic to Bragg's request than Secretary of War Conrad had been. In fact, Davis favored further reductions in artillery strength and the replacement of light batteries with heavy rifled guns; his answer to Bragg's request was to order Bragg's battery to Fort Gibson, in Indian territory.[36]

Bragg was furious. He believed the assignment of artillery units to frontier patrol duty was a waste of men and animals; batteries were unsuited to Indian warfare. Moreover, Bragg opposed frontier service because it would be uncomfortable for Elise. He did not want her to accompany him to Fort Gibson; living accommodations were primitive and there was always the possibility of an Indian attack, but she went along anyway.[37]

[34] Owen, *History of Alabama*, III, 200.
[35] Bragg to Davis, May 4, 1853, Letters Received, AGO.
[36] Birkhimer, *Historical Sketch*, pp. 51–52. Fort Gibson, Cherokee Nation, was located on the Arkansas River in what is now northeastern Oklahoma.
[37] Bragg and Elise arrived at Fort Gibson on October 31, 1853, Bragg to Jones, October 31, 1853, Letters Received, AGO; Mrs. Kate Kirkham to Elise, March 15, 1854, Bragg Papers, Rosenberg Library.

Fort Gibson met all of Bragg's apprehensions. Buildings crumbling with age and neglect provided inadequate shelter for troops and horses. Unless the fort were rebuilt immediately, he warned the War Department, winter weather would probably kill more men and animals than the Indians.[38]

After eight unhappy months at Fort Gibson, Bragg's battery moved to Fort Washita near the Texas border. It was as battered a post as Fort Gibson. The roofs on nearly all the buildings were old and leaky. Indeed, Bragg reported the hospital "unfit for use," the stables "insufficient and unsuitable for the accomodation of artillery horses," the storehouse "utterly unfit," and the magazine located "in a very unsafe position." Furthermore, there was no granary, workshop, or gunhouse at the post.[39]

Six months at Fort Washita were enough for Bragg. Years later Sherman recalled that "Bragg hated Davis bitterly" for sending him to the frontier, "as Bragg expressed it 'to chase Indians with six-pounders.'" In January 1855 he applied for sixty days' leave, and in April he and Elise left Fort Washita for Thibodaux.[40]

Clearly, what Bragg wanted most was to escape further frontier service. Not even a promotion, which came soon after he reached Thibodaux, could lure him back. On May 24, 1855, the commander of the First Cavalry wrote the adjutant general: "Will you please inform me if Bvt. Lt. Col. Braxton Bragg is a Major in the 1st Regt. of Cavalry. If he is, it is time for him to report." Twelve days before Bragg had declined the appointment because it would have forced him to return to the frontier. To avoid such duty, he requested an additional six months' leave and permission to visit Europe. "If ordered to

[38] Bragg to Jones, November 20, 1853, Letters Received, AGO.

[39] Bragg to "Assistant Adjutant General," July 13, 1854, *ibid.*; Bragg to "Quartermaster General," December 16, 1854, Army Papers, Missouri Historical Society, St. Louis.

[40] Sherman, *Memoirs*, I, 162; Bragg to Adjutant General Samuel Cooper, January 5, April 12, 1855, Letters Received, AGO.

Europe, we are to take a charming villa near *Florence*," wrote
Elise, though she feared this hope "will not probably be carried out." [41]

She was right; the War Department granted Bragg an additional six months' leave, but refused to approve his request to
visit Europe. He spent the rest of the year in Mobile, Raleigh,
and Thibodaux. This gave him ample opportunity to talk over
his problems with friends, to consider what he could do if he
resigned from the army, and to look at some farms which were
for sale.[42]

When he went to Washington in December to discuss his
case with the Secretary of War, Bragg apparently had no
thought of resigning; he merely hoped to get his battery transferred. "I miss our usual garrison excitment of preparing for
calls this morning—of beating up eggnogg & making apple
toddy," Elise wrote him on January 1. "I hope you will use
every exertion to be ordered to a post, where we can again
commence even our irregular housekeeping. I see the western
rivers are rising. The Arkansas is rising rapidly at Van Buren.
Your battery could be removed, Mr. Davis being willing." [43]

Davis was adamant; he insisted that Bragg's battery remain
on the frontier. Bragg probably tried to win some support for
his position in Washington, but it was difficult for him to hide
his distaste for politics. "I suppose you went . . . to pay your
respects to the President," wrote Elise. "It must be quite an
imposing sight, contrasted with the simplicity of the republic,
to see the ambassadors in their court dress with the insignia of

[41] Colonel E. V. Sumner to Cooper, May 24, 1855, *ibid.*; Bragg to
Cooper, May 12, 1855, *ibid.*; Elise to Bragg, December 17, 1855, Mrs.
Bragg Papers, University of Texas. In April 1855 Jefferson Davis did
order three officers to Europe to observe various military systems and
the Crimea War battlefields. Richard Delafield, *Report on the Art of
War in Europe in 1854, 1855, and 1856* (Washington, 1860), pp. v–vi.
[42] Bragg to Cooper, May 12, October 12, November 12, December 11,
1855, Letters Received, AGO; Elise to Bragg, December 17, 1855, Mrs.
Bragg Papers, University of Texas.
[43] Elise to Bragg, December 17, 1855, January 1, 1856, *ibid.*

rank & office. *I* who like looking at 'pomp & circumstance,' would enjoy it, tho' you agree with your friend Mr. Marcy in preferring the simple black." [44]

Bragg gave up his fight to get his battery transferred on December 31, 1855. To Adjutant General Samuel Cooper he sent this short note: "I have the honor to tender to the President of the United States the resignation of my commission in the Army." Across the bottom of the note Jefferson Davis wrote: "Accepted." [45]

Anger over Davis's intransigency probably provoked Bragg to resign his commission, but his decision was not wholly an emotional one. He had weighed carefully the advantages and disadvantages of civil and military life, for he was nearly forty years old and could not hastily abandon the only profession he had ever practiced. Eight years before, just after the Mexican War, he had hinted that he might leave the army if he could find a "rich wife." His marriage had provided the necessary money, but only after prolonged frustration had he resigned. Writing a few months after his resignation, Bragg explained that he had given up his "old profession under a pressure of outward circumstances which I resisted until disgusted & worn down. . . . Finding . . . my command . . . destroyed, my usefulness gone, and the department resolutely bent on substituting long range rifles for light artillery, I concluded to retire from the unequal contest." His "professional pride," he explained, forced him to resign after the "finest battery I ever saw was destroyed in two years at a cost of $100,000." [46]

Bragg had qualms about the future, but he refused "to repine over the past." It "was the duty of the department to carry out its own views," he believed, "and mine to obey or quit. The latter was my choice, and I do not regret it." If he

[44] Elise to Bragg, January 1, 1856, *ibid.*
[45] Bragg to Cooper, December 31, 1855, Letters Received, AGO.
[46] Bragg to [George Hay Stuart?], May 31, 1856, George Hay Stuart Papers, Library of Congress.

did not regret his decision, nevertheless he was happy to see that Davis had failed to inherit the executive office from Pierce. "I see no mention of my friend Davis [as a presidential candidate] now," Bragg observed with satisfaction. "He could drive me from the Army but not from my party." [47]

[47] *Ibid.*

CHAPTER VII

Give us all disciplined masters

1856–1861

On FEBRUARY 8, 1856, Bragg committed himself to a new career. He purchased a sugar plantation three miles north of Thibodaux for $152,000. It included 1,600 acres of land, "buildings, dwelling houses, sugar house mill, engine and the stock of cane and seed cane . . . horses, mules, cattle, hogs, sheep, farm utensils, agricultural implements," and 105 slaves. For this estate, which Bragg named Bivouac, he put up $24,912.40 in cash; agreed to pay another $30,000 before May 1, 1857, and the remainder, of $97,787.60, in eight yearly installments bearing 6 per cent interest.[1] The down payment was made with Elise's money,[2] but Bragg was the sole owner of the property. Of the 330 estates on the left bank of Bayou Lafourche listed by the Louisiana tax assessor in 1858, ten were considered more valuable than Bragg's. But only three of these estates were valued, for tax purposes, at more than one hundred thousand dollars; Bragg's was listed as worth $60,000. "My purchase was a large one," Bragg admitted to a neighbor. "Our prospects this year are gloomy indeed, the stubble is nearly all destroyed except in the region of your fine property. . . . The high price [of sugar] alone can save us," he concluded with characteristic pessimism.[3]

[1] Lafourche Parish Conveyance Book No. 3, pp. 35–48 (bound manuscript), Lafourche Parish Court House, Thibodaux, Louisiana.

[2] Bragg to William T. Sherman, January 25, 1867 (typescript), Walter L. Fleming Collection of David F. Boyd Family Papers, Louisiana State University.

[3] Lafourche Parish Real Property Tax Assessment, February 5, 1858, Zachary Taylor Papers; Bragg to [George Hay Stuart?], May 31, 1856, Stuart Papers.

Nevertheless, Bragg labored arduously to retire his heavy mortgage and to become a successful planter. "I would wish more to be with you dear love, did I not feel that just now I would be rather an encumbrance than a pleasure," Elise wrote Bragg before they moved to Bivouac. "You have so much business to attend to, I would only be in the way. Indeed, I have scarcely thought of my new home at all, but doubtless will have ample food for reflection when I get there." Bragg was never idle. He read to improve his knowledge of sugar cane culture, supervised the multiple operations of sugar making, and tried to predict the weather. His busiest time, of course, was in the late fall. "Until nearly Christmas," he wrote in November 1859, "I shall be overrun with business, or rather confined by it. We are in the midst of [sugar] manufacturing, and a cold spell is now on us which inflicts a heavy loss every day lost. I even work on Sunday from this time to the end." For five years he would have no holiday; only after his health deteriorated, and on doctor's orders, would he spend a few weeks in the mountains.[4]

No evidence suggests that Bragg was a cruel master, but he probably drove his slaves as hard as he drove himself. He certainly did not consider slavery a "peculiar institution." His father had been a slaveowner, and throughout most of his adult life Bragg had owned body servants. His views on slavery, according to the English reporter William H. Russell, were typical of southern planters: he believed that "neither he nor his family were responsible for the system"; slavery was

[4] Elise to Bragg, February 17, 1856, Bragg Papers, Rosenberg Library; Bragg to G. Mason Graham, June 27, 1860, Boyd Family Papers; Bragg to Sherman, November 13, 1859, June 14, 1860, Walter L. Fleming, ed., *General Sherman as a College President* . . . (Cleveland, 1912), pp. 53, 218. For excellent accounts of cane culture, sugar manufacturing, and Louisiana planter society, see J. Carlyle Sitterson, *Sugar Country: The Cane Sugar Industry in the South, 1753-1950* (Lexington, 1953), pp. 3-227; and Charles P. Roland, *Louisiana Sugar Plantations during the American Civil War* (Leiden, 1957), *passim*.

permitted under the "laws and constitution"; slaves were necessary for the cultivation of the southern crops; and if Northerners or foreigners "settled in Louisiana . . . they would discover that they must till the land by the labor of the black
race, and that the only mode of making the black race work,
was to hold them in a condition of involuntary servitude." [5]

Doubtless Bragg's army background influenced, indeed,
probably determined, the way he operated his plantation.
"The very plantation is a small military establishment, or it
ought to be," he wrote Sherman. By military, Bragg explained,
he did not mean "the old fogy notion of white belts, stiff
leather stocks and 'palms of the hands to the front,' but discipline, by which we secure system, regularity, method, economy of time, labor and material." He believed discipline would
"secure better health, more labor and less exertion, and infinitely less punishment, more comfort and happiness to the
laborer, and profit and pleasure to the master."

In Bragg's system of values discipline occupied a special
place. It not only insured harmonious master-slave relations,
but also the society Bragg admired. "We have a large class of
our population in subordination, [which is] just and necessary,"
he informed Sherman. "Where do we find the fewest mutinies,
revolts and rebellions? In the best disciplined commands.
Human nature is the same throughout the world," Bragg
argued. "Give us all disciplined masters, managers, and assis-
tants, and we shall never hear of insurrection—unless as an
exception. . . ." [6]

By 1860 Bragg's methods seemed successful. "My crop was
finished on the 12th, and is by far the most profitable one I
have made—giving me a net profit of $30,000," he boasted in
December 1859. The census of 1860 verified Bragg's pros-

[5] William Howard Russell, *My Diary North and South* (Boston, 1863),
p. 207.
[6] Bragg to Sherman, December 16, 1859, Fleming, ed., *Sherman*, p.
82.

perity. Listed as a farmer, he reportedly owned 1,640 acres of land conservatively valued, together with machinery and livestock, at $101,900, and he added several additional acres to his holdings when Congress confirmed his and Randal L. Gibson's claim to a disputed tract. Only two farms in Ward One of Lafourche Parish had a higher cash value than Bivouac, of which just eight hundred acres were improved. But these improved acres produced 28,000 gallons of molasses, 3,000 bushels of corn, 440 barrels (one thousand pounds each) of sugar, and fifty bushels of hay in 1859. Bragg owned 109 slaves; the estimated value of his personal estate was $120,000. By the standards of the time, he was a rich man.[7]

As Bragg became economically successful, he took a more active interest in public affairs. He had always been concerned with politics, and even as he struggled to master the art of planting he watched the national scene. "Our latest news is quite interesting," he wrote in 1856. "Nicaragua recognized . . . and old [Senator Charles] Sumner [of Massachusetts] severely chastised for his impertinence. You can reach the sensibilities of such dogs only through . . . their heads & a big stick." [8] When offered the local offices of "Levee Inspector and School Director," Bragg accepted. They were "trifles it's true," he admitted, but "my time is all occupied." [9]

Despite the demands politics made upon his time, he sought higher office. In 1859 he accepted the Democratic nomination for Second District Commissioner and was elected to the state's Board of Public Works. "I did not and do not wish the office, as it gives no prominence and little compensation," he wrote just after his election, "but friends, principally Richard Taylor, son of the old general, pressed me to accept a nomina-

[7] *Ibid.*, p. 80; Eighth Census of the United States, 1860, Louisiana, Schedule 1, p. 96, Schedule 2, pp. 53–54, Schedule 4, p. 7 (microfilm copy), Louisiana State University.

[8] Bragg to [Stuart?], May 31, 1856, Stuart Papers. Of course, Bragg was referring to Preston Brooks's attack on Sumner.

[9] Bragg to Sherman, June 14, 1860, Fleming, ed., *Sherman*, p. 219.

tion, as they could find no other man whose name could defeat the rogues. Under this pressure I gave up my privacy, and shall strive to inaugurate an honest administration." [10]

Bragg's explanation of his entry into politics sounds a bit strained, contrived to justify his course to friends and relatives who had heard his many blasts against politicians. His brother-in-law, Towson Ellis, wrote teasingly: "As the Col. has become so active a politician, and is willing to accept such an important responsibility for the good of the world, I suppose he must of course intend to sacrifice that very unprofitable plantation which persists in producing so much smarter cane than its neighbors." [11]

The duties of Bragg's new office were those previously administered by the Swamp Land Commissioner and other state officials, that is, to supervise and control "all state work, to support all officers and agents, etc. The duties are heavy," Bragg explained, "all expenditures large (over $1,000,000 a year) and the patronage extensive." Previously, "frauds, swindling and ignorance" had wasted much of the money intended for public works, and many serious charges had been made against the past administration. [12]

Bragg expected to produce "a new state of affairs." He had the strong support of State Senators F. S. Goode and Richard Taylor, "a very plain, straightforward man, of great independence, candid, honest and clearheaded." With their encouragement, Bragg attempted to run the Board of Public Works the way he had his plantation and battery, but one board member constantly frustrated Bragg's plans by the introduction of extraneous issues. "The other members are tender toward him,

[10] Bragg to Sherman, December 16, 1859, *ibid.*, pp. 80–81; Bragg to Edward G. W. Butler, December 27, 1859, Edward George Washington Butler Papers, Duke University.

[11] Towson Ellis to Elise Bragg, August 24, 1859, Bragg Papers, Rosenberg Library.

[12] Bragg to Sherman, December 16, 1859, Fleming, ed., *Sherman*, pp. 80–81; Bragg to Butler, December 27, 1859, Butler Papers.

and hope to conquer by mildness," wrote Bragg. "I prefer the military system and go at him rough shod." [13]

Soon Bragg realized that Louisiana's political affairs were worse than he had imagined. He liked the new governor, Thomas O. Moore, who took office in 1860. "The Gov. called in to see me last night," Bragg wrote Elise. "He is a very clear old gentleman—fond of his business, planting—and seems very moderate in his political sentiments. So far he is very popular, and contrasts very favorably with his predecessor." But Bragg disliked most of the public works commissioners. He complained to a friend: "Nobody is responsible, every disbursing officer keeps his own accounts, draws his own warrants on the treasury, and if he can only get a dishonest man to consent to sign a voucher and a warrant, they draw the money and there is the end of it. No one ever settles an account with the state." [14]

Such chicanery disgusted Bragg and made him ill. Boils broke out on his hand and he slept fitfully. "My hand is no worse," he wrote Elise in 1860, "the new boil not having broken is still a little troublesome, but with poultices & the many little conveniences so nicely prepared by you, I get on very well." [15]

After a year of frustration and controversy, he was "heartily tired of the honors of office." He confessed to his wife: "In our business we are at a *dead halt*—differences of opinion as to the powers &c given by law to members of the Board. The subject is referred to the Legislature and the Attorney General. I am getting . . . tired of being made a fool of at my own expense, and begin to think of resigning." [16]

One of the many favor-seekers to call on Bragg was St. John

[13] Bragg to Sherman, December 16, 1859, February 13, 1860, Fleming, ed., *Sherman*, pp. 80–81, 163.

[14] Bragg to Elise, February 8, 1860, Bragg Papers, Rosenberg Library; Bragg to Sherman, February 13, 1860, Fleming, ed., *Sherman*, p. 163.

[15] Bragg to Elise, February 8, 1860, Bragg Papers, Rosenberg Library.

[16] Bragg to Sherman, February 13, 1860, Fleming, ed., *Sherman*, p. 163; Bragg to Elise, February 8, 1860, Bragg Papers, Rosenberg Library.

R. Liddell, who had been expelled from West Point in 1835 for dueling. Liddell, upset over the possibilities of sectional conflict, insisted that the state government make "prompt preparation for defense," and that Bragg use his influence and office toward that end. Bragg recognized the possibility of civil war, recalled Liddell, but he "believed the danger to be distant; and . . . only wished *my* cooperation and assistance . . . in organizing and fostering the State Military School at Alexandria . . . with the express view of preparing young soldiers for this very emergency." [17]

Bragg's interest in the establishment of a good military college in Louisiana went beyond the training of young men for war. In fact, scientific instruction was his primary concern. "High literary institutions are growing around us," he wrote, "but in the scientific and military we are sadly deficient." Scientific knowledge was needed in nearly every phase of life in Louisiana: levee and canal construction, the operation of factory and plantation machinery, and even in the cultivation of the soil. Only a scientific education would overcome "our woeful deficiency and waste in our want of system in cultivation," he contended. "No class of people in the world are so dependent on Science and discipline as the Sugar planter, and we should prepare the means at home to perfect our young men." [18]

His hopes for the young school at Alexandria increased when he learned that Cump Sherman had been elected president. On receiving this welcome news, Bragg wrote: "The announcement gave me very great pleasure. . . . Had I known [of] your application I should have attended personally to forward your wishes." [19] He was certain Sherman would

[17] St. John R. Liddell, "Liddell's Record of the Civil War in N. America 1860 to 1866," Moses, St. John R. Liddell and Family Papers.
[18] Bragg to Sherman, December 16, 1859, Fleming, ed., *Sherman*, pp. 81–82; Bragg to Butler, December 27, 1859, Butler Papers.
[19] Before he learned of Sherman's candidacy, Bragg "united with many gentlemen in New Orleans to recommend Professor Sears . . . simply on the ground of his being a graduate of West Point." Bragg to

agree with his ideas on education. "The more you see of our society, especially our young men," wrote Bragg, "the more you will be impressed with the importance of a change in our system of education if we expect the next generation to be anything more than a mere aggregation of loafers charged with the duty of squandering their fathers' legacies and disgracing their names." [20]

Bragg did all he could to help Sherman and the school. He defended his old friend against charges of abolitionism, introduced him to a number of important politicians, and praised the school's positive effect upon several young men. "I am down here at the legislature log rolling for a bill to the interest of our institution," Sherman wrote a relative in February 1860. "I have no doubt of success. I cannot but laugh in my sleeve at the seeming influence I possess, dining with the governor, hobnobbing with the leading men of Louisiana, whilst John [Sherman, Cump's brother, a Republican Congressman from Ohio] is universally blackguarded as an awful abolitionist. No person has said one word against me, and all have refrained from using his name in vain. . . . Bragg and others here know me to be national, and they back me up too strong." To G. Mason Graham, Sherman admitted: "Bragg . . . put me in such good relation with his friends that really they overcome me with zeal." [21]

When Sherman was about to resign to accept a more profitable position, Bragg pushed a bill through the legislature that

---

Sherman, November 13, 1859, Fleming, ed., *Sherman*, p. 52. See also Bragg to C. B. Sears, July 28, 1859, Boyd Family Papers.

[20] Bragg to Sherman, February 13, 1860, Fleming, ed., *Sherman*, pp. 162–63; Bragg to G. Mason Graham, June 27, 1860, Boyd Family Papers.

[21] Bragg to Sherman, November 13, December 16, 1859, October 25, 1860, Fleming, ed., *Sherman*, pp. 53, 81–83, 299–300; Sherman to Thomas Ewing, Jr., February 17, 1860, *ibid.*, pp. 173–75; Sherman to Graham, February 17, 1860, *ibid.*, p. 172. See also Sherman to Mrs. Sherman, December 12 [1859], *ibid.*, p. 76; Sherman to Graham, December 31, 1859, January 13, 29, February 8, July 6, 1860, *ibid.*, pp. 90, 120, 130, 145, 239; Graham to Sherman, January 15, 1860, *ibid.*, pp. 123–24; Graham to Thomas O. Moore, February 9, 1860, *ibid.*, p. 156; Bragg to Sherman, February 13, 1860, *ibid.*, pp. 161–62.

increased Sherman's pay $500 a year by making the "seminary a State Arsenal," and tried unsuccessfully to get the federal government to donate his "Buena Vista battery" to the school. "I am coaxed and begged not to leave," wrote Sherman, "they [Bragg, Graham, and others] think that I can make . . . [the school] successful and famous." [22]

But the sectional crisis of 1860 soon overshadowed plans for the college, which seemed doomed after Abraham Lincoln's election to the presidency in November. On December 12 Governor Thomas O. Moore told a special session of the Louisiana legislature: "I do not think it comports with the honor and self respect of Louisiana . . . to live under the government of the Black Republican President." Secession, said Moore, was Louisiana's only choice. Money could no longer be spent on a state college; instead, the "militia should be reorganized, a Board of Military Affairs created and a half million dollars expended . . . in the purchase of modern arms and military equipment." [23]

Sherman, who would have none of this, decided to resign. "Your decision," Bragg wrote him, "does not surprise me; indeed, I do not see how it could be otherwise under the circumstances. . . . You are acting on a conviction of duty to yourself and to your family and friends. A similar duty on my part may throw us into an apparent hostile attitude, but it is too terrible to contemplate and I will not discuss it." [24]

The secession movement disturbed Bragg; he was—as St. John R. Liddell noted—a conservative who "believed in republics and thought no majority whatever could set aside written constitutions." Sherman later recalled: "Bragg, who certainly was a man of intelligence, and who, in early life, ridiculed a

[22] Bragg to Sherman, February 13, June 14, October 25, 1860, ibid., pp. 163, 219, 300–1; Sherman to Graham, February 16, July 16, 1860, ibid., p. 243; Sherman to Thomas Ewing, Jr., February 17, 1860, ibid., p. 175.
[23] Quoted in G. P. Whittington, "Thomas O. Moore: Governor of Louisiana, 1860–1864," Louisiana Historical Quarterly, XIII (1930), 7–8.
[24] Bragg to Sherman, December 26, 1860, Fleming, ed., Sherman, p. 319.

thousand times, in my hearing, the threats of the people of South Carolina to secede from the Federal Union, said to me in New Orleans, in February, 1861, that he was convinced that the feeling between the slave and free States had become so embittered that it was better to part in peace; . . . and, as a separation was inevitable, that the South should begin at once, because the possibility of a successful effort was yearly lessened by the rapid and increasing inequality between the two sections, from the fact that all the European immigrants were coming to the Northern States and Territories, and none to the Southern." The accuracy of Sherman's recollection is indicated by a letter he received in December 1860. "The Union is already dissolved," wrote Bragg. "The only question now is: can we reconstruct any government without bloodshed?" He doubted it; "a few old political hacks and barroom bullies are leading public sentiment. . . . They can easily pull down a government," he admitted, "but when another is to be built who will confide in them? Yet no one seems to reflect that anything more is necessary than to 'secede.' " Bragg would "continue to hope, though without reason, that Providence will yet avert the great evil. But should the worst come," he assured Sherman, "we shall still be personal friends." [25]

Reluctantly, Bragg prepared for war. On December 12, 1860, Governor Moore appointed him a member of the state military board, which the legislature had authorized. "We have had a preliminary meeting of our 'Military Board,' and laid down a plan for the formation of military companies," wrote Bragg in late December. "We have five thousand stands of arms—muskets; are to proceed to New Orleans to-morrow to see what can be done in enlarging it. All received from the government so far are gone—issued to volunteer companies and thrown away without the slightest accountability. Unless

[25] Liddell, "Liddell's Record of the Civil War," Moses, St. John R. Liddell and Family Papers; Sherman, *Memoirs*, II, 381–82; Bragg to Sherman, December 26, 1860, Fleming, ed., *Sherman*, pp. 319–20.

brought into service and kept under discipline how are we to prevent the same thing again? A regular force is the only alternative." [26]

Before an army could be organized, Governor Moore learned that Federal gunboats were secretly supplying forts on the Mississippi. From Baton Rouge, Bragg wrote Elise: "On Tuesday evening [January 8] I left [New Orleans] . . . on fifteen minutes notice to join the Governor here. Great excitement existed among those having special news from Washington . . . all urging Governor Moore to act at once in seizing the Forts and Arsenal. Expeditions were made up at other places to do it if he failed to act. Under . . . the circumstances he made up his mind on Wednesday to assume the responsibility. I have doubts of the policy but think it the only course he could adopt to avoid bloodshed." Bragg, in command of five hundred volunteers, persuaded the commander of the Baton Rouge arsenal to surrender on January 11. Because Bragg had no wish to start a conflict, he conducted the surrender negotiations with "prudence and conciliation," and assured himself that "the [Federal] officers left perfectly satisfied." Even so, he knew a dangerous step had been taken. He could only do his "duty and trust in Providence." [27]

Just as Bragg predicted, the secession convention approved the seizure of the forts and took Louisiana out of the Union. "The election returns are not as favorable to action as was expected," he wrote, "but still it seems a majority of the convention will decide to go with other Southern states." [28]

The convention also created a state army, and Governor

[26] The document which officially appointed Bragg a member of the state military board is in the Thomas Overton Moore Collection, Chicago Historical Society; Bragg to Sherman, December 26, 1860, Fleming, ed., *Sherman,* p. 320.

[27] Bragg to Elise, January 11, 13, 1861, William K. Bixby Collection of Braxton Bragg Papers, Missouri Historical Society, St. Louis.

[28] New Orleans *Crescent,* February 14, 1861; Bragg to Elise, January 11, 1861, Bixby Collection.

BRAXTON BRAGG
Library of Congress

Moore named Bragg its commander with the rank of major general. Louisiana would soon have a large force under arms, predicted Sherman, "and its commander will . . . dispose of your governor and legislature. . . . Our friend Bragg seems to be alert, and most likely he will soon be your king. You could not have a better." [29]

Bragg failed to become king, of course, but he worked as hard as any monarch to build an army. "I have no idea, my dear wife, when you may see me," Bragg wrote in January. "I must work day and night . . . and even then we shall not be ready." Thomas Bragg in North Carolina, though proud of his brother, confided to his diary: "I fear Braxton's military

[29] Bragg's appointment as major general in the service of Louisiana, February 6, 1861, Moore Collection; Sherman to G. Mason Graham, January 16, 1861, Fleming, ed., *Sherman*, p. 339.

duties will take him too much from his plantation and private business." Sherman, about to leave for the North, predicted: "I have seen a good deal of Bragg who goes quietly but steadily, organizing two regiments of regulars and mark my words when a time of strife comes he will be prepared." [30]

Bragg needed experienced soldiers to command and train his volunteer army, so he offered commissions to any professionals who would join him. To one of his letters, Mansfield Lovell, a West Point graduate who had resigned from the army to become New York City's deputy street commissioner, replied: "[Brevet Major P. G. T.] Beauregard [Superintendent of the United States Military Academy] can probably give you a better collection of names than I. [Gustavus W.] Smith [New York's street commissioner] is in Washington for a few days. When he returns I will ask him to mention some names of suitable persons, & will forward them to you. . . . In case highly recommended non-commissioned officers of the Army wish to join you," asked Lovell, "what might they expect in the way of rank?" [31]

Neither Lovell nor Smith accepted Bragg's offer of a commission, though both joined the Confederacy as major generals in the fall of 1861, and Beauregard smouldered because Bragg had been given command of the Louisiana forces. After all, Beauregard was a native Louisianian; though he had remained in the United States Army until February 20, 1861, he believed he deserved the state's highest military office. Bragg, in an attempt to placate the testy Creole, called at Beauregard's New Orleans office to ask his advice on the defense of the state and to offer him a colonelcy. Beauregard refused the commission, enrolled as a private in an aristocratic New Orleans regiment,

[30] Bragg to Elise, January 11, 1861, Bixby Collection; Thomas Bragg Diary, February 18, 1861, Southern Historical Collection, University of North Carolina; Sherman to David F. Boyd, February 23, 1861, Fleming, ed., *Sherman*, p. 366.
[31] Mansfield Lovell to Bragg, February 25, 1861, Palmer Collection.

and then got himself appointed a provisional brigadier general in the new Confederate Army.[32]

The Beauregard affair worried Bragg. Why, he asked himself, should Beauregard, a tardy patriot, become the first Confederate general? Perhaps because the President of the Confederacy, which Louisiana joined in February, was Jefferson Davis. When Sherman dined with the Braggs in New Orleans on his way to Ohio, he noticed that Bragg "seemed jealous" when they discussed Beauregard's appointment. And Elise remarked: " 'you know that my husband is not a favorite with the new president.' " [33] It seemed that Davis disliked Bragg enough to ignore him despite all he had done to prepare Louisiana for war.

But Bragg had no reason to be anxious; the Confederacy needed experienced officers too much for Davis to overlook him. On March 7, Bragg wrote Elise: "You will be astounded to hear I am off. . . . At 11 o'c[lock] this morning I received by telegraph, notice of my appointment as Brigadier General in the Confederate Army and orders to proceed to Pensacola and assume command." He wanted to see her before he left, but there was no time. "You know how unprepared I am for any such move," he reminded her. "My wants must be supplied by purchase here, and you must send by [Elise's brother] Towson all that you think I may require from home. Tell Towson to close up all my business, as far as he had orders, and bring with him the other accounts. I can settle them by letter." [34]

[32] Ezra J. Warner, *Generals in Gray* (Baton Rouge, 1959), pp. 22, 194, 281; T. Harry Williams, *P. G. T. Beauregard: Napoleon in Gray* (Baton Rouge, 1955), pp. 47–49.

[33] Sherman, *Memoirs*, I, 162. Doubtlessly Beauregard was more popular in Louisiana than Bragg. Fifteen Louisiana military organizations were named for Beauregard; only three were named for Bragg. See Andrew B. Booth, compiler, *Records of Louisiana Confederate Soldiers and Louisiana Confederate Commands* (2 vols., New Orleans, 1920), I, 7–8.

[34] Bragg to Elise, March 7 [1861], P. M., Carl Sandburg, ed., *Lincoln Collector* (New York, 1949), p. 314. See also *OR*, I, 448.

To Elise, Bragg admitted how concerned he was about the course of national events. "What is to become of all this I do not see except war," he wrote. "Mr. Lincoln says he will not recognize our government, and if he does not we must take the Forts in our limits; to do that is war, and when it commences it will rage from one end of the country to the other, God grant us a safe deliverance. Our cause is just, and we must triumph. I deplore the necessity, but neither you nor I could wish me out of it. Come what will I must be in it." [35]

Of course he had to be involved; he was too important, too patriotic, too ambitious to be a spectator. Whatever happened, it was his duty as well as his desire to participate. He would be missed in Louisiana. "All is wrong [here in Louisiana] since Genl. Bragg left," lamented an officer.[36] But Bragg was needed elsewhere. He had been assigned to Pensacola, Florida, because Beauregard had been sent to Charleston, South Carolina; their commands were equally important, for the only significant forts in the Confederacy still occupied by Federals were Fort Pickens, near Pensacola, and Fort Sumter, in Charleston harbor. If war came, it would likely begin either at Pickens or at Sumter.

Contemporaries considered Bragg and Beauregard ideally suited for such important posts. A newspaper, pleased that the Confederates had "wisely entrusted the command of their soldiers to officers who have served in the regular army," boasted that "these gentlemen [Bragg and Beauregard] are said to be the *élite* of the army of the late United States; none stand higher for skill, courage, and noble conduct in their profession." In July 1861 a West Point professor called Bragg "the best of all" the Confederate generals. Three months before, Theophilus H. Holmes, who would himself become a Confederate general,

[35] Bragg to Elise, March 7 [1861], P. M., Sandburg, ed., *Lincoln Collector*, pp. 314–15.
[36] Taylor Beatty Diary, March 12, 1861, Southern Historical Collection, University of North Carolina.

insisted that Bragg—though less colorful than Beauregard—
"possessed military capacities of a very high order." President
Davis, said Holmes, "had made most excellent selections in the
appointment of his first generals." [37]

[37] Richmond *Daily Dispatch*, February 22, 1861; Maria Lydig Daly,
Diary of a Union Lady, Harold E. Hammond, ed. (New York, 1962), p.
32; John B. Jones, *A Rebel War Clerk's Diary at the Confederate States
Capital* (2 vols., Philadelphia, 1866), I, 15.

CHAPTER VIII

War is inevitable

MARCH–APRIL, 1861

$\mathbf{B}$RAGG ARRIVED at Pensacola on March 10, 1861, and established his headquarters nine miles west of the town, at Fort Barrancas. "His unexpected appearance here has given universal satisfaction to the citizens and soldiers," announced a newspaper. "On his arrival at the [naval] yard, the officers and soldiers manifested their gratification at his presence by the most vociferous demonstrations of applause. We mingle our congratulations with those of the citizens generally upon the accession of one to the command here who has the unlimited confidence of all friends and the respect of those opposed to him." [1]

From Fort Barrancas, Bragg could see Federal troops at Fort Pickens on Santa Rosa Island, a mile and a half across Pensacola Bay. To his left as he faced Pickens were Barrancas Barracks, a naval yard, and the village of Warrington. To his right, on the mainland across the bay's entrance from Fort Pickens, were Fort McRee and its Confederate garrison.

The Federals in Fort Pickens seemed secure enough at the moment. After a badly planned and bloodless attempt by Alabama and Florida militia to capture the fort in early January, President James Buchanan and the Confederate government had agreed to a truce. Stephen R. Mallory, a former United States Senator from Florida, announced that the Confederates

---

[1] Bragg to Major George Deas, March 10, 1861 (copy), Palmer Collection of Bragg Papers; *OR*, I, 449; Richmond *Enquirer*, March 23, 1861. For a general account of military events at Fort Pickens, see Edwin C. Bearss, "Civil War Operations in and Around Pensacola," *Florida Historical Quarterly*, XXXVI (1957), 125–65.

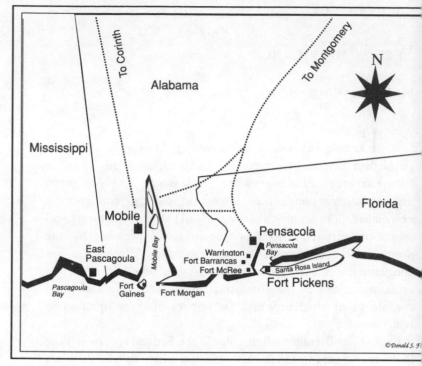

FORT PICKENS AND VICINITY

had no intention of attacking Fort Pickens, "but, on the contrary, we desire to keep the peace, and if the present status be preserved we will guarantee that no attack will be made upon it." Nine former senators, including Jefferson Davis and Judah P. Benjamin, joined Mallory in opposition to any Confederate attempt to take the fort. "We think no assault should be made," they wrote on January 18. "The possession of the fort is not worth one drop of blood to us." [2]

[2] OR, I, 354, 444–45.

President Buchanan also opposed any action that might appear aggressive. At his direction, the Secretaries of War and the Navy wrote the commander of the naval squadron off Pensacola on January 29: "In consequence of the assurances received from Mr. Mallory . . . that Fort Pickens would not be assaulted, you are instructed not to land the company on board the *Brooklyn* unless said fort shall be attacked." The day before this letter was written, the President asked Congress "to abstain from passing any law calculated to produce a collision of arms." Thereafter, through February, the Navy Department instructed the commanders of ships near Fort Pickens to "act strictly on the defensive." [3]

Buchanan's successor was less cautious. In the preliminary draft of his first inaugural address, Abraham Lincoln wrote: "All the power at my disposal will be used to reclaim the public property and places which have fallen; to hold, occupy and possess these, and all other property and places belonging to the government . . . but beyond what may be necessary for these, there will be no invasion of any State." Secretary of State William H. Seward begged the President to substitute for this strong statement a promise to use his power "with discretion in every case and . . . with a view and a hope of a peaceful solution of the national troubles and the restoration of fraternal sympathies and affections." Lincoln's friend Orville H. Browning also suggested that the phrase "to reclaim the public property and places which have fallen" was too strong. "On principle the passage is right as it now stands," Browning agreed. "But cannot that be accomplished as well, or even

[3] *Ibid.*, 355–56; James D. Richardson, ed., *A Compilation of the Messages and Papers of the Presidents, 1789–1910* (11 vols., New York, 1911), V, 662; Isaac Toucey to Captains James Glynn and Henry A. Adams, and Commander Charles H. Poor, January 21, 1861 (copy), Gustavus V. Fox Papers, New York Historical Society; Toucey to Captains James Glynn and William S. Walker, and Lieutenant Adam J. Slemmer, January 29, 1861 (copy), *ibid.*; Toucey to Walker, Adams, and Poor, February 16, 1861 (copy), *ibid.*

better without announcing the purpose in your inaugural?" Lincoln followed Browning's advice, but he left no doubt that he intended to hold Sumter and Pickens.[4]

By early March both Lincoln and Davis had decided to violate the truce, but neither knew what the other planned. Bragg had received instructions from the War Department on March 10 to report his "wants in respect to artillery and the munitions of war, having in view the . . . reduction of Fort Pickens." Two days later a Union ship had started south with an order for Captain Israel Vogdes aboard the U.S.S. *Brooklyn*. "At the first favorable moment," read the order, "you will land with your company, reenforce Fort Pickens, and hold the same till further orders."[5]

But the senior American naval officer off Pensacola, Captain Henry A. Adams, refused to obey the order. "I have declined to land the men . . . as it would be in direct violation of the orders from the Navy Department under which I am acting," he wrote Secretary of the Navy Gideon Welles on April 1. To reinforce Pickens, argued Adams, "would most certainly be viewed as a hostile act, and would be resisted to the utmost. No one acquainted with the feelings of the military assembled under Genl Bragg can doubt that it would be considered not only a declaration, but an act of war. It would be a serious thing to bring on by any precipitation a collision which may be entirely against the wishes of the administration. At present both sides are faithfully observing the agreement entered into by the U.S. Government with Mr. Mallory. . . ." Adams re-

---

[4] Roy P. Basler, ed., *The Collected Works of Abraham Lincoln* (8 vols., New Brunswick, 1953), IV, 254, 266. James G. Randall, *Lincoln the President: Springfield to Gettysburg* (2 vols., New York, 1945), I, 332, believed Lincoln would have ordered the evacuation of Fort Sumter if Buchanan had allowed the reinforcement of Fort Pickens.

[5] Bragg to Major George Deas, March 10, 1861 (copy), Palmer Collection of Bragg Papers; *OR*, I, 449; *Official Records of the Union and Confederate Navies in the War of the Rebellion* (30 vols., Washington, 1894–1927), Series 1, IV, 90.

minded Welles: "This agreement binds us not to reinforce Fort Pickens unless it shall be attacked or threatened. It binds them not to attack it unless we should attempt to reinforce it. I saw Genl Bragg on the 30th ulto., who reassured me the conditions on their part should not be violated." [6]

Bragg had been less than honest with Adams. Only insufficient means, not regard for the truce, prevented the Confederates from attacking Fort Pickens. When Bragg arrived at Pensacola his army was little more than a mob. These citizen-soldiers, independent and undisciplined, often deserted, and prominent civil officials sometimes hampered attempts to apprehend and punish them. Most of the troops, away from home for the first time, were intent upon having a good time. "Volunteers continue to arrive," bewailed Bragg. "How I am to manage them I hardly know. . . . Night before last we were near a general row all round." A large number of men got "drunk and a free fight commenced, and for awhile things looked badly. By the free use of the bayonet & hand cuffs applied by the *Zouaves* from *New Orleans,* they were soon quelled." Bragg immediately declared martial law throughout his command, raided the "grog shops" in the area, and captured enough whiskey "to have kept the Army drunk two months." [7]

Bragg soon had a sober command. He prohibited the sale of alcoholic beverages to his troops, and arrested all offenders. "An order was given last night that all the drinking saloons are to be kept closed," reported the New Orleans *Daily Picayune* on April 13, "and that no spirituous liquors are to be given or vended to any of the soldiers. . . . This is a wise and salutary precaution, which reflects credit upon the commanding officer, General Bragg." So effective was Bragg's campaign against

[6] Henry A. Adams to Gideon Welles, April 1, 1861, Fox Papers.
[7] Governor John J. Pettus to Bragg, May 28, 1861 (copy), Governors' Papers, Series E, No. 52, Mississippi Department of Archives, Jackson; Bragg to Elise, April 11, 1861, Bixby Collection of Bragg Papers.

drinking that the War Department issued a general order early in 1862 entreating commanders of all grades to follow Bragg's example and suppress drunkenness by every means in their power. Tipplers, of course, complained, but Bragg's suppression of whiskey won wide accord. Writing in 1862, a civilian offered Bragg his "most sincere thanks for the successful efforts you have made in arresting the fearful evil of the abuse of intoxicating liquor in our army." Everyone acknowledged that Bragg had rendered great service to the Confederacy, continued the writer, "but I feel that the greatest service you have done to the country, has been to put down the improper use of ardent spirits. You deserve & are now receiving the deep seated gratitude of every mother, wife & sister of our much afflicted country & God will bless you for it." [8]

"Most of my trouble here has been from election of officers," Bragg complained in early April. Confederate law allowed each unit to select its own officers, and since few volunteers had any military experience, command usually went to the most prominent or the most popular man. Democracy provided no insurance against incompetency, and frequently company, battalion, and even regimental commanders were unsuited for their position. It was reported, surely with some exaggeration, that the first man to make a mistake in drill was invariably elected captain of a volunteer company. The election of officers, whatever the circumstances, infuriated Bragg. He was equally irritated by the demands of Georgia's Governor Joseph E. Brown and the War Department. Brown insisted upon the right to commission a full quota of regimental officers although he sent only "skeleton" units to Pensacola. The War Department complicated Bragg's organization of the

[8] New Orleans *Daily Picayune*, April 13, 1861; Bragg to Richard Taylor, April 6, 1861, Urquhart Collection of Richard Taylor Papers, Tulane University; unidentified and undated newspaper clipping, Confederate Scrapbook, Alabama Department of Archives, Montgomery; *OR*, Series 4, I, 834–35; A. Mouton to Bragg, March 30, 1862, Palmer Collection of Bragg Papers.

army with instructions to keep men from the same state together.[9]

Bragg may have been angered most by the election of officers, but this was only one of the reasons why his army was unprepared to take Pickens. He lacked guns, specialists, transport, and money. By the end of March he had received few big guns and scarcely any trained artillery officers. Bureaucratic blunders in Montgomery were partly responsible. "I have at last received marching orders," Captain William Dorsey Pender, a West Point trained artillerist, wrote his wife from Montgomery on March 16. "I am off for Pensacola, Fla. tomorrow. . . . I am delighted to leave this place for it is not pleasant to loaf in a large city much less in a small one." But at nine o'clock that same evening Pender again wrote his wife: "The Sec.-of-War has just informed me that he does not want me to go to Pensacola, but remain here for the present, I suppose to work in the office. . . ." A few days later Pender was sent to Baltimore to assemble men who "enlisted in the Southern Army." This routine job required no special skill. "I merely inspect and ship them," Pender admitted. Thus, War Department carelessness or inefficiency deprived Bragg of a needed specialist. He did receive Captain Hypolite Oladowski, whose experience included European and American ordnance; Bragg admitted that he could "desire no more efficient officer" than Oladowski, but one specialist was insufficient. When Bragg could find no experienced quartermaster, he selected a man to train for the job. But all this took time. Furthermore, Bragg complained, "The [War] Department . . . is crowding me with men and giving nothing with them. They are useless without arms and munitions." What he needed was money or supplies. He repeatedly asked for funds during the first month he was at Pensacola, but he did not receive a dollar.

[9] Bragg to Taylor, April 6, 1861, Richard Taylor Papers; *OR*, I, 453, 455, 449; Louise Biles Hill, *Joseph E. Brown and the Confederacy* (Chapel Hill, 1939), pp. 51–52.

"With our empty purse and an exhausted credit it is pretty hard to feed . . . men on a barren sand bank," he wrote on April 6. "The most difficult question for us is that of money, and it seems to receive too little attention by our rulers," Bragg grumbled several weeks later. "War cannot be carried on without it, and yet it is unnecessary to waste it because we have war. In our private affairs we should merely use the necessities of life, and give all else to the cause." He assured President Davis: "We are using every effort to keep our expenditures down, and neither corruption nor extravagance will be tolerated, but you know too well that economy at the expense of efficiency is bad policy." [10]

By the end of March Bragg commanded an army of 1,116 men, and 5,000 additional troops were on the way to Pensacola, but he was not yet ready to fight. He believed that the erection of a new battery at Pickens was "a virtual violation of the [truce] agreement; and the threat of President Lincoln in his inaugural is sufficient justification of the means we are adopting." But Bragg "deemed it prudent not to bring the agreement to an abrupt termination." The Union fleet off Pensacola was too strong, and he was still unprepared. "According to my notions," he admitted to his wife, "things here are in a most deplorable condition. . . . Our troops are raw volunteers, without officers, and without discipline, each man with an idea that he can whip the world, and believing that nothing

[10] William W. Hassler, ed., *The General to His Lady: The Civil War Letters of William Dorsey Pender to Fanny Pender* (Chapel Hill, 1965), pp. 10–12; Bragg to Cooper, March 12, 1861 (copy), Palmer Collection of Bragg Papers; Bragg to Taylor, April 6, 1861, Richard Taylor Papers; Bragg to Elise, May 28, 1861, Bixby Collection of Bragg Papers; Bragg to Davis, April 7, 1861 (copy), Palmer Collection of Bragg Papers. Several months later, on the recommendation of his medical officers, Bragg substituted molasses for some of his army's usual meat rations. "Being a sugar planter," he wrote, "I do not advise it myself, but the troops are delighted with the change. Meat is scarce & high. Molasses abundant & cheap." See Bragg to Davis, October 22, 1861 (copy), Palmer Collection of Bragg Papers.

is necessary but go . . . take Fort Pickens and all the Navy."
It would not be that easy. The fort was on Santa Rosa Island, a
mile and a half across Pensacola Bay from the mainland. Bragg
had neither the firepower nor the ships necessary to isolate the
Federal garrison. Unless "the U. S. troops attack us," he confessed, "no fighting can occur here for a long time, as we are
totally unprepared. . . . Fort Pickens cannot be taken without a regular siege, and we have no means to carry that on.
. . ." [11]

Yet the Confederate War Department insisted that Bragg
submit a plan to take Pickens, and he suggested three possibilities—a regular siege, a flank attack upon the fort from Santa
Rosa Island, or a direct assault. If the operation was to be
undertaken immediately, he favored an infantry assault on the
fort after its walls had been broken by heavy guns and mortars. The other alternatives would require many more guns
and men than he had or could reasonably expect to have for
some time. Bragg explained to Adjutant General Samuel
Cooper on March 27: "I entertain little doubt of being able to
batter [the fort's walls] . . . down with 10 inch guns . . .
when an assaulting party from this side aided by a false attack
on the Island might carry the work with the Bayonet. It will
be difficult at this distance to determine when the breach is
fully effected . . . and should the enemy resist us by landing
heavy re-inforcements it would be a desperate struggle. A
knowledge, however, that success or entire destruction was
inevitable would nerve our men to the work." [12]

While Confederate authorities discussed what action, if any,
Bragg should take, the Federals prepared to reinforce Pickens.
On April 6, after Lincoln learned that his earlier reinforce-
ment instructions had not been obeyed, Gideon Wells in-

[11] OR, I, 454-55; Bragg to Cooper, March 13, 1861 (copy), Palmer
Collection of Bragg Papers; Bragg to Elise, March 11, 1861, Bixby Collection of Bragg Papers.
[12] Bragg to Cooper, March 27, 1861 (copy), Palmer Collection of
Bragg Papers.

formed Captain Henry A. Adams: "The [Navy] Department regrets that you did not comply with the . . . orders. . . . You will immediately, on the first favorable opportunity after receipt of this order, afford every facility to Capt. Vogdes . . . to enable him to land the troops under his command [at Fort Pickens]. . . ." [13]

When Bragg received reports that additional troops might soon land at Pickens, he was uncertain what he should do. On April 5 he wired Secretary Walker: "Should the agreement not to re-enforce be violated, may I attack?" Walker replied that same day with three questions: "Can you prevent re-enforcements being landed at other points on Santa Rosa Island other than the docks? Do you mean by 'attack' the opening of your guns upon the fort or upon the ships? If the former, would your operations be confined to battering the fort?" [14]

"I can control the dock," Bragg answered the next day, "but re-enforcements can be landed on the outside of Santa Rosa Island in spite of me. The ships, except the Wyandotte, are beyond my range. She can be driven off or destroyed. Any attack by us now must be secretly made by escalade. My batteries are not ready for breaching, and we are entirely deficient in ammunition. No landing should be made on Santa Rosa Island with our present means." [15]

It was still unclear to Bragg just what the War Department expected of him. In a letter to Adjutant General Cooper on April 5, Bragg asked how far he should "be governed by the articles of agreement now existing here?" He could not prevent the landing of reinforcements, but he might make it hazardous. Moreover, he might take Pickens by escalade before it could be reinforced. He would get ready for an escalade, "should it be deemed advisable at any time." Nevertheless, as "long as diplomatic intercourse is going on," he in-

[13] Gideon Welles to Henry A. Adams, April 6, 1861, Fox Papers.
[14] OR, I, 455–56.   [15] Ibid., 456.

formed Cooper, "I shall not feel authorized to bring on a collision, as now advised." Yet the next day Bragg seemed less certain. To Secretary Walker, he announced: "I do not hesitate to believe we are entirely absolved from all obligations under the [truce] agreement," and he wanted to know if he was "free to act when a favorable occasion might offer?" [16]

On April 6, the day he asked Walker for instructions, Bragg received from Jefferson Davis a remarkably candid letter, which historians have overlooked. It was written, in the President's words, "freely and hurriedly" by "your old comrade in arms, who hopes much, and expects much for you, and from you." Davis thought the tone of the northern press indicated a "desire to prove a *military* necessity for the abandonment of both Sumter & Pickens," but he believed the Lincoln government was determined to hold the forts. Informants in the North stated that Lincoln intended to reinforce Pickens, and would try to avoid a collision with Bragg by landing troops on the seaward side of Santa Rosa Island. "It is scarcely to be doubted," reasoned Davis, "that for political reasons the U. S. govt. will avoid making an attack so long as the hope of retaining the border states remains. There would be to us an advantage in so placing them that an attack by them would be a necessity, but when we are ready to relieve our territory and jurisdiction of the presence of a foreign garrison that advantage is overbalanced by other considerations. The case of Pensacola then is reduced [to] the more palpable elements of a military problem and your measures may without disturbing views be directed to the capture of Fort Pickens. . . . You will soon have I hope a force sufficient to occupy all the points necessary for that end. As many additional troops as may be

16 Bragg to Cooper, April 5, 1861 (copy), Palmer Collection of Bragg Papers; *OR*, I, 456–57. The same day he told Walker the Federals had broken the truce, Bragg wrote Richard Taylor: "Our truce remains in force. 'They are not to reinforce. We are not to attack.' It is being carried out by both parties so far." Bragg to Taylor, April 6, 1861, Richard Taylor Papers.

required can be promptly furnished." Davis concluded his letter with several suggestions on how Bragg could capture Pickens. The erection of a mortar battery on Santa Rosa Island might "prevent a junction of the land and naval forces," the President believed. "If that first step the establishment of a mortar battery was permitted you could establish gun batteries also, and then carry forward your approaches until you were attacked. Then all your batteries being opened, shells falling in the Fort from front and from rear must prove rapidly destructive to the garrison, and open to you several modes of success." [17]

This letter indicates that Davis was willing to start the war. He would have liked to do precisely what some historians claim Lincoln did—maneuver the enemy into firing the first

[17] Davis to Bragg, April 3, 1861, Palmer Collection of Bragg Papers. This letter is cited in only one of the many works on the first-shot controversy—Bruce Catton's *The Coming Fury* (New York, 1961), p. 492.

The historical literature on the crisis of 1861 is extensive. Besides Catton's volume, see: Charles W. Ramsdell, "Lincoln and Fort Sumter," *Journal of Southern History*, III (1937), 259–88; J. G. Randall, "When War Came in 1861," *Abraham Lincoln Quarterly*, I (1940), 3–42; Randall, *Lincoln the President*, I, 311–50; David M. Potter, *Lincoln and His Party in the Secession Crisis* (New Haven, 1942), pp. 315–75; Kenneth M. Stampp, "Lincoln and the Strategy of Defense in the Crisis of 1861," *Journal of Southern History*, XI (1945), 297–323; Stampp, *And the War Came: The North and the Secession Crisis, 1860–1861* (Baton Rouge, 1950), pp. 263–86; Allan Nevins, *The War for the Union: The Improvised War, 1861–1862* (New York, 1959), pp. 12–74; Richard N. Current, "The Confederates and the First Shot," *Civil War History*, VII (1961), 357–69; Current, *Lincoln and the First Shot* (Philadelphia, 1963), *passim*, but especially p. 201; John S. Tilley, *Lincoln Takes Command* (Chapel Hill, 1941), *passim*; Kenneth P. Williams, *Lincoln Finds a General: A Military Study of the Civil War* (5 vols., New York, 1949–1959), I, 16–59; W. A. Swanberg, *First Blood: The Story of Fort Sumter* (New York, 1957), *passim*; David R. Barbee, "The Line of Blood—Lincoln and the Coming of the War," *Tennessee Historical Quarterly*, XVI (1957), 3–54; Ludwell H. Johnson, "Fort Sumter and Confederate Diplomacy," *Journal of Southern History*, XXVI (1960), 441–77; and Ari Hoogenboom, "Gustavus Fox and the Relief of Fort Sumter," *Civil War History*, IX (1963), 383–98.

shot—but the Confederate President considered such a scheme, in his own words, "overbalanced by other considerations." In counseling action, Davis wrote, "your measures may without disturbing views be directed to the capture of Fort Pickens." And the tone of his letter implied that he expected Bragg to take the fort if he shot first.

Bragg could make no promise to capture the fort. In his reply to the President's letter on April 7, he stated: "Subsequent information has strengthened the opinion against the attack by way of Santa Rosa Island. . . . Regular approaches by any but veteran troops are very difficult under the most favorable circumstances, but when attended, as in this case, by a combination of the most unfavorable circumstances, they become almost impossible. . . . The placing of a mortar battery on the Island as you suggest would have a good effect," Bragg admitted, "but the same thing can be accomplished from this side without dividing our force." Bragg believed a Confederate landing on the island would result in the immediate reinforcement of Pickens. He could suggest only one possible and somewhat hazardous way to capture the fort before reinforcements landed. "The plan which just at this time might succeed," Bragg wrote, "is that of an escalade by ladders. My troops are eager, and will risk anything to avoid a long investment on this sand beach. Ignorant in a great degree of the danger they would go at it with a will, and with ordinary good luck would carry the point. Our greatest deficiency is the want of means to reach the Island properly and secretly." [18]

Davis doubtless considered an escalade too risky. If it failed, the Confederates would be branded as aggressors and have nothing tangible to show for it. Though Bragg prepared for an escalade, permission to assault Pickens never came. On April 8 Walker ordered Bragg to prevent the reinforcement of the fort at "every hazard." Bragg might have considered this per-

[18] Bragg to Davis, April 7, 1861 (copy), Palmer Collection of Bragg Papers.

mission to attack had Walker written nothing else, but in a subsequent message the Secretary of War warned: "The expression 'at all hazard' in my dispatch of this morning was not intended to require you to land upon the Island. The presumption is that reinforcement will be attempted at the Docks, and this I hope you can and will prevent, though it should lead to assault on your works. The belief here is that they will not only attempt to reinforce the Fort but also to retake the Navy Yard." [19]

Bragg, who had been less than enthusiastic in his recommendation that the Confederates attack Pickens, began to doubt his ability to check a determined Union assault on the Pensacola defenses. "[We] will do our best," he promised Walker on April 9, "but supplies are short for a continued resistance. [We also] want transportation to move guns, shot and troops." [20]

While Bragg strengthened his defenses, Confederate officials in Montgomery shifted their attention to Fort Sumter. Throughout March and early April they had ordered the Confederate commander at Charleston, General Beauregard, to prevent the reinforcement of Sumter but otherwise to remain on the defensive.[21] But on April 10, after it became clear that Pickens was an unlikely place to start the conflict and Lincoln had informed the Confederates that supplies were on the way to Sumter, Walker ordered Beauregard to demand the fort's "evacuation, and if this is refused proceed, in such manner as you may determine, to reduce it." [22]

[19] Walker to Bragg, 8 A.M. and 4 P.M., April 8, 1861, *ibid.*

[20] *OR*, I, 458; Bragg to Walker, April 9, 1861 (copy), Palmer Collection of Bragg Papers.

[21] On April 2, for example, Walker wrote Beauregard: "You are specially instructed . . . to keep yourself in a state of the amplest preparation and most perfect readiness to repel invasion, acting in all respects—save only in commencing an assault or attack, except to repel an invading or re-enforcing force—precisely as if you were in the presence of any enemy contemplating to surprise you." *OR*, I, 272, 285, 289, 291.

[22] *Ibid.*, 297.

The rest of the Sumter story is familiar enough. The Federal commander, of course, refused to evacuate the fort, and at 4:30 A.M. on April 12, Beauregard's guns opened fire. The next day Walker wired Bragg: "Sumter is ours." [23]

At that point Bragg was too busy with his own problems to rejoice. On the night of April 12 the first wave of Federal reinforcements reached Fort Pickens. One of Bragg's reconnaissance vessels discovered the landing on the seaward side of the island, but was detained by the Federals until their troops were safely ashore. Bragg reported that when the reinforcements landed he "was making every effort for an escalade, had my party all detailed, and was waiting notice of the readiness of the Engineers. . . . Of course," he asserted, "such a movement now is impossible. . . ." Five days later Colonel Harvey Brown, with four more companies of Union troops, landed to assume command of Fort Pickens. Bragg offered no opposition. [24]

"It comes now to a long contest of hard knocks," Bragg wrote Elise. "War is inevitable, and may be considered as existing." The South might lose many battles, he warned; "you must bear it all with the fortitude of a soldier, and pray for protection to our country and those who are dear to you. Our cause is just and must prevail, no matter how much individuals may suffer." [25]

Though war had come, there was still time for old friends on opposite sides to exchange opinions. Bragg wrote a cordial letter to Brevet Major Henry J. Hunt, who had arrived at Pickens on April 17 with his artillery company. "We have been united in our views of almost all subjects, public and

[23] *Ibid.*, 305; Walker to Bragg, April 13, 1861, Leroy Pope Walker Collection, Chicago Historical Society.

[24] Henry A. Adams to Gideon Welles, April 14, 18, 1861, Fox Papers; Harvey Brown to Adams, April 17, 1861, *ibid.; OR*, I, 460–61; Bragg to Cooper, April 13, 15, 1861 (copies), Palmer Collection of Bragg Papers; Bragg to Henry A. Adams, April 14, 1861 (copy), *ibid.*

[25] Bragg to Elise, April 24, 1861, Bixby Collection of Bragg Papers.

private," replied Hunt. "We still have . . . a personal regard for each other, which will continue, whatever course our sense of duty may dictate, yet in one short year after exchanging at your house assurances of friendship, here we are, face to face, with arms in our hands, with every prospect of a bloody collision. How strange!"

How had it happened? "My views on the immediate occasion of our troubles you know," wrote Hunt, "they are yours: they are those, too, of my family, all of whom have fought in the north, the battle of the south. . . ." Hunt, a supporter of John C. Breckinridge in the election of 1860, believed that secessionists purposely divided the Democratic party and then exaggerated the danger to the South of Lincoln's election. "I regret deeply that secession leaders should have pursued such a course," lamented Hunt. "I am not much surprised at it however. . . . I fear that war was considered a necessity to a final separation." Furthermore, he continued, "I have felt positively certain for the last six weeks that your president would force a collision, if possible under circumstances which would make the [Lincoln] government appear to be aggressor, before the election could take place in Virginia, and it has come to pass as I expected." [26]

Hunt was remarkably close to the truth. The first shot of the Civil War had been fired because neither Lincoln nor Davis tried very hard to avoid a collision. Lincoln had no desire to shoot first, but he was determined to hold the forts, and he readily broke the informal truce Buchanan had established. Davis too had little regard for the truce agreement. He supported it only when it seemed advantageous. He encouraged Bragg to attack Fort Pickens, but when Bragg insisted that the only possible way to take Pickens was by a reckless assault which might become an embarrassing failure, Davis

[26] Henry J. Hunt to Bragg, April 23, 1861, Palmer Collection of Bragg Papers.

shifted his attention to Sumter and directed Beauregard to open fire. Thus war came at Fort Sumter only because the Confederates were neither subtle enough nor strong enough to begin it at Fort Pickens.

CHAPTER IX

The highest administrative capacity

APRIL, 1861–MARCH, 1862

N<small>EITHER SIDE</small> was ready to fight at Fort Pickens. Colonel Harvey Brown, commander of the Federal garrison, notified the Confederates that he intended to remain on the defensive, and Bragg informed Elise he could not "attack Fort Pickens, simply because I have not and cannot get the necessary means. Men in abundance come, but they bring nothing, and only . . . eat my supplies." Bragg feared the fort would fall only after "a long siege, and a most difficult one. Indeed," he wrote, "I doubt the ability of our government to accomplish it. The enemy . . . can land when and what they please; have resources infinitely superior to us, and a supply of war material almost inexhaustible." Had means for an attack been furnished before reinforcements arrived, Bragg rationalized, "*possibly* they might have been driven off—but my calls for supplies &c. &c., brought nothing." Even now the force at Fort Pickens was small and "could we get at them," he boasted, "[they] would just last until breakfast, but there's the rub—how to get at them." [1]

Civilian strategists attempted to supply the answer. Bragg received numerous unsolicited suggestions on how Fort Pickens could be taken or what to look for when it was attacked. One lady, who had read in the newspaper that Union sappers and miners had landed, advised him that the Lincoln government intended "either to blow up Fort Pickens and desert it; or undermine it, so as to blow it up in case of an

[1] *OR*, I, 380; Bragg to Elise, April 24, 1861, Bixby Collection of Bragg Papers.

attack." She assured Bragg, "I have spoken of this to no one." After extensive observation through a telescope, a man warned that the Federals had cut Santa Rosa Island "in two by a large ditch." This ditch, Bragg learned, was "a gutter to entrap our poor boys . . . there is many cannon at the end of that ditch, already loaded, and rascals already appointed to apply the match whenever a goodly number of our poor fellows jump in they will be plowed out like shooting rats in a gutter." The *Mobile Register and Advertiser* facetiously suggested that Bragg "prepare tin or sheet iron shells . . . and charge them with rattle snakes, moccasins, adders, and copper-heads, lizards, tarantulas, scorpions, centipedes and congo eels." The shells would "break to pieces and liberate their contents upon falling." After a few shots "the fort would soon be evacuated." [2]

By the end of April Bragg had resolved some of his problems without adopting any outside advice. He had received some of the specialists he needed, and his engineers had partly blocked the entrance to Pensacola Bay with obstructions in the channel between Forts McRee and Pickens. Moreover, additional men and supplies arrived on the recently completed railroad between Montgomery and Pensacola. Bragg's army, more confident than ever but still largely unarmed and inadequately trained, was camped in a semicircle six miles long around the bay to guard the newly arrived siege guns and mortars. "Gen. Bragg, a gallant soldier, full of nerve and pluck, and with the sagacity of Beauregard, is equal to any emergency," announced a journal. "He is watching the movements of the enemy, and making his preparations accordingly." [3]

2 "A Southern Woman" to Bragg, April 24, 1861, Bragg Papers, Duke University; W. Smith to Bragg, May 23, 1861, *ibid.*; undated newspaper clipping, Confederate Scrapbook, Alabama Department of Archives.

3 *Richmond Enquirer*, May 3, 1861; *OR*, I, 466, 407; Bragg to Cooper, April 22, 1861 (copy), Palmer Collection of Bragg Papers.

"The Federal officers," wrote the famous English reporter William H. Russell, "have allowed General Bragg to work away at his leisure, mounting cannon after cannon, throwing up earthworks, and strengthening his batteries, till he has assumed so formidable an attitude, that I doubt very much whether the fort and the fleet combined can silence his fire." Bragg was everywhere. He supervised the instruction of his gunners, ruthlessly dismissed incompetent officers, cleared his camp of suspicious persons, threatened to suspend the mails out of Pensacola to maintain security, improved his hospital and medical arrangements, and gathered what information he could on Pickens from deserters and scouts.[4]

Confidently Bragg again proposed to the government a scheme to take Fort Pickens, but his plan was exactly what the Federals expected. He intended to land heavy guns on Santa Rosa Island five miles east of Pickens, drive off the Federal fleet, and bombard the fort into submission with guns on the island and the mainland. "If the enemy can make a lodgment and establish batteries so as to drive off the ships, he can then make regular approaches to the Fort and render our situation very precarious," wrote the Union commander of Pickens. "Major Towers, chief engineer, considers such a movement to be not only possible, but one that will almost certainly occur." Bragg believed he could take the garrison quickly; he would try as soon as he received two thousand additional men.[5]

Instead of additional troops, he received an order that upset his plan. The government wanted him to send men to Virginia,

[4] Russell, *My Diary North and South*, p. 205; Bragg to Cooper, April 22, 26, May 12, 1861 (copies), Palmer Collection of Bragg Papers; Bragg to Walker, April 16, 1861 (copy), *ibid.*; Thomas Butler to "Dear Father," May 4, 1861, Thomas Butler and Family Papers, Butler Family Papers (C), Louisiana State University; *Richmond Enquirer*, May 10, 1861.

[5] Bragg to Cooper, April 27, 1861 (copy), Palmer Collection of Bragg Papers; Bragg to Walker, May 6, 1861 (copy), *ibid.*; Harvey Brown to Henry A. Adams, May 19, 1861 (copy), Fox Papers.

which had seceded after Fort Sumter fell. Reluctantly, he postponed his attack and shipped off his three best-drilled and fully equipped regiments—2,800 men. Although Bragg had opposed the transfer of the Confederate government to Richmond, he considered Virginia important to the South and he thought Davis should go there "to look into military matters." Yet Bragg complained: "everything seems to tend in that direction; we are considered here as secondary." He was right, of course; only a few months later, Elise noted, a newspaper referred to Pensacola as a "forgotten petty province" which excited "as little interest in the public mind as if it were in . . . China or Japan." [6]

Bragg, sorely disappointed that his command had become relatively unimportant, probably agreed with the newspaper that wished he were in Virginia. "General Bragg is . . . one of the most accomplished, skilful and efficient officers in the Confederate service," announced the Richmond *Enquirer* on June 11, 1861. "How we would be delighted to have him in the field here in Virginia, in the important campaign of this summer! We expect to be able to make the enemy cry, 'hold, enough!' before many days; but we might make him succumb at a somewhat earlier day, by 'a little more grape' from Bragg's batteries. But General Bragg occupies a most important military position in the Confederate States, and there he will remain, we suppose, 'till the battle's fought and won.' " [7]

Bragg tried to comfort himself and Elise with optimistic forecasts about the outcome of the war. "England is with us most decidedly," he predicted. "A very large fleet is on its way over, and will soon pick a cause of quarrel about the block-

[6] Walker to Bragg, May 17, 1861, Palmer Collection of Bragg Papers; Bragg to Walker, May 18, 1861 (copy), *ibid.;* Bragg to Davis, May 28, 1861 (copy), *ibid.;* Bragg to Davis, June 1, 1861, Bragg Papers, Duke University; Bragg to Elise, May 25, 28, 1861, Bixby Collection of Bragg Papers; Elise to Bragg, October 13, 1861, Mrs. Bragg Papers, University of Texas.

[7] *Richmond Enquirer,* June 11, 1861.

ade." This was simply a rumor, but it was what Bragg and Elise wanted to believe. In any event, the Union blockade had caused no immediate problems because it was ineffective. "Our cotton is all gone [to Europe anyway]," Bragg exulted, "and we can get on without the Yankee notions we have heretofore wasted so much money on." He believed the North, hurt more by the loss of trade than the South, would soon ask for peace. But should Northerners "against all reason still pursue their own ruin to secure ours," he warned, "we must only make up our minds to fall together." He was certain there would be some action. Virginia probably would be invaded, and also the western Confederacy. But with Robert E. Lee, Joseph E. Johnston, and Beauregard in Virginia, contended Bragg, "we ought to whip them badly." By July he was convinced that "no peace can last in this country until New England fanaticism is well whipped. Still I shall favor it when it can be had on honorable terms—acknowledging our full independence—not before." [8]

Though Bragg saw no prospect of an immediate offensive, he continued those important tasks he could perform so well of drilling and disciplining an army. His methods were frequently harsh, but as "a disciplinarian he far surpassed any of the [other] senior Confederate generals," recalled Richard Taylor. An officer who reached Richmond from Pensacola in June, Colonel W. E. Starke, reported Bragg's army "in admirable condition," and a journalist remarked, "General Bragg has the entire confidence of officers and men, and has overcome what was regarded as almost insurmountable difficulties." [9]

Bragg drove himself even harder than he did his troops. Taylor called him "the most laborious of commanders, devoting every moment to the discharge of his duties." A mem-

[8] Bragg to Elise, June 17, July 7, 1861, Bixby Collection of Bragg Papers.
[9] Richard Taylor, *Destruction and Reconstruction: Personal Experiences of the Late War* (New York, 1900), p. 100; *Richmond Enquirer*, June 11, 1861.

ber of Bragg's staff stated: "He was untiring . . . methodical and systematic in the discharge of business." And a soldier wrote: "Bragg was industry personified." "Go to him on business," noted a chaplain, "and he promptly gives you a hearing. His manner indicates that you must be brief and speak to the point. If your request is reasonable and your cause is just, he decides for you and dismisses you at once. The promptness of his decision and the abrupt manner of his dismissal, not granting a moment of time to thank him, puts you in an ill humor with yourself; you feel when you rush out of his presence that it would be a relief if somebody would fight you." Bragg never learned to pace himself, and overwork made him abrupt and snappish. "You are overtasking your mind sitting so closely to your writing," Elise warned him. "I would write less, & exercise more." She was "seriously uneasy" that the life he was "leading joined to anxiety of mind" would make him ill, and her sister wrote: "We hope sincerely that sickness will not interrupt your work." [10]

They were right to caution Bragg. For years he had suffered from rheumatism, dyspepsia, nervousness, and severe migraine headaches. His poor health and wiry beard, shot with gray, made him look older than forty-five; William Russell, who visited Bragg at Pensacola, considered him elderly. Russell also described Bragg for a local newspaper as being "of a spare and powerful frame; his face is dark, and marked with deep lines, his mouth large, and squarely set in determined jaws, and his eyes, sagacious, penetrating, and not by any means unkindly, look out at you from beetle brows which run straight across and spring into a thick tuft of black hair, which is thickest

[10] Taylor, *Destruction and Reconstruction*, p. 101; William Preston Johnston, *The Life of Albert Sidney Johnston* (New York, 1878), p. 547; L. H. Stout, "Reminiscences of General Braxton Bragg," Palmer Collection of Bragg Papers (a slightly different version of this memoir was published in 1942 at Hattiesburg, Mississippi); Elise to Bragg, November 19, March 17, 1861, Mrs. Bragg Papers, University of Texas; Mary Ellis to Bragg, May 16, 1861, Bragg Papers, Rosenberg Library.

over the nose. . . . His hair is dark, and he wears such regulation whiskers as were the delight of our [British] generals a few years ago. His manner is quick and frank, and his smile is very pleasing and agreeable." When Bragg was unperturbed and well, most observers agreed, he could be sedate and soft-spoken. When ill or angry, he was ferocious; his eyes became cold and he was "a terror to all who incurred his displeasure." Throughout the war, as Bragg continued to overwork and to be burdened with increasing responsibilities and critical decisions, his chronic illnesses worsened and he often was "sour and petulant." [11]

But under his stern supervision the volunteers gradually began to look like soldiers. The amount of "activity and life" in camp impressed William Russell; troops were constantly "drilling, parading, exercising." In May a soldier observed that a number of units made "a fine appearance," and in June a chaplain reported to a newspaper: "Our encampment seems all alive with groups of happy soldiery scattered far and wide over the broad bosom of the beautiful fields which spread themselves around us; the duties of the day are over; the stirring notes of 'Pop goes the Weasel' are leading the last regiment, company by company, at double quicktime to their quarters, which dot the sloping sides of a neighboring eminence." [12]

Careful sanitation measures kept the men in good health. "No army in the world, I suppose, so hastily brought together and organized has enjoyed a greater exemption from disease," boasted Bragg. The camps were "models of neatness," re-

[11] Russell, *My Diary North and South*, p. 207; Russell quoted in *Mobile Advertiser and Register*, July 4, 1861; Taylor, *Destruction and Reconstruction*, p. 100; Irving A. Buck, *Cleburne and His Command* (New York, 1908), p. 209; Johnston, *Life of Albert Sidney Johnston*, p. 547; E. T. Sykes, "Walthall's Brigade . . . ," Mississippi Historical Society, *Publications*, centenary series, I (1916), 549.

[12] Russell, *My Diary North and South*, p. 206; Thomas Butler to "Dear Father," May 4, 1861, Thomas Butler and Family Papers; *Richmond Daily Whig*, June 15, 1861.

ported Russell; when barracks were unavailable, the troops slept in tents. "I like soldiering fine," wrote a private. "I have enjoyed the best of health since I have been in the army." [13]

Frequent parades also helped condition the men. "On last Thursday Gen'l Bragg reviewed all the troops under his command," wrote Thomas Butler, a young officer. "Our Regiment turned out in full force and looked well but the review was very severe upon us for we had to march nearly four miles through the deep sand & hot sun before we reached the parade ground and then we had to march round and stand in ranks for several hours. A great many officers & privates from every Regiment fell in the ranks from heat & exhaustion and I hear some had died but I believe it is not so." Proudly, Butler made his men "stand up to the mark" in spite of the heat. When several "almost gave out" he warned that if they fell he would give "them a course of training . . . that would improve their stamina." His threat caused them all to "hold out a little longer." [14]

By September Bragg commanded a disciplined army of some six thousand men, divided into four brigades. "I can truly say now," he wrote Elise, "that this army [is composed of] well organized and efficient soldiers." An officer agreed: "Our men are beginning to take a good deal of pride in themselves and feel and look like soldiers." [15]

Bragg was equally pleased with his officers. He had attempted to recognize and reward men of talent, whatever their background. None of his brigade commanders had previous military experience; he simply promoted them because they

[13] Bragg to Elise, May 25, 1861, Bixby Collection of Bragg Papers; Russell, *My Diary North and South*, p. 206; John H. Jefferies to Nat Jefferies, October 15, 1861, William Terry and Family Papers, Louisiana State University.

[14] Thomas Butler to "Dear Sister," September 23, 1861, Thomas Butler and Family Papers.

[15] *OR*, VI, 725; Bragg to Elise, September 1, 1861, Bixby Collection of Bragg Papers; Thomas Butler to "Dear Aunt," September 29, 1861, Thomas Butler and Family Papers.

were able men who had learned their duties well. Colonels James R. Chalmers, commander of the First Brigade, and John K. Jackson, commander of the Fourth Brigade, particularly impressed Bragg. Chalmers, a graduate of South Carolina College, had been a Mississippi lawyer and politician before he entered the Confederate service as commander of the Ninth Mississippi Regiment. Jackson, also a South Carolina College graduate, was a Georgia lawyer when the war began. Elected colonel of the Fifth Georgia, he made it the best regiment in Bragg's army. In fact, a captain reported, officers "who have seen most of the troops in the Confed Army say this Georgia regiment is the finest in the service." [16]

What success Bragg had achieved would have been impossible without the help of his staff—originally composed, according to William Russell, "of four intelligent young men, two of them lately belonging to the United States army," but soon supplemented by others. One of the most valuable was Richard Taylor, who served as a civilian staff member without rank from May until July. "He is cool, sagacious and devoted to the cause & to me," wrote Bragg. "I sincerely regret it," he complained when Taylor left to accept a command in Virginia. "He had become about a necessity to me," admitted Bragg. By October his staff consisted of nine men: two majors, three captains, three first lieutenants, and a surgeon. They were a mixed lot: some were exceptionally capable; others were only superficially competent. But a remarkable number of them rose to high rank in the Confederate army. Captain William R. Boggs, a West Point graduate, and Lieutenant James E. Slaughter, a Mexican War veteran, would become generals, and five others—George G. Garner, L. W. O'Bannon, Hypolite Oladowski, H. W. Walker, and Thomas W. Jones—would wear the stars of a colonel. Bragg's brother-in-

[16] Bragg to Elise, September 1, 1861, Bixby Collection of Bragg Papers; *OR*, VI, 779, 798, 810; Thomas Butler to "Dear Aunt," January 20, 1862, Thomas Butler and Family Papers.

law, Towson Ellis, an 1853 graduate of Yale University who had been traveling in Europe when Louisiana seceded, was an aide-de-camp. Contemporaries remembered Ellis as "modest, unassuming, courteous,"—a "calm, resolute and fearless" gentleman devoted to Bragg.[17]

Bragg or one of his staff officers were constantly about the camps. They checked, inspected, questioned, and even comforted the troops. How was the food? Did their uniforms fit? Did their tents leak? Were there problems at home? Bragg intervened to give a private a leave to marry his dying sweetheart after his regimental commander had refused. Another time, when the parents of a soldier received no news from their son, Bragg called the young man to his office and "threatened to issue an order" which would require him "to report to Head-Quarters once a week to write home." When the popular comedian Harry Macarthy, writer of several songs including "The Bonnie Blue Flag," came to Pensacola, Bragg allowed him to entertain the army.[18]

Periodically, Bragg inspected the hospital. "For the sick," he boasted, "we have a hospital unsurpassed in the world for its luxurious comforts and splendid appointments. It is supplied without regard to expense, with everything that can contribute to the health or comfort of the patients, and is attended by a full corps of the finest physicians the country can afford. Living in close proximity to this hospital, I see hourly what is going on; receive daily a written report from the chief physician, and on every Sunday pass through every ward, converse with every patient, ascertain every want, and, if practicable,

[17] Bragg to Cooper, April 29, 1861 (copy), Palmer Collection of Bragg Papers; Russell, *My Diary North and South*, p. 208; Bragg to Elise, May 25, July 4, 7, 1861, Bixby Collection of Bragg Papers; Bragg to Davis, June 1, 1861, Bragg Papers, Duke University; *OR*, VI, 752; XVII (pt. 2), 648; XXIII (pt. 2), 824-25; *Confederate Veteran*, IV (1896), 250-51.

[18] Undated and unidentified newspaper clipping, Kirkpatrick Scrapbook, Alabama Department of Archives; Thomas Butler to "Dear Father," June 22, 1861, Thomas Butler and Family Papers; New Orleans *Daily Picayune*, December 7, 1861.

gratify them." A reporter noted in October 1861: "Gen. Bragg was at the . . . Hospital this morning. He visited the bedside of every wounded soldier, and had a kind word for each." Bragg often tried to cheer the sick with his sometimes less than humorous jokes. On one visit he told some ladies who were attending the ill that if one of their sweethearts died "they must *hug the harder* with the one that was left." He wrote Elise: "The ladies seemed to enjoy my little jests as much as the men, and all were better for a little diversion." [19]

Sternness coupled with concern for the army's welfare characterized Bragg's command. As the strict routine toughened the troops they became proud of themselves and their commander. "Gen. Bragg," announced a journalist, "is well calculated to inspire the confidence reposed in him by the army, and withal he is a superb horseman." Probably the kindest remark ever made about Bragg's appearance came from a young officer at Pensacola. He wrote that Bragg, "mounted on a fine charger, looked every inch a commander in chief or as a Second Lieut expressed it 'just like a Gen'l you see in pictures.' " [20]

Not even his family could get military information from Towson Ellis after Bragg had instructed him to remain silent. "We were delighted and astonished beyond the reign of good sense to see Towsy," wrote Mary Ellis. "After a strict examination of his face we . . . acknowledge his individuality, at first a doubtful matter, from his copper colored resemblance to the Aboriginal tribes. He has acquired one soldier-like attribute to perfection, taciturnity in all things connected with military arrangements, for in spite of *three sisters,* he dared

[19] Bragg to Editor, Montgomery *Advertiser,* August 16, 1861, quoted in Richmond *Daily Dispatch,* August 28, 1861; *Mobile Advertiser and Register,* October 15, 1861; Bragg to Elise, October 14, 1861, Palmer Collection of Bragg Papers.

[20] Richmond *Daily Dispatch,* October 2, 1861; Thomas Butler to "Dear Sister," September 23, 1861, Thomas Butler and Family Papers.

profess ignorance of every question asked, and as you know, they were neither few nor far between." [21]

Later, after Bragg had lost the confidence of much of the country and had asked to be relieved of command, many of the soldiers who had served under him from the start of the war remained loyal. "I hear from many sources that the soldiers and many subaltern officers express indignation that it should have been said they did not like you as a commander," wrote General Joseph Wheeler in December 1863. "I have been serenaded twice in the last few days by Pensacola troops who said they had come to hunt up Genl. Bragg's friends, for whom they expressed the greatest devotion. It was to that alone I was indebted for the serenades. They said the only enemies you had were a few bad Generals and some newspaper editors." About the same time another officer wrote Bragg: "For myself I can say that I have seen no man in this war who looked, talked & acted on all occasions so much like my beau ideal of a General, as yourself. From the time when you moulded into an army at Pensacola the mass luxuriant in democracy & grotesquely verdant in all that makes the soldier . . . you have shown yourself a great military chieftain & history will give you an everlasting page in the records of the Southern struggle for independence." Of the many letters Bragg received from common soldiers after he retired from field command, perhaps the most charmingly simple was a note from J. H. Fraser of Company B, Fiftieth Alabama Volunteers. "Our camp is full of sorrow and sadness," he wrote on December 2, 1863, "for we had learned to love you as a child loves his father, and the thought of being separated from you, and losing perhaps forever your parental-like care sends pangs most bitter through our insides. Many of us have followed you with gladness from Mobile up to the present, and the longer

[21] Mary Ellis to Bragg, May 16, 1861, Bragg Papers, Rosenberg Library.

we remained with you the more we loved you, and the more confidence we had in your skill and ability as a military chieftain; and we always felt sure that while General Bragg commanded no evil could ever befall us." [22]

Bragg also won the confidence of the people around Pensacola. "Gen. Bragg has taken measures to meet and . . . repel . . . the enemy, and has shown in his every movement his great character for humanity and Christianity," wrote a newspaperman. "Brave, disciplined and empowered, he stands ready to defend and maintain his position against . . . the enemy; and when conflict comes . . . we feel satisfied that he will sustain his high character as a superior military officer and commander." Another correspondent suggested that Bragg be in the President's Cabinet: ". . . make him Secretary of War, Mr. Davis, and you will add not only to your own good fame but also place in that important position a soldier and a man competent to the great task. With Gen. Bragg as Secretary of War, not a Federal bayonet would be found on [Santa] Rosa Island forty days hence." [23]

As his army improved and he became popular with his men, Bragg worried more about Bivouac and Elise, who had to manage the plantation with the help of an overseer. Before Bragg left for Florida he had made every possible preparation to ease her tasks, including arrangements for credit with his banker. Neighbors and relatives also promised to help Elise, and Bragg sent her money when he could. "I sent you $400," he wrote on June 17. "You will need all I can send you for the plantation, if not for personal use. And if you do not others will. Let it be a common fund for all [our friends and relatives

[22] Joseph Wheeler to Bragg, December 26, 1863, Palmer Collection of Bragg Papers; James R. Chalmers to Bragg, December 19, 1863, *ibid.;* J. H. Fraser to Bragg, December 2, 1863, *ibid.*

[23] Unidentified and undated newspaper clipping, Overton Scrapbook, Alabama Department of Archives; *Mobile Advertiser and Register,* September 25, 1861.

to use]. I know they would share with us their last cent." [24]

Elise realized that it was her duty to remain behind and manage the plantation, though she really wanted to accompany Bragg to Pensacola. "I am rigidly economizing," she informed him. The low price of sugar, which dropped to two and one half cents a pound in October, and the "churlish" ways of her overseer were her biggest problems. "I am all alone, & find I am not such a coward after all," she wrote. "Indeed my mind has too many other things to dwell on, to think much about myself." But no amount of work satisfied her desire to see Bragg. When he failed to reply promptly to her letters, she scolded: "I have written three times a week, giving you every item of home business." Slyly she informed him, "The negroes want 'Master' to see his fine crop." And a few weeks later she admitted: "How I wish you could come home if [only] for one day." [25]

When she could bear her husband's absence no longer, Elise decided to visit Pensacola. Bragg tried to dissuade her, but she wrote: "The inconveniences of Pensacola are not greater than those I have borne, & be they what they are, they are preferable with you than luxuries without you." [26]

After her initial trip in the summer of 1861, she visited him frequently. Her presence cheered and delighted them both. He repeatedly paraded his army for her enjoyment, and the officers organized dinners and balls in her honor. Her humor and charm made Bragg's quarters seem less inhospitable. She often entertained and always laughed with and teased the

[24] Bragg to Elise, March 11, 14, April 11, 19, 24, May 25, 28, June 17, July 4, 7, 1861, Bixby Collection of Bragg Papers.
[25] Elise to Bragg, March 17 [April?] 28, August ?, October 13, 18, November 19, 1861, Mrs. Bragg Papers, University of Texas; Elise to Bragg March ?, 26, June 7, July 5 [August?] 7, 16, 1861, Palmer Collection of Bragg Papers.
[26] Bragg to Elise, July 7, 1861, Bixby Collection of Bragg Papers; Elise to Bragg, March 17, 1861, Mrs. Bragg Papers, University of Texas.

officers who called. One evening she told her young kinsman, Thomas Butler, that his family expected him home for Christmas and he must go. Butler protested that his application for leave had been rejected by his regimental commander. "Cousin Elise," Butler wrote, "then remarked in the hearing of . . . Genl [Bragg] that I ought to apply directly to him and [he] would let me go." Elise laughed, continued Butler, when Bragg "replied that I knew too well what I would get if I tried that experiment." [27]

Elise's visits diverted Bragg and some of his officers from their dull routine, but the army grew increasingly restless as the months passed without action. Brigadier General William H. T. Walker, Bragg's West Point classmate who became second-in-command of the army at Pensacola late in the spring, wrote his wife: ". . . I am here playing second fiddle to Bragg without the slightest sharing. If we fight I fight raw troops I never drilled behind sand bags I never put up." Walker considered his position "a d—g insult to me. I . . . have now to share the responsibility without even having had anything directly or indirectly to do with the arrangement here (for which I feel very proud entre nous). I feel very much discouraged at the tardy operations of the Powers that be." What really bothered him was that "though the enemy's guns are pointed at us and ours at them & we daily watch the operations of each other still there is no probability of an actual conflict. It seems to be a war of diplomacy." "This place is as barren of interest as anything you can imagine," complained Walker in July; "this sitting down and waiting to be

[27] A. H. Gladden to Elise [July ?, 1861], Bragg Papers, Rosenberg Library; Thomas Butler to "Dear Aunt," January 20, 1862, Thomas Butler and Family Papers; Mary Ellis to Elise, July 18, 1861, Bragg Papers, Rosenberg Library; Taylor Beatty Diary, July 23, 1861; an invitation to a ball given in Elise's honor by the officers from Louisiana, July 22, 1861, Confederate Scrapbook, Alabama Department of Archives; Thomas Butler to "Dear Father," January 3, 1862, Thomas Butler and Family Papers.

whipped . . . is to me the most disgusting." Nor could Bragg's attempts to entertain him allay Walker's discontent. "Today," he wrote on July 21, "my staff and I are invited to dine with Genl Bragg. I am not in a humor to dine on anything but files but I shall go as it may make me for the time being forget that I am here." News of the Confederate victory at Manassas, Virginia, in July caused even greater dissatisfaction in Bragg's army. Soldiers grumbled; officers requested— and some, like Walker, received—transfers to Virginia. Those West Pointers left behind were especially depressed.[28]

Bragg sympathized with them. "[The West Point men] have seen themselves overlooked by their government," he complained, "while their juniors in years of service and I think their inferiors in many cases, were put over them in rank in other armies." He was indebted to these officers for much of the success he had had in the organization and administration of his command. "You can see, then, how keenly I may share the mortification which has been inflicted on them," he informed Acting Secretary of War Judah P. Benjamin, "and I sincerely trust the department will be able to assist me in averting the calamity which threatens." Bragg would have liked to satisfy his army's impatience to fight by launching an attack, but he feared Fort Pickens was too strong; it was defended by heavy rifled guns, superior to any of his pieces, and nearly two thousand Federal soldiers. Moreover, the Union fleet which blocked the bay had been strengthened. Bragg estimated that with the best of luck he might lose half his force in an assault on the fort. Even then, success was uncertain and neither he nor the Confederate War Department considered the possession of Pickens worth the lives its capture might cost. Should the fort fall, the Union blockade of Pensacola could continue. Consequently, Bragg suggested an alternative that would sat-

[28] Walker to His Wife, June 15, July 3, 12, 21, 1861, Walker Papers; Bragg to Cooper, July 28, 1861 (copy), Palmer Collection of Bragg Papers.

isfy some of his men. He offered to exchange four of his best regiments for four newly organized ones.[29]

Whatever motivated Bragg's offer—an unselfish desire to promote the war effort, or perhaps a subconscious knowledge that he could organize and train troops better than he could direct them in battle—Davis was impressed. Commanders almost never relinquished troops without a protest; a man who would exchange trained soldiers for recruits was indeed rare. What Secretary Benjamin called this "noble and self-sacrificing spirit" was "fully appreciated and elicited the most heartfelt approval and admiration, not only of the president but of every member of the administration." In fact, Davis wanted to transfer Bragg to "some field of more active operation," but feared to do so because of the "disastrous effect" it would have on the morale of the Pensacola troops. Benjamin promised to promote Bragg's disgruntled officers, and concluded: "In the meantime . . . the President . . . suggested that it might be a partial relief to the tedium of your constant vigil to extend your command." [30]

Promoted to major general and given command of western Florida and the entire state of Alabama, Bragg viewed the extension of his authority with mixed emotions.[31] "This is a fearful responsibility," he informed Elise. He must defend more than fifty thousand square miles of additional territory with less than six thousand additional men. "My labors will be vastly increased," he wrote, "and my wife may be a loser by it occasionally—in not getting her letter as usual. If so she must

[29] Bragg to Davis, July 9, August 22, 1861, Bragg Papers, Duke University; Cooper to Bragg, July 23, 1861, Palmer Collection of Bragg Papers; Bragg to Benjamin, September 25, 1861 (copy), *ibid.;* Bragg to Cooper, July 28, 1861 (copy), *ibid.; OR,* I, 423, 427–28, 434–36, 469.

[30] Benjamin to Bragg, October 8, 1861, Palmer Collection of Bragg Papers.

[31] Bragg's promotion was dated September 12, 1861 (document in the Leroy Pope Walker Collection, Chicago Historical Society), while the order extending his command was issued on October 7, 1861 (*OR,* VI, 751).

stop a silent tear and charge it to ambition." What he really wanted was clear when Mansfield Lovell was appointed to command south Louisiana and New Orleans. "The command at New Orleans was rightly mine," Bragg complained to Governor Moore in October. "I feel myself degraded by the action of the government and shall take care that they know my sentiments. I am not surprised at the President, who, in his feeble condition, is entirely under the control of a miserable *petticoat* government as tyrannical as Lincoln's despotism. But from Benjamin I expected better things." [32]

When the government failed to make additional promotions in the Pensacola army, Bragg angrily charged that many of his veteran officers, some of whom had resigned from the United States Army "even before their States seceded," had been kept in subordinate positions by the War Department, "while their inferiors in rank," "eleventh-hour converts and civilians" had been placed above them. He had no wish to appear insubordinate, Bragg insisted: "All that I have, all that I am, shall remain in this cause whenever and wherever it may please the Government to employ me." Perhaps his officers had been neglected "without the knowledge of the President and against his wishes," Bragg admitted, "but it is nevertheless a rankling sore, which he only can cure. I am candid, perhaps harsh, but I am doing him more service than by permitting the evil to grow while he is in ignorance." [33]

Both Davis and Benjamin were conciliatory. Davis admitted that the "hard fate" of Bragg's army had caused many to apply for "more inviting service," but he appreciated all who had "cheerfully borne . . . the dull routine and cheerless watch at Pensacola," and he believed Bragg could keep up his army's morale. Three new regiments without field officers were on their way to Bragg. "This will give you an opportunity to

[32] Bragg to Elise, October 14, 1861, Palmer Collection of Bragg Papers; Bragg to Moore, October 31, 1861, Thomas O. Moore Papers, Louisiana State University.

[33] *OR*, VI, 758–60.

reward such of your officers as you think most worthy," wrote Benjamin. Though Bragg still thought "the Pres't & Sec'y of War . . . [were] not over well inclined towards him," Thomas Bragg, now a member of Davis's Cabinet, wrote in his diary: ". . . the President spoke with much concern of the state of things likely to exist next spring when the terms of many 12 m[onth]'s Volunteer Regiments expire. Many of them . . . would, he feared, refuse to remain in the service. He attributed bad feeling among the Volunteers, in a great measure, to want of management and knowledge of such troops on the part of our officers in command. He spoke of Gen'l Bragg as the only General in command of an Army who had shewn himself equal to the management of Volunteers and at the same time commanded their love and respect." [34]

The Federals soon gave Bragg an opportunity to test his army. Early on the morning of September 14 a few Union raiders crossed Pensacola Bay and burned a schooner which the Confederates were outfitting as a privateer. Outraged by the audacity of the enemy and the negligence of his own sentries, Bragg decided to retaliate with a sortie against the Federal camp on Santa Rosa Island. This would avenge the raid and give his troops a welcome taste of combat. He made careful preparations. First, he consolidated his four brigades into two, and assigned them to recently arrived Brigadier Generals Daniel Ruggles and Richard H. Anderson, West Point graduates with distinguished Mexican War records. Next, Bragg selected a thousand men for the expedition; a detachment from each unit, and some troops from every state represented in his army. To lead this force of three battalions under Colonels

[34] Davis to Gustavus W. Smith, October 29, 1861 (copy), Louisiana Historical Association Collection of Jefferson Davis Papers, Tulane University; Benjamin to Bragg, November 4, 1861, Braxton Bragg Papers, North Carolina Department of Archives and History; Thomas Bragg Diary, November 30, December 3, 1861, Southern Historical Collection, University of North Carolina.

Chalmers, Jackson, and J. Patton Anderson, Bragg picked Richard Anderson.[35]

After a Union deserter had reported all but two of the blockading vessels away on patrol, Bragg ordered a sortie made on the night of October 9. He supervised the loading of troops into steamers, watched them start for the island, and then returned to his quarters. There was nothing more to be done, but Bragg remained awake. There was too much for him to worry about; so many things could go wrong. The outcome of this minor action might well determine his future. As he saw it, the expedition "was a desperate affair, in which success" would be "commended, a failure unpardonable." [36]

By morning Bragg was extremely nervous, almost panicky. Since before dawn, when the first firing began, he had kept his field glasses on Santa Rosa Island. "For two hours I was intensely unhappy," he admitted. The action was too distant for him to observe closely but he could see his men being "pursued and fighting as they went," and he knew that they were exhausted after marching and fighting in the deep sand. He was heartened when they reached their boats and started for the mainland, yet he remained anxious until they landed. "Had one shot struck my steamer," he wrote Elise, "all was lost. The slightest wind blowing her on a sand bar would have ruined us. You can imagine how happy I was to see her move off." [37]

When the steamer landed safely, Bragg's confidence returned. "The expedition was entirely successful," he announced, "but attended, as I knew it must be, with considerable loss"—twenty killed, forty wounded, and thirty captured

[35] Bragg to Cooper, September 16, 1861 (copy), Palmer Collection of Bragg Papers; OR, VI, 750, 458-63; John H. Jefferies to Nat Jefferies, October 15, 1861, William Terry and Family Papers.
[36] Bragg to Elise, October 10, 1861, Palmer Collection of Bragg Papers.
[37] Bragg to Elise, October 14, 1861, ibid.

or missing. Union losses were fourteen killed, twenty-nine wounded, and twenty-four captured or missing. Bragg praised Richard Anderson, who was wounded, and his men; they had acted "in a very handsome manner." Their main attack, made on the Sixth New York Volunteer Infantry, which Bragg had "fondly hoped to destroy," caught the New Yorkers by surprise. They fled in their "shirt tails . . . at the first fire," he wrote, "and, as they started early and made Bull Run time, we caught but few of them." Instead of pursuing the enemy, the Confederates had burned the camp. "It was a grand illumination," crowed Bragg, "plainly visible to us all." When Union regulars hurried from Fort Pickens to halt the retreat, the raiders withdrew.[38]

Though pleased with his men, Bragg criticized some of their actions. He estimated that half the Confederate troops captured were those left to guard a Union hospital and forgotten when the main force retired. Nearly all of the men killed or wounded were stragglers. "One principle you never can teach volunteers," lamented Bragg, "[is the] *necessity for order and regularity in retiring.* They had fought gallantly and whipped the fight; they could see no impropriety in scattering about & enjoying the walk home. They could not be prevailed on to keep together. The regulars from the Fort followed them up and punished them for it." Perhaps the raid—admittedly, a small operation of no particular military significance—would convince both officers and men that they needed additional drill and better discipline.[39]

Despite the mistakes, Bragg was sure the action had improved the army's morale. Veterans of one skirmish were proud of themselves and looked upon their commander as a

[38] Bragg to Cooper, October 10, 1861 (copy), Palmer Collection of Bragg Papers; Bragg to Elise, October 14, 1861, *ibid.*; *OR*, VI, 438–63. See also Governor Thomas O. Moore to Elise Bragg, October 10, 1861, Bragg Papers, Rosenberg Library.

[39] Bragg to Elise, October 10, 1861, Palmer Collection of Bragg Papers.

military genius. "Gen. Bragg would have taken Pickens long ago," explained one of the raiders, "but he wants to save the Navy Yard, which would be burnt certain in the bombardment. The Navy Yard is the prettiest place I nearly ever saw. It is worth fifty millions of dollars and we will need it by & by." Devoted soldiers presented Bragg with various items—including "several hundred dollars," swords, pistols, and a "beautiful Crucifix"—which they had plundered from the Union camp.[40]

Bragg, satisfied that his troops could defend Pensacola against retaliatory attack, began an inspection tour of his new department on October 22. He found a "lamentable state of affairs" in the ordnance and transport departments at Mobile and Montgomery, and corruption and mismanagement in the quartermaster's offices. Supplies were being "misdirected, missent, or not sent at all," bewailed Bragg. He quickly assigned an officer to travel the state and check on shipments. Bragg also discovered that the resources of Mobile had been wasted on a "grand scheme for squandering money by digging ditches around the city, which would have required 40,000 men to defend." This criticism may have been an exaggeration, for Bragg never liked entrenchments and consistently underestimated their importance. Pleased that the new city commander, Brigadier General Jones M. Withers, had stopped the digging, Bragg decided that Mobile could be defended best by strengthening Fort Morgan, which guarded the entrance to Mobile Bay, with some regiments from Pensacola.[41]

To meet the supply needs of his department, Bragg ordered Mobile factory owners to make artillery harnesses, gun carriages, cannons, and ammunition; he directed that the partly

[40] John H. Jefferies to Nat Jefferies, October 15, 1861, William Terry and Family Papers; Bragg to Elise, October 14, 1861, Palmer Collection of Bragg Papers.
[41] Bragg to Davis, October 22, 1861 (copy), Palmer Collection of Bragg Papers; Bragg to Cooper, October 25, 1861 (copy), *ibid.*

constructed railroad between Mobile and Pensacola be completed within three weeks, so that troops, arms, and supplies could be hurried to any threatened point. He also sent all new regiments to instruction camps near Mobile where drillmasters could speed their training.[42]

Within a month there had been significant improvement in Bragg's department. The railroad between Pensacola and Mobile had been completed, factories in Mobile manufactured war material, and Bragg had what he called "an efficient force" of 12,000 men under his command. His only real shortage was in firearms; many of the recruits had to be equipped with shotguns or drilled with wooden rifles.[43]

The relative calm of the department was broken on November 22 when Fort Pickens batteries, supported by the guns of two Union warships, opened fire. The Confederate batteries on the mainland replied and for two days the firing continued. "It was grand and sublime," wrote Bragg. "The houses in Pensacola, 10 miles off, trembled from the effect, and immense quantities of dead fish floated to the surface . . . stunned by the concussion." Bragg concentrated his infantry just beyond range of the Union shells ready to repel the landing he expected. It never came. He also visited many batteries during the action and delighted his men with compliments "on their courage and skill." The bombardment satisfied the Federals. They expended some five thousand rounds of ammunition to the Confederates' one thousand, which proved what Bragg already knew: for long range action rifled guns and experienced artillerists were superior to smoothbore cannons and novice gunners. Nevertheless, his artillerymen had surprised him with their regular and accurate shots, and he praised their "coolness and gallantry" in his report. Of course, Fort Pickens and the Federal emplacements had escaped with less damage than had the Confederate works; Fort McRee was battered and fires were started in the navy yard and in Warrington, but casualties on both sides were light—forty Confederates and fifteen Federals. The way Bragg had dispersed his guns made them difficult targets.[44] During the next three months Bragg reorganized his command and improved his defenses. The enlistment of many veterans expired, but he kept most of them in the army by giving leaves of absence to those who reenlisted for the war. He extended General Withers's authority west of Mobile to Pascagoula, Mississippi, which had just been added to the department, and ordered General Leroy Pope Walker to Montgomery where he could do "less harm." Bragg had found Walker, the former Secretary of War, living comfortably in Mobile while his undisciplined brigade suffered in crowded tents and huts fifteen miles away. When Brigadier General Samuel Jones arrived from Virginia in January, Bragg assigned him to the command of the Pensacola forces. Arms were still in short supply, but by February 1, 1862, Bragg had 16,000 men guarding the coast.[45]

With his department relatively secure, Bragg might have relaxed a bit, but developments elsewhere intruded. The western Confederacy was in danger. On November 8, 1861, General Ben McCulloch, who had helped check a Union advance at Wilson's Creek, Missouri, in August, suggested that Bragg be sent to Missouri to reorganize and command Confederate forces. Davis, favorably disposed, had asked Bragg on December 27 to take command of "everything west of the Mississippi except the coast defenses." Secretary Benjamin added: "The President and myself have anxiously scanned every name on our army list, and . . . we invariably fell back on yours." Bragg owed it to the country to accept the command, argued Benjamin, for no other "name and reputation" could save the

[44] *Ibid.*, 469–95; Thomas Butler to "Dear Father," November 26, 1861, Thomas Butler and Family Papers; A. C. Bledsoe to "Dear Parents," November 24, 1861, William Clark Doub Papers, Duke University.

[45] Thomas Bragg Diary, January 20, 1862; *OR*, VI, 778–79, 780, 793, 815–16, 819, 821.

West. Even so, the job would not be forced upon Bragg against his wishes.[46]

Bragg had no desire to go to the Trans-Mississippi Department. The western Confederacy was important, he admitted, but the prospect of victory there was "most gloomy." It would be difficult to defend or to supply because the region was huge and had a miserable railroad system. Bragg had heard that the troops in the area lacked arms, equipment, discipline, and able officers; he distrusted his ability to make good soldiers of troops "so long accustomed to . . . freedom and license." Perhaps Bragg was unusually pessimistic because he was ill. "I had a long and interesting letter from Gen'l Bragg tonight," Thomas Bragg noted on December 19. "I am sorry to hear that his health is suffering. Two years ago he was troubled with carbuncles. He tells me that he again has one on his left hand & one on his left leg, greatly troubling him." From such a painful perspective the Trans-Mississippi Department certainly seemed "a most unpromising field of operations. But should the President decide on it," wrote Bragg, "I will bend all my energies and faculties to the task, and offer myself (as a sacrifice, if necessary) to the great cause in which we are engaged." [47]

The President, confronted with such reluctance, decided he could not spare Bragg. Major General Earl Van Dorn went to command the Trans-Mississippi Army, and soon Bragg was needed elsewhere.[48]

In February Union General Ulysses S. Grant captured Forts Henry and Donelson on the Tennessee and Cumberland Rivers. This broke the center of the vital Confederate defense line across Kentucky and northern Tennessee, divided Con-

[46] Ben McCulloch to Judah P. Benjamin, November 8, 1861 (copy), Barret Collection of Albert Sidney and William Preston Johnston Papers; Benjamin to Bragg, December 27, 1861, Confederate Civil War Papers, Missouri Historical Society, St. Louis.

[47] Thomas Bragg Diary, December 19, 1861; OR, VI, 797–98.

[48] Thomas Bragg Diary, January 8, 1862.

federate General Albert Sidney Johnston's army, and opened central and western Tennessee to the Federals. As Grant followed his success with a drive up the Tennessee River, Johnston and the right wing of his army retreated toward northern Alabama. Beauregard, who had just arrived from Virginia, led the army's left wing toward northern Mississippi.

A map revealed the extent of the disaster; Bragg knew that unless Johnston could rally his forces for a stand the Federals would follow the rivers—the Cumberland, the Tennessee, and the Mississippi—deep into the South. Soon Union armies might control some of the best railroads and waterways; they might invade Mississippi and Louisiana, capture Nashville, Memphis, even New Orleans, and cut the Confederacy in two. Bragg had sent a staff officer to find Johnston's army and to ascertain its condition and needs. Upon receipt of a glum report, Bragg sent some of his own troops north as reinforcements without awaiting permission from the War Department.[49]

Bragg also advised the President to change his military strategy. Davis must abandon his attempt to defend every Confederate state and concentrate all "means and resources" in the most vital regions of the country. Only a few strategic points along the Atlantic and Gulf coasts should be defended. Missouri, and the "whole of Texas and Florida, should be abandoned," insisted Bragg, who believed it would be better to yield territory rather than to sacrifice "men and means in a futile attempt at defense." [50]

What Bragg proposed was a Napoleonic strategy of rapid concentration and attack. "It is a great misfortune that our limited means should be so much dispersed," he wrote General

---

[49] OR, VI, 824, 834; Bragg to Benjamin, February 27, 1862 (copy), Palmer Collection of Bragg Papers. For details on the Union advance and the Confederate retreat see Charles P. Roland, *Albert Sidney Johnston: Soldier of Three Republics* (Austin, 1964), pp. 279-302; Bruce Catton, *Grant Moves South* (Boston, 1960), pp. 75ff; and Williams, *Beauregard*, pp. 115-16.

[50] OR, VI, 826-27.

Mansfield Lovell on February 16, 1862. "We are being whipped in detail, when a vigorous move with our resources concentrated would be infinitely more damaging to the enemy. . . . I have urgently advised our government to cease *protecting property*, and apply all its means to the discomfiture of the enemy—the only strategic points to be held in the gulf are New Orleans, Mobile & Pensacola. All else should be abandoned at once. It would double our resources, and enable us to aid those behind us." [51]

For a time Davis seemed ready to adopt Bragg's suggestion that the Confederacy abandon certain territory and concentrate its forces for a major offensive. On February 19 Thomas Bragg confided to his diary: "The Prest said [in Cabinet meeting] the time had come for diminishing the extent of our lines —that we had not the men in the field to hold them and we must fall back." [52] But within a few months the President would return to a defensive-offensive strategy designed to protect all parts of the Confederacy. [53]

At the outset Davis had planned to fight a strictly defensive war. He explained: "the Confederate Government is waging this war solely for self-defense . . . it has no design of conquest or any other purpose than to secure peace and the abandonment by the United States of its pretensions to govern a people who have never been their subjects and who prefer self-government to a Union with them." But southern sentiment overwhelmingly favored an invasion of the North. "Our policy is to be defensive, and it will be severely criticized, for

[51] Bragg to Lovell, February 16, 1862, Mansfield Lovell Collection, Henry E. Huntington Library. On Napoleonic strategy see Robert S. Quimby, *The Background of Napoleonic Warfare* (New York, 1957), pp. 255–57.

[52] Thomas Bragg Diary, February 19, 1862.

[53] Archer Jones, *Confederate Strategy From Shiloh to Vicksburg* (Baton Rouge, 1961), is the most elaborate account of Davis's strategic decisions; for their effect upon the war's outcome, see Grady McWhiney, "Who Whipped Whom? Confederate Defeat Reexamined," *Civil War History*, XI (1965), 5–26.

a vast majority of our people are for 'carrying the war into Africa' without a moment's delay," noted War Clerk John Jones in June 1861. "The sequel will show which is right, the government or the people. At all events, the government will rule." Jones was wrong; the government did not rule. Confederate Secretary of State Robert Toombs announced that he was for "taking the initiative, and carrying the war into the enemy's country." He opposed any delay. "We must invade or be invaded," he insisted. And in July 1861, just after First Manassas, Davis indicated in a public speech that he was ready to abandon a solely defensive strategy. "Never heard I more hearty cheering," recorded Jones. "Every one believed our banners would wave in the streets of Washington in a few days. . . . The President had pledged himself . . . to carry the war into the enemy's country. . . . Now . . . the people were well pleased with their President." [54]

Davis's defensive-offensive strategy, which was intended to satisfy both the advocates of invasion and the politicians who demanded that their states be defended, divided the Confederacy into military departments, with armies dispersed to protect important points or likely invasion routes. A British visitor was shocked to learn in 1863 that even though there were over 350,000 men in the Confederate service General Robert E. Lee's army mustered only 60,000 effectives. When the visitor asked where all the other troops were, he was told that "on account of the enormous tract of country to be defended . . . the South was obliged to keep large bodies of men unemployed, and at great distances from each other." Nor did Davis really change this policy after 1863. In December 1864 less than half of the 196,016 Confederate soldiers present for duty were with either of the two major armies; the majority of them were scattered from Virginia to Texas in small

[54] Dunbar Rowland, ed., *Jefferson Davis, Constitutionalist: His Letters, Papers and Speeches* (10 vols., Jackson, 1923), V, 338; Jones, *Rebel War Clerk's Diary*, I, 51, 66.

units.[55] The President's cordon defense plan allowed offensives, but only those of a limited and usually uncoordinated type; it encouraged static rather than elastic defenses. Clearly, it was not the bold strategy of massive consolidation and attack which Bragg advocated.

In February 1862 Davis would allow only a limited concentration of Confederate strength; Bragg's force together with a few other units from the Gulf went to join Johnston. On February 28 Bragg started north. With him went approximately 10,000 soldiers, whom one officer considered "the finest and best disciplined body of troops the Confederacy ever had." [56] Perhaps they were; Bragg could train soldiers, and he had had nearly a year to drill them.

Even if his men were not quite the Confederacy's best, Bragg left the coast with an enviable military reputation.[57] "My desire is to be attached to your command," wrote former Confederate Congressman Robert H. Smith, who was raising a regiment of Alabamians. And Representative James L. Pugh, formerly a soldier at Pensacola, wrote that he "was delighted to find" in Richmond "the highest confidence in my old Genl Bragg. It gives me great pleasure to assure you that no General in the army has more of public confidence and admiration. Your praise is on the lips of every man. Mr Benjamin told me that you were 'the greatest General we had.' President Davis said that 'you had shown a most self sacrificing devotion to the cause, and was about the only General who had accomplished all you undertook.' " To a Cabinet member Davis also "spoke [favorably] of Gen'l Bragg—said he had put down drinking

[55] Walter Lord, ed., *The Fremantle Diary* (Boston, 1954), p. 165; *OR*, Series 4, III, 989.

[56] Benjamin to Bragg, February 18, 1862, Palmer Collection of Bragg Papers; *OR*, VI, 836; Sykes, "Walthall's Brigade," p. 546.

[57] The Mobile defenses rapidly deteriorated after Bragg left, claimed John Forsyth: "I feel it my painful duty to say to you that in the military arranty & confusion which I find here, Mobile is only waiting for the enemy to come & take it." Forsyth to Bragg, November 3, 1862, Palmer Collection of Bragg Papers.

and that his had been the only well disciplined and managed army in the field. That he set a proper example to his men. In speaking of the other Generals, their qualities &c, he [Davis] ranked him [Bragg] with Sidney Johns[t]on [the President's favorite]." Even Bragg's old competitor Beauregard, now sick and distraught, had telegraphed the War Department from Tennessee on February 28: "Bragg ought to be sent here at once. I will, when well enough, serve under him rather than not have him here." From a man as vain as Beauregard, this was extraordinary praise. "General Bragg brings you disciplined troops," Davis reassured Johnston, "and you will find in him the highest administrative capacity." [58]

Only a single demur seemed to offset this acclaim. "General Bragg [is] . . . a good officer, a man of fair capacity," wrote General Jones M. Withers, "[but he is] self-willed, arrogant, and dictatorial." [59]

If Withers's judgment appears somewhat harsh, it should be remembered that Bragg could be obstinate, haughty, and authoritative. Moreover, he had displayed at Pensacola other characteristics, thus far overlooked or undetected by the government, which would be detrimental to any field commander: poor health, moodiness, and a tendency to spend too much time on trivia.

[58] Smith to Bragg, April 2, 1862, Palmer Collection of Bragg Papers; Pugh to Bragg, March 16, 1862, *ibid.*; Thomas Bragg Diary, January 8, 1862; *OR*, VII, 912, 258.
[59] Withers to C. C. Clay, February 13, 1862, Clement C. Clay Papers, Duke University.

CHAPTER X

Dictatorial measures are necessary

MARCH 4–APRIL 5, 1862

THE MILITARY SITUATION was critical when Bragg reached Jackson, Tennessee, on March 4, 1862. One Union army under Don Carlos Buell occupied Nashville; another under Ulysses S. Grant was moving up the Tennessee River toward the vital railroad which connected Virginia with the Mississippi River. Confederate forces in the western theatre were divided and demoralized. Albert Sidney Johnston, who was withdrawing his troops from Nashville toward the rail junction at Corinth, Mississippi, was still a hundred miles away. Until he arrived, Beauregard was in command of a rapidly deteriorating southern defense line stretching across western Tennessee to Island No. 10 in the Mississippi and New Madrid on the Missouri side.[1]

"If we can keep [the enemy] . . . back on the Miss[issippi]," Bragg wrote his wife, "I shall not despair at all of our success elsewhere. We are to a great extent, however, reduced to the Fabian policy. Our troops and our supplies are so limited and so disorganized that offensive operations are out of the question unless we now have a little time to restore tone and confidence."[2]

Beauregard himself was a problem. He welcomed Bragg and gave him command of all troops south of Jackson, but Bragg was too concerned about his commander's health to leave

---

[1] OR, VII, 920–21; X (pt. 2), 297; Williams, *Beauregard*, pp. 120–21; Roland, *Johnston*, pp. 300–3. Some of the material in this and the following chapter appeared in Grady McWhiney, "Braxton Bragg at Shiloh," *Tennessee Historical Quarterly*, XII (1962), 19–30.

[2] Bragg to Elise, March 20, 1862, Bragg Papers, Duke University.

town. Beauregard seemed almost incapacitated by illness and worry; he issued dramatic appeals to the public for reinforcements as well as for plantation bells to make cannons. "I must ask your assistance and general supervision in the turning of these bells into cannon we most need," Beauregard wrote General Mansfield Lovell. "Genl. Bragg and myself think the Napoleon twelve-pounder, smooth bore, and rifle six pounder . . . are the most efficient guns; and we have determined to have the bells moulded accordingly." Though he humored Beauregard, Bragg considered the request "for plantation bells . . . somewhat . . . sensational. We have more guns now than instructed men to serve them," he admitted. "And metal in New Orleans for many more." Beauregard was unduly "distressed and worried" by the military situation, and so was the commander of Confederate forces north of Jackson, Major General Leonidas Polk, former Episcopal Bishop of Louisiana and West Point schoolmate of Jefferson Davis. "Every interview with Genl Polk turns [Beauregard's recovery] . . . back a week," noted Bragg. "But for my arrival here to aid him I do not believe he would now be living." [3]

Given sufficient time, Bragg believed he could restore the army's confidence. He had reassured anxious citizens and preached professionalism on his trip north from the coast. "At every station on the railroad," noted a reporter, "as soon as it was known that [Bragg] . . . was on the cars, he was loudly and repeatedly called for by the people to show himself and to say something to them. The desire to see him was intense." At Meridian, Mississippi, Bragg said: "This is a time for acts, not words. Experience has taught me, too, that every man should stick to his trade. In many efforts, I believe I never made but one successful speech—and that was, in a few words, when I courted my wife—the result then being due less to any merit either in the speech or the speaker than to an unfortunate habit

[3] Thomas Bragg Diary, February 19, 1862; Beauregard to Lovell, March 23, 1862, Lovell Collection; Bragg to Elise, March 20, 1862, Bragg Papers, Duke University.

with young ladies of deciding more from impulse than reason, by which, as in my case, they are too apt to be unfortunate. Ponder well, then, my fellow-citizens, this piece of advice: never call on an old soldier for speeches; and, if you will pardon me the liberty, I will add, never send politicians to command your armies." [4]

Beauregard was no politician, but at the moment Bragg considered him too upset to be left alone. It was necessary, therefore, for Bragg to organize his command from Jackson. He directed General Ruggles, who had brought a division north from New Orleans, to assemble all troops in the vicinity of Corinth and to entrench. Furthermore, Bragg established rendezvous points for recruits and reinforcements, put all railroads under military control, had unauthorized passengers arrested, declared martial law in Memphis, and prohibited the sale of liquor within five miles of any camp or railroad station occupied by troops or within a mile of any public highway used for military purposes. He also ordered a reserve ammunition depot constructed at Grand Junction, between Corinth and Memphis, where the Tennessee and Ohio Railroad crossed the Memphis and Charleston. At this point 1,500,000 rounds of ammunition were assembled for quick supply to troops operating along rail lines to the east, north, or west. To increase his force's mobility, Bragg restricted each regiment to eleven wagons, soldiers to a knapsack, and officers to a valise. In addition, he instructed Ruggles to establish a hospital; to keep scouts out at all times; to collect supplies, forage, and wagons; to issue axes to each regiment, one hundred rounds of ammunition to each soldier, and two hundred rounds to each cannon crew. Above all, Bragg wrote, Ruggles should "preserve the best discipline possible with our men, preventing the plundering of our people, which is now too common." [5]

[4] New Orleans *Daily Picayune*, March 13, 1862.

[5] *OR*, X (pt. 2), 297–98, 299, 300, 301, 305, 328; Bragg to Ruggles, March 7, 10, 11, 1862 (telegrams), Daniel Ruggles Papers, Duke University. See also Ruggles to Bragg, March 4, 5, 9, 10, 1862 (copies), *ibid*.

This was about all Bragg could do in Jackson to prepare his command, but Elise still worried. "I have lost the little confidence I ever had in the President's favorite S. Johnston, & he *ranks you*," she wrote Bragg on March 3, 1862. "Beauregard is an egotist—Polk a wild enthusiast & both *rank you*. Could you have had command, I might hope—but as it is, we almost despair. Beauregard is . . . calling for a *mob* for any number of days. An army composed of such a mass cannot be effective, to meet the splendidly armed & equipped forces of Buell, now flushed with victory—*western* men too, not *Yankees*. One thing I trust, he [Johnston] will not commit the fatal mistake of again *separating our forces*. The retreat from Nashville is represented as disgraceful—everything sacrificed by an early departure, *four* days before an enemy appeared." Never hesitant to offer her views, Mrs. Bragg concluded: "How I wish dear husband that you could be [commander of Confederate forces in the West] . . . not for the gratification of any personal vanity, but because I truly feel, & the President knows, & *has acknowledged*, you are the only one capable of managing volunteers. God knows your being a *General*, has given me more anxiety & suffering than pleasure. I have had to feel not only for your individual safety, but for the deep responsibility of your position. One thing alone has & will ever console me. You know your duty, & will under every circumstances faithfully discharge it."

A few days later Elise again insisted that a change in command was necessary. She wrote Bragg: "Can you not . . . *urge* upon our President, either to come himself, or appoint you or Beauregard to the sole command, giving *one head* to our important movements in the West? Can Mr. Davis still remain impassive, & still infatuated with Johnston? I have a great mind to go to him myself & tell him the plain unvarnished truth." [6]

[6] Elise to Bragg, March 3, 12, 1862, Mrs. Bragg Papers, University of Texas. Mrs. Bragg was not Johnston's only critic. "I have been with and near General Johnston's army ever since he was assigned command;

Bragg may have agreed with Elise, but he kept quiet; John-ston remained in command,[7] and the enemy continued to ad-vance. When Beauregard and Bragg received reports of Union gunboats on the Tennessee River and troops ashore at Pitts-burg Landing and other points southeast of Jackson, Bragg rushed to Bethel station on the Mobile and Ohio Railroad some twenty miles north of Corinth, and about the same dis-tance northwest of Pittsburg Landing. Beauregard ordered the divisions of Polk and Withers to follow Bragg "with utmost speed," and for a short time Bragg appeared ready to act boldly. On March 15 he notified Ruggles: "Hold your force in hand, with transportation for any point. Should the enemy give us a chance, it is our policy to fight him as early as possible." The next day Bragg proposed to join Ruggles and drive the Federals into the river: "You will please inform me immediately what the effective strength of your command is, amount of ammunition, &c; whether you have enough trans-portation to move against the enemy. Troops are now arriving [here]. . . . If the result of the reconnaissance [to determine the enemy's movements from Pittsburg Landing] be satisfac-tory, I desire to march from this point with this army and unite our forces at a point between this and the enemy." [8]

What Bragg did not know was that if he and Ruggles had

---

have been his admirer and defender; still admire him as a man; but in my judgment his errors of omission, commission, and delay have been greater than any general who ever preceded him in any country," Congressman E. M. Bruce wrote President Davis. "If your presence [in Tennessee] is impossible, for God's sake give immediate command to Beauregard, Bragg, or Breckinridge, or all will be irretrievably lost." *OR,* X (pt. 2), 314.

[7] "My confidence in you has never wavered," Davis informed John-ston on March 26, 1862, "and I hope the public will soon give me credit for judgment rather than continue to arraign me for obstinacy." *OR,* X (pt. 2), 365.

[8] Ruggles to Bragg, March 11, 1862 (copy), Ruggles Papers; James E. Slaughter to Ruggles, March 16, 1862 (telegram), *ibid.; OR,* X (pt. 2), 310, 312, 318, 319, 320, 328, 330, 331, 332.

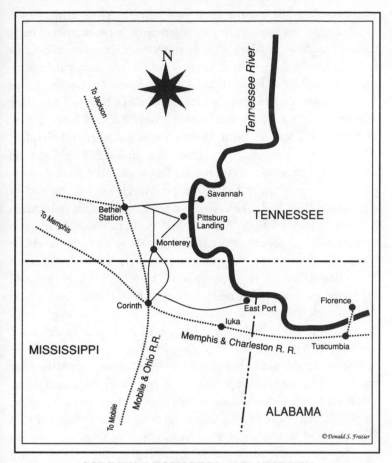

CORINTH, MISSISSIPPI, AND VICINITY

moved toward Pittsburg Landing on March 16 they almost surely would have encountered a Union division commanded by Bragg's old friend William T. Sherman which disembarked that day and marched to Monterey, about ten miles from

Pittsburg Landing on the road to Corinth. After dispersing a Confederate cavalry regiment, Sherman's men marched back to the Landing on March 17. In such an encounter, the Confederates probably would have enjoyed a numerical superiority, though it is impossible to fix numbers precisely in this case. Sherman's division, which probably had an effective strength of about 8,000 men, was the only Federal force ashore at Pittsburg Landing until March 18, when General Stephen A. Hurlbut's approximately 7,000 men landed.[9] Ruggles, who had 9,536 men in his division on March 31, may have had no more than 7,000 ready for action on March 16. By the end of the month Polk had 9,136 effective troops under his command, but how many of these had reached Bethel Station by March 16 is unknown, probably no more than three or four thousand. Withers's division of Bragg's army, which had been ordered from Island No. 10 via Memphis on March 13, likely was still en route to Bethel Station.[10] Perhaps the Confederates could have struck Sherman with 11,000 men. If so, that might well have been enough, if they had been well managed, to drive the Federals into the river.

But no attack was made on March 16. Bragg, disturbed by the condition of his troops as well as by divergent intelligence, lost his determination during the day. He telegraphed Ruggles: "Your information of this morning confuses me much. From the scouts of as late an hour as yesterday evening . . . we are assured the enemy was not at Pittsburg in any force. Upon information so conflicting we cannot safely predicate a military movement, though I am anxious and decided to strike a blow as soon as we can do so, consistent with any sense of security." Bragg, unwilling now to act rashly, decided to go to

[9] *OR*, X (pt. 1), 26, 27, 28, 112; Sherman, *Memoirs*, I, 228. On April 4, 1862, Sherman's division had an aggregate strength of 8,830; Hurlbut's was 7,302. Even on March 21, some of Grant's divisions had not landed at Pittsburg Landing. See *OR*, X (pt. 2), 52–56.

[10] *OR*, X (pt. 2), 378, 382, 318.

Corinth and wait for Albert Sidney Johnston. "I am glad to hear General Johnston is joining us," Bragg admitted to Ruggles. "With his force we certainly ought to crush any force the enemy can now bring." Three days later from Corinth, Bragg explained his failure to attack to Beauregard: "You will have seen my entire change of purpose. . . . The troops arrived too slowly, were too poorly supplied, and too badly organized, instructed, and disciplined, to justify a hope of even carrying them to the point desired, much less a success against a well-organized foe." [11]

Bragg found "disorder and confusion" in Corinth. Many troops were "without supplies, and greatly disorganized by hasty and badly conducted arrangements." The sick were without accommodations, and bad weather added to the chaos. "The Hotel," Bragg wrote, "was a perfect pandemonium— thousands of hungry men standing against the barred doors ready to rush in and sweep the tables—regardless of sentinels or officers. Even the kitchen was not safe—meats were removed from the fire, and the life of the Hotel keeper threatened for expostulating." [12]

Elise expected as much. She had warned Bragg that he was putting too much confidence in Ruggles, who "did not leave N. Orleans with the same high reputation he did Pensacola. His brigade states, he lived at the St. Charles [Hotel], paying but little attention to their comfort or drilling. . . . For two days they were kept at the depot in a pelting rain, waiting for transportation, the charitable citizens supplying the troops with food. Gen. R. never came near them, & his two aids . . . were twice sent down to see about his *horses*." Elise had heard that Ruggles could not "drill two hours without being laid up, he is so old & feeble." [13]

[11] *Ibid.*, 332, 341.
[12] Bragg to Elise, March 20, 1862, Bragg Papers, Duke University.
[13] Elise to Bragg, March 12, 1862, Mrs. Bragg Papers, University of Texas.

Bragg reprimanded Ruggles for letting the men get out of hand and quickly restored order. He had several plunderers, including a colonel, arrested and ordered General Adley H. Gladden's Louisianians, who had served at Pensacola, to drive "the swine" back to their camps with bayonets. "No plundering has taken place since [Gladden's men went into action]," Bragg informed Elise.[14]

The town was quiet when Johnston arrived on March 23. Bragg wrote: "Johnston almost embraced me when I met him, saying 'Your prompt and decisive move, Sir, has saved me, and saved the country. But for your arrival, the enemy would have been between us.'" After Johnston had thanked Bragg and Beauregard for their efforts to concentrate forces at Corinth, the talk turned to strategy. Bragg, delighted that his opinions had "some weight with both Johnston & Beauregard," urged that General Earl Van Dorn's army in Arkansas be ordered to Corinth, and insisted upon new commanders for Island Number 10 and Fort Pillow, the remaining Confederate forts on the upper Mississippi. "I offered my whole force," explained Bragg, "saying I could put any one of my Genls. there and knew they would never be stampeded." And to his wife, he complained: "I ought to have the whole command myself, and take my Pensacola & Mobile troops there. . . . But that point I could not urge, of course, as Genl. Polk, who commands is my senior." [15]

After a discussion of various strategic alternatives, Johnston decided that Bragg and his troops—indeed, the bulk of the army—would remain in Corinth and prepare for an offensive. The latest intelligence reports indicated that a Union army of nearly 40,000 men under General Grant was encamped near Pittsburg Landing awaiting General Buell, who was marching from Nashville with 25,000 troops. Johnston was determined

[14] Bragg to Elise, March 20, 1862, Bragg Papers, Duke University.

[15] *OR*, X (pt. 2), 361; Bragg to Elise, March 25, 1862, Bixby Collection of Bragg Papers.

to attack and crush Grant before Buell joined him; the Confederates must not allow these two Federal forces to unite.[16] The problem was not so much what to do, as how to do it. The 40,000 Confederates assembled at Corinth were still disorganized. Most of them were untrained and undisciplined, some were unarmed, and many were demoralized by recent defeats. A few days before Johnston reached Corinth, Bragg admitted to Beauregard: "In the present condition of this army, without transportation, supplies, discipline, or organization, no move toward the enemy can be made. We can only try and keep him in check whilst we labor to correct these radical defects." Van Dorn's force, beaten at Pea Ridge, Arkansas, on March 8, was dispirited and also hampered by transportation difficulties. Johnston and his generals knew it would take an Atlantean effort to organize the forces at Corinth, to unite two widely separated Confederate armies, and to overwhelm Grant before Buell arrived. But additional disasters, the Southerners agreed, were almost certain unless they could keep the Federal armies apart. So Van Dorn's force was ordered to Corinth, and preparations for the Confederate offensive began. Johnston, painfully aware that he had led his men only in retreat, magnanimously offered Beauregard command of the army. Beauregard graciously declined, but Johnston delegated much of the responsibility of organizing, arming, disciplining, and training the army to Beauregard and Bragg. He appointed Beauregard second-in-command of the army, and made Bragg chief of staff and a corps commander.[17]

It is unclear what Johnston expected his chief of staff to do, if anything, besides help reorganize the army. Johnston merely informed the President: "General Bragg is chief of staff for this army and department. There will be a thorough reorganization of the army as soon as possible." But Bragg's appointment also may have been a way to give him authority over General Polk, who was Bragg's senior in rank, but a less expe-

16 Roland, *Johnston*, pp. 311–13.   17 *OR*, X (pt. 2), 354, 370–71.

rienced soldier.[18] Thomas Jordan, assistant adjutant-general of Johnston's army, recalled after the war that "Bragg was nominally appointed chief of the general staff, a position borrowed from continental European armies, although there was no such office provided by law . . . in the Confederate military organization, which, however, was not regarded as material at the time, as General Bragg was not to be detached or at all diverted from the command of his corps; and in fact his assignment to the position was in order simply to enable him, at some possible exigent moment on the field, to give orders in the name of General Johnston, a power which both the Commander-in-Chief and . . . [Beauregard] desired that General Bragg should have in certain exigencies." Another staff officer, David Urquhart, recalled: "Genl Bragg was appointed Chief of Staff & explained to me that Genl Johnston so desired it to enable Beauregard & himself to carry out their plans." [19]

Johnston's most obvious aim in appointing Bragg chief of staff was to improve army administration. Davis had praised Bragg's high "administrative capacity" to Johnston; Beauregard probably told how he had relied upon Bragg's administrative ability since March 4. Johnston knew that the reorga-

[18] *Ibid.*, 372. Polk had resigned from the United States Army soon after graduation from West Point in 1827 to study for the ministry. An Episcopal bishop and a Louisiana sugar planter when the Civil War began, he was appointed a major general in the Confederate army after a visit with his old friend Jefferson Davis in June 1861. There is no indication that Polk ever read a book on military science after he left West Point. "Of classics [and theology] he knew little," admitted a close friend. "Of canon law, with the exception of our small American code, he knew nothing at all." Nor did Polk have any understanding of economics; he had failed as a planter, but he could be "wonderfully charming" in conversation. For a sympathetic study, see Joseph H. Parks, *General Leonidas Polk, C.S.A.: The Fighting Bishop* (Baton Rouge, 1962), pp. 41, 43, 113, 166, 169.

[19] Thomas Jordan, "Recollections of General Beauregard's Service in West Tennessee in the Spring of 1862," *Southern Historical Society Papers*, VIII (1880), 409; David Urquhart to Beauregard, August 14, 1878, Beauregard Papers, Duke University.

nization of his army needed close supervision, but he had neither the time nor the inclination for such detailed work. As Bragg explained after the war, Johnston was "not in the habit of descending to minutia." Therefore, Bragg, a compulsive worker who delighted in details, must have seemed to Johnston an ideal man for chief of staff.[20] But Johnston should not have given Bragg command of a corps if he expected him to be more than nominally chief of staff. To find a man capable of doing either job was hard enough; to expect one man to perform both was asking too much.

Yet other officers regarded Bragg's appointment as chief of staff as "an admirable arrangement. Bragg possesses many qualities which particularly fit him for that position," wrote General William J. Hardee. And years later a staff colonel who had served in the East as well as in the West claimed Bragg could discipline, organize, feed, and move troops better than any other Confederate general. "Sidney Johnston," according to this testimony, "weighed . . . [Bragg] aright when he assigned him a position hitherto unknown in American warfare, but essential to the proper organization of a great army, and so recognized by the European powers." [21]

For all his administrative talent, Bragg faced an impossible task. In the weeks since March 4 before he became chief of staff, he had tried to supply, equip, and put into combat condition the mass of men gathering at Corinth. But most of the troops remained unprepared. "Stern, dictatorial measures are necessary, and as far as my influence goes will be adopted,"

[20] OR, VII, 258; Bragg to William Preston Johnston, December 16, 1874, Barret Collection of Johnston Papers. Confederate armies nearly always needed better administration. To achieve this, Senator Louis T. Wigfall introduced a staff bill later in the war which would "enable [a commander] . . . to select from his Generals . . . an officer to relieve him from details." Wigfall to Joseph E. Johnston [April 1864?], Joseph E. Johnston Papers, Huntington Library.

[21] Hardee to Mrs. Felicia Lee Shover, April 3, 1862, William Joseph Hardee Papers, Library of Congress; J. Stoddard Johnston quoted in Johnston *Life of A. S. Johnston*, p. 546.

Bragg wrote his wife. "But great labor is before us, and we need not conceal the fact that great danger also threatens us. Our people, our generals, with few exceptions, and our troops are not up to the emergency." Except for the soldiers he brought from the coast, Bragg considered the army hopelessly undisciplined. "I thought my Mobile Army was a *Mob*," he informed Elise, "but it is as far superior to Polk's and Johnston's as the one at Pensacola was to it." A lack of uniform ordnance added to Bragg's problems; he discovered a variety of weapons in every regiment—"rifled and smooth bore muskets, some of them originally percussion, others hastily altered from flint locks by Yankee contractors, many still with the old flint and steel, and shot guns of all sizes and patterns." Supplies were difficult to obtain because the railroad system was utterly deranged, and plundering by Confederate soldiers was still prevalent. An attempt to increase the army's riflemen by hiring slaves for noncombatant tasks failed because local planters refused to let their Negroes serve as teamsters, laborers, or cooks. Nor would local people lend their mules to the army. Bragg lamented: "Such has been the outrageous conduct of our troops that the people . . . prefer seeing the enemy." Bishop-General Leonidas "Polk & Johnston do nothing to correct this. Indeed the good Bishop sets the example, by taking whatever he wishes. . . ." [22]

With his characteristic disregard for high rank and political influence, Bragg tried to restore order. Beauregard, with Johnston's approval, had reorganized the army into four corps of unequal size: the First Corps, assigned to Polk, consisted of 9,136 men, divided into four brigades; Bragg commanded the Second Corps, which numbered 13,589 men and six brigades; the Third Corps, under Hardee, included three brigades and

[22] Bragg to Elise, March 25, 1862, Bixby Collection of Bragg Papers; Bragg, "General Albert Sidney Johnston and the Battle of Shiloh," Barret Collection of Johnston Papers; Roland, *Johnston*, pp. 315–16; *OR*, X (pt. 2), 339-40.

6,789 men; the Reserve Corps, three brigades and another 6,439 men, was commanded by George B. Crittenden, son of Senator John J. Crittenden of Kentucky. Some historians believe that Beauregard's arrangements were superior to what had existed; this is true, but hardly praiseworthy, for almost any organization would have been better than the previous hodgepodge. Actually, Beauregard made two errors in reorganizing the army. His major mistake was assigning nearly 14,000 men (one third of the army) to Bragg's corps. A more equal distribution of troops would have encouraged tighter battlefield control and prevented much of the overlapping of units and command confusion so prevalent at Shiloh. Beauregard's second error was giving General Crittenden command of a corps. Bragg remedied that mistake on March 31 by arresting Crittenden and one of his brigadiers, William H. Carroll, for drunkenness, neglect of duty, and incapacity. John C. Breckinridge, formerly Vice President of the United States, replaced Crittenden. Bragg knew it was risky' to change generals just before a battle, but probably he was correct in his belief that retaining Crittenden and Carroll in command would be even more dangerous, and that their removal would improve army discipline.[23]

Bragg's efforts to discipline the army caused many complaints. Furthermore, he made the mistake of following the advice of his wife. Her views were often based on whim or rumor, but she constantly instructed him. "Dear husband please *do not trust* the Tennessee troops," she wrote. "Put the Tennesseeans where your batteries can *fire* upon them if they attempt to run. Lead them into action yourself, & *shame* them into fighting." Elise believed Bragg could rely only on Louisiana and Mississippi soldiers. The Creoles, she claimed, were "obedient, good marksmen, habituated to exposure, & free from the besetting sin of the Confederacy, drunkenness." The entire South, she contended, praised the Mississippians: ". . .

[23] *OR*, X (pt. 2), 370–71, 372, 279.

they will never fail you." Bragg replied that he was scattering
Tennesseeans "among better men" in his corps. "I never realized the full correctness of your appreciation of them until
now," he wrote. And Private Sam R. Watkins reported that
before Bragg sent his corps into battle, he placed other units
behind the Tennessee troops "to shoot us down if we ran."
Watkins admitted that the men in his regiment were "in no
condition to fight." "They loved the Union anyway," he confessed, "and were always opposed to this war. But breathe
softly the name . . . Bragg. It has more terror than the
[enemy] army." [24] Certainly Bragg's determination to enforce
discipline, combined with his utter tactlessness, offended independent Southerners and gained him many enemies. Later in
the war he would be falsely accused of atrocities.

On the night of April 2 Johnston decided that even though
the army needed more drill he could delay no longer; the
Confederates must attack Grant at once for scouts reported
that Buell was rapidly approaching the Tennessee River. Johnston, accompanied by Colonel Thomas Jordan, roused Bragg
to discuss the situation. It was clear that Van Dorn would not
arrive in time to help; Johnston would have to make the attack
with the men at hand. Jordan later wrote that Bragg, despite
his belief that the troops were still unready, approved Johnston's decision to attack at once. After a lengthy discussion,
Johnston announced that the army would advance the next
day. Jordan immediately "turned to a table in . . . Bragg's
chamber, and wrote a circular order to the . . . corps commanders . . . directing that each should hold his corps under
arms by 6 A.M., on the 3d of April, ready to march, with
one hundred rounds of ammunition; three days' cooked provisions per man in their haversacks, with two more to be trans-

[24] Elise to Bragg, February 16, March 12, 1862, Mrs. Bragg Papers,
University of Texas; Bragg to Elise, March 20, 1862, Bragg Papers, Duke
University; Sam R. Watkins, *"Co. Aytch." Maury Grays First Tennessee
Regiment* . . . (Jackson, Tenn., 1952), pp. 71–72.

ported in wagons. This circular also prescribed the ammunition for the artillery, and the number of tents each company should be provided with; all of which was approved by General Johnston," recalled Jordan, "when I read the rough draught of it. Afterward the copies were made by an aide-de-camp on the staff of General Bragg." [25]

Most of the morning of April 3 was spent preparing to advance. Bragg and the other corps commanders met after breakfast for a briefing with Beauregard, whom Johnston authorized to make battle plans. Reconnaissance indicated that Grant's force of about 37,000 men was encamped between Owl and Lick Creeks near Pittsburg Landing on the west side of the Tennessee River. It was a strong natural position of "rolling uplands, partially cultivated, interspersed with . . . forests." In such terrain the maneuver of troops would be difficult, but a tactical surprise might be possible. The Federals had not entrenched; indeed, Grant's campsites were open and unaligned.[26]

Beauregard expected the army to march from Corinth on two dirt roads which converged at a house called Mickey's about eight miles from Pittsburg Landing. Verbal orders were given for the advance to begin at noon with each corps following an assigned route. Corps commanders, Beauregard promised, would receive written orders later. Hardee was to march on the Ridge Road, bivouac that night at Mickey's, and move forward at 3 A.M. on April 4 to deploy in line of battle. Bragg would follow the Monterey Road as far as the hamlet of

[25] OR, X (pt. 2), 388; Thomas Jordan, "Notes of a Confederate Staff-Officer at Shiloh," *Battles and Leaders*, I, 594–95. Roland (*Johnston*, pp. 316–17) shows that Jordan overemphasized his own and Beauregard's role in Johnston's decision to attack without further delay.

[26] OR, X (pt. 1), 567; David Urquhart to Beauregard, August 14, 1878, Beauregard Papers, Duke University; Jordan, "Notes of a Confederate Staff-Officer at Shiloh," p. 596; G. T. Beauregard, "The Campaign of Shiloh," *Battles and Leaders*, I, 581; Catton, *Grant Moves South*, p. 220.

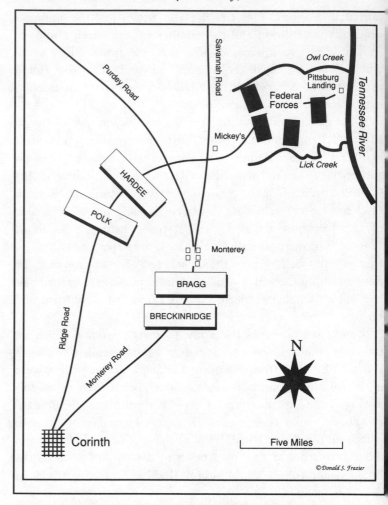

**ROUTE OF THE CONFEDERATE
ADVANCE ON PITTSBURG LANDING**

Monterey, where his two divisions would separate and march
on different roads (the Purdy and Savannah Roads that inter-
sected the Ridge Road south of Mickey's). Bragg's first division—Ruggles's, which was composed of brigades commanded

by General J. Patton Anderson, Colonel Preston Pond, Jr., and Colonel Randall L. Gibson—was supposed to reach Mickey's before sunset; Withers's division of three brigades commanded by Generals Gladden, Chalmers, and Jackson was expected to arrive at the intersection of the Ridge Road by night. The next morning Bragg would unite his command and form a second battleline behind Hardee. Polk was to leave Corinth on the Ridge Road half an hour after Hardee, halt at the Purdy Road intersection until Bragg's second division had passed, advance the next morning, and form a third battleline. Breckinridge would follow Bragg to Monterey, and then move forward by the quickest route to form a fourth battleline.[27]

Beauregard's marching plan had obvious faults. It sent more than half the army by the longer route, and it required nearly perfect timing for the orderly meshing of units on the battlefield, an unreasonable expectation considering the inexperience of many officers and soldiers. A sounder plan would have been to send Bragg, followed by Hardee, over the shortest road, and Polk and Breckinridge over the longer. After the war Bragg wrote: ". . . Johnston gave verbal instructions for the general movement, General Beauregard's Chief of Staff, Jordan . . . had been accepted unfortunately by General Jonnston, as Adjutant General of the Army. Over his [Jordan's] signature these elaborated details reached the Army. The general plan (Johnston's) was admirable—the elaboration simply execrable." "To be candid with you," Bragg informed Johnston's son, "I believe Beauregard, or his man Jordan, is entitled to all the blundering of those details."[28]

The march to Pittsburg Landing indicated that Beauregard's plan was too complicated for inexperienced officers and men to execute properly. Instead of starting on time, soldiers

[27] OR, X (pt. 1), 382–83, 292–95; (pt. 2), 387.
[28] Bragg to William Preston Johnston, December 16, 1874, Barret Collection of Johnston Papers. See also Thomas Lawrence Connelly's excellent *Army of the Heartland: The Army of Tennessee, 1861–1862* (Baton Rouge, 1967), pp. 152–57.

jammed the streets of Corinth. Hardee, blocked by Polk's troops and baggage train, did not get out of town until the afternoon of the third. Bragg was even later getting started for he also had difficulty disentangling his corps from the rest of the army. He cursed the green troops, who had never marched or "performed a day's labor" before, the inexperienced teamsters, and the inferior quality and insufficient number of impressed wagons.[29] The problem was simply that the Confederate commanders expected too much; neither they nor their troops were capable of executing a complex march and attack without numerous delays and mistakes.

More trouble followed the initial congestion in Corinth. Hardee reached Mickey's twelve hours late. The other corps fell even further behind schedule. Much to their commander's exasperation, Bragg's men seemed to creep along. His first division, which was supposed to arrive at Mickey's at sundown on the third, had to march all night to get there on the morning of the fourth. All of his second division did not reach Monterey until the evening of the fourth. On his own authority, Bragg changed Beauregard's marching instructions, sending his second division to Mickey's via the Savannah Road instead of the Purdy Road as originally planned. This was an attempt not to delay Polk's corps, but Polk had been waiting three hours when Bragg's courier reached him with word to go ahead. "Bad roads, inefficient transportation badly managed," complained Bragg, were too much for the army to overcome. Some of the difficulties of the march are recorded by Lieutenant Taylor Beatty who near Monterey on April 3 was "put under arrest—together with most of the other officers by Genl. Gladden because our men burned some rails." Released from arrest the next day, Beatty and his regiment "Marched very slowly . . . not marching more than four or five miles," he noted. "Just as we were going into camp, artillery in front opened and we were ordered forward—slow work—met some

[29] *OR*, X (pt. 1), 463.

prisoners coming back. Camped in a mud hole—terrible raw—cold and disagreeable." Amidst such confusion, Johnston soon realized he must modify Beauregard's original timetable. After a conference with Bragg and Beauregard about 5 P.M. on April 4 at Monterey, Johnston rescheduled the attack for the morning of April 5.[30]

Bragg rode to Mickey's after dark on the fourth and prepared for the battle he expected the next day. To his assembled division and brigade commanders, he explained what he knew about the country's topography and the enemy's position, ordered that troops be ready to move forward at 3 A.M. the next morning, and read aloud Beauregard's battle plan. It would send the army into action with one corps behind the other across a three-mile front. The tactical objective was to turn the enemy's left flank, drive the Federals from the Tennessee River, and pin them against Owl Creek where they could be destroyed or captured.[31]

The plan was sound except for the arrangement of forces. Bragg later observed that Beauregard, rather than spreading each corps across a three-mile front, should have concentrated the bulk of the army on the enemy's left. But there is no indication that Bragg told his superiors or his subordinates this on the night of April 4. In fact, the evidence suggests that he only later realized the weaknesses of Beauregard's troop arrangement. Writing to Johnston's son after the war, Bragg insisted that Johnston had intended to concentrate on the enemy's left, but Beauregard muddled the details and Johnston hesitated to rearrange the troops on the eve of battle. Under Beauregard's arrangement of forces, Bragg explained, "no commander, in a wooded country, could possibly exercise supervision over his own troops, even, and he had no control over those in his front or rear." Bragg also complained that the

---

[30] *Ibid.*, X (pt. 2), 390–91; Taylor Beatty Diary, April 3–4, 1862; Roland, *Johnston*, p. 319.

[31] *OR*, X (pt. 1), 464, 397, 494–95.

army's artillery was badly organized. Because batteries were scattered among brigades and divisions before the march from Corinth no concentration of guns was possible; artillery was not organized by battalions, as the drill manuals directed; nor was there a chief of artillery. Yet just before the battle all artillery batteries were "placed under the nominal orders of one of the Corps Commanders, a trust it was simply impossible for him to execute." [32]

Bragg apparently had no control over the assignment of artillery or the arrangement of units; though he remained nominally chief of staff, Beauregard and several junior officers, principally Jordan, seemed to have assumed all the army's staff work after the advance began. Relief from staff responsibilities allowed Bragg to concentrate his full energy upon corps command, but it deprived the staff at a critical moment of a man whose greatest military talents were organizational and administrative, not tactical. Bragg probably would have been more useful to the army behind the lines coordinating movements and communications, organizing stragglers, and forwarding reinforcements and ammunition. If he had continued his staff duties after the army left Corinth, Beauregard, a full general and a more experienced combat commander than Bragg, would have been free to lead the Confederate assault on the Union left. Instead, Beauregard remained behind the lines doing what Bragg could have done just as well, if not better. Perhaps Beauregard stayed in the rear because he was still too ill for field command. In his own words, "at the time I was greatly prostrated and suffering from the prolonged sickness with which I had been afflicted since early in February. The responsibility [of army command] was one which in my physical condition I would have gladly avoided. . . ." [33] Perhaps too Johnston was unwilling to separate Bragg from the troops

---

[32] Bragg to William Preston Johnston, January 7, 1875, Barret Collection of Johnston Papers; Roland, *Johnston*, pp. 321–23.
[33] *OR*, X (pt. 1), 387, 390–91.

he had trained and brought to Corinth. Most Confederates preferred field command to staff duties and there is no reason to believe Bragg was an exception.

About 2 A.M. on April 5 a heavy rain began. It soaked Bragg and his men, filled creeks and ravines, and made movement impracticable until dawn. "So dark we can't see to move," a soldier wrote in his diary, "so we had to stand under arms in a pelting rain until daylight." The men were already tired from the march and because they had been kept awake all night by what Bragg called the sporadic firing of "undisciplined troops . . . in violation of positive orders." But not all the noise was by soldiers testing to see if their weapons were wet. Sometime during the night Bragg had received a note from Hardee; his men had repulsed an attack by several Federal companies.[34] A surprise attack by the Confederates no longer appeared possible.

When it was light enough to see, Bragg advanced and deployed his corps eight hundred yards behind Hardee's battle-line. The wooded terrain, the size of Bragg's corps, and the crowded road slowed the movement; not until Johnston ordered Polk's troops, who were blocking the road, to move aside could Bragg get all his men in line. It was then nearly 10 A.M. and still no attack order came. Bragg did send one brigade ahead after Hardee wrote that his corps was not large enough to cover the front and Beauregard wanted one of Bragg's brigades placed on Hardee's right to fill out the line. By now the sun had appeared; the soldiers were dry and in better humor. One noted: "It seems the fight won't come off today. Warm and bright. Our bed clothes and mess things came up and we have prospects of a good night." [35]

It would not be a good night for Bragg. He had paced nervously all day while the army waited for Breckinridge's

---

[34] Taylor Beatty Diary, April 5, 1862; OR, X (pt. 1), 464; Hughes, Hardee, p. 103.
[35] OR, X (pt. 1), 464; Taylor Beatty Diary, April 5, 1862.

corps which had been delayed by muddy roads and did not arrive until late in the afternoon. Before dark Johnston, Beauregard, Bragg, and Polk met at a crossroad and began discussing their situation. Beauregard was most upset. He said Polk was responsible for the delay; Polk, in turn, censured Bragg, who blamed bad weather, untrained troops, and poor planning. Some soldiers had already eaten in three days rations intended to last five. As the conversation continued Bragg and Beauregard became more pessimistic. Beauregard suggested that the Confederates return to Corinth without a fight; he had given up hope of surprising the enemy. "Now they will be entrenched to the eyes," he warned. Bragg agreed. A staff officer noted in his diary: "5 P.M. Bragg and B[eauregard] think provisions short, and the delay of 36 hours will cause failure." [36]

With the army poised for a battle that might save the Confederacy, Bragg and Beauregard had momentarily lost their nerve. Perhaps the strain of the past few weeks had been too severe: the tensions and the responsibilities of command, the frustrations and the fatigue of the march from Corinth combined with Bragg's and Beauregard's poor health may account for their vacillation. At times Bragg and Beauregard could be frightfully unstable, with quick changes in mood from cocksureness to despair.

This hesitancy of Bragg and Beauregard, considering what was at stake, indicates that they lacked that necessary resolution good field officers must have. What they believed a retreat would accomplish is uncertain. If it was essential to crush Grant before Buell joined him, as both Bragg and Beauregard argued before the Confederates left Corinth, then why wait? It seemed unlikely that there would ever be a better chance to

36 Bragg to Elise, April 8, 1862, Bixby Collection of Bragg Papers; *OR*, X (pt. 1), 464, 407; Alfred Roman, *The Military Operations of General Beauregard in the War Between the States, 1861–1865* (2 vols., New York, 1884), I, 277–79; William Preston Diary, April 5, 1862, War Department Collection of Confederate Records, National Archives.

overwhelm Grant. What Bragg and Beauregard apparently feared was that an attack would fail because the element of surprise—so essential, they believed, to the plan's success—had been lost. They ignored or overlooked the effect another retreat without a fight might have on the Confederate army's morale. They warned of disaster and placed the terrible responsibility of whether to fight or withdraw squarely upon Johnston.

"Gentlemen," Johnston said after listening to everyone, "we shall attack at daylight tomorrow." He still hoped the enemy might be surprised. In any event, he told a staff officer as the generals dispersed, "I would fight them if they were a million. They can present no greater front between these two creeks than we can, and the more men they crowd in there, the worse we can make it for them." [37]

Johnston would have been right in 1847; attackers had enjoyed an advantage over defenders in the Mexican War, particularly when defenders crowded together and were unable to maneuver. But on April 5, 1862, Johnston was wrong. Technological changes in the 1850s had modified warfare far more than Johnston or his generals realized. They had no idea how unsuited the tactics they had learned at West Point and practiced in Mexico were for Civil War battles. An awful truth awaited them.

[37] William Preston Johnston, "Albert Sidney Johnston at Shiloh," *Battles and Leaders,* I, 555; Roland, *Johnston,* pp. 323–25; Williams, *Beauregard,* pp. 131–32. Later that evening, the senior generals gathered in Johnston's tent where "a further discussion elicited the same views, and the same firm determination." Bragg implied that at this meeting he agreed with Johnston's decision to attack the next day. Braxton Bragg, "General Albert Sidney Johnston and the Battle of Shiloh," Barret Collection of Johnston Papers.

CHAPTER XI

It is our own fault

APRIL 6–8, 1862

SHORTLY AFTER DAWN on April 6, while Confederate forces aligned for battle, Bragg and "several generals" again met at Johnston's camp. Beauregard still opposed an offensive, but Bragg recalled: "The enemy did not give us [much] time to discuss the question of attack, for soon . . . he commenced a rapid musketry fire on our pickets." At which point Johnston said: "The battle has opened, gentlemen; it is too late to change our dispositions." [1]

Though the fire of Federal patrols had sounded the alarm, the Union generals were still unprepared for battle. Shiloh, as a careful student noted, "was one of the greatest strategic surprises in all military history." No defense line existed; not a single Union soldier was entrenched. Grant's six divisions were scattered; one, commanded by General Lew Wallace, was four miles downriver from the rest of the army. Grant himself was at his headquarters nine miles from Pittsburg Landing. The senior general on the field was Sherman, who had ignored the considerable evidence of enemy activity. The day before he had assured Grant: "I do not apprehend anything like an attack on our position." [2]

Bragg hurried from Johnston's camp to lead his corps. "My line was three miles long thro' a dense forest, cut by ravines & creeks & bogs," he later explained to Elise. His troops advanced some two miles before encountering their first heavy

[1] *OR*, X (pt. 1), 464; Bragg, "General Albert Sidney Johnston and the Battle of Shiloh," Barret Collection of Johnston Papers.
[2] Roland, *Johnston*, p. 328; *OR*, X (pt. 2), 93–94.

opposition about 7:30 A.M. near a little log church called Shiloh, from which the battle took its name. Bragg ordered a vigorous assault and soon the Federals retreated.[3]

All day the Confederates advanced, but much less rapidly than at first, for as layers of Federals fell back they were joined by fresh units moving up to the front. After the initial shock, the Union troops fought stubbornly, and the Confederate advance slowed. As the resistance stiffened, the Southerners became tangled, with corps, divisions, and brigades pell-mell. Lines ceased to exist as men lost interval, dropped out of ranks to rest, to pillage the Federal camps, or to return to Corinth. "There were many battles but no one line of battle," noted a historian. "Shiloh was a grab bag full of separate combats in which divisions, brigades, and even regiments fought on their own, each one joined by fragments of other commands that had fallen apart in the shock of action, most of them fighting with their flanks in the air, knowing nothing of any battle except the fragment which possessed them—great waves of sound beating on them, smoke streaking the fields and making blinding clouds under the trees, advance and retreat taking place sometimes because someone had ordered it and sometimes on the impulse of the untaught soldiers who were doing the fighting." [4]

Beauregard's battle plan made such muddling "inevitable," Bragg later charged; "commanders found themselves leading strange battalions, and the troops saw . . . leaders . . . whom they did not recognize, and whose rank and authority they did not even know. So great was this confusion and disorder, that commands were not again united under their own officers for several days." Bragg considered an attack by corps sensible only if "each corps is held by its own commander so as to be handled. But the order for Shiloh required each corps to cover the whole line of battle, about three miles, and to be

---

[3] Bragg to Elise, April 8, 1862, Bixby Collection of Bragg Papers.
[4] Bruce Catton, *Terrible Swift Sword* (New York, 1963), p. 232.

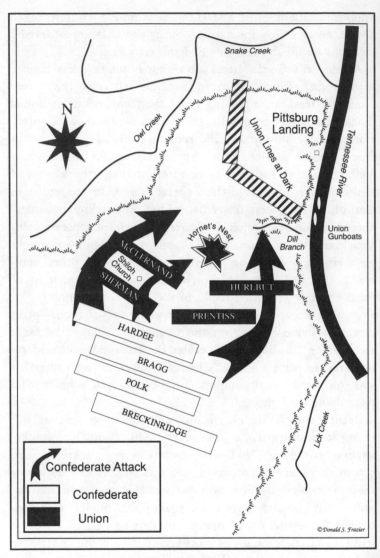

Snake Creek

N

Owl Creek

Pittsburg
Landing

Union Lines at Dark

Tennessee River

Hornet's Nest

Dill
Branch

Union
Gunboats

McCLERNAND
Shiloh
Church

SHERMAN

HURLBUT

PRENTISS

HARDEE

BRAGG

POLK

BRECKINRIDGE

Lick Creek

Confederate Attack

Confederate

Union

©Donald S. Frazier

BATTLE OF SHILOH, April 6, 1862

supported in succession by the corps in rear, each attenuated in like manner. Thus arranged, no commander, in a wooded country, could possibly exercise supervision over his own troops, even, and he had no control over those in his front or rear, so as to afford or require support when needed." [5]

The Confederate attack also gradually lost force for another reason, a reason neither Bragg nor his colleagues understood. They had learned—from Napoleon, or Jomini, or Mahan—the dogma of the offensive. "The bayonet has always been the weapon of the brave and the chief tool of victory," Napoleon had written. "A charge by column, when the enemy is within fifty paces, will prove effective, if resolutely made," preached Mahan.[6] And the American experience in combat against Indians and Mexicans before the Civil War reinforced these pronouncements. Taylor and Scott had often relied upon bayonet attacks for victory.

Such attacks had been successful before the Civil War because the basic infantry firearm, the smoothbore musket, was quite inaccurate. A soldier might fire a smoothbore musket at a man all day from a distance of a few hundred yards and never hit him.[7] Yet through the 1840s field commanders had favored smoothbores over rifles for general infantry use. Rifles required too much time and effort to load because each bullet had to be slightly larger than the bore; otherwise, when the weapon was fired, the bullet would fail to spin through the barrel along the rifled grooves. These rifled grooves gave the rifle both its name and its superiority in range and accuracy over the smoothbore. But before the 1850s it took as much as two minutes to load a rifle. Equipped with either inaccurate smoothbore muskets or hard-to-load rifles, troops usually could be routed by a disciplined bayonet assault.

[5] Bragg to William Preston Johnston, January 7, 1875, Barret Collection of Johnston Papers.

[6] Herold, ed., *The Mind of Napoleon*, p. 218; Mahan, *An Elementary Treatise on Advanced-Guard*, p. 11.

[7] Grant, *Personal Memoirs*, I, 95.

What Bragg and most of his contemporaries failed to realize on the morning of April 6, 1862, was that a technological innovation had negated the lessons they had learned about the advantages of bayonet attacks. The technological change that finished the smoothbore as the standard infantry arm and created a tactical lag was the development in the 1850s of the Minie "ball." It was neither Captain Minie's invention nor a ball; the projectile actually was an elongated bullet with a hollow base which was small enough to fit easily into the rifle's bore, but would expand automatically when fired and fit snugly into the rifled grooves. The Minie bullet made the rifled muzzleloader a practical military weapon. Compared with pre-Civil War shoulder weapons, the rifled muzzleloader was a firearm of deadly accuracy. It could be fired two or three times a minute; it could stop an attack at up to four hundred yards, and could kill at a distance of one thousand yards. The rifle was to become the great killer of the Civil War. Because of its range and accuracy, Civil War infantry assaults were always bloody; sometimes they were suicidal. Defenders, for the first time in over a century, had a decisive advantage. "One rifle in the trench was worth five in front of it," recalled Union General Jacob D. Cox. Perhaps he exaggerated a bit, but a few entrenched men armed with rifles did hold positions against great odds. The rifle and the spade made Civil War defenses at least three times stronger than offenses.[8]

In April 1862 neither Bragg nor anyone in either army knew how much the rifle would modify traditional tactics. Shortly before the Civil War army officials noted the rifle's range and precision, but they believed that these could be offset simply by teaching soldiers to move more quickly in battle. "They are introducing the light infantry tactics this spring, a new thing," wrote Cadet Henry A. du Pont from West Point on

---

[8] Jacob D. Cox, *Atlanta* (New York, 1909), p. 129. For a more elaborate discussion of the impact of the rifle and the results of the Confederacy's tactical lag, see McWhiney, "Who Whipped Whom?" pp. 5-26.

March 28, 1857. "There are a great many very rapid movements in it, and many of them are performed in double quick time, that is running. Within the last week [Colonel William J.] Hardee [author of the new tactics book and Commandant of Cadets] has had the whole battalion going at double quick with the band. . . . It will take time for everyone to learn to keep step. I expect that they will almost run us to death when the board of visitors come." Two months later du Pont admitted that the new tactics were "no doubt better in some respects, that is to say that troops drilled to them would be more efficient, but they do not look so well, for it is impossible to attain . . . the same precision and accuracy with all this running and quick movements, as was possible under the old system, and besides it is much harder work." [9]

If the new tactics had stressed dispersal as well as speed then attackers might have had a chance to overcome the advantage rifles gave defenders, but dispersal of forces without loss of control was difficult to achieve in the 1860s. In some ways the Civil War was a modern struggle: in minutes generals communicated with each other by telegraph over thousands of miles; trains quickly carried large armies great distances, and piled mountains of supplies at railheads. But, in other ways, the war was strikingly antiquated: men walked or rode horses into battle, and their supplies followed in wagons. Few attempts were made to connect combat units with each other or with field headquarters by telegraph; nearly all battlefield messages went by courier on horseback. This traditional system of combat communication bound Civil War generals to close order formations. They had no desirable alternative; the dispersal of forces to avoid the rifle's firepower and accuracy would have made communication even more difficult, and further weak-

[9] Major Richard Delafield, "Report on the Art of War in Europe in 1854, 1855, and 1856," *Senate Executive Document*, 36 Cong., 1 sess., No. 59, pp. 6–8; Ambrose, ed., "West Point in the Fifties: Letters of Henry A. du Pont," pp. 306–7.

ened a commander's control of his men in battle. Even when troops were tightly bunched, communication between units was difficult enough.

Except for the quicker movements required of troops, the new tactics were much like the old ones. Both emphasized close order formations, and taught men to rely on the shock effect of bayonet assaults. A Prussian officer who visited the South in 1863 reported: "There was diligent drilling in the camps according to an old French drill manual that had been revised by Hardee, and I observed on the drill field only linear formations, wheeling out into open columns, wheeling in and marching up into line, marching in line, open column marching, marching by sections, and marching in file. . . ." [10]

When the Confederates attacked at Shiloh, Bragg and the other generals employed essentially the same tactics they had learned at West Point and practiced in Mexico. "I led the center [of the battleline] until 11 o'clock carrying everything before us with small loss," boasted Bragg, but the first advances were more costly than his letter to Elise indicated. "Waked up early this morning and ordered into line to attack the enemy," wrote Taylor Beatty of the First Louisiana Regiment. "After advancing some half mile ahead we encountered the enemy and after engaging them for about 20 minutes drove them from their position. Capt. Wheat & Lt. Levy were killed here—& we lost a great many men." Colonel W. A. Stanley, whose Ninth Texas Regiment was part of Ruggles's division, reported: ". . . we advanced in line of battle under a heavy fire of artillery and musketry from the enemy's first encampment. Being ordered to charge [a] . . . battery with our bayonets, we made two successive attempts; but finding . . . it is almost impossible to withstand the heavy fire directed at our ranks, we were compelled to withdraw for a short time,

[10] Captain Justus Scheibert, *Seven Months in the Rebel States During the North American War, 1863,* William Stanley Hoole, ed. (Tuscaloosa, 1958), pp. 37–38.

with considerable loss." A subsequent charge routed the enemy, and Stanley's men hurried through two other encampments before they were again checked by the "galling fire" of a second battery and its infantry support. Here additional men and Stanley's horse were killed. Early in the battle Lieutenant Colonel Charles Jones, who commanded the Seventeenth Louisiana, was ordered to make a bayonet assault on a Federal battery. "A Tennessee regiment . . . was in front of us," he recalled. "We were delayed a moment by this regiment, when I gave the order to charge. When we reached the top of the hill the enemy poured into us a murderous fire. The Tennessee regiment . . . retired by the flank through our lines, cutting their way through the center of our fourth company, separating our right from our left, and throwing us into some confusion." Jones's men retreated, reformed, and attacked again. But "a destructive flank fire from another of the enemy's batteries, as well as from his small-arms," forced the Seventeenth Louisiana to withdraw after it sustained heavy losses. The Fourth Louisiana suffered an even greater shock. "While drawn up in line of battle and awaiting orders a Tennessee regiment immediately in our rear fired into us by mistake, killing and wounding a large number of my men," reported Colonel Henry W. Allen. "This was a terrible blow. . . . It almost demoralized the regiment, who from that moment seemed to dread their friends much more than their enemies." [11]

For several hours Bragg directed assaults near the center of the battlefield. Union resistance was now even more determined. Sherman and other Federal commanders had "directed the men to avail themselves of every cover—trees, fallen timber, and a wooded valley to our right." As Confederate units broke against these strong positions, Bragg stubbornly rallied and sent them forward again. Before 10 A.M. his horse was killed and fell on him. He escaped with only a bruised leg.

[11] Bragg to Elise, April 8, 1862, Bixby Collection of Bragg Papers; Taylor Beatty Diary, April 6, 1862; OR, X (pt. 1), 508–9, 505, 489–90.

Mounting another animal, Bragg saw a regiment belonging to what he called "Polk's mob" break, and he rushed to halt them. An hour later his second horse was killed.[12]

About this time Polk joined Bragg. They agreed that the battle was not developing as Beauregard had planned; Hardee, on the left, was gaining ground more rapidly than other Confederate units. The Federals were being enveloped and pushed back toward Pittsburg Landing instead of away from the river. This situation had to be remedied quickly; there was no time to consult Johnston, even if Bragg and Polk had known where to find him. Command arrangements and communications had become chaotic. Polk later reported: ". . . I sought out General Bragg . . . and asked him where he would have my command. He replied, 'If you will take care of the center, I will go to the right.' It was understood that General Hardee was attending to the left." [13]

Bragg soon discovered why the Confederate right wing had stalled. Remnants of three Union divisions—Stephen A. Hurlbut's, Benjamin M. Prentiss's, and W. H. L. Wallace's—were making a determined stand in a densely wooded area of thick undergrowth which was flanked on either side by open fields. The Confederates, after repeated failures to capture this strong point, called it the Hornets' Nest. "Here," admitted Bragg, "we met the most obstinate resistance of the day, the enemy being strongly posted, with infantry and artillery, on an eminence immediately behind a dense thicket." General Hurlbut reported: "For five hours these brigades maintained their position under repeated and heavy attacks. . . ." Of one such Confederate assault, Hurlbut wrote: ". . . the enemy appeared on the crest of the ridge, led by the Eighteenth Louisiana, but were cut to pieces by the steady and murderous fire of

12 *OR*, X (pt. 1), 465, 250, 389; Bragg to Elise, April 8, 1862, Bixby Collection of Bragg Papers. Thomas Bragg's son, who was at Shiloh, claimed his Uncle Braxton "was much exposed—had 3 horses shot under him and yet was not hit." Thomas Bragg Diary, April 28, 1862.

13 *OR*, X (pt. 1), 408, 465–66.

our artillery." The Louisianians had advanced to within 150 yards of the enemy, stopped to fire a volley, then continued forward yelling, "but the only effect it had on the men of this battery," commented a Union artillerist, "was to cause them promptly to move their guns by hand to the front . . . pouring into [the Confederates] . . . a shower of canister, causing both the yelling and the firing of the enemy to cease." The Eighteenth Louisiana, part of Ruggles's division, lost 207 men (41 per cent of its total strength) in this single charge.[14]

Thomas Hindman's division had just retreated after an unsuccessful attack when Bragg arrived opposite the Hornets' Nest. Yet Bragg remained unconvinced that the position was too strong to be taken by bayonet attack. First, he directed General Charles Clark to charge a worrisome Union battery with one of his regiments. "The Eleventh Louisiana . . . being most convenient," recalled Clark, "I led it forward. The battery was concealed from us by a ridge and distance about 300 yards. The . . . [men] moved up the ascent, with fixed bayonets, at a double-quick, and when on the crest of the ridge we were opened upon by the enemy's battery with shot and canister and by a large infantry support with musketry at easy range. Our men were compelled to fall back behind the ridge, where they were promptly reformed." This regiment, which started the attack with 550 men, made several subsequent charges, but the next day its commander could muster only some sixty men. The rest were casualties or stragglers. Bragg had expected too much of a regiment; it ultimately took a whole brigade to drive back the battery and its support which Clark had attacked.[15]

Bragg next sent a brigade of Louisiana and Arkansas regiments commanded by his Lafourche Parish neighbor, Randall Gibson, against the Union position. "The brigade moved forward in fine style, marching through an open field under a heavy fire and half up an elevation covered with an almost

[14] *Ibid.*, 204–5, 273, 521.   [15] *Ibid.*, 415, 420–22.

impenetrable thicket, upon which the enemy was posted," reported Gibson. "On the left a battery opened that raked our flank, while a steady fire of musketry extended along the entire front. Under this combined fire our line was broken and the troops fell back; but they were soon rallied and advanced to the contest. Four times the position was charged and four times the assault proved unavailing. The strong and almost inaccessible position of the enemy—his infantry well covered in ambush and his artillery skillfully posted and efficiently served—was found to be impregnable to infantry alone. We were repulsed." But Bragg believed the failure of the attacks was "due entirely to want of proper handling" of the brigade by Gibson. After the battle Bragg complained that he and his staff had to rally the brigade. "I . . . took their flag and led them in," he claimed, "but it was no use—they were demoralized and nothing would induce them" to drive the enemy.[16]

Several months later Gibson and several of his regimental commanders challenged Bragg's charges. Gibson denied that Bragg or his staff had rallied the brigade. So did the commanders of two Louisiana Regiments. "I never heard that any part of that brigade was rallied by General Bragg or his staff," stated E. M. Dubroca of the Thirteenth Louisiana. "General Bragg, staff, and body guard retired to a ravine [when an enemy battery opened fire]," insisted Colonel Henry W. Allen of the Fourth Louisiana. "I saw nothing more of them during that day. No member of his staff ever rallied any of my men, nor do I believe any of them at any time rallied your brigade." Gibson and all his subordinate commanders agreed that their men had fought gallantly; they had failed because Bragg refused to give them artillery support, and because of the enemy's "severe artillery fire, advantageous position, superior numbers, and the almost impenetrable thicket through which we had to advance." [17]

[16] *Ibid.*, 466, 480; Bragg to Elise, April 8, 1862, Bixby Collection of Bragg Papers.
[17] *OR*, X (pt. 1), 482–87.

Gibson and his men had a strong case. Perhaps in the strictest sense they were not rallied by Bragg nor by any of his staff. Bragg's claim that he took the flag and led the brigade into battle may have been an embellishment for Elise; he made no such statement in his official report. But Colonel Samuel H. Lockett, who was Bragg's chief engineer at Shiloh, recalled being sent by Bragg to rally the brigade and to take its flag forward. "The flag must not go back again," said Bragg. When Lockett seized the Fourth Louisiana's colors, Colonel Allen objected. "What are you doing with my colors, sir?" asked Allen, who had been shot in both cheeks and had blood running from his mouth. Told of Bragg's order, Allen replied: "If any man but my color-bearer carries these colors, I am the man. Tell General Bragg I will see that these colors are in the right place. But he must attack this position in flank; we can never carry it alone from the front." [18]

Allen proved to be correct, but Bragg failed to act at the time on this advice or on requests for artillery support. Gibson stated: "I . . . sent Mr. Robert Pugh [who acted as Gibson's aide-de-camp at Shiloh] to the general after the first assault for artillery; but the request was not granted, and in place of it he brought me orders to advance again on the enemy." Colonel B. L Hodge of the Nineteenth Louisiana sent a staff officer to inform Bragg "that I thought it impossible to force the enemy from this strong position by a charge from the front, but that with a light battery playing on one flank and a simultaneous charge of infantry on the other the position could be carried with but small loss." Hodge concluded his report with the bitter comment: "I may be permitted to add, sir, that this formidable position of the enemy, after having withstood the repeated attacks of various regiments, was only carried at last by a charge upon the right flank, supported by a battery on the left." [19]

[18] S. H. Lockett, "Surprise and Withdrawal at Shiloh," *Battles and Leaders*, I, 605.
[19] *OR*, X (pt. 1), 483, 493.

Criticism of Bragg certainly was justified. He had made several serious tactical mistakes. In his desire to drive back the Federals, he forgot Mahan's warning about the dangers of frontal assaults on a strong position. Bragg had tried to overwhelm the enemy with the bayonet. He would have saved time and lives if he had immediately used enfilading artillery fire or infantry attacks on the enemy's flank, as some of his subordinates suggested. Even his frontal assaults were poorly conceived; they might have been more effective if the troops had been massed before they attacked. But Bragg sent them forward in driblets. Also, in anger and frustration, he made an unfair charge against Gibson and his men. "*Entre nous*," Bragg wrote Elise soon after the battle, "he [Gibson] is an *arrant coward*." This was untrue, as were many of Bragg's impulsive judgments; Gibson proved his courage in later battles. Nor were Bragg's harsh comments on Gibson's brigade justified. The unit lost 682 men, nearly a third of the brigade, at Shiloh.[20]

For several hours the Union defenders of the Hornets' Nest checked every Confederate assault. About 2:30 P.M. General Johnston, who had come forward to see the situation himself, was hit in the leg by a bullet and bled to death. Beauregard, upon whom command of the Confederate army devolved, was far from the front. Earlier some Kentuckians had seen him near Shiloh church "standing on a stump . . . he cheered the boys as we passed telling us we had them whipped and to fall in on them—keep cool and shoot low." When Beauregard learned of Johnston's death, he ordered that the attack be continued.[21]

After Johnston's death Bragg left the troops he had been with and rode toward the Confederate right flank. There,

[20] Bragg to Elise, April 8, 1862, Bixby Collection of Bragg Papers; *OR*, X (pt. 1), 466, 395, 481.
[21] *OR*, X (pt. 1), 464–65; Roland, *Johnston*, pp. 335–39; Nathan Parker Diary, April 6, 1862 (photostatic copy), University of Kentucky; G. T. Beauregard, "The Campaign of Shiloh," *Battles and Leaders*, I, 590.

facing one side of the Hornets' Nest, he found Withers's division; Benjamin F. Cheatham's division, of Polk's corps; and Breckinridge's corps—"without a common head." Bragg immediately took command. "I . . . gave them a talk," he later wrote, "moved forward the whole, with a general order, 'let everything be forward, and nothing but forward.' " [22]

Bragg's tactics were the same he had used earlier; he simply overwhelmed the Federals with repeated attacks. "Neither battery nor battalion could withstand . . . [our] onslaught," he wrote. It was not as easy as Bragg's report made it sound. Actually it was slow, bloody work. "The enemy advanced steadily in two lines, about 200 yards apart," wrote Union Colonel William T. Shaw of the Fourteenth Iowa Regiment. "I ordered my men to lie down and hold their fire until they were within thirty paces. The effect of this was, that when the order to fire was given, and the Twelfth and Fourteenth [Iowa] opened directly in their faces, the enemy's first line was completely destroyed." Still the Confederates advanced. Unit after unit crashed against the Federal lines. Gradually these attacks drove back the less favorably placed Union units and ultimately isolated the defenders of the Hornets' Nest. "We maintained . . . [our] position until 3 o'clock P.M.," recalled Colonel I. C. Pugh of the Forty-first Illinois Regiment, "when we fell back slowly, forming lines of battle frequently, and making great slaughter among the enemy. . . ." [23]

The brigades of Withers's division were particularly conspicuous in these attacks. Gladden's brigade remained in the fight despite the loss of its commander and his successor. One of the brigade's regiments suffered 67 per cent casualties; another, "exposed at times to a perfect hurricane of shot and shell," its commander noted, lost five different color bearers. "This was the fourth fight in which my brigade had been engaged during the day," recalled General James R. Chalmers,

[22] *OR*, X (pt. 1), 466; Bragg to Elise, April 8, 1862, Bixby Collection of **Bragg Papers.**
[23] *OR*, X (pt. 1), 466, 153, 212.

"and after a severe firing of some duration, finding the enemy stubbornly resisting, I rode back for General Jackson's brigade, which was lying down in reserve in my rear and to my left." Chalmers instructed his men "to lie down and rest until they received further orders"; he then followed Jackson's brigade back into battle, where he met "Bragg, commanding in the thickest of the fight." Soon some Confederate troops retreated in disorder, and Bragg shouted: "bring up Chalmers' brigade." Chalmers wrote: "I rode back immediately to where I had ordered my men to halt, and found that they had not understood the orders and had pressed on after the retreating foe. Riding rapidly after them, I reached them just after the enemy had raised the white flag. . . ." Finally, about 5 P.M., pressure by Polk and by Bragg on the flanks of the Hornets' Nest had forced what was left of Prentiss's command—some 2,200 men—to surrender. Their magnificent stand probably saved Grant's army.[24]

"The order was now given by General Bragg, who was present on the right during the fierce fight which ended in the capture of Prentiss, to sweep everything forward," remembered Withers, but the Confederates did not advance immediately. Some time passed while they disarmed Prentiss's command, organized, and sent them under guard to the rear. "Not only that," recalled a staff officer, "the news of the capture spread, and grew as it spread; many soldiers and officers believed we had captured the bulk of the Federal army, and hundreds left their positions and came to see the 'captured Yanks.'" Additional time was lost because some Confederate units had to replenish their ammunition. When, at last, the Confederates advanced, Bragg reported, the "sun was about disappearing."[25]

Yet he believed it was not too late to "sweep the enemy

[24] *Ibid.*, 533–34, 537–38, 541–42, 550, 408; Catton, *Terrible Swift Sword*, p. 236.
[25] *OR*, X (pt. 1), 533–34, 466, 550; Lockett, "Surprise and Withdrawal," p. 605.

from the field." A staff officer reported: "I was with General Bragg, and rode with him along the front of his corps. I heard him say over and over again, 'One more charge, my men, and we shall capture them all.' " Bragg explained to his wife two days later: ". . . we literally swept . . . [the enemy] before us capturing his camps, artillery, men, horses, arms &c. &c. One whole battery was brought to me with the officers, men & horses all complete, and marched to the rear as if on parade. It was a sight rarely seen, and very impressive. It was now nearly sun set. We were close on the bank of the river just above Pittsburg, the landing place, driving . . . [the enemy] back, full well." At this point Bragg's chief engineer remembered only a single enemy position still resisting, and the Confederates could see confused Union masses huddled near the river bank.[26]

Bragg's men were still advancing when a message arrived from Beauregard directing that the pursuit end. Colonel Lockett recalled that Beauregard's order, as relayed by the messenger, was: ". . . the victory is sufficiently complete; it is needless to expose our men to the fire of the gun-boats." Bragg reportedly cried: "My God, was a victory ever sufficiently complete? Have you given the order to any one else?" The messenger said he had. Bragg, looking to his left, saw Polk's forces withdrawing. "My God, my God, it is too late!" he sobbed.[27]

[26] OR, X (pt. 1), 466; Lockett, "Surprise and Withdrawal," p. 605; Bragg to Elise, April 8, 1862, Bixby Collection of Bragg Papers.

[27] Lockett, "Surprise and Withdrawal," p. 605. A member of Beauregard's staff told a completely different story, claiming Bragg rode to Beauregard's headquarters shortly after the Hornets' Nest fell and said in "an excited manner: 'General, we have carried everything before us to the Tennessee River. I have ridden from Owl to Lick Creek, and there is none of the enemy to be seen.' Beauregard quickly replied: 'Then, General, do not unnecessarily expose your command to the fire of the gun-boats.' " Alexander Robert Chisolm, "The Shiloh Battle-Order and the Withdrawal Sunday Evening," Battles and Leaders, I, 606. Other than Chisolm's reminiscence, there is no contemporary evidence that Bragg met Beauregard during the battle.

Bragg objected to the withdrawal order, though his words may not have been exactly as Lockett recalled them. "We drove the enemy from every position, captured nearly all his artillery, and were hotly pursuing him under my command when we were recalled," Bragg wrote Elise two days after the action. Beauregard, told by General Prentiss that the Federals "were defeated and en route across the river," thought "it best no doubt to spare our men, and allow them to go." When Bragg wrote his official report on April 20 he admitted that his troops were "exhausted by twelve hours of incessant fighting" at the time the order to withdraw arrived, but he insisted that a final attack had "every prospect of success." Years later, Johnston's son wrote that Bragg believed Beauregard's order cost the South the battle.[28]

Nor was Bragg the only officer surprised by the recall order. A fourth of the brigade commanders and a fifth of the regimental commanders operating under Bragg's supervision later reported that their men were "worn with fatigue," or were "quite exhausted," when the withdrawal order arrived, but most of the units Bragg commanded were moving forward at that time, and none of the corps or division commanders on the extreme right flank thought the assault should have been stopped. General Daniel Ruggles was "advancing toward the river" with a "considerable force" of stragglers he had assembled when a messenger stopped him with Beauregard's order to retreat. Ruggles could scarcely believe the messenger. General Jones M. Withers reported that he was carrying out Bragg's assault order when, to his "astonishment, a large portion of the command was observed to move . . . [away] from . . . the enemy. Orders were immediately sent to arrest the commanding officers and for the troops to be promptly placed in position for charging," wrote Withers. "Information was

[28] Johnston, "Albert Sidney Johnston at Shiloh," p. 568; Bragg to Elise, April 8, 1862, Bixby Collection of Bragg Papers; *OR*, X (pt. 1), 467.

soon brought, however, that it was . . . General Beauregard's order . . . that the troops [withdraw]. . . ." [29] Beauregard never explained precisely why he issued this withdrawal order. In a telegram to the War Department later that evening, he claimed the battle was over and the Confederates had won decisively: "We . . . gained a complete victory, driving the enemy from every position." In his report, written on April 11, he failed to say why he ended the attack, though he noted: "Darkness was close at hand; officers and men were exhausted. . . ." [30]

Beauregard's defenders have accepted their hero's opinion that the Confederates were too exhausted to destroy the enemy.[31] But such a view fails to explain how Beauregard, who was not with the attacking units, had a better knowledge of their condition than Bragg and most of the generals who were leading them.

Perhaps the best explanation of what happened is that Beauregard misunderstood the situation at the front. He knew that many Confederates were tired and disorganized, and he doubtless believed Prentiss's statement that the Federals were beaten; certainly that is what Beauregard wanted to believe. He must have thought that what remained of Grant's army was retreating across the river while Federal gunboats bombarded the advancing Confederates. Beauregard could see barrages landing between his position and his men, and he believed they were suffering unnecessarily from this shelling. Since the Confederates, who had no boats, could not pursue the Federals across the river, Beauregard decided to "withdraw the troops from under fire of the Federal gun-boats." Actually, though Beauregard did not know it, few of the enemy shells were hitting the Confederates. Bragg reported that the

[29] OR, X (pt. 1), 488, 491, 509, 522, 538, 546, 551, 480, 493, 499, 555, 472, 534.
[30] Ibid., 384, 387.   [31] Williams, Beauregard, pp. 141-42.

enemy's fire, "though terrific in sound and producing some consternation at first, did us no damage, as the shells passed over and exploded far beyond our positions." General Polk explained the situation more fully. He wrote that after his forces joined those of Bragg and Breckinridge "the field was clear; the . . . forces of the enemy were driven to the river and under its bank. We had one hour or more of daylight still left; were within from 150 to 400 yards of the enemy's position, and nothing seemed wanting to complete the most brilliant victory of the war but to press forward and make a vigorous assault on the demoralized remnant of his forces." At this juncture, enemy gunboats "opened a tremendous cannonade." The guns, elevated to fire over the high river bank, could hit only points some distance from the river's edge. "They were comparatively harmless to our troops nearest the bank," continued Polk, "and became increasingly so as we drew near the enemy. . . . Here the impression arose that our forces were waging an unequal contest; that they were exhausted and suffering from a murderous fire, and, by an order from the commanding general, they were withdrawn from the field." [32]

No one can be sure what the results would have been if Beauregard had let the fight continue. But before stopping it, he should have consulted the commanders at the front. He could not have known, of course, that by nightfall a fresh division had reinforced Grant's tired troops or that the first units of Buell's army were being ferried across the river. But Beauregard might have guessed as much; he should have realized that time was against the Confederates.

The Confederates spent the night of April 6 in considerable disarray. "Our force was disorganized, demolished, and exhausted," wrote Bragg; "hungry, some of them, because they were too lazy to hunt the enemy's camps for provisions." Most

[32] *OR*, X (pt. 1), 466, 410.

of the Confederate troops were "out of ammunition, and tho' millions of cartridges were around them, not one officer in ten supplied his men, relying on the enemy's retreat." Shortly after dark rain fell, adding to the low-spirited soldiers' discomfort, and making it impossible to assemble scattered units. At least 6,500 Confederates had been killed, wounded, or captured; that many more had strayed. Without orders or arrangements for the next day, troops bivouacked "where night overtook them." Polk marched with Cheatham's division back to where he had camped the previous night. Bragg and Beauregard shared a tent occupied the night before by Sherman.

Beauregard made few plans for the morrow. He appointed Bragg second-in-command of the army and wrote President Davis: "I earnestly and urgently recommend Major General Bragg for immediate appointment to General A. S. Johnston's place." Apparently, Beauregard meant he wanted Bragg promoted to full general rather than to army commander. Beauregard seemed confident of total victory the next day. He believed a false report that Buell's army was marching toward northern Alabama rather than Pittsburg Landing, and was so optimistic that he forgot one of Professor Mahan's favorite admonitions: to reconnoiter. Apparently Bragg forgot too. Colonel Nathan Bedford Forrest, who reported heavy Union reinforcements crossing the river to Hardee, was ordered to tell Beauregard. Unable to find the commander's headquarters, Forrest awoke Hardee again, but was told to return to his regiment and to keep watch.[33]

Confederate illusions of easy victory were shattered on April 7. Awakened by heavy firing, Bragg rushed to the left flank and took command of Ruggles's division and several units belonging to other corps. He ordered an attack that pushed the

[33] Bragg to Elise, April 8, 1862, Bixby Collection of Bragg Papers; OR, X (pt. 1), 384–85; Beauregard to Davis, April 6, 1862 (copy), Palmer Collection of Bragg Papers; Williams, Beauregard, pp. 143–44; Hughes, Hardee, pp. 109–10.

ATTACK ON A CONFEDERATE BATTERY, APRIL 7, 1862
Library of Congress

Federals back nearly a mile, and secured his left flank on a creek. Here Bragg formed a battleline across an open field and held his position against repeated assaults. "We fought them with . . . success for eight hours," he wrote, "our generals having to lead in person one half the troops." But about 2:00 P.M. the Confederate lines began to collapse. "Beauregard rallied several thousand," noted Bragg, "and formed a second line, behind mine, and when part of mine gave way, he led on the rear, but they would not stand. I rallied and led back a part of mine but it was no use. No earthly power would keep them up. My staff were imploring me not to expose myself so much, but there was no alternative." [34]

By early afternoon the Confederates were fought out. When the Second Texas, of Bragg's corps, was ordered to counterattack, it moved so slowly that General Hardee remarked: "Those men don't move as if they would fight." Soon the regiment broke and fled in disorder. Hardee instructed an aide: "Stop those men—the cowards." But the aide was unable "to rally the regiment or to induce a single man to return to the field." He told an officer and some men who were hiding behind a tree that Hardee considered them "a pack of cowards," but "they refused to stir; and when the officer was upbraided with his conduct . . . he replied that he didn't care a damn." [35]

Beauregard, who now considered the situation irremediable, ordered a general withdrawal. Bragg admitted to himself that "there was no hope of success against such odds," but he refused to retire until a staff officer sent to Beauregard confirmed the order. Bragg then took command of the army's rear guard. Captain William H. Ketchum of the Alabama State Artillery recalled "Bragg remaining with the battery up to the last moment of the fight, and after our infantry had withdrawn from the field, he ordered me to withdraw by sections in good order, covering the retreat, and taking position for any advance of the enemy." [36]

The enemy did not pursue in force; they were as exhausted as the Confederates. Years later Sherman said: "So help me God, you boys never had a fiercer fight than we had [at Shiloh]." In two days the Federals had suffered 13,000 casualties; the Confederates had lost nearly 11,000 men. Confederate losses in every corps were over 20 per cent of the men en-

[34] *OR,* X (pt. 1), 467; Bragg to Elise, April 8, 1862, Bixby Collection of Bragg Papers.
[35] *OR,* X (pt. 1), 571–73, 563–64. [36] *Ibid.,* 388, 467–68, 528.

gaged. Some units were nearly destroyed. Only one of the First Louisiana's thirty-five officers returned to Corinth with the army: twenty-three had fallen in battle; the others were missing. The regiment's total losses were 279 out of 440.[37]

"Our condition is horrible," wrote Bragg, who was in charge of the "irregular & disastrous" retreat. Hungry and demoralized, the troops clogged the muddy roads, throwing away blankets, knapsacks, and even rifles. Many wounded men and much ammunition were left behind, while "tents and officer's trunks filled the wagons." Some of the officers, complained Bragg, "had baggage enough for a trip to Saratoga." Abandoned artillery and wagons dotted the road, Bragg reported to Beauregard from three miles south of Mickey's the morning after the retreat began. "It is most lamentable to see the state of affairs," he admitted, "but I am powerless and almost exhausted." He had posted a rear guard at Mickey's under Breckinridge, but questioned how long the position could be held without supplies. Droves of famished soldiers had already deserted. When Beauregard sent no assistance, Bragg assigned working parties to do what they could to improve the roads and to salvage equipment and he proceeded to Corinth. He arrived shortly before 2 P.M. on April 8 and immediately sent out provisions, wagons, tools, and fresh troops. What was left of the army finally reached Corinth.[38]

The night he arrived in Corinth Bragg began a postmortem on Shiloh. "Our failure is due entirely to a want of discipline and a want of officers," he informed Elise. "Universal suffrage —furloughs & whiskey, have ruined us. If we fall it is our own fault." Later he gave additional reasons for Confederate defeat: Beauregard's poor planning, the loss of time following John-

37 *Ibid.*, 468, 108, 396; Lewis, *Sherman*, p. 232; Taylor Beatty Diary, April 8, 1862.
38 *OR*, X (pt. 2), 398–99; Bragg to Elise, April 8, 1862, Bixby Collection of Bragg Papers; Taylor Beatty Diary, April 7–8, 1862.

ston's death before the Confederate offensive resumed, and the arrival of Buell's troops.[39]

There is some merit in this analysis,[40] but it is incomplete because Bragg overlooked his own mistakes, his contribution to Confederate defeat at Shiloh. He had sent troops forward piecemeal in bayonet attacks against strongly held positions; for hours he had hammered away at stubborn Union defenders with frontal assaults instead of outflanking or bypassing them. The tragedy for the Confederacy was not that Bragg had lied or tried to hide these tactical mistakes from others; it was his total unawareness that he had made any errors. Nor was he alone. Hardee, who had written a book on tactics, wrote three days after Shiloh: "I am not so much impressed as many respecting the invincibility of our volunteers & of their determination to be free—they are good for the dash, but fail in tenacity. I don't think we can yet regard ourselves as soldiers —our men are not sufficiently impressed with a sense of honor that it is better to die by far than to run." A reporter wrote from the battlefield that "Bragg has . . . most admirably . . . handled [his men] . . . throughout the entire day. Gallant and chivalric, yet cool and sagacious, he knows, when and where to plant his terrible blows." And scarcely a month after Shiloh the editor of an army newspaper advised troops:

[39] Bragg to Elise, April 8, 1862, Bixby Collection of Bragg Papers; *OR*, X (pt. 1), 469–70. After the war Bragg continued to censure Beauregard's actions at Shiloh. "Johnston decides on battle and gives the general outline of his plan," wrote Bragg. "This is elaborated by a subordinate who mars it by faulty details, then opposes execution and predicts failure. The chief boldly determines to execute [the plan anyway] and leads his forces to a brilliant victory—falling in the moment of triumph. That wonderful victory is rapidly converted by a successor into disaster. . . ." Bragg to William Preston Johnston, December 16, 1874, Barret Collection of Johnston Papers.

[40] The Confederates definitely were hampered by a poor arrangement of forces, but the delay which followed Johnston's death may not have been as important in the battle's outcome as Bragg thought. Yet the delay occurred at a crucial moment and gave the Federals time to regroup. The arrival of Buell's force, of course, was decisive.

"Whenever it is necessary to charge, charge impetuously. No Federal regiment can withstand a bold and fearless bayonet charge. We believe that when every ounce of powder and lead is shot away, our army, if properly drilled, will really be stronger than it ever was. The greatest minds in the South are coming to the conclusion, that our liberties are to be won by the bayonet. Those regiments or companies that most distinguished themselves in bayonet charges will march on the true road to honor and preferment." [41] Bragg, like most of his contemporaries, completely missed the major tactical lesson of Shiloh—that frontal bayonet attacks were too costly against determined riflemen occupying a naturally strong defensive position and supported by artillery firing grape or canister.

The "valuable lesson" Bragg did learn at Shiloh, "by which we should profit," he stated in his report, was "never on a battle-field to lose a moment's time, but leaving the killed, wounded, and spoils to those whose special business it is to care for them, to press on with every available man, giving a panic-stricken and retreating foe no time to rally, and reaping all the benefits of a success never complete until every enemy is killed, wounded or captured." [42] An important lesson, to be sure, but scarcely so vital to the fate of the Confederacy as the one Bragg missed.

[41] William J. Hardee to Mrs. Felicia Lee Shover, April 9, 1862, Hardee Papers; Richmond *Daily Enquirer*, April 19, 1862; Corinth *Missouri Army Argus*, May 12, 1862.
[42] *OR*, X (pt. 1), 470.

CHAPTER XII

Round into Tennessee

APRIL 9–JULY 28, 1862

W HILE THE ARMY recuperated at Corinth, Bragg received considerable praise. A newspaper announced: "Gen. Bragg and staff were the last to leave the ground, though he was frequently urged before to retire, saying that he would never leave the battlefield so long as one of his soldiers remained before him. His heroic valour and generalship throughout the battle has won for him imperishable fame." On April 12 Jefferson Davis appointed Bragg a full general, the fifth ranking officer in the entire Confederacy.[1] Governor John Gill Shorter of Alabama proclaimed Bragg "a master genius," congratulating him "for the brilliant part performed" at Shiloh, his efforts to organize the army, and his promotion. "The honored title of *General* was proudly won and the country rejoices that it was so promptly bestowed." A poem honoring Bragg was published, and several citizens demanded that he be given command of Confederate forces in Louisiana. Governor Moore sent word that he had more confidence in Bragg than in any "other military (or civil) man." [2] Congressman Jabez L.M. Curry of Alabama also applauded Bragg. "It is for less noticeable achievements that I desire espe-

[1] New Orleans *Daily Picayune*, April 18, 1862; George W. Randolph to Bragg, April 15, 1862 (telegram), Palmer Collection of Bragg Papers; document in George Wythe Randolph Collection, Chicago Historical Society.

[2] Shorter to Bragg, April 22, 1862, Palmer Collection of Bragg Papers unidentified and undated newspaper clipping in Kirkpatrick Scrapbook, Alabama Department of Archives; John Williams to Bragg, May 17, 1862. Palmer Collection of Bragg Papers; Thomas C. Manning to Bragg, May 5, 1862, *ibid*.

cially to assure you of the cordial gratitude of one man," wrote Curry. "The high state of discipline, and thorough organization of the men under your command, acquired and maintained under such disadvantages," impressed the congressman. "The rigid impartiality with which all have been required to conform to regulations essential to success: the commendable efforts to secure a loftier moral sentiment and the abandonment of personal vices . . . the Napoleonic energy with which resources have been deduced, when the government was weak or remiss in supplying them, have challenged my admiration, and I rejoice and take courage at the fact, that the Confederacy has an officer so capable and so successful." A religious soldier lauded Bragg for encouraging troops to attend church services; a nun blessed him for the preparations made for his sick and wounded, and trusted that "our dear Lord will protect you and all your undertakings." A soldier, thanking his homefolk for what they had sent him, wrote: "The whiskey you may depend will be used moderately as I belong to the Temperance Society of whom Gen Braxton Bragg is president." [3]

Bragg also received some criticism. Resentment against him grew among volunteers who had been kept in the service by the newly enacted Conscription Act after their one-year enlistment had expired. Bragg strictly enforced the law; he granted no furloughs. Several newspapers denounced his "uncalled-for brutality, and unjust and improper treatment of volunteers." Some soldiers supported Bragg, but others, especially those in certain Tennessee regiments, hated him. Rumors spread that he was "fishing for favour at the War Department, and it was hinted that he was trying to undermine and super-

[3] Curry to Bragg, May 14, 1862, Palmer Collection of Bragg Papers; Richard L. Pugh to Mary Williams Pugh, May 20, 1862, Richard L. Pugh Papers, Louisiana State University; Sister Philomena to Bragg, May 25, 1862, Palmer Collection of Bragg Papers; Isaac Alexander to His Family, June 27, 1862, quoted in Bell Irvin Wiley, *The Life of Johnny Reb* (Indianapolis, 1943), p. 187.

sede" Beauregard. Denied furloughs, the men in one Tennessee regiment "laid down their arms and refused duty." Bragg had the men surrounded and "gave them five minutes to take up their arms and return to duty," recalled Private William Watson. The Tennesseeans "sullenly obeyed, each muttering to himself that it would be but little service that he would ever get out of them, and this was true." Watson noted that a "good many deserted, but some were caught attempting to desert . . . and were summarily shot without any trial." Only a few days after the Tennesseeans were forced to return to duty, Watson "first observed something like secret disaffection among the troops." Men discussed "the state of affairs and the action of General Bragg," continued Watson, "and I heard something like propositions that the whole army should break up . . . and march off in bands, taking their arms with them; and they seemed to be sounding the feeling among the different divisions." [4]

When Elise heard criticism of Bragg she begged him to defend himself. "Conscious of having done your duty, of having too, borne the duties & burdens of others, you are indifferent to public praise or blame," she wrote. "But is that right or fair? If you are silent & require others to be so, your power of doing good, the sphere of doing your duty, will be circumscribed. . . ." Now that Bragg was a full general, Elise reasoned: "Your usefulness is thereby increased, & you are relieved from obeying the commands of our vain glorious Bishop [Polk]. What you can *now do*, or indeed any one, is the important question." [5]

What the Confederates would do depended upon what the Federals attempted. Beauregard's scouts reported that General Henry W. Halleck, commander of all Union forces in the West, had arrived at Pittsburg Landing and was starting to-

[4] William Watson, *Life in the Confederate Army* . . . (London, 1887), pp. 368–70. See also Watkins, *"Co. Aytch,"* pp. 71–72.
[5] Elise to Bragg, April 15, 1862, Mrs. Bragg Collection.

ward Corinth with over 100,000 men. It might be possible to stop them. The Corinth defenses were strong; after Van Dorn's forces arrived in mid-April the trenches were filled with over 50,000 Confederates. "No one must fall back unless compelled to . . . do so," Beauregard announced; "we are fighting for our homes and firesides. When necessary, one place is as good as another to die." [6] But Beauregard did not wait passively in his trenches for the Federals.

Twice he tried to divide and destroy part of Halleck's army as it advanced. Early in May General John Pope rashly pushed his force ahead of the main Union mass. Part of Bragg's corps went out to attack Pope while some of Van Dorn's forces moved to assail his rear. "You are again about to encounter the mercenary invader who pollutes the sacred soil of our beloved country," read Bragg's pre-assault proclamation to his troops. "We have, then, but to strike and destroy, and, as the enemy's whole resources are concentrated here, we shall not only redeem Tennessee, Kentucky, and Missouri at one blow, but open the portals of the whole Northwest." If Bragg really expected that an attack on one part of Halleck's army would accomplish so much, he deceived himself; if not, he deceived his troops. Probably the optimistic predictions of his proclamation were merely Bragg's idea of how to build his men's morale. If Confederate hopes rose, they fell soon enough. Bragg's men advanced on time, but Pope escaped from the planned trap because Van Dorn's troops did not get into position soon enough. Later Pope again exposed some units; Bragg's forces attacked the Federals, but Van Dorn's men could not get into action.[7]

These frustrations plus the usual strains of campaigning began to tell on Bragg. In late April Thomas Bragg noted that his brother's "health is not good." Elise, about the same time, became aware that her husband's letters reflected "the deepest

[6] OR, X (pt. 2), 146–51, 436, 439, 440, 443, 465, 451.
[7] Ibid., 484–91, 502–7, 517–21, 523–41; (pt. 1), 674, 803–4, 807–15, 852–55, 762–63.

despair." She tried to cheer him. "Rouse & be yourself again," she urged. "If we are to have a S[outhern] Confederacy you will be spared, for it cannot be without you—if we are not, you will not wish to live, nor I either." He must take courage, she added, from her little niece, who often sang, "I bet my money on Braxton Bragg." [8]

Beauregard, whose health was as bad as Bragg's, was no more optimistic; nor had a meeting with his highest ranking generals on May 25 made him feel better, for they had advised, and Beauregard had agreed, that Corinth must be abandoned. Otherwise the Confederates would be trapped in the town and captured. They could either stay until Corinth was surrounded, or retreat before the siege began. Beauregard decided to move immediately. "But everything that is done must be done under the plea of the intention to take the offensive," he explained. "Every commandant of corps must get everything ready to move at a moment's notice, and must see to the proper condition of the roads and bridges his corps is to travel upon." [9]

The retreat began on May 29. To avoid panic Confederate leaders spread a rumor among the troops that they were about to advance. Heavy equipment and the sick and wounded started south by rail. Bragg took charge at the railroad depot. "It will be impossible to save all," he informed Beauregard at 11:30 A.M. on May 29. "Army, ammunition, and the sick, I fear, will be all we can do; but hospital things and provisions will be saved if possible. I find trunks enough here to load all trains for a day. They are being piled for burning, and great is the consternation. My [body]guard have . . . to prevent plundering; but all is going on well. If we had trains, all could be well by 12 o'clock to-night; but there is great want of cars," Bragg lamented. "Nothing in our power will be left undone. It is the first time I have played chief quarter-master,

[8] Thomas Bragg Diary, April 28, 1862; Elise to Bragg, April 20, 1862, Mrs. Bragg Collection.
[9] OR, X (pt. 2), 544–47.

but it is no difficult task." By 1 A.M. on May 30 the whole
army was under way. Left behind was a token force, which
spent the night traveling up and down the lines in a train.
Stopping frequently, the men cheered loudly to give the impression that reinforcements were arriving. "Deserters" had
been sent through the lines with "confidential information"
that the Confederates would attack the next day. Before the
ruse was discovered Beauregard's army was miles away.[10]

The Confederates reached Tupelo, some fifty miles south of
Corinth, on June 9 without serious difficulty. On the first day
of the retreat, Bragg reported from his camp fifteen miles
south of Corinth that his rear guard was holding back the
enemy's cavalry, but six trains loaded with supplies had been
lost. They were late leaving and did not reach the Tuscumbia
River bridge until just after it had been burned. Bragg believed
the march to Tupelo improved the "moral and physical" condition of his troops. Nevertheless, many men straggled, and
Bragg had to issue orders against the "indiscriminate pillage of
the country," and the "practice of officers and soldiers billet-
ing themselves upon citizens." He promised that offenders
would receive "the severest penalty known to the military
code." A soldier recalled passing nearly a thousand men who
had dropped out of ranks and were lying in the woods. "We at
first thought they were the rear-guard," wrote William Watson. "They were quite indifferent and defiant, and said they
were going no further with Bragg, and told us if we saw Bragg
that day to tell him to come back and see them, and they
would make a bargain with him. I quite believe they would,
and it would have been a final settlement so far as Bragg was
concerned." [11]

At Tupelo Bragg's popularity continued to decline. One

[10] Ibid., 557; (pt. 1), 762–73; Williams, Beauregard, p. 154.
[11] OR, X (pt. 2), 563, 570, 574, 576, 580, 588, 601; Watson, Life in the
Confederate Army, p. 378. Other accounts mention the desertion of
Tennessee troops; see, for example, John Buckner to Mrs. Simon B.
Buckner, June 24, 1862, Simon B. Buckner Papers, Huntington Library.

soldier wrote in his diary: "Genl Bragg is trying to get the army under strict discipline—he is not liked much by the boys on account of having several men shot for being absent without leave and desertion." A Tennesseean boasted of violating Bragg's orders against stealing from civilians and then complained bitterly when culprits were whipped. Private Sam Watkins heard that Bragg was having men shot every day, although he actually saw only two executions. "So far as patriotism was concerned," wrote Watkins, "we had forgotten all about that, and did not now so much love our country as we feared Bragg." [12]

There was reason to fear Bragg for he never hesitated to shoot deserters. "A deserter . . . attempted this morning to join the enemy, but was captured and promptly executed," Bragg wrote Beauregard on May 22. But Bragg was not as bloodthirsty as some people believed. Mary Boykin Chesnut noted in her diary that Bragg had executed a soldier for shooting a chicken. This story caused considerable indignation; like so many others told about Bragg, claimed Colonel David Urquhart, it was false. "At Tupelo," wrote Urquhart, "an order had been issued forbidding the men firing their muskets when in camp. One of the volunteers shooting at a chicken killed a man; he was tried and shot, not, as unjustly stated, for disobedience of orders, but for killing a man." [13]

After the spring of 1862, however, many people believed that Bragg was unmerciful. A soldier claimed Bragg "sedulously avoided giving public evidence of the tender feeling which he entertained for the suffering and unfortunate"; most men knew him only as "an earnest military disciplinarian and chieftain of rough and somewhat forbidding exterior," but no man who came to Bragg "appealing for justice or pleading for

[12] John Euclid Magee Diary, June 10, 1862, Duke University; Watkins, "Co. Aytch," pp. 76–78.

[13] OR, X (pt. 2), 538; Chesnut, A Diary from Dixie, p. 268; Urquhart, "Bragg's Advance and Retreat," Battles and Leaders, III, 609. Stout (Reminiscences, p. 12) claimed a drunk soldier wounded a Negro child.

mercy, ever went away unheard or without a prompt and decisive answer, if the facts . . . were fully and fairly stated." Colonel J. Stoddard Johnston, who served on Bragg's staff, wrote: "I was too frequently cognizant of his good deeds of mercy to delinquents, for light offenses, and commutations, reprieves, and pardon for capital ones to let him rest under the imputation of a heartless man, or one who wielded his great power cruelly." [14]

Shortly after the troops reached Tupelo Bragg had the opportunity to exercise even more power than ever before; he replaced Beauregard as army commander. On June 14 Bragg received a telegram from Richmond directing him to relieve General Mansfield Lovell, who had recently surrendered New Orleans to the Federals. Beauregard, quite ill and at odds with the President, refused to let Bragg leave. He could not be spared, Beauregard informed Davis; Bragg must command at Tupelo while Beauregard took a short rest. The following day Beauregard departed for an Alabama health resort. Bragg, who was on friendly terms with both Beauregard and Davis, realized he was in an awkward position. He immediately wired Richmond for instructions, and wrote a letter explaining why he had not relieved Lovell. Back came a telegram on June 20 assigning Bragg permanent command of the Western department.[15]

Bragg seemed somewhat embarrassed. "I envy you and am almost in despair," he informed Beauregard, who replied: "I cannot congratulate you, but am happy for the change." He offered Bragg the temporary use of his staff, and later spoke of him as "a personal friend, of whom I know not a superior in

[14] Stout, *Reminiscences*, pp. 21, 7; Stoddard Johnston quoted in Johnston, *Life of A. S. Johnston*, p. 547.

[15] OR, XVII (pt. 2), 599, 601, 606, 614; Bragg to Davis, June 19, 1862, Bragg Papers, Duke University. On July 4, 1862, Thomas Bragg wrote in his diary: "Beauregard has been relieved from command on account of ill health & Gen'l Bragg now commands. . . . I learn that . . . the change is favorably regarded, it is said, by all."

the service." With equal grace, Bragg wrote that no "two men living ever served together more harmoniously or parted with more regret. And few men possess my confidence & esteem to the same extent, as a General & a Gentleman. None of us are free from our faults & weaknesses, but among mine will never be found a jealousy which would detract from so pure a man and eminent a General as Beauregard." Either Bragg was being less than candid, or he had forgotten his former jealousy of Beauregard. Bragg admitted, nevertheless, that "Genl Beauregard has never been physically equal to the labors of his position since I joined him in March last, and has often said to me he could not get on with its labors without the cordial & earnest assistance I gave him. Our intercourse was daily, free, unrestrained and as harmonious as if we had been brothers. Upon the urgent appeal of his physicians, after arriving here, when it was supposed we should not be assailed by the enemy for a few weeks, he retired to seek some relief from the toils which have made him an old man in the short space of one year." [16]

Bragg may not have realized that he could expect a similar fate, but he did know he faced a mass of problems. No new enemy advance seemed imminent, but army morale was low, and desertion was still a problem. Nor was it easy to feed soldiers at Tupelo. With most of the area west of the Mississippi cut off, food was scarce and citizens (especially those visited by pillagers) were reluctant to sell at prices the army would pay. Wagons had deteriorated, and were difficult to replace. The loss of Corinth had severed direct rail communications between Mississippi and the East, severely handicapping the army's mobility. Bragg, certain that any strategic movement of troops eastward depended upon adequate rail connections through the central Confederacy, urged imme-

[16] Williams, *Beauregard*, pp. 159, 162; Bragg to John Forsyth, July 17, 1862 (copy), Braxton Bragg Papers, Samuel Richey Confederate Collection, Miami University, Oxford, Ohio.

diate completion of an unfinished railroad between Meridian, Mississippi, and Selma, Alabama. When the government apparently ignored his suggestion, he seized the railroad property, but returned it when company officials agreed to let his appointee act as general military superintendent of the project.[17]

Bragg believed the army's major weakness was a lack of capable officers. Too many promising young officers had been killed at Shiloh or driven from the service by what Bragg called "the elective feature of the conscript law." To improve the quality of commanders, he established brigade promotion boards which promoted good officers on the company and regimental levels. He struck at the conscript law, which allowed units to elect their officers and to displace rigid disciplinarians, by arbitrarily stipulating that if the elected officers were not accredited by the brigade boards the "elective franchise would be considered exhausted." Bragg was no less dissatisfied with his senior officers. After he had sent Van Dorn and Breckinridge to check the Federal advance on the Mississippi River, Bragg reported that Hardee was the only "suitable" major general "now present." Such a remark was a deliberate slap at Polk, whose military ability Bragg distrusted. Bragg also considered seven other generals unqualified: Major Generals George B. Crittenden, Benjamin F. Cheatham, and John P. McCown, and Brigadier Generals William H. Carroll, James M. Hawes, Lucius M. Walker, and James H. Trapier. Five of these men were West Point graduates. "Among the junior brigadiers we have some excellent material," wrote Bragg, "but it is comparatively useless, being overshadowed. Could the [War] Department by any wholesome exercise of power or policy relieve this army from a part of this dead-weight it would surely give confidence to the troops and add much to

[17] For a more detailed account of the Meridian-Selma project, see Robert C. Black III, *The Railroads of the Confederacy* (Chapel Hill, 1952), pp. 156–57.

our efficiency." Bragg did what little he could to improve the situation. He deprived Polk of the active control of troops by assigning him as second-in-command of Bragg's department. This enabled Bragg to give Hardee command of all the forces that had fought at Shiloh.[18] The problem of army organization was allied with the difficulty of finding competent officers. Many regiments had few men on the rolls. Bragg suggested the consolidation of some regiments and the discharge of less efficient officers, but such actions—as President Davis's special inspector, Colonel William Preston Johnston, observed—was "not in accordance with the law." [19]

No law prevented Bragg from reorganizing his staff. "Persevering and industrious as he was in his efforts to organize the staff," wrote a contemporary, "it is no wonder that . . . Bragg's enemies, who were smarting under the lash of his discipline, were . . . spreading falsehoods about him. They often spoke of him as 'tigerish,' and bloodthirsty. They distorted facts and invented stories in confirmation of their unfavorable opinion of him." [20]

On June 27 Congressman Jabez L. M. Curry protested that Bragg, whom he had praised a month before, had prohibited the election of officers in his army and caused discontent among his troops. Although Curry admitted that he had voted against the election bill, he nevertheless insisted that the law be enforced. Adjutant General Samuel Cooper forwarded a copy of Curry's protest to Bragg, adding: "charges of this sort have become so frequent, as greatly to concern the President, and the Department. The Department is far from giving credit to these allegations, but considers it due to you that you should have an opportunity to refute them." [21]

Bragg replied that he had been attacked because he denied

[18] OR, XVII (pt. 2), 647–48.   [19] Ibid., 627–28, 673; X (pt. 1), 780.
[20] Ibid., XVII (pt. 2), 648; Stout, Reminiscences, p. 12.
[21] Cooper to Bragg, July 10, 1862, Palmer Collection of Bragg Papers.

Curry a staff position. "I had no use for fawning sycophants on my staff or in my command," Bragg informed Davis. Nor did Bragg conceal his disagreement with the government's policy of allowing troops to elect their own officers: "I have not hesitated to express my opinion, and to declare, I had neither the capacity nor the desire to command troops, where the officers were made subservient to the men by this disorganizing and ever recurring universal suffrage." Yet, "however much I may regret the injury resulting to our discipline and efficiency," he continued, "the laws will be enforced to the extent of my ability." Doubtless there were some dissatisfied officers and men in the army, Bragg admitted, "but, that they exist to any extent, I do not believe, except with those who were last in the victories and foremost in the retreats." He hoped that if any congressmen visited his army they would not come as Curry had to "pervert facts, assert falsehood, and engender discord and mutiny." [22]

What Bragg may not have realized was that his honeymoon with Congress and the press was over. For over a year he had received little but praise from politicians and reporters. No longer would Bragg be exempted; in fact, each month after July 1862, he came increasingly under attack—sometimes unjustly, but not always. Curry's criticism was merely a hint of what was ahead for Bragg.[23]

Bragg's methods, despite some discontent and criticism, improved the condition of his forces. "A thorough reorganization of the whole army took place [under Bragg], and constant

[22] Bragg to Davis, July 31, 1862, James A. Seddon Papers, Duke University; Bragg to Davis, July 5, 1862 (copy), Palmer Collection of Bragg Papers.

[23] John Bragg blamed Thomas H. Watts, whom Braxton had arrested at Corinth, for an Alabama newspaper's attack on Braxton in July, but Jefferson Davis thought William L. Yancey was responsible. See Thomas Bragg Diary, July 18, August 8, 1862; Jefferson Davis to Braxton Bragg, August 5, 1862, Richey Collection of Bragg Papers.

drill was our daily avocation," noted John Magee. "The health of the whole army improved materially." Private William Watson agreed, and even Sam Watkins, the Tennesseean who hated Bragg, admitted that the "troops . . . recovered their health and spirits." In July Lieutenant John H. Maury wrote: "There has been a marvelous change for the better in the condition, health, discipline & drill of the troops of this army since it left Corinth, it was a perfect rabble there, & would I think have done much more running than fighting, if they had been put to the scratch." Bragg alone was responsible for this improvement, thought Colonel Philip B. Spence: "Under this stern, strict disciplinarian the army was soon greatly improved, and the morale and spirits of the men were as cheerful as before our disastrous defeat on the second day's battle at Shiloh. Officers and men at this time had the utmost confidence in Gen. Bragg." A soldier concurred. "Bragg is beyond doubt the best disciplinarian in the South," wrote John Buie. "When he took command . . . the Army was little better than a Mob. The din of Firearms could be heard at all hours of the day. *Now* a gun is never fired without orders from the Brigade Commanders. Bragg had one man shot for discharging his gun without orders. . . . Since that time the discipline of the troops was improved very much. Men are not apt to disobey orders when they know death is the punishment." On July 15 Colonel William Preston Johnston reported to the President: "The discipline of the army seems excellent. The ordinary forms of respect to officers seem cheerfully paid. The respect for private property is very creditable." "The older regiments," Johnston continued, "show great skill and promptness in drill and the progress of the new levies is satisfactory. The daily exercise occupies five hours, which is ample. The carriage of the men is soldierly and guard duty is apparently well performed. The great improvement which I learn has been made since the retreat from Corinth in these details, as well as in police and other duties, is due in some measure to the better and more rigid system of inspection that has been inaugurated." [24]

Bragg was pleased with what he had accomplished. "The great changes of command & commanders here has well nigh overburdened me," he wrote Elise, "but . . . I . . . hope yet to mark the enemy before I break down. Since our arrival here great and marked improvement has taken place in the Army, so that we are now in a high state of efficiency, health and tone. We shall be on the move very soon and you may expect to hear from us before very long." [25]

What Bragg had in mind was an offensive. In early June the huge Union army that had captured Corinth broke up. Forces under Generals Grant, Sherman, and William S. Rosecrans still threatened central Mississippi, but an army commanded by Buell was moving across northern Alabama along the line of the Memphis & Chattanooga Railroad toward Chattanooga, Tennessee. When Bragg learned of this division of Union forces, he knew he should act. But it was difficult for him to decide what to do. The Confederate commander in East Tennessee, Major General Edmund Kirby Smith, lacked sufficient men to stop Buell. If Bragg went to Smith's aid would this open central Mississippi to invasion? And if Grant could not be held in northern Mississippi what would happen to Van Dorn at Vicksburg? He was strong enough to guard the river approaches to the town, but doubtless he could not withstand attack from two sides. On the other hand, loss of Chattanooga would open the road to Georgia and might ultimately divide the Confederacy. To Smith's appeal for help, Bragg sent

[24] John Euclid Magee Diary, July 23, 1862; Watson, *Life in the Confederate Army*, pp. 381, 385–86; Watkins, "*Co. Aytch*," p. 79; John H. Maury to Matthew F. Maury, July 29, 1862, Richard L. Maury Papers, Duke University; *Confederate Veteran*, VIII (1900), 500; John Buie to His Father, September 30, 1862, John Buie Papers, Duke University; *OR*, X (pt. 1), 781.

[25] Bragg to Elise, July 22, 1862, Bixby Collection of Bragg Papers.

McCown's division (3,000 men) to Chattanooga by rail on
June 27 as a stopgap, but when Colonel William Preston John-
ston left Tupelo on July 4 Bragg was still undecided where to
strike his major blow. "He deliberated between attacking at
Corinth and leaving that [Federal] army behind to cross the
Tennessee and attack Buell," Johnston informed President
Davis. "The danger of the latter plan was, being assailed while
crossing [the river]. . . ." Johnston believed Bragg favored
"attacking the enemy on the flank by a movement . . . on
Corinth." [26]

Perhaps Bragg had favored an attack on Corinth, but he
soon changed his mind. As early as June 24 Bragg had written
to Van Dorn that "no greater disaster could befall" the Confederacy than the loss of Chattanooga. By July 22 Bragg had
decided to shift half of his army to Chattanooga. Such a move,
he informed Beauregard, would allow Bragg, "in conjunction
with Major General Smith, to strike an effective blow through
Middle Tennessee, gaining the enemy's rear, cutting off his
supplies and dividing his forces so as to encounter them in
detail." [27]

One reason why Bragg decided to invade Tennessee from
Chattanooga may have been a suggestion he received from
Elise. She had constantly urged him to advance. In March she
wrote: "Use all your influence dear Husband . . . to *advance*
when we can." In April she advised: "if the enemy retreat,
pursue until you are before *Cincinnati*." And on June 8 she
concluded that of "all the fatal mistakes we have committed
during this war, none will prove so disastrous as a *Fabian
policy*—what was done in the heathenish days of Rome, will
not answer in the nineteenth century, with R. Roads, rivers,

[26] OR, XVI (pt. 2), 681, 695, 701, 709; XVII (pt. 2), 626, 629, 630, 656;
X (pt. 1), 785.
[27] Bragg to Van Dorn, June 24, 1862, Miscellaneous Personal Papers,
Library of Congress; OR, LII (pt. 2), 331. See also Bragg's letter to
Cooper of July 23, 1862, *ibid.*, XVII (pt. 2), 656.

steam navigation. . . . Why not . . . take our army round into Tennessee & thence into Kentucky. You leave our enemy in your rear—true, but is not that better than an enemy in your midst, starvation." [28] It is of course impossible to determine if this strategic concept was Elise's own idea or merely one she had learned from Bragg.

Another likely reason for Bragg's decision to go to Chattanooga was the successful movement of McCown's men. Bragg apparently had two things in mind when he sent these troops: to reinforce Smith, and to test the feasibility of moving a larger force east by rail. Bragg selected McCown's division because he considered the men poorly disciplined and their commander incompetent. "I must urge on you the propriety of assuming command in person at Chattanooga," Bragg wrote Smith. "The officer I sent you, I regret to say, cannot be trusted with such a command, and I implore you not to intrust him . . . with any important position. New Madrid fell by his errors and want of decision and firmness . . . while other prominent instances . . . of his want of capacity and nerve . . . have been brought to my notice." If McCown's division could make the trip successfully, other units would have no difficulty. The journey, via Mobile, Montgomery, and Atlanta, was woefully circuitous, covering 776 miles over six railroads. Through trains could not be used because some of the roads were of different gauge, and troops had to cross Mobile Bay on ferries. Careful planning, however, got the first trainload of McCown's men to Chattanooga just six days after orders for the movement had been issued. [29]

On July 23 additional units began the trip. In all Bragg ordered some 30,000 soldiers to Chattanooga; he left Major General Sterling Price with 16,000 troops at Tupelo to support

[28] Elise to Bragg, March 16, April 2, 1862, Palmer Collection of Bragg Papers; Elise to Bragg, June 8, 1862, Eliza Brooks Bragg Collection, Chicago Historical Society.
[29] *OR*, XVII (pt. 2), 651; Black, *Railroads of the Confederacy*, p. 181.

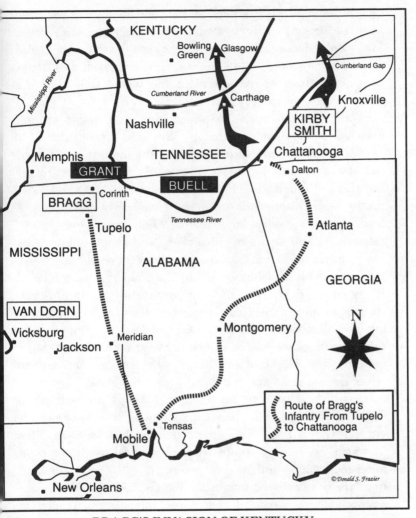

BRAGG'S INVASION OF KENTUCKY

Van Dorn's 16,000 men at Vicksburg. The overall plan, Bragg informed Adjutant General Cooper, was to unite his force with Smith's army and move between Buell and his supply base at Nashville. At the same time, Van Dorn and Price would combine their armies and invade western Tennessee. Most of Bragg's infantry would travel over the same route McCown's division had taken; the artillery, cavalry, and wagon trains would follow more direct, dirt roads to Chatta- nooga, for Bragg dared not place the whole weight of the movement on the rickety railroads.[30]

On the whole, it was a disciplined trip. "Your transports and detached portions of your troops have been passing daily for more than two weeks through one of the interior counties of this state . . . and I have been pleased at the generally re- spectful and orderly conduct of the teamsters, and the gentle- manly bearing and deportment of most of the officers and men," wrote a resident of Alabama. "The policy you inaugu- rated of putting a stop to debauchery and drunkenness in the army and as far as possible among volunteers on the highways has been of incalculable service to the country," he informed Bragg. "Before then, our now comparatively quiet and orderly steamboats and railroad cars presented daily the most disgust- ing and demoralizing scenes." But not all of Bragg's men moved as quickly or were as well behaved as this report might indicate. John Magee, whose battery took twenty-two days to cover the 432 miles across country, recorded in his diary what appears to have been an enjoyable trip. Magee ate well, often free, in hotels or homes; he went swimming at least five times, got his watch fixed, and attended several dances. At Blue Mountain Station the troops were entertained by "some right good musicians"—and "a great many ladies"; Magee admitted that "the boys enjoyed themselves hugely." At Aberdeen, Mis- sissippi, Magee wrote: "There was some lewd women in town—some of the boys were about them all night." In an- other town the officers got "up a dance," but "many of them

[30] OR, XVII (pt. 2), 656–57. Both Van Dorn and Price understood that an invasion of western Tennessee was an important part of Bragg's plan and they promised to cooperate. See ibid., 662, 664–66, 675; Van Dorn to Bragg, July 24, 1862, Palmer Collection of Bragg Papers. The best biography of Van Dorn is Robert G. Hartje's Van Dorn: The Life and Times of a Confederate General (Nashville, 1967).

got drunk and behaved very badly," and in Talladega, Alabama, several soldiers "got tight and wanted to fight." At one point, after his unit had moved on, Magee stopped with a friendly family for "3 or 4 hours, had a long talk—read poetry —heard music on the Piano," and enjoyed himself "very much." Several times officers fired cannons for the amusement of women who gathered to see the troops. Taylor Beatty, whose company went by rail as Bragg's escort, mentioned no such entertainment, but he did note one unpleasant incident. "Left Mobile at 3 P.M.," he wrote on July 27. "At the R. R. had a difficulty with an unknown Captain of a Texas regiment who insulted me because I ordered him out of the cars. I had to slap him." [31]

Despite these and probably a few other lapses in discipline by the men, Bragg had reason to rejoice. When his first infantry units reached Chattanooga on July 29 Buell's army was still miles away. [32] Bragg had moved men farther faster than troops had ever been moved before; he had united two armies whose direct line of communication had been severed by the enemy. More important, Bragg's strategic use of the railroad had reversed the direction of the war. No longer were southern leaders confronted with only the objectionable alternatives of retreating before overwhelming odds or attacking strongly held Union positions. Not only were Buell's flank and rear exposed; all Federal armies in the lower Mississippi Valley— Buell's, Grant's, Sherman's, Rosecrans's—were menaced, for if Bragg advanced into Tennessee he might cut their communications with the North and force them to fight separated from each other and on unfavorable ground. The Confederates, thanks to Bragg, now had a chance to regain all they had lost. Up to this point in his offensive he had done everything right.

31 J. W. Lapsley to Bragg, August 21, 1862, Palmer Collection of Bragg Papers; John Euclid Magee Diary, July 23–August 14, 1862; Taylor Beatty Diary, July 23, 27, 1862.
32 OR, XVI (pt. 2), 741.

CHAPTER XIII

By marching, not by fighting

JULY 29–SEPTEMBER 22, 1862

At CHATTANOOGA Bragg found Kirby Smith ready to discuss strategy. Smith, who considered Bragg "a grim old fellow, but a true soldier," agreed to cooperate. They decided that while Bragg awaited his artillery and wagons Smith would recapture Cumberland Gap, an important mountain pass bordering Virginia and Kentucky, which he had lost in June; then he and Bragg would invade Middle Tennessee. Cavalry would harass the enemy and screen Bragg's army until it was ready to move.[1]

If their initial scheme succeeded, Bragg and Smith planned to advance into Kentucky. "When I called on Gen Bragg [at Chattanooga in July 1862] . . . to tell him that I thought it a good time to go to Ky," wrote J. Stoddard Johnston, "he told me it was [for] . . . that purpose . . . he was then moving his troops from Alabama to Chattanooga. . . ." It was a bold plan which seemed worth the risk involved. President Davis wrote Bragg on August 5: "If, as reported, the railroad has been effectually broken in rear of Buell, it may enable you to fight the enemy in detachments. Buell being crushed, if your means will enable you to march rapidly on Nashville Grant will be

[1] OR, XVI (pt. 2), 741. Smith later claimed he opposed an attack on Cumberland Gap. See Joseph Howard Parks, *General Edmund Kirby Smith, C.S.A.* (Baton Rouge, 1954), pp. 201–2. Some of the material in this and the following chapter appeared in Grady McWhiney, "Controversy in Kentucky: Braxton Bragg's Campaign of 1862," *Civil War History*, VI (1960), 5–42.

compelled to retire to the river, abandoning middle and east Tennessee and Kentucky." [2]

At first relations between Bragg and Smith were cordial, but the campaign was handicapped from the outset because Smith commanded an independent department and a separate army. Before Bragg left Tupelo he had tried, with unusual tact, to get East Tennessee included in his department. He had argued that as commander of General Albert Sidney Johnston's old army he also commanded Johnston's old department, which included East Tennessee. But Davis refused Bragg's request. "In Gen'l E. K. Smith you will find one of our ablest and purest officers," Davis informed Bragg. "Upon your cordial co-operation I can, therefore confidently rely." So far there had been no difficulties, yet Bragg felt "much embarrassed" because he was in Smith's territory, and he hesitated to display too much authority. Instead of orders, Bragg gave Smith advice and frequently as the campaign progressed Smith's independent actions forced Bragg to modify his plans.[3]

Scarcely a week after Smith and Bragg had conferred, Smith decided not to cooperate in an invasion of Middle Tennessee. He intended to leave behind a force to invest Cumberland Gap and to march with the bulk of his army directly to Lexington, Kentucky. Such a move, he informed Bragg, would bring the "most brilliant results." A report from Colonel John H. Morgan, who had just returned from a cavalry raid in Kentucky, doubtless influenced Smith's decision. According to Morgan, as soon as a southern army entered the state Kentuckians

[2] J. Stoddard Johnston Diary, afterthought added to entry of August 14, 1862, Filson Club, Louisville; Jefferson Davis to Bragg, August 5, 1862, Richey Collection of Bragg Papers.

[3] *OR*, XVII (pt. 2), 619, 627; XVI (pt. 2), 746; LII (pt. 2), 335; Davis to Bragg, August 5, 1862, Richey Collection of Bragg Papers. Davis refused to give Bragg undisputed authority over Smith because the President favored a rigid departmental system of command. See Jones, *Confederate Strategy from Shiloh to Vicksburg*, and Vandiver, *Rebel Brass*.

would overthrow their Union government and join the Confederate service.

Smith's determination to move independently meant that Bragg had to scrap his original plan. He feared that an invasion of Kentucky by Smith's army alone would be too risky; Smith might be overwhelmed without support. Consequently, Bragg warned him not to advance too far until Cumberland Gap had been taken and Buell's army had been either whipped or outmarched. To prevent Buell from taking Chattanooga or hurrying to Kentucky to crush Smith, Bragg decided to move northward, keeping his forces between Buell's and Smith's. Such an alignment of troops would save Chattanooga, Bragg believed, because Buell would retreat to protect his supply line. If a favorable opportunity occurred, Bragg would attack Buell's army; if not, he would try to maneuver it out of Tennessee. Within two weeks Bragg promised to march either toward Nashville or Lexington. "My inclination is now for the latter," he wrote Smith, "Van Dorn and Price will advance simultaneously with us from Mississippi on West Tennessee, and I trust we may all unite in Ohio." [4]

While Bragg waited for his artillery and wagons to arrive, he reorganized his army. He had approximately 30,000 effective troops, not including detached cavalry, directly under his command. He divided his infantry into seventy-three regiments, sixteen brigades, four divisions, and two corps (called wings). From three to six regiments formed a brigade; the largest, John K. Jackson's brigade, boasted 2,800 effective soldiers divided into four regiments, but most brigades could expect to take between 1,200 and 1,600 men into battle. Four brigades constituted a division; each corps consisted of two

[4] *OR*, XVI (pt. 2), 743, 741, 749; Cecil Fletcher Holland, *Morgan and His Raiders* (New York, 1943), pp. 126–27. Smith claimed (Smith to Jefferson Davis, August 11, 1862, E. Kirby Smith Papers, Duke University) he convinced Bragg that an invasion of Kentucky was worthwhile. The most detailed criticism of Smith for his failure to cooperate with Bragg is Connelly, *Army of the Heartland*, pp. 205–20.

divisions. A battery of artillery was assigned to each brigade; a small brigade of cavalry to each corps.[5] With only slight modifications this would be the organization of the army as long as Bragg commanded. It was a sound arrangement, eventually adopted by both Union and Confederate commanders, and vastly superior to the unbalanced organization used by Beauregard at Shiloh or the awkward divisional grouping used by Robert E. Lee during the Seven Days' Battle in Virginia.

Bragg, as usual, was dissatisfied with some of his subordinates. His senior major general both in rank and in age was fifty-six-year-old Leonidas Polk, who commanded one corps. Polk's affable manner reminded English Colonel A. J. L. Fremantle of a "grand Seigneur." To others Polk appeared pompous, theatrical in action and speech, and lacking military ability. "He is great at talk, but is monstrous uncertain," wrote Dr. D. W. Yandell in November 1862. "I saw enough of [him] . . . at Shiloh & Perryville to cause me to place no great confidence in him. He will *prevaricate*." "He did say he was going to do this and going to do that, but the old man forgets." Unless "he is transferred to house *duties* [some unimportant post]," concluded Yandell, "we will all go to the Devil out here."[6] Bragg made no secret of his belief that Polk was unsuited for field command, but the Bishop's high rank and his

---

[5] Estimates of strength are computed from returns found in OR, XVI (pt. 2), 772, 782, 784, 877, 886, 890, 893, 896, 900. Exact figures are impossible to determine because the number of effectives varied from day to day. On August 27 Colonel Joseph Wheeler's cavalry brigade consisted of 700 effectives; Colonel John F. Lay's cavalry brigade mustered 550 effectives. Colonel John A. Wharton soon took command of Lay's brigade.

[6] Lord, ed., *Fremantle Diary*, p. 111; St. John R. Liddell, "Liddell's Record of the Civil War," Moses, St. John R. Liddell and Family Papers; D. W. Yandell to William Preston Johnston, November 8, 1862, Barret Collection of Johnston Papers. Yandell, formerly Beauregard's surgeon, was no Bragg partisan. Bragg, according to his brother John, considered Yandell "a *miserable dog*." John Bragg to William T. Walthall, November 26, 1874, William T. Walthall Papers, Mississippi Department of Archives.

friendship with the President forced Bragg to retain him.[7] The other corps commander was Major General William Joseph Hardee, a broad-shouldered man, forty-five years old, who looked "rather like a French officer." Author of a book on tactics, which was used by both Union and Confederate armies, he was also a close friend of President and Mrs. Davis. Men admired Hardee because he was "kind and considerate of the wants of his soldiers"; often he would "give up his horse to some barefooted or sick soldier and walk for miles." A cadet wrote in 1856, when Hardee was commandant at West Point: "I do not suppose it would be possible to find a kinder man in the army than . . . Hardee." And in 1862 a soldier stated: "Of all the men in the army I most admire Gen Hardee." He was modest, and "not a warrior by instinct," recalled a contemporary. In fact, a critic called Hardee "a man of mediocre talent," and a friend admitted that before the war ended Hardee's men "began to have as little confidence in his ability as he seemed to have himself." But in the summer of 1862 Bragg considered Hardee an able officer.[8]

Major Generals Benjamin F. Cheatham and Jones M. Withers commanded divisions in Polk's corps. Bragg considered Cheatham, a former militia officer who had served as colonel of a regiment of Tennessee volunteers in the Mexican War, an incompetent political appointee. A "stout, rather

[7] Richard Taylor, who visited Bragg in Chattanooga, heard him call one of his high ranking generals "an old woman, utterly worthless." Taylor did not name the "old woman," but apparently it was Polk. Taylor, *Destruction and Reconstruction*, p. 100.

[8] Lord, ed., *Fremantle Diary*, p. 110; Ambrose, ed., "West Point in the Fifties," p. 302; E. John Ellis to His Father, November 4, 1862 (typescript), E. John, Thomas C. W. Ellis and Family Papers (B), Louisiana State University; Albert Brackett, *History of the United States Cavalry . . . to June, 1863* (New York, 1865), pp. 147–48; R. M. Gray, "Reminiscences," (typescript), pp. 70–72, Southern Historical Collection, University of North Carolina, Chapel Hill. On Hardee, see also Hughes, *Hardee*, and Thomas Conn Bryan, ed., "General William J. Hardee and Confederate Publication Rights," *Journal of Southern History*, XII (1946), 264–66.

rough-looking man," Cheatham sometimes drank too much, but most of the men in his division, mainly Tennesseeans, liked him. Withers, on the other hand, was a West Point graduate who had fought in Mexico in a regular army unit. At Shiloh he had won Bragg's praise, but he was handicapped as a field commander by poor health.[9]

Hardee's division commanders were Samuel Jones, a West Pointer who had been Beauregard's chief of artillery at First Manassas, and Simon B. Buckner, who had surrendered Fort Donelson to Grant. Recently exchanged and promoted to major general, Buckner would become one of Bragg's most determined enemies.[10]

Before the troops left Chattanooga Bragg made several additional changes in army organization. He ordered Samuel Jones, who was ill, to remain behind with Brigadier General Samuel B. Maxey and a mixed brigade of cavalry and infantry. Jones's job was to defend the town, apprehend spies, and forward expected reinforcements. Bragg directed him to establish martial law in Chattanooga and to list the occupation of every inhabitant. This order may have been partly responsible for much of the local newspaper criticism of Bragg.[11] To command what had been Jones's division Bragg appointed a member of his old Pensacola army, Brigadier General Patton Anderson, a strict disciplinarian who had once practiced medicine; Bragg considered Anderson "as noble and true a soldier and gentleman as any age can boast." When Smith requested reinforcements, Bragg happily sent him McCown's division. Then, after Smith asked for more men, Bragg detached Patrick R. Cleburne's and Preston Smith's excellent brigades. All of

[9] Lord, ed., *Fremantle Diary*, p. 116; Sykes, "Walthall's Brigade," p. 614; Warner, *Generals in Gray*, pp. 47-48, 342-43; *OR*, X (pt. 1), 468-70.

[10] Warner, *Generals in Gray*, pp. 38-39, 165-66. See also Stickles, *Buckner*.

[11] *OR*, XVI, (pt. 2), 742, 761-62; John K. Jackson to Bragg, January 14, 1863, Palmer Collection of Bragg Papers. See also *Confederate Veteran*, XL (1932), 140-42.

these detachments left Bragg only 27,000 effective troops with which to oppose Buell's 50,000 men.[12]

Bragg believed his army would be stronger, whatever its numbers, if he could rid it of men he considered incompetent. For this reason, he ordered Generals Crittenden and Carroll court-martialed, and he removed Generals Trapier, Hawes, and Lucius M. Walker from command. Yet Bragg did not believe he had done enough. "I do not hesitate to assert that a fourth of our efficiency is lost for want of suitable brigade and division commanders," he informed President Davis on August 6. "No appointing power can avoid errors through which in time each grade must become encumbered with some incapable and inefficient officers, who cannot be employed without material prejudice to the service." Bragg asked permission to select his commanders on the basis of ability rather than rank; he also wanted to break up small regiments and distribute the troops among other units from the same state. If the government would allow him to do this, he would keep only the competent officers; indeed, Bragg wanted to discharge all officers who stayed on sick leave over ninety days, unless they were recovering from wounds.[13]

When the President, for political reasons, refused to grant these requests, Bragg complained to Richard Taylor, who had stopped at Chattanooga on his way to Louisiana. Taylor, shocked by some contemptuous remarks Bragg made about his generals, warned him that he could hardly expect cooperation from them. "I speak the truth," answered Bragg. "The government is to blame for placing such men in high position." Taylor recalled that he henceforth "had misgivings as to General Bragg's success." [14]

Bragg of course had a point; Davis had appointed a number of amateur generals, but Bragg only worsened the situation

[12] *OR*, XVI (pt. 2), 744–45; Sykes, "Walthall's Brigade," p. 612; Williams, *Lincoln Finds a General*, IV, 42.

[13] *OR*, XVII (pt. 2), 627–28, 654–55, 658, 673, 668, 671–72.

[14] Taylor, *Destruction and Reconstruction*, p. 100.

when he denounced men he could not remove from command. Had he been more tolerant of mistakes men learning a new profession were certain to make, he might have had fewer critics and much of the dissension that developed in his army might have been avoided. In many cases, Bragg was too quick to judge men. Obviously, he never realized that his own generalship often fell far below the ideal standards he tried to impose upon others.

Bragg even made staff changes at Chattanooga. He sent his chief of staff, Thomas Jordan, and his inspector general, James E. Slaughter, back to Mississippi to organize exchanged prisoners into regiments and to hurry them forward. The exchanged men reached Tennessee too late to be used against Buell; nor did Jordan and Slaughter rejoin Bragg for the campaign. Yet this detachment of his only staff generals just before the army advanced was not as shortsighted as it might appear. Jordan, disabled by rheumatism, planned to relinquish his post anyway. He wanted to serve on Beauregard's staff, not Bragg's. Also, if Jordan, who was something of a gossip, can be believed, Slaughter was incompetent. "He means well," wrote Jordan, "but has neither the education nor natural ability for the important place he holds." [15]

When the government refused Bragg's request for Richard Taylor to fill Jordan's position, Bragg made a serious mistake. He decided to act as his own chief of staff.[16] He thought he could add to his already heavy duties of command the details of organization and administration without injury to himself or to his army. But he was wrong. He needed a number of experts—each a specialist with clearly assigned duties—super-

[15] *OR*, XVI (pt. 2), 740, 756–57, 762; XVII (pt. 2), 640–41, 679; *Confederate Veteran*, XXVI (1918), 164.

[16] Confederate Army regulations did not provide for the position of chief of staff until June 1864; before then the office existed illegally. *OR*, Series 4, I, 114–15, 163–64; III, 498. Much of my discussion of Bragg's staff is based upon the research of June I. Gow, one of my graduate students, who is writing a dissertation on the organization and administration of the Army of Tennessee.

vised by a chief of staff to help him keep his army together, to feed and equip it, and to plan its movements. What Bragg settled for was a mixed group of experienced and inexperienced men who followed his instructions to the best of their knowledge or ability.[17] For example, Jordan claimed that Bragg's chief quartermaster, Lieutenant Colonel L. W. O'Bannon, might have done well as quartermaster of "a two-company post on the Texas frontier," but he could not handle the transportation and supply problems of a large army.[18] Neither Bragg nor the Confederate authorities in Richmond understood just how important competent staffs were to their cause.

Bragg delegated work erratically, and frequently did it himself. "I do not average four hours rest in twenty-four," he informed his wife. Nor was it always easy to work with him. He sometimes made no distinction between staff officers; he might assign work to one that was more properly the duty of another. On the day Lieutenant Colonel George William Brent joined Bragg's staff, he wrote: "Gen Bragg is said to be difficult to please. He told me that he was exacting 'but tried to be just.' " [19]

After Bragg had made all detachments and transfers his subordinates included five major generals and thirteen brigadiers.[20] The average age of the major generals was forty-six years; that

[17] Lee also tried to do most of his own staff work. "Colonel Chilton remained titular chief of staff, but . . . Lee was his own principal staff officer," noted Douglas S. Freeman (*Lee*, III, 229).

[18] *OR*, XVII (pt. 2), 669–70.

[19] Bragg to Elise, September 18, 1862, Bixby Collection of Bragg Papers; George William Brent Diary, October 2, 1862, Palmer Collection of Bragg Papers. This diary, catalogued as the work of "J. Stoddard Johnson," was identified as Brent's by June I. Gow, "The Johnston and Brent Diaries: A Problem of Authorship," *Civil War History*, XIV (1968), 46–50.

[20] This number does not include any of the generals removed, detached, or transferred by Bragg. Nor does it include Generals Slaughter and Jordan of Bragg's staff, or cavalry Generals Nathan B. Forrest and Abraham Buford who were on patrol.

of the brigadiers, thirty-nine years. Six generals were from Tennessee, five from Louisiana, two each from Alabama and Georgia, and one each from Mississippi, Florida, and Kentucky. All of the major generals except Cheatham, who had served as colonel of volunteers in the Mexican War, were graduates of the United States Military Academy. But less than a third of the brigadiers were West-Point trained.

Though Bragg was dissatisfied with many of his subordinates, he directed his army northward on August 28 to participate in the only multi-army offensive the Confederates ever launched. Smith's army was already in Kentucky; in less than two weeks Lee's Army of Northern Virginia would be in Maryland; and Van Dorn and Price were expected to advance into western Tennessee. "Move as soon as practicable," Bragg telegraphed Van Dorn on August 25. "Buell is falling back. Is now in Nashville. Price reports movements from Corinth to reinforce Buell. Destroy them as they cross the rivers. Kirby Smith is in Kentucky moving on Lexington. We move in a few days to sustain him . . . or fight Buell if he stands." [21]

Bragg knew that without overall supervision and coordination this offensive was a dangerous gamble. Since 1861 he had recommended concentration of Confederate forces, which the President's independent departmental organization of armies had prevented. Bragg had disregarded his own recommendation when he moved with only part of his army from Tupelo to Chattanooga, but he still hoped for a concentration of Confederate forces in either Tennessee or Kentucky. Indeed, he believed that the success of his offensive depended upon successful maneuvers and a junction with Smith, Van Dorn, and Price. [22] The weakness of this plan was that Bragg had no control over Smith's movements and only nominal control over Van Dorn's and Price's. Moreover, as each army

[21] Bragg to Van Dorn, August 25, 1862 (telegram), James W. Eldridge Papers, Huntington Library.
[22] *OR*, XVI (pt. 2), 782.

advanced from its base, communication between army commanders became more difficult.

If the campaign failed, Bragg knew, he would receive most of the criticism. "Gen. Bragg's army is now said to be located at a point where it can and will soon strike an important and telling blow," reported a newspaper. "At Buena Vista, at Pensacola, and at Shiloh, General Bragg won immortal honors. We expect even greater things of him in the blow he is about [to] strike the insolent but now greatly disheartened foe." Bragg also received a letter of warning from the President. "You have the misfortune of being regarded as my personal friend," wrote Davis, "and are pursued, therefore, with malignant censure by men regardless of truth, and whose want of principle . . . renders them incapable of conceiving that you are trusted because of your known fitness for command and not because of friendly regard." [23]

The route of the army's advance was across Walden's Ridge and along the Sequatchie River to Pikeville, and then over the Cumberland Plateau to Sparta. It was a hard march. "On reaching [a mountain] . . . summit," noted a newspaper correspondent, "a weary soldier of the 6th Arkansas Regiment, a red-headed, rough-bearded specimen . . . pausing to wipe the perspiration from his face . . . remarked: 'Well this is about the steepest game of *Bragg* I ever come up with, they thought they'd *bluff* this chicken, but he stood the *raise* though he only had one *little pair* (slapping his legs) to come in on.'" An artilleryman reported men and horses suffering for want of food. "Some of the boys . . . were punished for disobeying orders and going into peach orchards," wrote John Magee on August 28; as punishment they were forced to "carry a heavy rail 4 miles [or] . . . put a flour barrel over them, and . . . carry it." Yet Colonel H. W. Walter, Bragg's judge advocate, wrote from near Sparta (where Bragg and his staff spent the night of September 4 in the open air, without tents) that the

[23] *Richmond Enquirer*, August 26, 1862; *OR*, LII (pt. 2), 335.

army was in splendid condition. "Health & happiness prevail in its ranks," claimed Walker. "The wild shouts of welcome which marks the approach of the General shows how well they love him, whilst their strict discipline & cheerful bearing show them to be equal to any emergency." [24]

At Sparta, where the Confederates stopped for a few days, several Tennesseeans who were with the army, including Governor Isham G. Harris, urged Bragg to move directly on Nashville, but he refused to be diverted from his plan to stay between Buell and Smith. When the army reached Carthage, some forty miles east of Nashville, on September 9, reports indicated that the Federals were evacuating Nashville; Buell seemed to be withdrawing toward Louisville, Kentucky. "We cannot possibly overtake him," Bragg informed Polk, "but must head him off from General Kirby Smith." Bragg ordered Polk to move promptly to Glasgow, Kentucky, seize the railroad leading north, and wait for the arrival of Hardee's corps. Bragg advised Smith, who had reached Lexington after overwhelming a force of Union recruits on August 30, to fall back toward Glasgow if pressed by the enemy. Smith's army consisted of nearly 20,000 men, but between 6,000 and 8,000 of these were investing Cumberland Gap. "Combined we can thrash them all," Bragg predicted.[25]

By September 14 Bragg's entire army, "foot-sore and tired," rested at Glasgow. Morale was high. Shabbily dressed Confederates had marched smartly through each town behind bands playing "Dixie" and the "Bonnie Blue Flag," while citizens had

[24] Unidentified and undated newspaper clipping, M. J. Solomons Scrapbook, p. 406, Duke University; Magee Diary, August 28, 1862; Johnston Diary, August 31—September 4, 1862; H. W. Walter to Mrs. Bragg, September 4, 1862, Palmer Collection of Bragg Papers.

[25] Johnston Diary, September 7—8, 1862; J. Stoddard Johnston, "Bragg's Campaign in Kentucky: From Chattanooga to Munfordville," J. Stoddard Johnston Military Papers, Filson Club, Louisville; OR, XVI (pt. 2), 804, 806, 811; Parks, Smith, pp. 211, 231. Actually, Buell left 6,000 troops entrenched at Nashville.

shouted "Hurrah for our Southern boys," and had cheered the troops even more with gifts of wine and cider. Some men had been able to see their families; others, including Bragg, had enjoyed quick visits with old friends; and many had made new friends. "I remember how gladly the citizens of Kentucky received us," wrote a Tennesseean. "I thought they had the prettiest girls that God ever made." [26]

"My army is in high spirits and ready to go anywhere the 'old general' says," Bragg happily informed Elise. "With but one suit of clothes, no tents, nothing to eat but meat and *bread*, or when we can't get that *roasting ears* from the corn fields along the road, we have made the most extraordinary campaign in military history." [27] Bragg's men agreed. "The march from the Tennessee River is without parallel in the history of the war," wrote Private John Buie. "Gen. Bragg's march . . . will be recorded as one of the most remarkable in history," exclaimed John Forsyth, a newspaper editor who was with the army. "With a vast train of ordnance and supplies he has traversed two mountains, crossed two rivers, and marched three hundred miles. At ever step he has outgeneralled and outflanked Buell. . . ." Indeed, such statements were only slightly exaggerated. Without fighting a battle Bragg had forced the Union evacuation of northern Alabama and central

[26] *OR*, XVI (pt. 2), 815; H. W. Walter to Mrs. Bragg, September 4, 1862, Palmer Collection of Bragg Papers; John Buie to His Father, September 30, 1862, Buie Papers; Bragg to Mrs. W. K. Williams, September 2, 1862, William H. Polk Papers, North Carolina Department of Archives and History; Watkins, "*Co. Aytch*," p. 79.

[27] Bragg to Elise, September 18, 1862, Bixby Collection of Bragg Papers. Bragg's army certainly traveled light. "The regiments moved with but three wagons each, and . . . the officers were allowed to carry little or no baggage," reported a spy. "The troops were provided with large tarpaulins, which they stretched from tree to tree, and under which whole companies can sleep with comfort. The wagons were used to haul forage, the ten tarpaulins of a regiment taking up but little room. The men lived off the country." Louisville *Journal*, September 13, 1862, quoted in Richmond *Daily Dispatch*, September 23, 1862.

Tennessee. "Not often has boldness and hard marching accomplished more," concluded a careful student of the campaign.[28] The last Confederate unit had scarcely reached Glasgow when Bragg again issued orders to march; he sent James R. Chalmers's Mississippi Brigade to Cave City, ten miles northwest of Glasgow, to cut the railroad leading north from Bowling Green. This would hamper Buell's army, which was at Bowling Green, in its retreat northward. After Chalmers completed his mission, he rashly proceeded to Munfordville, some twenty miles north of Glasgow, and unsuccessfully attacked what he mistakenly believed was a force of less than two thousand Federals. Bragg condemned this attack as "unauthorized and injudicious," but he was unwilling "to allow the impression of a disaster to rest on the minds" of his men. So, on September 15, he moved his weary and scantily provisioned army to Munfordville.[29]

The next day, after reconnoitering the enemy position and placing his artillery, Bragg demanded the unconditional surrender of the garrison. In an exchange of notes, the Union commander, Colonel John T. Wilder, asked for proof of Bragg's superior force. Bragg refused to reveal the exact size of his army, but he promised to prove his strength if necessary. He allowed Wilder an hour to decide. When the time was up, wrote a staff officer, Bragg "nervously looked at his watch and said he would give five minutes grace, and, if he heard nothing from Wilder, he would issue orders for the attack at daylight." Before midnight Wilder came to Bragg's

---

[28] John Buie to His Father, September 30, 1862, Buie Papers; *Mobile Register and Advertiser*, October 14, 1862; Williams, *Lincoln Finds a General*, IV, 62.

[29] *OR*, XVI (pt. 1), 971–80, 1090. Bragg softened his censure of Chalmers in an endorsement on the Mississippian's report: ". . . the conduct of the troops and commander in action reflects credit on both, and adds but another proof of the many of their distinguished gallantry." *Ibid.*, 980.

headquarters, toured the Confederate lines with Buckner, and agreed to capitulate.[30]

In a dispatch to Richmond, Bragg announced the capture of Munfordville, 4,000 prisoners, 4,000 small arms, ten pieces of artillery, and a large quantity of munitions. He paroled the prisoners and sent them to Bowling Green in hopes of demoralizing Buell's army. "My position must be exceedingly embarrassing to Buell and his army," boasted Bragg. "My junction with Kirby Smith is complete. Buell [is] still at Bowling Green." [31]

Bragg's imprudent announcement of September 17 was wrong on two counts. First, Bragg had not joined Smith; their armies were still a hundred miles apart.[32] Second, Buell was no longer at Bowling Green; he was at Cave City, only ten miles to the south, moving toward Munfordville.

For a time Bragg seemed determined to fight. Using the captured Union fort as part of his defense line, he posted most of his army just below Munfordville on the south side of Green River to await Buell's advance. "Early on the morning of the 18th," wrote Joseph Wheeler, who then commanded Hardee's cavalry brigade, "General Bragg sent for me and explained his plans. I never saw him more determined or more confident. The entire army was in the best of spirits. I met and talked with Generals Hardee, Polk, Cheatham, and Buckner,' continued Wheeler; "all were enthusiastic over our success and our good luck in getting Buell where he would be com-

30 J. Stoddard Johnston, "Bragg's Campaign in Kentucky," newspaper clipping, Barret Collection of Johnston Papers; OR, XVI (pt. 1), 968-71.

31 OR, XVI (pt. 1), 968.

32 A letter from Bragg's chief engineer, explaining the best route from Glasgow to Bardstown, indicates that Bragg intended moving toward Bardstown rather than toward Bowling Green as early as September 15 David B. Harris to Bragg, September 15, 1862, David Bullock Harris Papers, Duke University. See also J. Stoddard Johnston, "Bragg's Campaign in Kentucky: From Munfordville to Frankfort," Johnston Military Papers.

Legend

.... Railroad

- - - Road

Forty Miles

Ohio

Indiana

Cincinnati

Ohio River

N

Louisville

Shelbyville

Frankfort

Mount Sterling

Taylorsville

Versailles

Lexington

Shepherdsville

Mount Washington

Harrodsburg

Bryantsville

Elizabethtown

Bardstown

Perryville

Danville

Munfordsville

Brownsville

Morgantown

Cave City

Green River

Bowling Green

Glasgow

Kentucky

Cumberland Gap

Louisville & Nashville R.R.

To Nashville

Tennessee

©Donald S. Frazier

ROADS FROM BOWLING GREEN TO LOUISVILLE

pelled to fight us to such a disadvantage. It is true our back
was to a river, but it was fordable at several places, and we felt
that the objection to having it in our rear was fully compensated by the topographical features, which, with the aid of the
fort, made our position a strong one for defense. So anxious

was Bragg for a fight that he sent Buckner's division to the front in the hope that an engagement could thus be provoked. . . ." There were several flaws in Bragg's scheme. It was undertaken for the wrong reason. Bragg did not decide to defend because he knew that, all other things being equal, Confederate losses would be less and Union losses greater if Buell attacked. Bragg resolved to defend, as he later explained, only because he "could not prudently afford to attack"; his supplies were too limited and his men too exhausted. Even if he defeated the Federal army, which he believed was twice as large as his own, Buell could retreat to prepared fortifications at Bowling Green, where he had ample supplies. The Confederates, short of food, could not besiege Bowling Green; nor could they maintain their defensive position very long. Buell, whose route to Louisville and reinforcements was not blocked, refused to be enticed into attacking the Confederates. After two days passed without action, Bragg became pessimistic. His rations were so low he decided to withdraw from Munfordville. "This campaign must be won by marching, not by fighting," he told Colonel David Urquhart. On September 20 Confederate units started toward Bardstown, where Bragg hoped to obtain supplies and to unite with Kirby Smith for a campaign against either Louisville or Cincinnati.[33]

Bragg has been severely criticized for abandoning Munfordville as well as for allowing Buell's army to reach Louisville. "When a final appraisal of his generalship is made," wrote Stanley F. Horn, "his inadequacy in this crisis should weigh more heavily against him than some of his more conspicuous failures elsewhere." Horn insisted: (1) Bragg could and should have reached Louisville before Buell; (2) Bragg had or could have secured plenty of supplies—"a supply train from Kirby Smith did reach Bragg on the nineteenth"; (3) Bragg should

[33] OR, XVI (pt. 1), 1090; (pt. 2), 848, 849, 855; Joseph Wheeler, "Bragg's Invasion of Kentucky," Battles and Leaders, III, 10; David Urquhart, "Bragg's Advance and Retreat," ibid., III, 601; Bragg to Elise, September 18, 1862, Bixby Collection of Bragg Papers.

have ordered Smith to join him at Munfordville; and (4) Bragg, even without Smith's help, should have fought Buell at Munfordville—he "had close to 30,000 men and Buell was supposed to have 38,000." "The conclusion is inescapable that Bragg was simply unequal spiritually to the responsibility of precipitating a battle," asserted Horn, "and, as an afterthought, he invented the scarcity of supplies as a cloak for timidity." [34]

Bragg's failure to prevent Buell's army from reaching Louisville without a fight deserves criticism, but the charge that Bragg "invented the scarcity of supplies" is refuted by contemporary evidence. The Federals at Bowling Green, wrote J. Stoddard Johnston, were "protected by works of our own construction, the nature of which, as offering means of defense . . . was too well known to many of our officers high in command who had been there the preceding winter under General Sidney Johnston, to make an assault feasible, while the necessities of the commissariat and the impoverished condition

[34] Horn, *Army of Tennessee*, pp. 170–72. As a source for his conclusion, Horn cites Basil W. Duke, who was not present at Munfordville. Other critics of Bragg's actions include Parks (*Smith*, p. 229; *Polk*, pp. 259–62) and William M. Polk (*Leonidas Polk: Bishop and General* [2 vols., New York, 1915] II, 130–31), who claim that Bragg wasted five days vacillating over whether to fight or run, and that such wavering shocked his subordinates. According to Polk, the arrival of George H. Thomas's division on September 20 finally frightened Bragg into retreating. Some of Polk's charges are repeated in Thomas Robson Hay's "Braxton Bragg and the Southern Confederacy," *Georgia Historical Quarterly*, IX (1925), 270. Wheeler ("Bragg's Invasion of Kentucky," p. 10) also wrote that after Thomas's arrival "Bragg did not deem it advisable to risk a battle with the forces then under his command." Bragg did vacillate over whether or not to fight at Munfordville, but the fact that on September 19 he issued orders for Polk's corps to march north at daylight the next day proves that he had decided to withdraw from Munfordville before the arrival of Thomas's division on September 20. See *OR*, XVI (pt. 2), 849. On September 18 Bragg wrote Elise (Bixby Collection of Bragg Papers): ". . . tomorrow we march—full of hope and zeal." A message from Hardee to Wheeler on September 23 (*OR*, XVI [pt. 2], 868) also suggests that Bragg's subordinates were not yet displeased with their commander's actions. "Our affairs, except our men being jaded, are prosperous," wrote Hardee.

of the country from the occupation of the previous fall and winter, rendered a siege impracticable. In fact, so powerful were the reasons against moving to the attack of Buell that among officers whose rank led them into consultation with the general commanding, I remember none who deemed it necessary to the success of the campaign that Buell should be attacked. On the other hand, it was believed that his army would be effectually disposed of without a battle." On September 21 General Jackson, whose brigade escorted the army's wagons to Bardstown, reported from New Haven that supplies were scarce. "The country is very barren," he informed Bragg. From a few miles north of Munfordville on the same day, Bragg wrote Polk: "Do not push your troops to-day. As I hear nothing from the rear it is presumed we are not pressed, and, in any event, our troops are jaded so that too great a pressure will be worse than a fight with superior numbers. Send ahead and see if subsistence or forage in small quantities can be had for our wants to-night. . . ." A newspaper account, written soon after the campaign, described the region around Green River as a "naturally unproductive" area, "affording slender supplies." [35]

Nor is Horn's statement correct that a supply train from Kirby Smith reached Bragg's army on September 19. Actually, on that day Smith wrote Bragg: "I have to-day ordered 50 wagons for you; 30 will be loaded with flour and hard bread, and will be ready to leave Danville by the morning of the 21st instant." Danville was three or four days' march from Munfordville. At 4 P.M. on September 18, J. Stoddard Johnston left Munfordville by buggy with a request from Bragg for Smith "to send, with all dispatch, a heavy train of provisions to

[35] Johnston, "Bragg's Campaign in Kentucky: From Munfordville to Frankfort," Johnston Military Papers; John K. Jackson to Bragg, September 21, 1862, Palmer Collection of Bragg Papers; OR, XVI (pt. 2), 859; unidentified newspaper clipping, November ?, 1862, Palmer Collection of Bragg Papers. Buell also admitted that the region around Munfordville was unproductive. OR, XVI (pt. 1), 46.

Bardstown." Johnston arrived at Smith's headquarters in Lexington at 11 A.M. on September 20; he had made the trip of 135 miles in forty-three hours. In response to the message Johnston delivered, Smith wrote Bragg on September 21: "A supply train of all the wagons that could be collected . . . will load immediately for Bardstown. The train sent by way of Danville has been ordered also to Bardstown." [36]

Horn's contention that Bragg should have attacked Buell near Munfordville is equally questionable. Instead of the 30,000 effective troops Horn assigned him, Bragg had nearer 26,000. Buell probably had about 40,000.[37] Had Bragg attacked he probably would have been repulsed. The most he could have hoped to accomplish by assaulting the Federals would have been Buell's withdrawal to the fortifications at Bowling Green where the enemy had collected supplies for twenty or thirty days.[38]

Nor could Bragg have prevented Buell from reaching Louisville by merely maintaining a defensive position and awaiting the supplies Smith promised to send. "I could have avoided the enemy [at Munfordville] by passing to either side of him," wrote Buell.[39]

It is true that the presence of Kirby Smith's army at Munfordville would have improved the Confederate situation, but its absence cannot be blamed on Bragg. The original campaign plan was for Bragg and Smith to combine their armies against

[36] Johnston, "Bragg's Campaign in Kentucky: From Munfordville to Frankfort," Johnston Military Papers; *OR*, XVI (pt. 2), 850, 861.

[37] Hard marching and irregular diet cost Polk over five hundred effectives between August 27 and September 25. Returns from Hardee's corps are unavailable, but it seems reasonable to assume that his losses equalled Polk's. If so, Bragg had about 26,200 effective men. *OR*, XVI (pt. 2), 784, 877. Buell stated in an article he wrote after the war ("East Tennessee and the Campaign of Perryville." *Battles and Leaders*, III, 42) that he had 47,500 men at Munfordville. *OR*, XVI (pt. 1), 14.

[38] For a careful analysis of the situation see Williams, *Lincoln Finds a General*, IV, 108-9.

[39] *OR*, XVI (pt. 1), 48.

Buell in Tennessee. This scheme was upset when Smith, acting as an independent departmental commander, decided to march to Lexington before Bragg left Chattanooga. When Bragg's army reached Munfordville, Smith's forces were over a hundred miles away, scattered from Lexington to Cumberland Gap. Busy gathering supplies, Smith did not want to march to Munfordville. Instead, he proposed a junction of forces nearer Lexington. Nor should Bragg be blamed for not summoning Smith's troops quickly to his assistance. "Surely," wrote Kenneth P. Williams, "it would have been the height of folly for Bragg to order Smith to join him without knowing the aspect of affairs about Lexington and elsewhere to the north." [40]

Up to the time his army left Munfordville, Bragg had made no irreparable strategic or tactical mistakes. He had neither blocked Buell's retreat to Louisville nor lured the Federals into destroying themselves by rash assaults against strong Confederate positions; nevertheless, Bragg had achieved much—he had protected Smith from Buell and at the same time maneuvered Buell out of Tennessee. Yet the campaign was far from finished. Bragg still had formulated no precise plan for defeating Union forces in Kentucky or for holding the state. Whether he and Smith could defend what they had won depended upon their ability to cooperate and how much help they received from Kentuckians.

[40] Williams, *Lincoln Finds a General*, IV, 108.

CHAPTER XIV

Many blame Gen. Bragg

SEPTEMBER 23–NOVEMBER 2, 1862

F ROM MUNFORDVILLE Bragg marched to Bardstown where he expected Smith's army to join him. He selected the town as a rendezvous point because it was about halfway between Munfordville and Lexington. But when Bragg arrived on September 23 he found a letter from Smith instead of that general's army. Smith insisted that his troops must remain near Lexington to protect that "valuable region"; Federal General George Morgan who had evacuated Cumberland Gap might withdraw northward through central Kentucky. Smith also believed a Federal force might advance into central Kentucky from Cincinnati. His army was still badly scattered: General Humphrey Marshall, commanding 3,000 men, was at Mount Sterling, some thirty-five miles east of Lexington; General Carter L. Stevenson's 8,000 men were at Cumberland Gap, 170 miles from Lexington; and Smith's main force of about 10,000 men was divided into detachments occupying Lexington, Frankfort, and Danville. Considering the disposition of his army, Smith's promise to "hold my force in readiness to co-operate with you [Bragg] upon Louisville if needed" was meaningless. Though Smith wrote Bragg, "I regard the defeat of Buell before he effects a junction with the force at Louisville as a military necessity," he expected Bragg alone to defeat Buell. Furthermore, Bragg should act quickly, advised Smith, for Kentuckians would not support the Confederacy until Buell had been beaten. Smith did promise to return Cleburne's and Preston Smith's brigades (less than 3,000 men), which he had borrowed before leaving Tennessee, but the next day he changed his mind. He wrote Bragg: "I have ordered my entire force to Mount Sterling to try to intercept General Morgan." [1]

Even without Smith's aid, Bragg still hoped to defeat Buell and capture Louisville,[2] but he had lost much of his boldness and drive. "The long, arduous, and exhausting march [from Chattanooga] renders it necessary for my troops to have some rest," he wrote. His most aggressive cavalry commander, General Nathan B. Forrest, reported that he could not carry out an order to destroy the railroad between Elizabethtown and Louisville "on account of the condition that my horses are in." Bragg and his men were simply fatigued; they made no attack on Buell's army, which reached Louisville safely on September 25. "It is a source of deep regret," Bragg informed General Cooper that same day, that "want of provisions" had forced the army to march to Bardstown and enabled "Buell to reach Louisville, where a very large force is now concentrated." Without Smith's help, Bragg admitted, he could not attack Louisville.[3]

In letters to Cooper and Davis written three days after reaching Bardstown, Bragg revealed for the first time that he had serious apprehensions about the outcome of the Kentucky invasion. He was still tired and somewhat discouraged. Nearly a month of campaigning without sufficient rest, commanding an army and at the same time acting as his own chief of staff, had doubtless sapped his reserve of energy and self-confidence

[1] OR, XVI (pt. 2), 850, 866; Smith to Bragg, September 24, 1862, Palmer Collection of Bragg Papers. This letter is reproduced in OR, XVI (pt. 2), 873, but with the incorrect date. "Thus," wrote Kenneth P. Williams (Lincoln Finds a General, IV, 112), "Smith bowed himself out of the Louisville scheme."

[2] A memorandum showing the best routes to Louisville was prepared on September 24 by Captain Davis B. Harris, chief engineer, on orders from Bragg. This document is in the Harris Papers.

[3] OR, XVI (pt. 2), 876, 863; Buell, "East Tennessee and the Campaign of Perryville," p. 42. On Federal strength at Louisville, see Connelly, Army of the Heartland, p. 240.

and increased his willingness to criticize. His strategy of concentration, the timely meshing of widely separated units, had failed. None of those he had counted on—Smith, Van Dorn, Price, or Breckinridge—had joined him. He had expected Breckinridge to reinforce the army with a division. Now it was clear that Breckinridge, delayed by Van Dorn in Mississippi, would not arrive in time to participate in the campaign.[4] "The failure of Genl Breckinridge to carry out his part of my program has seriously embarrassed me, and moreover the whole campaign," wrote Bragg. "I regret to add," he informed Davis, "that there has been a want of cordial cooperation on the part of Genl Van Dorn since his department was merged in mine." "The general is most true to our cause and gallant to a fault, but he is self willed, rather weak minded & totally deficient in organization and system. He never knows the state of his command," concluded Bragg, "and wields it only in fragments." [5]

But what discouraged Bragg most was the failure of Kentuckians to join his army. "Our prospects here, my dear sir, are not what I expected," he wrote Davis on September 25. "Enthusiasm runs high, but exhausts itself in words." Even Kirby Smith had lost much of his confidence in a general uprising among Kentuckians. On September 18 he wrote Bragg: "The Kentuckians are slow and backward in rallying to our standard. Their hearts are evidently with us, but their blue-grass and fat cattle are against us." [6] At Bardstown, wrote

[4] *OR*, XVI (pt. 2), 995–1002. Breckinridge finally reached Knoxville in early October with 6,000 men, but before he could march to Kentucky Bragg withdrew.

[5] Bragg to Davis, September 25, 1862 (copy), Braxton Bragg Papers, United States Military Academy.

[6] *Ibid.*; Parks, *Smith*, p. 225. Smith, it will be remembered, had urged the Kentucky invasion because he believed a large army could be recruited in the state. Even after Bragg reached Glasgow, Smith continued to believe Kentuckians would enlist. On September 14 General McCown, who had been left in East Tennessee, wired Cooper: "General E. K. Smith calls for arms .for the Kentuckians flocking to his standard.

a soldier, "the women all kissed Gen Buckner and strong men wept like infants," but nobody enlisted. "There are a great many persons who come into camp professing a desire to join the army . . . but who are really seeking protection," reported the commander of the Kentucky Partisan Rangers on September 26. "I have now about eleven hundred men mustered into service," he admitted, but "some of them have been in service for twelve or fifteen months." "We have so far received no accession to this army," Bragg informed Cooper on September 25. "General Smith has secured about a brigade —not half our losses by casualties of different kinds. We have 15,000 stand of arms and no one to use them. Unless a change occurs soon we must abandon the garden spot of Kentucky to its cupidity." Bragg estimated that he would need 50,000 recruits to hold the state.[7]

Bragg tried to encourage enlistment in several ways. In a proclamation issued on September 14 he announced that his soldiers had entered Kentucky not as "conquerors or as despoilers," but as liberators. "I shall enforce rigid discipline and shall protect all in their persons and property," he promised. "Kentuckians, we have come with joyous hopes," continued his appeal. "Let us not depart in sorrow, as we shall if we find you wedded . . . to your present lot. If you prefer Federal rule, show it by your frowns and we shall return whence we came. If you choose rather to come within the folds of our brotherhood, then cheer us with the smiles of your women and lend your willing hands to secure . . . your heritage of liberty." In a second appeal, issued September 26, Bragg offered peace, trade, and free navigation of the Mississippi to

---

Could arm 20,000 men if he had arms. . . . General Smith (dated 5th, from Lexington) says Kentucky is rising *en masse*." *OR*, XVI, (pt. 2), 821.

[7] E. John Ellis to His Mother, October 2, 1862 (typescript), E. John, Thomas C. W. Ellis and Family Papers (B); Colonel A. R. Johnson to Bragg, September 26, 1862, Palmer Collection of Bragg Papers; *OR*, XVI (pt. 2), 876.

the people of the entire Northwest.[8] He also assigned Buckner, a popular Kentuckian, to command a special camp for
recruits, established along with a new supply depot near
Bryantsville. "I have done my best," Bragg wrote Davis, "but
must acknowledge my deficiencies in the field of statesman-
ship. A plain, unvarnished argument based on their [the Kentuckians's] interests I presumed would have the most effect."[9]
When appeals failed to bring in recruits, Bragg decided to
introduce conscription. But to conscript Kentuckians legally,
he had to turn governormaker and replace the existing Union
state government with the pro-southern regime that had fled
some eight months before. The exiled government, or enough
of it for Bragg's purpose, had followed Confederate forces
back into the state. In fact, the Confederate governatorial
claimant, Richard Hawes, had just arrived in Danville.[10] "I see
no hope but in the conscript act," Bragg wrote Davis on October 2, "and I propose to enforce it immediately after installa-
tion of the provisional civil government. . . ."[11]

Temporarily, until he could inspect the resources and military possibilities of central Kentucky, confer with Smith, in-
stall a pro-Confederate governor, and raise an army of Ken-

[8] OR, XVI (pt. 2), 822; LII (pt. 2), 363–65. Horn (Army of Tennessee, p. 177) claimed, without citation, but probably correctly that
John Forsyth wrote the second appeal. But see "Gen. Bragg's Address to
the People of the Northwest," unidentified and undated newspaper clipping, M. J. Solomons Scrapbook, pp. 354–55, Duke University.

[9] OR, XVI (pt. 2), 887; Bragg to Davis, September 25, 1862 (copy),
Bragg Papers, USMA.

[10] The pro-southern Kentucky government though never completely
organized, was recognized by the Confederacy and was represented in
the Confederate Congress. Lieutenant Governor Hawes claimed he was
the legal successor to Governor George W. Johnson, who had been
killed at Shiloh. The Union government of Kentucky, of course, denied
that Johnson or Hawes had any right to office. See E. Merton Coulter,
The Civil War and Readjustment in Kentucky (Chapel Hill, 1926), pp.
136–39.

[11] Bragg to Davis, October 2, 1862, Bragg Papers, USMA. On September 5 Bragg had ordered the conscript law enforced in Tennessee. OR,
XVI (pt. 2), 797–98.

tuckians, Bragg decided to adopt a defensive strategy. On September 28 he left his army at Bardstown, under Polk's command, and started for Danville. As it happened, leaving Polk in command was a mistake, but Bragg had no choice; Polk was his senior subordinate. Thus Bragg gambled on Union inactivity while he sought Smith's cooperation and reinforcements.[12]

At Danville, where Bragg spent a day, he was greeted "with a reception which would have been flattering to the pride of anyone," and some bad news. Kirby Smith had failed to intercept Morgan; moreover, Bragg found fewer supplies at Danville than he had expected. He was pleased, of course, that Stevenson's command had just arrived from Cumberland Gap, and that several prominent Kentuckians had returned from the south. Bragg made arrangements for Hawes's inauguration, and welcomed General William Preston Johnston. "He has great influence here and will forward our recruiting," Bragg wrote.[13]

Kirby Smith, just back from his unsuccessful hunt for Morgan, met Bragg and Hawes at Lexington on October 1. They "rode through the streets to the Phoenix Hotel, amid the booming of artillery and the welcoming demonstrations of the citizens," recalled J. Stoddard Johnston. Bragg made a short speech in which he announced his intention to inaugurate Hawes. "It is generally believed, that [Bragg] . . . will take command of all the forces in Kentucky," wrote Colonel George W. Brent, who had just been transferred from Smith's to Bragg's staff. "The reception of Genl. B. in Lexington was quite enthusiastic," noted Brent. "But it is only manifested by words and shouts. There is no action on the part of Kentuckians to take an active armed effort to sustain us." Bragg agreed. "Enthusiasm is unbounded but recruiting at a dis-

[12] OR, XVI (pt. 2), 886, 891; (pt. 1), 1091; Johnston, "Bragg's Campaign in Kentucky: From Munfordville to Frankfort," Johnston Military Papers.
[13] OR, XVI (pt. 2), 891-92; Johnston, "Bragg's Campaign in Kentucky: From Munfordville to Frankfort," Johnston Military Papers.

count," he complained. "Even the women are giving reasons why individuals should not go." [14] Convinced now that Kentuckians would join his army only after he had proved its strength, Bragg decided that he must defend the state, for a time at least, with the men already in his and Smith's armies. But where should he establish his defense line? No place seemed satisfactory for Bragg tried to do too much with too few men. He wished to hold as much of the state as possible, and he tried to cover all the roads from Louisville over which Buell's army might march into eastern Kentucky. Bragg also wanted to protect Frankfort, where his pro-Confederate government would legislate, as well as the supply depot at Danville, some fifty-five miles south of the state capital. Before he left Danville he had dispatched instructions to Polk. "I consider it best to move your troops forward [toward Frankfort]," Bragg had written; "camp your main bodies" near Taylorsville, twenty miles northeast of Bardstown. Bragg sent Stevenson's troops to Shelbyville to replace Cleburne's and Preston Smith's brigades, which he ordered to join Polk. These orders suggest that Bragg wanted most of his army stationed about half way between Bardstown and Frankfort. But on October 1 he advised Polk: "It will never do to allow the enemy . . . to gain our rear. It is very important that we hold the road at Elizabethtown." [15] Probably Bragg only meant for Polk to send cavalry to Elizabethtown, about twenty miles southwest of Bardstown, but even a small force placed there would have spread the army over nearly a fifty mile front.

[14] Johnston, "Bragg's Campaign in Kentucky: From Munfordville to Frankfort," Johnston Military Papers; Brent Diary, October 1, 1862; George W. Brent's Memoranda of Events Connected with the Kentucky Campaign, October 1, 1862, Palmer Collection of Bragg Papers; Bragg to Polk, October 1, 1862 (microfilm copy), Leonidas Polk Papers, Southern Historical Collection, University of North Carolina. On the authenticity and authorship of Brent's Memoranda, see Gow, "The Johnston and Brent Diaries."

[15] OR, XVI (pt. 2), 891–92; Bragg to Polk, October 1, 1862 (microfilm copy), Polk Papers, University of North Carolina.

Before Polk had moved troops to either Taylorsville or Elizabethtown, Bragg issued new orders. On October 2, while still at Lexington, he received reports that the enemy, in "considerable force," had compelled Cleburne to abandon Shelbyville and to retire toward Frankfort. Bragg reacted to this news with surprising confidence. He was in one of his optimistic moods—ready, as frequently happened at such times, to abandon his defensive strategy and to strike the enemy. His plan, as noted by a member of his staff, was for "Polk at Bardstown to move on the enemy via Bloomfield & assail him in flank & rear; whilst . . . Smith, with the Army of Kentucky would move directly on his front." Bragg directed Polk to prepare his army to march northward with cooked rations. If Polk learned that a large Union force was advancing on Frankfort, he must "strike [that force's right flank] without further orders." Smith's army would be at Frankfort the next day. At 1 P.M. Bragg sent Polk additional instructions: "The enemy is certainly advancing on Frankfort. Put your whole available force in motion by Bloomfield & strike him in flank, and rear. If we can combine our movements he is certainly lost." [16]

Bragg's plan of a Napoleonic concentration of forces on the battlefield was bold, but it was based upon inadequate intelligence. Bragg, who had only vague reports on the location of the Federal forces, misunderstood Buell's strategy. The Union movement on Frankfort "may be a reconnaissance," Bragg admitted to Polk on October 2, "but should it be a real attack we

[16] Colonel W. G. M. Davis to Bragg, October 2, 1862 (telegram), Palmer Collection of Bragg Papers; Brent Diary, October 3, 1862; *OR*, XVI (pt. 2), 896–97. The original 1 P.M. dispatch is in the Leonidas Polk Papers, Library of Congress. Joseph Parks (*Smith*, p. 233, and *Polk*, pp. 262–63) accepted Kirby Smith's claim, which is unsupported by contemporary evidence, that at Lexington Smith and "Buckner tried to persuade Bragg to give up the inaugural ceremony and begin concentrating all available forces for an all out engagement with Buell. But Bragg expressed confidence that his army at Bardstown, now commanded by Polk, could take care of Buell."

have them. . . . With Smith in front and our gallant army on the flank I see no hope for Buell if he is rash enough to come out. I only fear it is not true." Bragg was too cocksure. Actually, the Federals had advanced from Louisville on four roads over a sixty mile front. "The plan of my movement," Buell explained after the war, "was to force the enemy's left back and compel him to concentrate as far as possible from any convenient line of retreat, while at the same time making a strong demonstration against his right, so as to mislead him as to the real point of attack, and prevent him from moving upon my left flank and rear." [17]

On October 3, confident that Polk was moving north to join Smith in an attack on the Federal advance, Bragg and his staff left Lexington by train for Frankfort. They were accompanied by "Hawes & many ladies." Bragg seemed cheerful. "The impression strongly prevails that the great Battle will be fought in this vicinity," wrote Colonel Brent.[18]

But at Frankfort, after Bragg had read the latest reports from the front, he became less certain of Federal plans and he decided to halt Polk's march temporarily. At 8 P.M. on October 3 Bragg wrote Polk: "I have sent you several dispatches since yesterday morning desiring you to move your force on the enemy, who was making a descent on this point. That move has proved to be only a feint and has ceased. You will act accordingly, but I desire you to hold your command ready for a junction at any moment, and if possible place one flank at Taylorsville." [19] Again Bragg had mistaken Federal intentions; the Union movement against Frankfort was a feint, as he indicated to Polk, but it had not ceased.

Nor was Polk preparing to march to Frankfort, as Bragg

[17] *OR*, XVI (pt. 2), 896–97; Buell, "East Tennessee and the Campaign of Perryville," p. 47.

[18] Johnston, "Bragg's Campaign in Kentucky: From Munfordville to Frankfort," Johnston Military Papers; Brent Diary, October 3, 1862; Brent's Memoranda, October 3, 1862.

[19] *OR*, XVI (pt. 2), 903.

expected when he sent his 8 P.M. dispatch. The Bishop had not even moved to Taylorsville, as ordered on September 30; he was still at Bardstown on October 3 when he received instructions to march northward. Furthermore, Polk had sent neither aid nor orders to Cleburne, at Shelbyville, though Polk had known for more than a day that Cleburne's force was threatened. Yet Polk had the temerity to write Bragg at 10 A.M. on October 2: "It seems to me we are too much scattered." [20]

Polk was right; Confederate forces were too far apart—but he was about to separate them further. He had decided that Bragg's order to march toward Frankfort was based on faulty knowledge of the Federal army's location; reports from Polk's cavalry indicated that Buell's entire force was converging on Bardstown. Polk, who had not yet received Bragg's order to suspend the march to Frankfort, told his highest ranking generals that he had decided to retreat toward Danville in defiance of Bragg's order of October 2; he asked and received their support for this extraordinary decision. Although Hardee and Cheatham later refused to reveal what they had advised, Sterling A. M. Wood readily admitted counseling Polk to disregard Bragg's order and to retreat. Apparently only Patton Anderson, the junior officer present at the meeting and a strong Bragg supporter, favored obeying the order. Anderson pointed out that if Polk failed to march to Frankfort and cooperate with Smith the results might be disastrous for the Confederates.[21] But Polk disregarded Anderson's opinion. At 3 P.M. on October 3 Polk wrote Bragg: "The last twenty-four hours have developed a condition of things on my front and left

[20] At 10 P.M. on October 1 Cleburne informed Polk that the enemy was advancing on Shelbyville and asked for instructions. Cleburne to Polk, October 1, 1862, Palmer Collection of Bragg Papers; Polk to Bragg, 10 A.M., October 2, 1862, *ibid.* Hardee also wrote (10 A.M., October 2, 1862, *ibid.*) Bragg: "I judge you will deem a concentration of your force essential in the present juncture."

[21] *OR*, XVI (pt. 1), 1101, 1107; Wood to Bragg, April 13, 1863, Palmer Collection of Bragg Papers; Anderson to Bragg, April 15, 1863, *ibid.*

flank which . . . makes compliance with this order not only eminently inexpedient, but impracticable. I have called a council of wing and division commanders, to whom I have submitted the matter, and find that they . . . indorse my views. I shall therefore pursue a different course, assured that when the facts are submitted to you you will justify my decision." [22] Polk not only disobeyed orders; he failed to explain why he thought it was necessary to retreat to Danville. His letter to Bragg was too vague. For some reason Polk kept what he knew or guessed about Buell's advance from his commander.

Yet most Civil War writers have condoned Polk's disobedience of orders. Bragg, they point out, mistakenly believed Buell's army was concentrated near Frankfort, when actually it was converging on Bardstown.[23] Had Polk moved toward Frankfort on October 3 as ordered, wrote his son, the Confederates would have been "speedily" attacked by "all of Buell's army." This statement is nonsense. Nor would a march to Smith's aid have necessarily exposed the Confederate flank to attack, as Polk claimed. Buell's army was not concentrated on October 3, and Polk's cavalry, if properly used, could have screened the army's march. All these objections were afterthoughts to justify Polk's action. The Bishop even claimed he disobeyed no order; Bragg directed him to move with all his "available" force, but none of his troops were available for a march to Frankfort.[24]

What Polk's partisans have overlooked is that Buell's army from October 3 through October 5 occupied positions which just might have allowed Bragg's original plan to work. Buell's force of about 82,000 men had marched from Louisville on October 1 in four columns: General Thomas L. Crittenden's corps toward Shepardsville, General Charles C. Gilbert's corps

[22] OR, XVI (pt. 1), 1094-95.
[23] See, for example, Williams, Lincoln Finds a General, IV, 126; Horn, Army of Tennessee, pp. 178-79; Parks, Smith, p. 233, and Polk, p. 265; Connelly, Army of the Heartland, p. 248.
[24] Polk, Leonidas Polk, II, 140; OR, XVI (pt. 1), 1101.

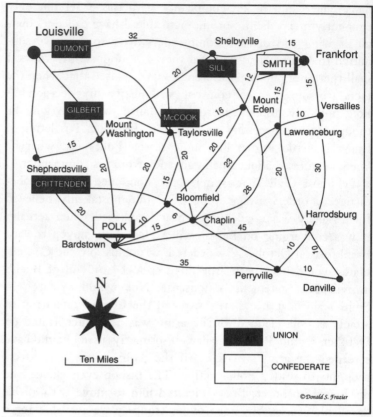

LOCATION OF FORCES, October 3, 1862

toward Mount Washington, General Alexander M. McCook's corps toward Taylorsville, and General Joshua W. Sill's division (detached from McCook's corps), as well as General Ebenezer Dumont's division, toward Frankfort. These two divisions marching on Frankfort totaled approximately 22,000 men. On October 3, when Polk decided to retreat to Danville, each of Buell's columns was about a day's march apart.

McCook, Gilbert, and Crittenden were advancing toward Bardstown on three different roads; they were still twenty miles away. Buell, convinced that Bragg would concentrate at Danville, was moving cautiously.[25] Bragg, of course, did not know all this, but he did realize on October 4 that he had been mistaken about the Federal advance on Frankfort; it had not ceased. At that time, had he not received word of Polk's retreat, Bragg probably would have ordered Polk to join Smith's army near Frankfort. Bragg had every reason to believe, until he learned of the retreat, that Polk already had at least one division at Taylorsville and was prepared to march to Smith's support.

Had Polk moved rapidly to Frankfort on October 3 or 4 and cooperated with Smith the outcome of the Kentucky campaign might have been different. The Confederates, who would have outnumbered Sill and Dumont, might have crushed these two Union divisions or at least forced them to retire to Louisville. In any event, the armies of Bragg and Smith would have been united and better able to meet Buell's main force. Buell might have gained the Confederate rear by marching to Danville, but such a move would have left his supply line open to attack and uncovered Louisville. As the campaign up to this point had already proved, Bragg's forces were less tied to supply lines than Buell's. A junction of Confederate forces near Frankfort certainly would have surprised Buell and upset his plans for it was not what he expected.

The essential question, of course, is whether or not Buell could have prevented Polk from reaching Frankfort. It seems unlikely for two reasons: Buell's army was too scattered on October 3 for effective control, and Buell believed Polk would retreat toward Danville. The only Federal force in a position to block Polk's march to Frankfort was McCook's two divisions at Taylorsville. As late as October 5, by which time Polk could have bypassed the Federals and joined Smith, McCook

[25] *OR*, XVI (pt. 1), 1024: (pt. 2), 566.

had no idea whether the Confederates had gone to Frankfort or to Danville. "I am in blissful ignorance," he admitted.[26] Granted, however, that McCook might have blocked the roads to Frankfort; it is still doubtful that his 10,000 men, nearly half of them recruits, could have halted 20,000 Confederate veterans. Less than a week later McCook's men broke when attacked by only 5,000 of Polk's troops.

Polk's argument that he did not disobey orders because he was instructed to march with only his "available" force has no merit. It is the argument of a bishop, not a general. If his command was available for a retreat it was also available for a march to Frankfort. Polk and some historians contend that Bragg's order was unclear, but Patton Anderson disagreed. "On the 3rd of October, 1862, I was present at General Polk's quarters in Bardstown," he informed Bragg. "Your dispatch from Frankfort of date 1 P.M. Oct 2nd was read and after an interchange of views in regard to our military condition, as junior officer present, I was called upon by General Polk to give my views as to what was best to be done. I hesitated to do so, whereupon General Polk enquired as to the cause of my reluctance to advise a course which seemed to be so clear: And I replied, that your order just read did not seem to admit of any other course than that of compliance, and that if any other alternative than that of obedience to the order was adopted, it might involve you and the forces with you near Frankfort in great embarrassment if not defeat—that in your dispatch you distinctly stated that Genl. Kirby Smith would attack the enemy then in your front, and that *we* must move through Bloomfield upon him and 'strike him in flank and rear. . . .' " [27]

Though a retreat was the safest course to follow, it was precisely what Buell expected. Thus Polk's move made it easier for Buell to execute his own strategy while it forced Bragg to

26 *Ibid.* (pt. 2), 575.
27 Anderson to Bragg, April 15, 1863, Palmer Collection of Bragg Papers.

cancel his plan to protect Frankfort and the new government he had installed. The decision of Polk to retreat demonstrated more than mere cautiousness; it evidenced a distrust of his commander's judgment totally unsuitable in a second-in-command. Older than Bragg, and closer to the President, Polk probably had been a bishop too long to be a successful subordinate. "With all his ability, energy and zeal, General Polk, by education and habit, is unfitted for executing the orders of others," Bragg informed Davis. "He will convince himself his own views are better, and will follow them without reflecting on the consequences." [28]

One of the strangest claims made by Polk's supporters is that Bragg refused to follow the Bishop's suggestion of October 2 to concentrate Confederate forces. Bragg's orders to Polk, which he disobeyed, were intended to unite the armies or to keep them within supporting distance of each other. Polk's movements after October 3 were away from Frankfort and Smith's army.

The most serious consequence of Polk's disobedience was that it forced the Confederates to abandon Frankfort at a most inopportune moment. On October 4, the day Bragg told Kentuckians he had "driven the invaders" from the state capital, the unexpected news of Polk's retreat arrived. Bragg kept this information from the citizens, but after Governor Hawes had been inaugurated the Confederates abandoned Frankfort. Bragg ordered a concentration of troops at Harrodsburg, ten miles northwest of Danville. If Polk would not come to Frankfort, Bragg and Smith would have to go to Polk; Kentucky's capital was no longer tenable. About 5 P.M. Bragg left the town. "So well was the purpose of the evacuation kept a secret," recalled J. Stoddard Johnston, "that when the order was given for our horses to be brought from the stables, the

[28] OR, XVI (pt. 2), 566; (pt. 1), 1091; Bragg to Davis, May 22, 1863 (copy), Palmer Collection of Bragg Papers. There is also a typescript of this letter in the Bragg Papers, Duke University.

general impression was that we were going to the front on the Shelbyville road, and it was only when General Bragg and his staff rode off in the opposite direction that the truth was revealed. A wonderful change ensued. Where all had been cheerfulness and anticipation of pleasure, alarm and dismay seized upon our friends who did not belong to the army." After dark flames from a railroad bridge Bragg had ordered burned alarmed the countryside. "The news spread with electric speed," noted Johnston. "The evacuation of the State was regarded as a fixed fact. A paralysis of gloom settled upon the people at large, and the name of Bragg became odious. The cause of his sudden change of position was not known, and, as usual, he incurred the obloquy which falls to the lot of a general who does not meet public expectations." [29]

When Bragg reached Harrodsburg at 1 P.M. the next day he discovered that Polk was still determined to concentrate at Danville. Bragg sent him a sharp message. "The general commanding instructs me to renew the directions . . . to you to concentrate your command at this point as rapidly as possible," wrote Colonel Brent. "He does not desire them to move to Danville, as he is withdrawing forces from there." [30]

Polk finally followed orders and started his troops northward, but at this point Bragg made a strategic mistake. At 11 P.M. on October 6 Polk sent Bragg a note that was to cause considerable misunderstanding. Hardee and part of Bragg's army were still some ten miles southwest of Harrodsburg, at Perryville. "I have directed General Hardee to ascertain, if possible, the strength of the enemy which may be covered by his advance," wrote Polk. "I cannot think it large." [31] In other

[29] *OR*, XVI (pt. 2), 904-5; Brent Diary, October 4, 1862; Johnston, "Bragg's Campaign in Kentucky: From Frankfort to Perryville," Johnston Military Papers.

[30] *OR*, XVI (pt. 2), 912. This was the third order sent Polk to evacuate Danville. See *ibid.*, 904, 905, 911.

[31] *OR*, XVI (pt. 1), 1095. William Polk (*Leonidas Polk*, II, 149) insisted his father meant that only the Union advance guard was not large,

words, Hardee faced few Federals. Earlier that same day Bragg had received dispatches from Kirby Smith, near Versailles, "begging for help." He was certain the enemy had concentrated "evidently with a design on Frankfort and Lexington." These reports convinced Bragg that he should unite his and Smith's army and advance toward Lawrenceburg, some twenty miles northwest of Harrodsburg and about ten miles southwest of Versailles. Bragg ordered Withers's and Cheatham's divisions to march northward the next day; Hardee and the rest of Bragg's army would follow as soon as possible. "The enemy's front seems extended & dispersed," noted Colonel Brent. "A good opportunity to strike a blow." [32] But the information Bragg relied upon to make this decision was faulty—the product of his inadequately organized and administered intelligence system. Rather than direct reports from his own cavalry, Bragg received only Hardee's, Polk's, and Smith's evaluations of these reports which misinformed Bragg on the whereabouts of Buell's main army.

A dispatch from Hardee, written at 3:20 P.M. on October 7, caused Bragg to modify his plan. "Tomorrow morning early," Hardee wrote, "we may expect a fight. If the enemy does not attack us you ought unless pressed in another direction to send forward all the reinforcements necessary, take command in person, and wipe him out. I desire earnestly that you will do this. The enemy is about two miles from us; my advance of infantry, Liddell's Brigade, about one mile. If Buckner is with you send him forward. I want him. Liddell has just reported that the enemy is endeavoring to turn his right flank." Since Hardee reported no heavy concentration in his front, Bragg still believed Smith faced most of the Federal army. Even so, Bragg sent reinforcements to Hardee. At 5:40 P.M. Bragg

---

but that is not what Polk wrote. Nor is it likely that Polk knew where Buell's main army was.

[32] Brent's Memoranda, October 6, 1862; *OR*, XVI (pt. 2), 918; (pt. 1), 1095–96; Brent Diary, October 6, 1862.

wrote Polk: "In view of the news from Hardee you had better move with Cheatham's division to his support and give the enemy battle immediately; rout him, and then move to our support at Versailles." "No time should be lost in these movements," Bragg reminded Polk.[33]

Later, both Polk and Hardee claimed they knew most of Buell's army was near Perryville on October 7. His 3:20 P.M. dispatch, Hardee insisted in his report, informed Bragg "that the enemy was moving in heavy force against my position" and "urged the concentration of the whole army at Perryville." Actually, Hardee's message merely stated that the enemy was advancing; though his dispatch failed to mention the size of the Union force, Hardee implied that it was not large. He did not say he was threatened by a "heavy force," nor did he "urge the concentration of the whole army at Perryville." Neither Polk nor Hardee suggested that most of Buell's army was near Perryville. On October 7 Polk wrote his wife from Harrodsburg: "We have come here to concentrate our army with that of E. Kirby Smith. It has been done and now we shall give the Enemy battle whenever he presents himself." These are hardly the words of a man who knew the location of the main Federal army. It seems clear that Hardee and Polk were as poorly informed about the enemy's location as Bragg. Months later, after Polk and Hardee charged that their advice had been ignored, the inspector general of the army, Colonel William K. Beard, wrote Bragg: "I had occasion to see you frequently during the few days preceding the battle of Perryville & well recollect that you were led to believe from the information given you by the officers commanding both at Perryville & Versailles that the main attack would be in the direction of the latter place." Colonel David Urquhart also remembered that Smith pleaded for reinforcements, "confident that the feint was against Perryville, and that the main

33 Hardee to Bragg, 3:20 P.M., October 7, 1862 (copy), Palmer Collection of Bragg Papers; Brent Diary, October 7, 1862; OR, XVI (pt. 1), 1096.

attack would surely fall on him. Thus urged, General Bragg, against his own judgment, yielded, and detached two of his best divisions. . . ." [34]

Near midnight on October 7 Bragg received another message from Hardee, written at 7:30 P.M. "Permit me, from the friendly relations so long existing between us, to write you plainly," he begged. "Do not scatter your forces. There is one rule in our profession which should never be forgotten; it is to throw the masses of your troops on the fractions of the enemy." This advice was taken directly from a nineteenth-century military textbook. It may have been wrong, but it was what Napoleon, Jomini, and Mahan had taught, and it was what both Hardee and Bragg believed. "If it be your policy to strike the enemy at Versailles," reasoned Hardee, "take your whole force with you and make the blow effective; if, on the contrary, you should decide to strike the army in front of me, first let that be done with a force which will make success certain. Strike with your whole strength first to the right then to the left. I could not sleep quietly tonight without giving expression to these views," Hardee continued. "If you wish my opinion, it is that in view of the position of your depots you ought to strike this force first." [35]

If Bragg resented this lecture, his immediate actions did not reveal it. He was nevertheless concerned. Hardee still failed to mention the size of the force he faced, but he now implied that it was sizable. If Buell's main army threatened Smith, it would be a mistake to evacuate Versailles and uncover the Confederate supply base at Lexington. On the other hand, if Buell confronted Hardee, the evacuation of Perryville and Harrodsburg would endanger the supply depot at Bryantsville. With apparently conflicting reports before him, Bragg decided it

[34] *OR*, XVI (pt. 1), 1102, 1109, 1120; Polk to His Wife, October 7, 1862, Polk Papers (microfilm copy), University of North Carolina; Beard to Bragg, April 24, 1863, Palmer Collection of Bragg Papers; Urquhart, "Bragg's Advance and Retreat," p. 602.

[35] *OR*, XVI (pt. 1), 1099. The original letter is in the Palmer Collection of Bragg Papers.

was too late to modify his orders to Polk. Withers's division could not be recalled; it was nearing Versailles. But Bragg ordered Preston Smith's brigade, the only unit within reasonably quick marching distance of Perryville, to join Polk instead of Kirby Smith. Furthermore, Bragg prepared to ride south instead of north at dawn.[36]

Bragg, usually "a rapid rider," hurried to Perryville. On the way he received a message from Polk, written at 6 A.M., promising to attack "vigorously" at daylight, but no attack was underway when Bragg arrived at 9:30 A.M. Polk, who met Bragg outside the town, explained that after consultation with his highest ranking subordinates he had decided to adopt what he called "the defensive-offensive, to await the movements of the enemy, and to be guided by events" rather than by Bragg's orders.[37]

Bragg must have been furious, especially after he reconnoitered and saw Polk's disposition of the army. Three roads fanned westward from Perryville: one went northwest to Mackville, another due west to Springfield, and the other southwest to Lebanon. Each crossed an almost dry stream

[36] Brent's Memoranda, October 8, 1862; Brent Diary, October 7, 1862; Beard to Bragg, April 24, 1863, Palmer Collection of Bragg Papers. Preston Smith's brigade arrived at Perryville in time to guard the wagon train, but did not participate in the battle.

[37] OR, XVI (pt. 1), 1092, 1096, 1110, 1120; Brent Diary, October 8, 1862; J. Stoddard Johnston, "Battle of Perryville," Johnston Military Papers. The officers whom Polk consulted on October 8 were Hardee, Buckner, and Cheatham. Later each refused to say what he had advised. OR, XVI (pt. 1), 1101, 1105–7. Six months after the event Polk said he had not received an order to attack. He insisted that the letter directing him to go to Perryville with Cheatham's division and "give the enemy battle immediately" was "not mandatory, but simply suggestive and advisory." He claimed he "already knew . . . that three-fifths of Buell's army" was near Perryville before he left Harrodsburg, and consequently that "great caution" was justified. OR, XVI (pt. 1), 1102. If Polk knew that most of Buell's army was at Perryville, why did he keep this information from Bragg? Moreover, why did Polk write at 6 A.M. on October 8 that he would attack immediately if he considered "great caution" necessary?

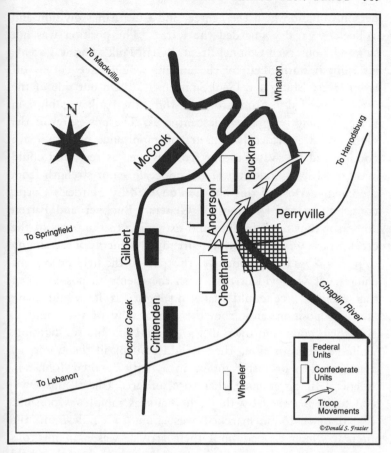

POSITION OF FORCES AT PERRYVILLE, 10 a.m., October 8, 1862

called Doctor's Creek, which trickled northeast into Chaplin River about two miles above Perryville. Between the town and Doctor's Creek Polk had placed the 15,000 Confederates in a concave line facing west. Buckner's division and Colonel John A. Wharton's cavalry brigade, which protected the infantrymen's flank, occupied the extreme right of the battleline; Anderson's division held the center; and Cheatham's division and Wheeler's cavalry guarded the left.[38] "The position was not so good," observed Colonel Brent. "Genl Polk's line was weak, his right if outflanked by the enemy would have cut us off from Harrodsburg and Genl Smith. . . ." "On our side of the creek," recalled J. Stoddard Johnston, "the bank was bluff in places, sloping by gradual descent. . . . The possession of the bluff . . . was evidently a matter of importance, as with it, we commanded the water in our front as well as rear, and could mask our forces under the slope, concealing our strength from the enemy. Most of this line was covered by Hardee's Corps, consisting of the Divisions of Generals Buckner and Patton Anderson, but to their right and extending to the forks of the creek, there was a gap, which already the enemy were aiming to possess." As Bragg rode over this part of the field he saw the danger. "It was evident that, with the enemy in possession of this position, we could make no fight, as it would flank Hardee's position, and from the topography of the country, give them command over all the ground suitable for fighting, while at the same time, they would control all the water, an item never to be lost sight of in a battle," noted Johnston. "General Bragg at once, therefore, ordered Cheatham's Division to be marched by the right flank as rapidly as possible. The distance to be marched was about two miles, and the interval which elapsed until their arrival, was a momentous one, as should the enemy in force occupy the height then held by their skirmishers, it would . . . compel us to take up position on the east side of the creek, which was wooded and unavailable for offensive operations." [39]

[38] Unless otherwise noted description of terrain and combat is based upon the reports in *OR*, XVI (pt. 1), 1087–1134, and the manuscript reports of Brigadier Generals George Maney and Alexander P. Steward (Palmer Collection of Bragg Papers), which were not printed.

[39] Brent's Memoranda, October 8, 1862; Johnston, "Battle of Perryville," Johnston Military Papers.

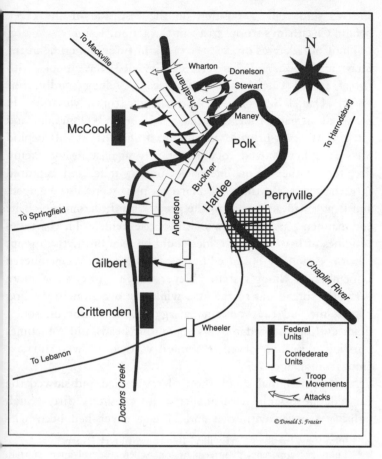

BATTLE OF PERRYVILLE, October 8, 1862

After Cheatham's men arrived "at the double quick" about
noon and drove the enemy skirmishers from the creek bank,
Bragg decided to continue the advance. He ordered Polk to
send Cheatham's brigades across the creek in echelon;
Hardee's command would follow "to take advantage of the
confusion . . . Polk's unexpected attack would cause." Bragg

and his staff took a position on the east side of the creek behind Cheatham's troops to await the action.[40]

The Confederates crossed the creek in force sometime in the early afternoon.[41] Wharton's cavalry led the attack with "great fury." Cheatham's Tennesseeans, yelling loudly, followed: Daniel S. Donelson's brigade in front, Alexander P. Stewart's brigade four hundred yards behind Donelson, and George Maney's brigade one hundred and fifty yards behind Stewart. They moved forward bravely against heavy enemy fire, forced the Union line back about a mile, and captured three batteries. By this time Hardee's men were also engaged, and Bragg had advanced to the creek's bluff, "from which he commanded a perfect view of the battle-field." "The batteries and lines of battle of both sides could be seen distinctly, except when occasionally obscured by the dense smoke," remembered a member of Bragg's staff. "Never was a battle scene more perfectly spread out to the eye, while the occasional whistling of a minie and the constant passage of shells near us, sometimes cutting the cedar twigs above our heads and sometimes bursting close by, served to remind us that we were not exempt from danger." [42]

After their initial shock the Federals rallied and slowed the Confederate assault with artillery and musketry fire. "Such fighting I never witnessed and in fact never had been wit-

[40] Johnston, "Battle of Perryville," Johnston Military Papers.

[41] There is apparent disagreement on when the advance started. Colonel Brent noted (Brent Diary, October 8, 1862): "At 12½ PM the ball regularly opened & for 7 hours, the most hotly contested battle I ever saw took place." But J. Stoddard Johnston recalled ("Battle of Perryville," Johnston Military Papers): "It was expected that the battle would open at one o'clock, but that hour passing, staff officers were sent to ascertain the cause of the delay, and to order immediate attack. Another half hour elapsing, General Bragg rode to the extreme right himself, and directed the movement of the line at once. General Polk was, at the time . . . making final arrangements for the . . . attack and reconnoitering the ground. It was a few minutes after two p.m., when Cheatham's noble Division . . . moved forward, as if on dress parade. . . ."

[42] Johnston, "Battle of Perryville," Johnston Military Papers.

CONFEDERATE ATTACK ON STARKWEATHER'S BRIGADE
Library of Congress

nessed on the battlefields of America," wrote a Shiloh veteran. "There was no cringing, no dodging. The men stood right straight up on the open field, loaded and fired, charged and fell back as deliberately as if on drill." The Confederates used the same tactics and assault formations they had employed at Shiloh with similar results. A regiment of Donelson's brigade lost 199 men trying to capture a Federal battery. "Genls Bragg & Hardee & all the regulars pronounced it the severest struggle ever witnessed," noted a staff officer. "Gen Hardee said to me, on the field, that it was 'Nip & Tuck' & he once thought 'Nip' had it." [43]

[43] *OR*, XVI (pt. 1), 1038–49, 1155–56; E. John Ellis to His Mother, October 21, 1862, E. John, Thomas C. W. Ellis and Family Papers; John H. Savage, *The Life of John H. Savage, Citizen, Soldier, Lawyer, Congressman* (Nashville, 1903), p. 116; Brent Diary, October 8, 1862.

The Confederates lost momentum after they had driven the enemy back nearly two miles and had captured fifteen guns. Bragg rode to the front to encourage his men, but it was no use—the attack had stalled. "A ghastly scene of dead and dying [met] . . . our view at each step," remembered a staff officer; "the blue and the grey mingled together in sickening confusion." [44] Stewart's brigade was out of ammunition. Nearby Maney tried unsuccessfully to urge his tired men forward. The brigades of S. A. M. Wood and John Calvin Brown were shattered, their commanders severely wounded. Other badly battered units could only hold the ground they had already gained.

At this point, late in the afternoon, Bragg committed the last of his reserves, St. John R. Liddell's brigade of Arkansans. As Liddell's men advanced in the twilight Polk saw them fired upon by what he believed to be another Confederate unit. "Dear me, this is very sad, and must be stopped," Polk muttered as he cantered over to the erring commander and asked why he was shooting his friends. "I don't think there can be any mistake about it," replied the surprised officer. "I am sure they are the enemy." "Enemy," exclaimed Polk, "why I have only just left them myself—cease firing, sir; what is your name, sir?" After the officer gave his name and his Union regiment, he asked, "and pray, sir, who are you?" Polk, realizing his mistake, brazenly shook his fist in the Federal officer's face, and said: "I'll soon show you who I am. Cease firing at once." Polk then turned his horse and rode slowly back to join Liddell. "They are enemies; fire upon them," Polk yelled as he reached the Confederate line. Liddell's men responded with deadly volleys, which routed the startled Federal regiment, but it was now dark and the battle was almost over. Artillery fire continued until about 8 P.M.; then, wrote an observer, "all was the stillness of death." [45]

44 Johnston, "Battle of Perryville," Johnston Military Papers.
45 OR, XVI (pt. 1), 1157–60; Polk, Leonidas Polk, II, 161–62; John-

At his headquarters, about half a mile from Perryville on the Harrodsburg Road, Bragg consulted his principal subordinates. "It was evident that we had gained a victory, but against great odds and at a heavy loss," recalled a member of Bragg's staff. "It was also evident that the main body of the enemy was in our front, our intelligence from prisoners, of whom we had a number, giving us all needed information." Bragg decided to withdraw from Perryville and to unite his forces with Kirby Smith's. Near midnight Bragg's troops retired to a position east of Perryville, and early the next morning they started for Harrodsburg.[46]

The Confederates had gained only a limited tactical success at Perryville. It was not a victory because they achieved nothing and suffered almost as many casualties as they inflicted on the Federals: 3,396 Confederates and 4,211 Federals were killed, wounded, or captured (or were missing). Cheatham's division lost 30 per cent of its effectives, including 40 per cent of Maney's brigade. Eight days after the contest a Union officer thought the battlefield "the most horrid sight that ever man beheld. Today," he wrote his wife, "there are hundreds of men being eaten up by the buzzards and hogs." [47]

The battle proved that Bragg was no better at commanding an army in combat than he had been at leading a corps. He had fought blindly, unaware that nearly 60,000 Union troops were

---

ston, "Battle of Perryville," Johnston Military Papers. One scholar believed the "skillful handling of Confederate artillery" accounted for much of the success Bragg's army achieved. Ralph A. Wooster, "Confederate Success at Perryville," *Register of the Kentucky Historical Society*, LIX (1961), 318–23. Wooster's conclusion has been challenged by Charles W. F. Bishop, "Civil War Field Artillery in the West, 1862–1863" (M.A. Thesis, University of British Columbia, 1967), pp. 49–54.

[46] Brent Diary, October 8–9, 1862; Johnston, "Battle of Perryville," Johnston Military Papers; *OR*, XVI (pt. 1), 1093.

[47] Confederate losses were: 510 killed, 2,635 wounded, and 515 captured or missing. *OR*, XVI (pt. 1), 1112, 1036. Captain Alexander M. Ayers to His Wife, October 16, 1862, Alexander M. Ayers Papers (in possession of Professor W. Darrell Overdyke, Centenary College of Louisiana).

near Perryville. He could blame others—Polk, Hardee, and Smith—for giving him incorrect or inadequate information on the whereabouts of Buell's main force,[48] but the responsibility for a faulty intelligence service and the absence of a staff of experts to analyze reports rested squarely upon Bragg, as army commander.[49] Perhaps even more important, Bragg showed no talent for tactical innovation. He tried to beat the enemy by direct bayonet attacks, just as he had done at Shiloh. He used all his reserves in an attempt to crush the enemy's flank, a tactical maneuver he would employ repeatedly in his battles; he committed his men recklessly, regardless of casualties, but in driblets. Such action might have been disastrous had Buell handled his troops effectively. But he did not realize a battle was underway until 4 P.M., and he got less than two thirds of his men into the fight. Wheeler's cavalry, which screened the Confederate left flank, kept one entire Federal corps out of action.[50]

Bragg halted his forces at Harrodsburg, where Kirby Smith's army and Withers's division joined them on October 10. To oppose Buell's advance, Bragg placed his and Smith's troops in a battleline two miles south of Harrodsburg on the

---

[48] In his initial report, written two days after the battle, Bragg generously gave Polk, Hardee, Cheatham, Buckner, and Anderson credit for "the brilliant achievements on this memorable field. Nobler troops were never more gallantly led." Bragg was less gracious, however, after some of his generals criticized his campaign. In their reports Polk and Hardee claimed that they had informed Bragg several times on October 7 that most of Buell's army was near Perryville. Bragg called them liars and gathered documents to prove it. He also pointed out that Polk had repeatedly disobeyed orders during the campaign. OR, XVI (pt. 1), 1088, 1091–93, 1101–3, 1109–12, 1119–22; Bragg to Hardee, April 24, 1863, Palmer Collection of Bragg Papers.

[49] Bragg apparently expected Kentuckians to keep him informed on the enemy's movements, but they did not. "Information from citizens it seems impossible to obtain," wrote a member of Bragg's staff, "and so far as that was concerned, we were in an enemy's country." J. Stoddard Johnston's Memoranda, January 8, 1863, Johnston Military Papers.

[50] OR, XVI (pt. 1), 556, 464, 477, 898, 656, 660, 51.

west bank of Salt Creek. But when reports, which arrived during the night, suggested that Buell was moving toward Danville and Bryantsville, Bragg ordered a withdrawal to Bryantsville to protect his supply depot.[51]

On October 11 the Confederates reached Bryantsville, and Bragg soon announced his intention to abandon Kentucky. Discouraged by the few recruits obtained in the state, he now feared that autumn rains would make all roads leading south "utterly impassable." Moreover, reports that a Union army was marching from Cincinnati to join Buell's force disturbed Bragg. But a report that Van Dorn and Price, whom Bragg expected to advance into Tennessee, had been defeated at Corinth on October 4 prompted Bragg's decision to quit Kentucky. "The news of this disaster reached General Bragg on the 12th of October," noted an officer. "His mind was immediately made up. The cause of the whole country required that he should return and that the fate of the Confederacy should not be staked upon an unequal engagement with the enemy, nor by the dangers of a delay." There was still another reason to retreat: Bragg discovered that the Bryantsville depot contained few supplies. Despite orders issued on September 27, Bragg's and Smith's quartermasters had failed to transfer sufficient food from Danville and Lexington. Only four days' rations were on hand at Bryantsville.[52]

Kirby Smith later insisted that the army had plenty of "supplies & provisions," but his claim is refuted by contemporary

[51] Brent Diary, October 10, 1862; Joseph Wheeler to Brent, October 10, 1862, Palmer Collection of Bragg Papers. Kirby Smith later claimed that he favored remaining at Harrodsburg. "For God's sake, General, let us fight Buell here," Smith quotes himself as saying to Bragg. See Parks, *Smith*, pp. 237–38.

[52] Brent's Memoranda, October 11, 1862; *OR*, XVI (pt. 1), 1093; (pt. 2), 883; Brent Diary, October 11, 1862; Johnston's Memoranda, January 8, 1863. Bragg's brother noted (Thomas Bragg Diary, October 7, 1862): "I fear Gen'l Bragg has risked a good deal upon other movements in combination from the Miss. Army, which were not made, or if so not in time. . . ."

evidence. A few days before the Confederates arrived at Bryantsville, the depot there contained, in addition to some candles and soap: 33,000 pounds of hardtack, 10,000 pounds of bacon, 500 pounds of lard, 3,000 barrels of pork, 250 barrels of flour, 130 barrels of sugar, 702 cattle, 75 sacks of coffee, 5 sacks of salt, and 1 sack of rice. The Bryantsville depot contained insufficient food for an army of 45,000 men, even Confederates, who were accustomed to a scant diet.[53]

The Confederates started for Cumberland Gap on October 13, traveling in two columns. "Smith and Marshall are said to be opposed to this movement," noted Colonel Brent. "But what else can be done. We are outnumbered, & far removed from our base. The enemy is near his, drawing ample supplies of men & subsistence. Kentucky has not furnished us men. The prime object of the invasion . . . has failed; & finally painful rumors prevail that Price has been defeated by Rosecrans, so that nothing but retreat is left to us." Kentuckians charged "fabulous prices" and demanded gold for the food and clothing they supplied "our hungry and naked soldiers," Bragg complained to Elise, and half of the 2,000 Kentuckians who enlisted during the invasion had deserted. Therefore, Bragg believed it would be foolish to continue risking the lives of his "handful of brave Southern men" fighting "for cowards." In answer to a report that thirty-two regiments had been organized in Kentucky, Captain E. John Ellis wrote: "We found indeed 32 men who were willing to be Colonels, 32 willing to serve as Lieut Cols and Majors, any quantity ready to tack on their collars the bars of a Captain or Lieut, but few, very few willing to serve in the ranks. *Kentucky is*

[53] Parks, *Smith*, p. 238; Captain Isaac Scherck's Memorandum, October 7, 1862, Palmer Collection of Bragg Papers. Colonel Brent also mentioned the scarcity of supplies, and on October 12 Bragg sent Withers to Tennessee "for the purpose of procuring supplies for the forces here." Brent Diary, October 12, 1862; Brent's Memoranda, October 19, 1862; *OR*, XVI (pt. 2), 938.

subjugated." [54] This, of course, was true, but it was also a fact that Bragg and many of his disappointed soldiers wanted to blame Kentuckians for most of the failures of the campaign.[55]

The Confederates, protected by Wheeler's cavalry, made the long march to East Tennessee safely. "Thus terminates the Ky campaign," wrote Colonel Brent from Cumberland Gap on October 19. "It failed owing to several causes. The failure of Ky to co-operate actively and efficiently, the scarcity of subsistence stores &c., the overwhelming superiority of the enemy's force, the failure of Van Dorn at Corinth which exposed our left, clearly indicated the propriety and wisdom of the retreat at the very moment the General decided upon it." [56]

But not everyone agreed with Colonel Brent. As the fatigued and hungry troops [57] trudged southward soldiers and civilians cursed Bragg. Few were as restrained as the officer who wrote: "Many blame Gen. Bragg [for the failure of the campaign], I will not till I know that he is the proper man." Polk and Hardee openly censured Bragg, and their remarks confirmed General Liddell's suspicions "that Bragg was not well supported and encouraged by his generals." Generals Kirby Smith and Henry Heth "came to the conclusion that General Bragg had lost his mind," recalled Heth, "and Smith

[54] Brent Diary, October 12–13, 1862; Seitz, *Bragg*, p. 207; Ellis to His Mother, October 21, 1862, E. John, Thomas C. W. Ellis and Family Papers. Marshall wrote a letter to the War Department criticizing Bragg (Jones, *A Rebel War Clerk's Diary*, I, 193), and Smith repeatedly censured Bragg for withdrawing from Kentucky (Parks, *Smith*, pp. 239–43).

[55] Thomas Bragg Diary, October 30, 1862; Atlanta *Confederacy*, quoted in *Richmond Whig*, October 28, 1862.

[56] Brent's Memoranda, October 19, 1862; John P. Dyer, *"Fightin' Joe" Wheeler* (Baton Rouge, 1941), pp. 64–69.

[57] Horn (*Army of Tennessee*, p. 183) suggested that the soldiers ate well on the retreat. For a different view, see Watkins, "Co. Aytch," pp. 85–86, and Assistant Quartermaster Lemuel O. Bridewell to Colonel L. W. O'Bannon, October 12, 1862, Palmer Collection of Bragg Papers.

said he would so state in his report to Mr. Davis." Nor were
the generals the only ones who questioned Bragg's sanity and
competence. "General Bragg is either stark mad or utterly
incompetent," wrote Dr. D. W. Yandell. "I do not doubt Gen.
Bragg's loyalty as some have done," stated a Kentuckian, "nor
question his sanity, as others have done; but, believing him to
be both sane and loyal, I concur in the judgement already
rendered by the people and the army . . . that as a military
commander he is utterly incompetent." Congressman Henry S.
Foote, of Tennessee, told a South Carolinian: ". . . if Bragg is
kept in command of the Western Army, the whole country of
the Mississippi Valley will be lost." And Senator G. A. Henry
wrote his colleague Louis T. Wigfall from Knoxville on October 25: ". . . never have I heard so much dissatisfaction as
this army expresses at the result of Bragg's campaign into Ky.
Even common soldiers say he ought to have whipped Buell at
Munfordville. . . . The army is clamoring for Joe E. Johnston
to lead them, or for Beauregard." "They don't object to
Bragg, on account of his discipline: not at all, but because of
the failure of the campaign. . . . I write the result of my
observations and you may rely on it. I am not deceived. . . .
The greatest blunder of all was for Bragg to have his forces
scattered all over Ky when he fought at Perryville. If his army
had been massed there, he would have totally routed the enemy. The safety of the army depends upon a change of *commanders*." Even Mrs. Bragg joined the critics. "We feel the
greatest anxiety concerning your army," she wrote Bragg on
October 16. "You have it is true made a very rapid march but
without defeating your wary foe. . . . I have a very high
opinion of Gen Buell's abilities, & feel that he has drawn you in
a very precarious position. I had hoped he could have been
overtaken & *driven out* [of Kentucky], his army disorganized.
You have left Nashville strongly garrisoned by Yankees in
your rear, & the fear is, Rosecrantz [*sic*] will soon effect a
junction with them, & thus place you between two enemies. It

will be very hard for you to have to assume the defensive, & to have to fall back when so much was expected from your army. . . . I hoped you would have cleared Tennessee as you advanced." [58]

When Bragg, who was ordered to Richmond on October 23, arrived in the capital he found himself as unpopular with the citizens as a Union general. "At once the dogs of detraction were let loose upon me," he wrote Elise, "and the venal press . . . decided I was removed from my command. . . ." On October 20 the *Richmond Whig* had announced that "something more than boastful orders" had been expected of Bragg, but his "long delay at Tupelo, his hesitancy at Chattanooga, his tardy advance into Kentucky had shaken the public confidence; but few were willing to condemn so long as opportunity yet remained for a consummation of the grand objects of the campaign. It is all over now. The Kentucky movement in the hands of Gen. Bragg has turned out to be simply a fizzle." Bragg was too cautious to command an army, concluded the Richmond *Daily Dispatch* on October 23: ". . . a cautious general is the most dangerous of all generals in the world—to his own friends." [59]

[58] E. John Ellis to His Mother, October 21, 1862, E. John, Thomas C. W. Ellis and Family Papers; Liddell, "Liddell's Record of the Civil War," Liddell Papers; Morrison, ed., "The Memoirs of Henry Heth," pp. 23–24; Yandell to William Preston Johnston, November 8, 1862, Barret Collection of Johnston Papers; A Kentuckian to Editor, November 5, 1862, unidentified and undated newspaper clipping, Kirkpatrick Scrapbook; James Hemphill to His Brother, November 19, 1862, William R., J. C., and R. R. Hemphill Papers, Duke University; Henry to Wigfall, October 25, 1862, Louis T. Wigfall Family Papers, University of Texas; Elise to Bragg, October 16, 1862, Palmer Collection of Bragg Papers.

[59] Brent Diary, October 23, 1862; Seitz, *Bragg*, p. 206; *Richmond Whig*, October 15, 20, 1862; Richmond *Daily Dispatch*, October 23, 1862. Bragg's brother wrote (Thomas Bragg Diary, October 19, 1862): "I see the Raleigh Standard in every number is swearing at Gen'l Bragg as extremely tardy, cautious &c. All this is owing to the hatred of [Editor William W.] Holden, to me. He is the meanest, basest man alive—that is & has been for a long time my deliberate opinion."

The President was cordial, despite all the clamor against Bragg, and gave him the opportunity to defend himself. "I went to Richmond Monday morning the 27th [of October] to see Gen'l Bragg," wrote Thomas Bragg. "I found him looking well & in good spirits. He was in daily conference from 10 A.M. to 4 P.M. with the Pres, & Sec'y of War. I believe the Pres. is entirely satisfied as to the propriety of his withdrawing the Army from Kentucky." [60]

Thomas Bragg was correct; his brother's actions had not displeased Davis. "Gen Bragg returned from Richmond," noted Colonel Brent on November 2. "He brought the gratifying fact, that his conduct in Kentucky had been approved by the President. That the President had expressed his delight at the safe return of the Army." [61]

Perhaps Davis dismissed most of the complaints against Bragg as the anticipated grumblings of administration critics; unpleasant, certainly, but nothing to worry about. For months anti-Davis congressmen had castigated Bragg. "Gen'l B. was assailed by [James L.] Orr [of South Carolina], [John B.] Clark of Missouri & [William L.] Yancey [of Alabama]—all 'sore heads,'" noted Thomas Bragg on September 12. "Orr denounced Gen'l B. as a tyrant, assassin, murderer &c. He was defended by [Clement C.] Clay [of Alabama], [James] Phelan [of Mississippi], [Louis T.] Wigfall [of Texas], [Henry C.] Burnett [of Kentucky] and others." [62]

Only the charge that Bragg had lost the confidence of his army really disturbed Davis. Hoping to stop such talk, he ordered Polk and Kirby Smith to Richmond. Both told the President they considered Bragg responsible for the failure of the Kentucky campaign. They also repeated their accusation that Bragg had lost the confidence of his men and suggested

---

60 Thomas Bragg Diary, October 30, 1862.
61 Brent Diary, November 2, 1862. See also Jones, *A Rebel War Clerk's Diary*, I, 176.
62 Thomas Bragg Diary, September 12, 1862.

that he be replaced by Joseph E. Johnston, who had been without command for several months while recovering from a wound. Polk acknowledged Bragg's great ability as an organizer and disciplinarian, but he insisted his commander lacked "the higher elements of generalship." Smith said he preferred not to be associated with Bragg in any future campaign.[63]

But Davis refused to change his mind. In a letter to Kirby Smith, the President explained why he had decided to retain Bragg. "I have held long and free conversations with Genl. Bragg," Davis wrote on October 29; "he uniformly spoke of you in the most complimentary terms, and does not seem to imagine your dissatisfaction. He has explained in a direct and frank manner the circumstances of his campaign and has evinced the most self denying temper in relation to his future position." Bragg's modesty and candor obviously impressed Davis. "That another Genl. might excite more enthusiasm is probable," admitted the President, "but as all have their defects I have not seen how to make a change with advantage to the public service. His administrative capacity has been felt by the Army of [Mississip]pi, his knowledge of the troops is intimate and a new man would not probably for a time with even greater ability be equally useful." Davis meant that he had no one he wanted to put in Bragg's place. "Of the Generals," he explained, "Cooper is at the head of the Bureau, Lee is in command of the army in Va., Johnston still disabled by the wound received at Seven Pines, Beauregard was tried as Commander of the army of the West and left it without leave, when the troops were demoralized and the country he was sent to protect was threatened with conquest. Bragg succeeded to the command and organized the army and marched to your support with efficient troops," the President reminded Smith. "The retreat from Kentucky was not so bad as that from

[63] OR, XVI (pt. 2), 981; Parks, Smith, pp. 242-45; Polk, Leonidas Polk, II, 165.

. . . Corinth." Bragg had achieved much; clearly he deserved support not censure. Nor would Davis transfer Polk or Smith. The President appealed to their patriotism, attempted to placate them with promotion, and asked them to stop complaining and to cooperate with Bragg.[64]

Davis's attempt to compromise differences was not very successful, even though Bragg apparently tried to be conciliatory. On the train back to Knoxville he encountered Smith. Though "every one prognosticated a stormy meeting," Smith wrote his wife, Bragg "spoke kindly to me & in the highest terms of praise and admiration of 'my personal character and soldierly qualities'—I was astonished but believe he is honest & means well." Perhaps, as Davis noted, Bragg did not know what Smith had said about him. Maybe, for once in his life, Bragg had decided that a quarrel would serve no useful purpose. At this time, his brother noted, Bragg seemed "indifferent, too indifferent it may be to all [his] . . . assailants." [65]

Smith claimed that after he left Richmond neither he nor his staff "uttered a recorded word of criticism of Bragg's Kentucky campaign for the duration of the war," but Polk seemingly was not so willing to reconcile differences.[66] To his brother-in-law Polk denounced Bragg's Kentucky campaign and boasted that if he "had been in chief command, the strategy of the campaign would have been very different—and the practical operation, as to tactics would have been very different." [67] According to several reports, Polk fostered

[64] Davis to Smith, October 29, 1862, E. Kirby Smith Papers.

[65] Parks, *Smith*, p. 245; Thomas Bragg Diary, October 30, 1862.

[66] Parks, *Smith*, p. 245. Although Bragg denied that he charged Polk with negligence at Shiloh, Polk may have heard such a rumor. See Bragg to Judge Milton Brown, February 27, 1863, and Brown to Bragg, March 3, 1863, Palmer Collection of Bragg Papers. On March 25, 1863, Colonel Brent noted in his diary that Bragg referred to Polk's report as the "Romance of Shiloh."

[67] The strategy Polk outlined revealed how quickly he forgot what actually happened as well as some of his shortcomings as a general. "He was in favor of a more rapid and energetic campaign," explained the Bishop's brother-in-law. "Instead of the long detour of 400 miles around

opposition to Bragg and schemed to have him removed from command. "There has been an organized effort to break you down," Congressman James L. Pugh, of Alabama, wrote Bragg from Richmond on March 5, 1863. "This city has been the focal point of all the malignity against you—false representations have been made [by Polk and his friends] to members of Congress, and a dissolute press has teemed with communications originating with these croakers and malcontents." On January 17, 1863, General Preston Smith informed Bragg: "Some two months since, I advised you of what I believed then would occur, an intended effort to supersede you in this command." "I sincerely hope for the discomfiture of those disorganizing schemers now at work for your disadvantage," remarked Smith. Although he had not been approached by "the secret combination" against Bragg, General John K. Jackson believed such a group existed. He had "suspected for some time that an undercurrent had been set in motion, which was intended to sweep [Bragg] . . . away." [68]

Historians have generally accepted the charge that the Kentucky campaign caused nearly every Confederate except Davis to lose confidence in Bragg. There is some evidence for this belief besides the testimony of Kirby Smith and Polk. On November 14, 1862, a soldier wrote: "Genl Bragg . . . still commands this army, though everybody seems to have lost all confidence in him since his Ky. raid." Yet this same soldier

---

by Chattanooga, he was for a more direct and vigorous plan of falling first on one corps of the enemy, and then on another and thus destroying them in detail. Instead of marching on a line, nearly parallel with that of Buell, he was in favor of a cross march, and falling on his flank and crushing him before he could get to the relief of Louisville. And instead of fighting the battle of Perryville with divided forces, he was in favor of concentrating our forces then falling on one corps of the enemy, and after crushing that, the crossing Green River and crushing the other corps—all of which he insisted could have been easily done." Quoted in Parks, *Polk*, p. 280.

[68] Pugh to Bragg, March 5, 1863, Palmer Collection of Bragg Papers; Smith to Bragg, January 17, 1863, *ibid*.; Jackson to Bragg, January 17, 1863, *ibid*.

admitted that Bragg was "*the man* to drill and discipline an army. I am sorry to say that our army, or rather individuals in it act almost as badly as the Yankees, that is they take forage and many other things with[out] either asking or paying for them; but these things are not done when 'Bragg is about' as Death would be the penalty if such acts were brot before his notice." "We do nothing in this department nor will the matter be mended as long as our poor partisan President keeps this miserable tyrant Bragg at the head of affairs," wrote another soldier on November 29. Two weeks later this same man desperately wanted to visit his family, but he reported: ". . . old Bragg would rather see a man hung than have a leave of absence and Bragg is right for we need every man at his post now." [69]

Such letters probably expressed the ambivalent attitude of many men toward Bragg, who seems to have had somewhat similar feelings toward his troops. St. John R. Liddell remembered Bragg telling him about this time: "Genl. I have no children and hence I look upon the soldiers of my army as my own, as my children." Liddell repeated this remark to some soldiers, who replied, Bragg "has a very large family and sometimes causes his boys to be shot." [70]

It would be a mistake, however, to conclude that Bragg had completely lost the confidence of his army. Of the twenty generals directly under his command in Kentucky, apparently only Polk and Hardee openly expressed dissatisfaction with their commander at this time.[71] Thirteen generals and numerous colonels, either in their own words or in those of their

[69] John Buie to His Father, November 14, 1862, Buie Papers; E. John Ellis to His Father, November 29, 1862, E. John, Thomas C. W. Ellis and Family Papers; Ellis to His Sister, December 12, 1862 (typescript), E. John, Thomas C. W. Ellis and Family Papers (B).

[70] Liddell, "Liddell's Record of the Civil War," Liddell Papers.

[71] Hardee wrote Polk (*OR*, XVI [pt. 1], 1098): "If you choose to rip up the Kentucky campaign you can tear Bragg into tatters." See also Dr. D. W. Yandell to William Preston Johnston, November 8, 1862, Barret Collection of Johnston Papers.

contemporaries, declared themselves supporters of Bragg.[72] "My opinion of Genl. Bragg remains unchanged," wrote General Jackson on November 7. "I still think he is as good a general as we have in the Confederacy. The newspaper and street-corner warriors abuse everybody in relation to the conduct of the war, about which they know nothing. It is certainly true that the army was disappointed when we were ordered to fall back, but every officer and man is now satisfied that it was the very *best* thing that could have been done." "The opinion of the army sustains Genl. Bragg, he is the idol with them notwithstanding the censure of newspapers," concluded Jackson.[73]

Nor were all civilians against Bragg. In December 1862, Senator James Phelan advised Bragg not to "let attacks such as was made upon you in the Senate by Mr. Orr disturb your patriotic efforts to save the country. . . . Time will set all that even." Congressman Francis S. Lyon, of Alabama, wrote Bragg in January 1863: "Your campaign in Kentucky in the estimation of those who will take the trouble to inform themselves of the facts leaves you nothing to regret and the public no just grounds of complaint." Two months later Congressman James L. Pugh informed Bragg: ". . . so far as Congress is concerned the majority in your favor is overwhelming." A resolution praising Bragg's Kentucky campaign, continued Pugh, "passed the House by 78 to 2—the Kentucky feeling broke out with three or four but they found no encourage-

[72] I could not determine whether Cheatham, Buckner, Maney, Wood, or Bushrod Johnson had lost confidence in Bragg at this time. Some of them, at least, probably had. The generals on record as Bragg supporters were: Donelson, Withers, Stewart, Brown, Jackson, Chalmers, Cleburne, Anderson, Liddell, Adams, Preston Smith, Franklin Gardner, and Johnson K. Duncan. Some Bragg partisans among the regimental commanders and the colonels commanding brigades were: Wheeler, Thomas M. Jones, Robert C. Tyler, J. G. Coltart, Edward C. Walthall, Henry D. Clayton, Henry Maury, and Zachary Deas.

[73] Jackson to "Dear Frank," November 7, 1862, Charles Colcock Jones Papers, Duke University.

ment or sympathy and their clamor was soon hushed. The two Kentucky Senators [William E. Simms and Henry C. Burnett], old [John B.] Clark of Missouri, Orr of S. C. & Wigfall of Texas will vote against you in the Senate. All the other Senators are for you strongly." Of course, Bragg would always be criticized by "mobocratic mouthpieces" for his determination to "produce that discipline so necessary to the effectiveness of the troops and without which they were little better than an armed mob," announced a citizen in March 1863. But he assured Bragg that his "Kentucky campaign, in spite of Generals ambitious for separate command; in spite of Kentucky growlers, whose people dared not to aid you in defending their own homes, is now proclaimed by the country as conducted with masterly skill and correctness, as it was so appreciated from the first by the President." [74]

Kentuckians continued to be Bragg's most vocal critics. What upset them most, but they hated to admit, was the failure of their own people to join the Confederate army. Richard Hawes, governor-in-exile, railed for three columns in the Richmond *Examiner* against Bragg and John Forsyth, the Mobile editor who had accompanied the Confederates to Kentucky. Hawes claimed Forsyth's reports were "replete with erroneous statements of assumed facts and distortions." Stung by Forsyth's statement that "the campaign was based upon the most positive and reliable promises of a general insurrection in Kentucky, upon the appearance of the Confederate Army, and a rush of 50,000 troops to its standard," Hawes charged: first, that Bragg should have beaten Buell before he got to Louisville; second, that Bragg should have fought at Perryville with 25,000 or 30,000 men instead of with 15,000; third, that Bragg should not have retreated from Perryville; and fourth, that there was no reason for Bragg to

[74] Phelan to Bragg, December 4, 1862, Palmer Collection of Bragg Papers; Lyon to Bragg, January 22, 1863, *ibid.;* Pugh to Bragg, March 5, 1863, *ibid.;* Jenkes Campbell to Bragg, March 1, 1863, *ibid.*

abandon Kentucky when he did. Because Kentucky had been occupied by Federal troops for a year, argued Hawes, "it was natural that our people should be slow in believing our power to hold the State." Yet he admitted: ". . . our rich men, of Southern affinities, loved their estates more than their liberties; but there were many, and very many, shining exceptions." [75] One exception was J. Stoddard Johnston, a Kentuckian who defended Bragg. "[I]t grates harshly to hear Kentuckians reflect unjustly upon him," wrote Johnston. "It was my fortune to accompany him in his campaign, to witness his untiring vigilance, his sleepless industry, his wonderful equanimity under all shades of fortune. That his expedition did not meet the high expectations conceived for it, all admit, but that its failure was owing to causes for which he is censurable is, to say the least, extremely doubtful." [76]

But his friends were too willing to exculpate Bragg. Aside from his failure to hold Kentucky or to destroy Buell's army, Bragg had exhibited certain characteristics during the invasion which made his ability for high field command questionable. At times dauntless, he had also been hesitant and despondent. Too often he had acted on impulse, without sufficient information about the enemy's location or plans, for he had neither an adequate intelligence system nor an experienced staff. He had overworked, devoting so much time to administrative detail that he had exhausted mind and body. Yet he had relied heavily—too heavily because he had failed to win their loyalty—upon the cooperation of his principal subordinates and Kirby Smith. Outguessed by Buell, upset by Polk's disobedience of orders, and confused by conflicting reports, Bragg had fought blindly at Perryville with only a fragment of his force. And a few days later at Bryantsville he had become

[75] Hawes to Editor, Richmond *Examiner*, n.d., clipping, M. J. Solomons Scrapbook, p. 359. See also *Mobile Register and Advertiser*, November 16, December 5, 1862; *Richmond Enquirer*, December 12, 1862.
[76] Johnston's Memoranda, January 8, 1863, Johnston Military Papers.

completely disheartened when inexperienced staff officers failed to provide enough food for the army. "Gen. Bragg is unquestionably an excellent disciplinarian, and a very brave man," admitted a newspaper account while he was in Richmond, "but he seems to have been greatly deficient in some of the other qualities which constitute a great commander. No doubt, serving under some man of great military genius, he would have made an excellent subordinate. The talent of separate command, however, is very rare, and he at least does not seem to possess it." [77] Perhaps President Davis should have heeded this warning and removed Bragg from field command.

On the other hand, there were several reasons why Bragg deserved another chance. He had made some serious mistakes during the Kentucky campaign, but it was the first time he had commanded a large army in the field. Considering his inexperience, he had done reasonably well, better certainly than Albert Sidney Johnston had in his first campaign, and better by all evidence than Polk or Kirby Smith would have if either had been in command. Bragg might have been more successful if Polk and Hardee had given him the support he needed and had a right to expect, or if Kirby Smith had cooperated fully. A divided command, for which Jefferson Davis was primarily responsible, had been a major impediment to Confederate success throughout the invasion. His failure to give Bragg control over Smith's army at the campaign's outset may have been one of the President's biggest military errors. A unified command would not have insured victory, of course, but it would have allowed Bragg to coordinate troop movements and to make plans which would not have to be modified frequently just to fit Smith's independent actions. Hindsight seems to indicate that Bragg should have insisted upon command unity at the outset. Yet, despite a divided command, Bragg and Smith had conceived and executed the most successful Con-

[77] Richmond *Daily Dispatch*, October 23, 1862.

federate offensive. A sympathetic editor called it "one of the
most extraordinary movements in history," and the five Union
generals who investigated Buell's conduct during the invasion
concluded: "History of military campaigns affords no parallel
to [Bragg's] army throwing aside its transportation, paying no
regard to its supplies, but cutting loose from its base, marching
200 miles in the face of and really victorious over an army
double its size." [78]

Lee's invasion of Maryland, just concluded, had failed;
nevertheless, the public praised Lee and denounced Bragg,
though he had achieved more. A young officer, infuriated by
such invidious comparisons, complained to a newspaper editor:
"Gen. Bragg, instead of hearing on his return, the universal
thanks of his countrymen for relieving them . . . of the
insolent presence of their most bitter and unrelenting foes, is
greeted with the upbraidings of an almost unanimous press,
and reproaches of an ungrateful people, for not accomplishing,
with the *inadequate* means at his command, an impossibility,—
That is, the holding of Kentucky against overwhelming odds."
Comparing Lee's and Bragg's invasions, the officer continued:
". . . tell me, Mr. Editor, (for you are the mouth-piece of the
public), which campaign of the two has been the most profitable to the country!—The victories of Gen. Lee, with the
spilling of oceans of blood? or the successes of Gen. Bragg
. . . ? Yet, no bitter jeers, and scornful upbraidings greeted
the retreat of the army from Maryland." Bragg avoided
comparisons when he wrote his final report, but he pointed out
that he and Smith had redeemed northern Alabama and much
of central Tennessee; recovered possession of Cumberland
Gap, "the gate-way to the heart of the Confederacy"; killed,
wounded, or captured not less than 25,000 Union troops; taken
over thirty pieces of artillery, hundreds of wagons, horses and

[78] Unidentified and undated newspaper clipping, Palmer Collection of
Bragg Papers; *OR*, XVI (pt. 1), 16.

mules, 17,000 small arms, and 2,000,000 cartridges; subsisted for two months off the country; and secured enough material in Kentucky to clothe the army.[79]

[79] An Officer to Editor, *Atlanta Intelligencer*, n.d., clipping, M. J. Solomons Scrapbook, p. 358; *OR*, XVI (pt. 1), 1094. Douglas Southall Freeman (*Lee*, II, 405–14) preferred to call Lee's Maryland campaign "unsuccessful," rather than a failure.

CHAPTER XV

Fight . . . and fall back

NOVEMBER 3, 1862–JANUARY 3, 1863

WHILE THE VERBAL controversy over his military competence raged, Bragg prepared for a new campaign. Union armies still threatened Mississippi and Tennessee: one under Grant was about to move south from Corinth; another under Rosecrans, who had replaced Buell, had concentrated at Nashville. President Davis wanted Bragg and Kirby Smith to combine their forces for an advance toward Nashville. "Genl. Bragg cannot move into Middle Tenn. with prospect of success without your cooperation," the President informed Smith on October 29. From Knoxville on November 7 Bragg wrote John C. Pemberton, who had just been assigned command in Mississippi: "We are moving our available forces as rapidly as possible into middle Tennessee, to resume the offensive. . . . This throws us in rear of your opponents, and ought to create some diversion. I would prefer striking the enemy in rear at Corinth . . . but the Tennessee [River] is a barrier we cannot overcome." [1]

But the Confederates, delayed by rickety railroads and the necessity of refitting many soldiers, moved slowly, and before Bragg reached his temporary headquarters at Tullahoma he apparently changed his mind. His letter to Beauregard of November 12 mentioned no proposed offensive; Bragg merely promised: ". . . should the enemy move out of his intrenchments at Nashville, we will soon fight him." [2]

[1] Davis to Smith, October 29, 1862, E. Kirby Smith Papers; *OR*, XX (pt. 2), 394.
[2] *OR*, XX (pt. 2), 400.

On November 17, after Bragg conferred with his generals, he definitely decided against an immediate offensive. Nearly 50 per cent of his troops were absent: many of them were hospitalized; others had simply deserted. "Some of my regiments are down to 100 privates," complained Bragg, who insisted that he had not received a single conscript during the seven months the law had been in effect. He wrote: "This is to me the most serious question to be solved." To attack the enemy's "strong works [at Nashville] garnished with the heaviest guns, and defended by numbers superior to my own," he informed General Cooper, "would be an act of imprudence, to say the least. . . . Should the [War] Department differ with me, however, I will undertake it, as I have troops ready to dare anything their leaders may order." [3]

Bragg's hesitancy to advance may have prompted Davis to appoint an overall commander of Confederate forces between the Blue Ridge Mountains and the Mississippi River, but his decision to name Joseph E. Johnston to that position on November 24 seems to have been the result of instigation by several generals as well as by Secretary of War George W. Randolph and his successor, James A. Seddon. Even Bragg claimed that while he was in Richmond he asked Davis to assign Johnston command of all the Southwest, "with plenary powers." "General Joseph E. Johnston . . . has been ordered to the command of our forces now in Tennessee," noted Virginia's governor on November 25. "His presence will inspire confidence in that army. Bragg has lost sadly in popular estimation, and not less in the estimation of the army. I have not seen an officer or private who is not loud and open in his condemnation of him and his military capacity." [4]

---

[3] Ibid., 416, 386–87, Brent Diary, November 17–24, 1862. Bragg expected a battle at any time. "I shall go forward to-morrow," he wrote Davis on November 24, "and remain with the front, as the slightest change with either party may precipitate an engagement. . . ." OR, XX (pt. 2), 422.

[4] Jones, Confederate Strategy from Shiloh to Vicksburg, pp. 95–96;

From the outset Johnston was displeased with his assignment. "A great mistake has been made in the arrangement of
my command," he informed Senator Louis T. Wigfall. "Mississippi & Arkansas should have been united to form it. Not
this state [Tennessee] & Mississippi, which are divided by (to
us) an impassable river & impracticable country. The troops
in Middle Tennessee could reach Fredericksburg [Virginia]
much sooner than Mississippi." Johnston, an advocate of
coordinated military movements, had hoped to unite the forces
of Pemberton and Theophilus H. Holmes, who commanded
the Trans-Mississippi Department. So had Secretary of War
Randolph, who had resigned on November 15 after the President rebuked him and countermanded his order to Holmes to
cross the river and join Pemberton. "[I]t seems to me that our
best course would be to fall upon . . . Grant with the troops
of . . . Holmes and Pemberton united for the purpose,"
Johnston explained to the Richmond authorities on November
24. "This suggestion was not adopted, nor noticed," complained Johnston, who could not understand why Davis
rejected a proposal that seemed so sound. "I have been dream-
ing of crushing Grant with Holmes & Pemberton's troops,
sending the former into Missouri; & with the latter, Bragg &
Kirby Smith marching to the Ohio," Johnston wrote Wigfall
on December 15. "You perhaps see no special object on my
part in troubling you with this, in truth I have no other than
putting my troubles before one who has a head to comprehend
grand war & a heart to sympathize with me." [5]

Historians disagree on what Davis expected of Johnston. He
was supposed to supervise the departments of Bragg, Kirby

OR, XX (pt. 2), 492; John Letcher to William Weaver, November 25,
1862, William Weaver Papers, Duke University.
[5] Johnston to Wigfall, December 15, 1862, Louis T. Wigfall Family
Papers, University of Texas; Joseph E. Johnston, *Narrative of Military
Operations* (Bloomington, 1959), pp. 148-50; OR, XX (pt. 2), 436, 441,
460.

Smith, and Pemberton, yet their orders would continue to come directly from Richmond; Johnston was given only limited control over strategy. The President resorted to this "strange military procedure," hint some writers, because he wanted a scapegoat in case of military disaster in the West, and because he distrusted Johnston.[6] But other scholars see Johnston's appointment as an honest attempt by Davis and Seddon to create command unity in the West.[7]

In early December, when the War Department suggested that some of Bragg's troops be sent to reinforce Pemberton, Johnston refused. "The map convinces me that General Holmes' troops can re-enforce [Pemberton] sooner than General Bragg's," Johnston wired Adjutant General Cooper on December 4. It would take a month to transfer men from Tennessee to Mississippi, argued Johnston; besides, Bragg's army was weak enough already. The most Johnston would agree to was what Bragg had already planned—the sending of about 6,000 cavalrymen under Forrest and Morgan north and west of Nashville to destroy railroads and to disrupt Union communications. These raids, Johnston wrote, "may delay General Grant." Bragg was even more confident. On November 24 he had informed the President that Morgan and Forrest would "create a diversion in favor of Pemberton," and might "force the enemy to retire from Mississippi."[8]

Bragg's incredible prediction was right. Forrest destroyed over fifty miles of railroad in western Tennessee and severed

[6] Gilbert E. Govan and James W. Livingood, *A Different Valor: The Story of General Joseph E. Johnston, C.S.A.* (Indianapolis, 1956), p. 164; Williams, *Beauregard*, p. 242.

[7] Jones, *Confederate Strategy from Shiloh to Vicksburg*, p. 97; Vandiver, *Rebel Brass*, pp. 34–35.

[37] OR, XX (pt. 1), 495–96, 305–6, 314–15, 319–21, 325–26, 394–95, ordered Forrest's brigade to western Tennessee to "harass" the enemy, to destroy his "depots and lines of communications." The next day Bragg wrote Cooper: "Col. John H. Morgan is peculiarly suited for the special service in which I propose to employ him—partisan war on the enemy's lines in Kentucky."

Grant's communications for ten days. At the same time Van Dorn, who commanded Pemberton's cavalry, hit Grant's supply depot at Holly Springs, Mississippi, and destroyed over $1,500,000 worth of supplies. Grant retreated from Mississippi after these raids had completely upset his plans to take Vicksburg.[9]

Morgan also made a spectacular raid. He estimated that his men destroyed over two million dollars worth of property, including the Louisville and Nashville Railroad from Munfordville, Kentucky, to within eighteen miles of Louisville. He lost only ninety men and captured nearly 2,000 prisoners, but Morgan's efforts failed to dislodge the Federals from Nashville. Moreover, these raids by Forrest and Morgan deprived Bragg of over half his cavalry during the ensuing campaign.[10]

While Bragg waited for his cavalry to force the Federals to retreat from Nashville,[11] he tried to solve his manpower problems. What particularly bothered him was a lack of officers. Four brigade and fifteen regimental commanders were absent for various reasons. Nor had the War Department

[9] *OR*, XVII (pt. 1), 592; Bruce Catton, *Never Call Retreat* (New York, 1965), pp. 30–34.

[10] *OR*, XX (pt. 1), 153–58. Horn (*Army of Tennessee*, p. 194) claimed "Bragg made good use of his cavalry while encamped on the Murfreesboro line. . . ." Cecil F. Holland (*Morgan*, pp. 165–66) disagreed. He believed Bragg should have sent his raiders off earlier, before Nashville was well supplied. John P. Dyer, who disagreed with both Horn and Holland, insisted (*Wheeler*, pp. 72–73) that Bragg nullified the usefulness of his cavalry by sending Forrest to western Tennessee. If Bragg had concentrated all his horsemen north of Nashville, concluded Dyer, the Confederates could have kept the railroad to Louisville cut and thus delayed "almost indefinitely the Federal advance." Kenneth P. Williams (*Lincoln Finds a General*, IV, 540–41) doubted Dyer's conclusion, because the Cumberland River soon became navigable and supply by rail became less vital for the Federals at Nashville.

[11] Nearly a month later Bragg still thought his horsemen would compel the Federals to abandon Nashville. "Rumors afloat of the evacuation of Nashville," Colonel Brent noted in his diary on December 19. "Gen Bragg feels confident of it. Thinks it certain, because enemy can not subsist there. I doubt it much."

helped matters by transferring four experienced generals—Buckner to Mobile; Samuel Jones, Franklin Gardner, and Samuel Maxey to Mississippi. Capable staff officers were as hard to find as line officers. Bragg wanted to replace Quartermaster O'Bannon, whose inadequate handling of supplies had been one reason for abandoning Kentucky, but no one better qualified was available. So O'Bannon retained his post with only a reprimand from Bragg. Dr. J. C. Nott, protesting O'Bannon's censure, wrote Bragg: "Your best friends admit that your temper is irritable—that under excitement you are sometimes harsh when there is no necessity for it & sometimes even wound an innocent man, as I think you did O'Bannon." [12] Neither Generals Jordan nor Slaughter had returned to duty. Jordan, at his own request, had been transferred to Beauregard's department, and Slaughter was ill. To secure a trained soldier who could supervise all staff work, Bragg relieved General Johnson K. Duncan from brigade command and appointed him chief of staff. Soon, however, Duncan became ill and on December 18 he died. Desperately, Bragg asked the War Department to assign the position to his old West Point classmate and Mexican War comrade, General William W. Mackall, who was stationed at Mobile. For months, however, the Richmond authorities vacillated and during the critical winter campaign Colonel George Brent, who lacked formal military training, continued to serve as Bragg's acting chief of staff.[13]

Bragg tried several expedients to fill the depleted ranks of his

[12] "I know you have made some enemies in this way, but these very men, are generally less opposed to you than the lazy fellows whom you have never harmed," continued Nott. "But whatever amount of harshness, justly or unjustly may be charged to you, it is certain that it has not done a thousandth part of the injury to the service, that has been done by those smooth tongued, popularity seeking individuals who have joined the hue & cry against you & who have failed to perform their duties." Nott to Bragg, January 31, 1863, Palmer Collection of Bragg Papers.

[13] *OR*, XX (pt. 2), 417, 508, 403; LII (pt. 2), 385, 396.

army. He secured permission to induct into the service all draft-age Kentuckians then in Tennessee who did not volunteer. Many of these emigrants entered the army unwillingly. Bragg also sent officers from each regiment to conscript camps in Alabama, Georgia, Mississippi, and Louisiana "to take charge of such recruits as may be furnished." He directed parolees to report to a training camp near Chattanooga, where they would be drilled and ready for immediate assignment when exchanged; he insisted that all absent officers and soldiers, who were not sick or disabled, return to duty; and he had every man in his army vaccinated against smallpox, as a precaution against future sickness.[14]

In reorganizing his command, Bragg shifted various units about, consolidated eighteen undermanned regiments into nine, convened examination boards to eliminate "disqualified, disabled, and incompetent" officers, and requested the promotion of several promising men. Contrary to army tradition, Bragg suggested that certain officers be promoted ahead of those who outranked them. He especially wanted Daniel S. Donelson and Patrick Cleburne advanced to major general. Donelson was the army's senior brigade commander, but seven other brigadiers outranked Cleburne. Donelson "is ever devoted to duty, and conspicuously gallant," wrote Bragg; "Cleburne is young, ardent, exceedingly gallant, but sufficiently prudent; a fine drill officer, and, like Donelson, the admiration of his command as a soldier and gentleman." Bragg also asked that six infantry and two cavalry colonels be promoted.[15]

[14] Ibid., XX (pt. 2), 392–93, 426.
[15] Ibid., 395, 447, 448, 456, 508–9; (pt. 1), 676–81. The infantry officers Bragg wanted promoted were (in "their order of merit"): Roger W. Hanson, Edward C. Walthall, Zachary C. Deas, Arthur M. Manigault, Thomas H. Hunt, and Lucius E. Polk. The cavalry officers were: Morgan and Wharton. Early in October President Davis had promoted Kirby Smith, Polk, and Hardee to lieutenant general. Later that same month Wheeler became a brigadier.

The President, without stating his reasons, struck three names from the promotion list Bragg submitted. Donelson's was one of them. Another was that of Colonel Arthur M. Manigault, who apparently was not promoted because a letter of his criticizing the Davis administration was published. "I admit having written the letter & must abide the consequences," Manigault explained to Bragg. "It is a matter of as great surprise to me as to yourself, its publication in any newspaper, the more so, as to the best of my recollection, I placed it in the post office at Knoxville myself." [16]

Bragg's forces, now called the Army of Tennessee, numbered about 47,000 men when General Johnston arrived at Murfreesboro on December 5. Several days before Kirby Smith had come from East Tennessee with two divisions (12,000 men), and Bragg had divided his troops into three infantry corps (commanded by Polk, Hardee, and Smith), some twenty-eight batteries of artillery, and Wheeler's 4,000-man cavalry division. [17] After Johnston had inspected the army, he wrote a friend: "Bragg's troops are in fine condition. Healthy looking & well clothed. In fine spirits too. I see no evidence of the want of confidence & dissatisfaction of which we heard so much in Richmond." [18]

Despite its excellent condition, the Army of Tennessee was not strong enough to be divided. On this Bragg and Johnston agreed; they estimated Rosecrans's strength as 65,000 men at Nashville and 35,000 distributed along the railroad to Louis-

[16] OR, XX (pt. 2), 449; Manigault to Bragg, November 30, 1862, Palmer Collection of Bragg Papers. Hunt was the other officer denied promotion by Davis. Colonel Brent (Brent Diary, December 14, 1862) thought all the men who received promotions deserved their new rank except Lucius E. Polk and Roger W. Hanson.

[17] Smith brought two thirds of the troops in his department to Middle Tennessee; this amounted to six brigades. OR, XX (pt. 2), 413, 433, 441.

[18] Johnston to Louis T. Wigfall, December 15, 1862, Wigfall Family Papers.

ville,[19] but they could not convince President Davis, who arrived at Murfreesboro on December 12 determined to send troops from Tennessee to Mississippi. Johnston told the President that weakening the Army of Tennessee might mean loss of the entire state to Rosecrans, and Bragg insisted that "Grant's campaign would be broken up by . . . cavalry expeditions" before Confederate infantry from Tennessee could reach Mississippi. Davis listened, "but he was inexorable," Bragg recalled. The President ordered Johnston and one division (9,000 men from Smith's corps) to start for Mississippi immediately. "It is quite a loss," noted Colonel Brent. If Rosecrans advanced, Davis told Bragg: "Fight if you can, and fall back beyond the Tennessee." [20]

The departure of reinforcements for Pemberton dampened the merriment of the Murfreesboro Christmas season, though Bragg remained surprisingly cheerful and maintained his sense of humor. As he arrived at a party one evening Dr. D. W. Yandell, of Hardee's staff, was impersonating him in one of his sterner moods. Bragg, who watched in silence until seen by the embarrassed performer, simply smiled and the party continued. Kirby Smith, who returned to his own department after Johnston went to Mississippi, left Bragg "in good spirits; he has been in constant receipt of information indicating the evacuation of Nashville," wrote Smith on December 26, "and feels confident he will soon be in possession of the city." [21]

Others were not so sure. "The Yankees seem to want time for preparation and I guess they can have as much as they want for Gen Bragg will never attempt to take Nashville at

[19] *OR*, XX (pt. 2), 441. On December 20 Rosecrans's army consisted of 90,441 men present for duty, so Bragg's and Johnston's estimate of Union strength was not an exaggeration. *Ibid.*, 213.

[20] *OR*, XX (pt. 2), 441, 449-50, 493; Johnston to Louis T. Wigfall, December 15, 1862, Wigfall Family Papers; Brent Diary, December 12, 16, 19, 1862.

[21] Holland, *Morgan*, p. 177; *OR*, XX (pt. 2), 461, 462.

least such is my opinion," wrote an officer. "That place is growing stronger all the time. . . ." And Wheeler, whom Bragg sent out to scout on December 20, reported "no indications on the part of the enemy to retire." [22]

The day after Christmas it became clear that Rosecrans was moving out of Nashville, but not in retreat. Wheeler reported the enemy advancing toward Murfreesboro. On December 25 Rosecrans had told his corps commanders—Thomas L. Crittenden, Alexander M. McCook, and Bragg's old friend, George H. Thomas—"We move tomorrow, gentlemen! We shall begin to skirmish, probably as soon as we pass the outposts. Press them hard! Drive them out of their nests! Make them fight or run! *Fight them! Fight* them! Fight, I say!" [23]

The Confederates Rosecrans wanted to drive were not in "nests," or intrenchments, or even field fortifications. Bragg's army was spread over a thirty-mile front when the Federal advance began. The Confederates retired toward Murfreesboro in cold rain that soaked their uniforms. Wheeler's cavalry skirmished repeatedly to delay the Federals while Bragg concentrated his infantry and artillery. "Everybody is anxious," noted Colonel Brent on December 27.[24]

The next day Bragg selected a position some three miles northwest of Murfreesboro and began placing his forces in a battleline arching northeast to the Lebanon Pike and southwest

[22] E. John Ellis to His Father, November 29, 1862, E. John, Thomas C. W. Ellis and Family Papers; Brent Diary, December 20–21, 1862.

[23] Wheeler to George W. Brent, December 26, 1862, 2 P.M. and 9:30 P.M., December 27, 1862, 2:10 A.M., Palmer Collection of Bragg Papers; Joseph Wheeler, "The Battle of Murfreesboro," Joseph Wheeler Collection, Chicago Historical Society; Rosecrans quoted in William M. Lamers, *The Edge of Glory: A Biography of General William S. Rosecrans, U.S.A.* (New York, 1961), p. 201.

[24] *OR*, XX (pt. 1), 663; Brent Diary, December 26–27, 1862. In his official report of the campaign, Bragg wrote (*OR*, XX [pt. 1], 669): ". . . the weather had been severe from cold and almost constant rain, and we had no change of clothing, and in many places could not have fires."

to the Triune Road. Near the line's center, the Nashville Pike crossed the Nashville & Chattanooga Railroad a few hundred yards west of fordable Stone's River. Bragg ordered Hardee's corps east of the river; Polk's west. Several hundred yards behind the center of his line, Bragg stationed his reserves: McCown's division, all that remained of Kirby Smith's corps, and Jackson's small brigade, recently recalled from guard duty near Chattanooga.[25]

The position Bragg selected was not particularly well suited for defense. Most of the area was open farm country without natural barriers. Where there were trees, they grew in thick patches which could conceal the enemy and hamper Confederate cavalry and artillery movements. Furthermore, should the river rise, a likely event after the heavy rain on December 27,[26] the Confederates might be in an awkward position. But if Bragg was aware of these disadvantages, he evidently did not consider them determinative. He wanted to hold Murfreesboro because it was his supply depot and because the surrounding country fed his army. He also feared a retreat southward would expose East Tennessee to invasion. He selected his battleline because it was the only place he could concentrate his army and still cover the roads from Nashville. "Owing to the convergence upon . . . Murfreesborough of so many fine roads by which the enemy could approach," reported Bragg, "we were confined in our selection to a line near enough the point of juncture to enable us to successfully cover them all until the real point of attack should be developed." [27]

Even if his defensive position was the best available under

[25] *OR*, XX (pt. 2), 457, 458, 462, 464; (pt. 1), 672, 682. Kirby Smith sent one regiment to Bragg's aid from East Tennessee, but it did not arrive in time to be used against Rosecrans. *OR*, XX (pt. 2), 468.

[26] It rained nearly every day between December 27 and January 4. Brent Diary, December 27, 1862—January 4, 1863. A soldier recalled (Watkins, "*Co. Aytch*," p. 92): "Line of battle was formed on the north bank of Stone's River—on the Yankee side. Bad generalship, I thought."

[27] *OR*, XX (pt. 1), 663.

the circumstances, which seems questionable, Bragg neverthe-less committed a serious tactical error; he failed to intrench his army. Bragg apparently missed the most obvious lesson of Shiloh and Perryville: that defenders in a strong position generally lost fewer men than attackers. Like many Civil War generals, he never fully understood the advantage of defensive tactics nor realized that intrenched troops supported by artillery could often repulse twice their number. Perhaps Bragg believed his men did not have time to use their spades to good advantage at Murfreesboro, but more likely he under-estimated the value of field works. "General Bragg says heavy intrenchments demoralize our troops," wrote President Davis's military aide in April 1863. Bragg would have agreed with a young officer who wrote just before the Murfreesboro campaign: ". . . we want Stonewall Jackson fighting and that sort of strategy which hurls masses against fractions of the enemy's army, and destroys it in detail. The policy of in-trenching and evacuating will ruin our cause if adopted here. The truth is it never paid anywhere." [28]

Bragg became impatient between December 27 and 30 as the two armies skirmished and groped into close contact. He seemed bold and determined, strikingly different from the way he sometimes acted in a crisis. When it became apparent that Rosecrans would not attack on December 29, Bragg sent Wheeler around the enemy's left flank to destroy supply trains. The raid, which began about midnight, was brilliantly executed. Without one of his men being killed, Wheeler rode completely around the Union army in forty-eight hours,

[28] *Ibid.*, XXIII (pt. 2), 761; E. John Ellis to His Father, November 29, 1862, E. John, Thomas C. W. Ellis and Family Papers. "The Engineers are busy . . . strengthening the field works around Tullahoma," Colonel Brent noted in his diary on April 13, 1863. "Gen. Bragg has never shown much confidence in them—Murfreesboro for example." Without specific orders from Bragg, apparently only a few units made any attempt to fortify their positions. *OR*, XX (pt. 1), 689; unpublished reports, Palmer Collection of Bragg Papers.

destroyed over four hundred wagons filled with supplies, captured six hundred prisoners, remounted a portion of his command, and secured enough weapons to arm a brigade. But a cavalry raid was only the preliminary to what Bragg had in mind. On December 30 Colonel Brent wrote in his diary: "Gen Bragg determined to await no longer the tardy movements of the enemy & resolved to attack him." That night Bragg called Polk and Hardee to headquarters. The army would assail the enemy's left flank at daylight the following day, Bragg announced. Polk objected and proposed instead an assault on the Union right, which he believed could be more easily outflanked. Bragg deferred to this suggestion and issued the necessary orders for the rearrangement of his forces.[29]

The Confederates spent the night of December 30 getting into position to attack. Polk's corps (13,633 effectives) remained where it was (in two lines—Withers's division in front, Cheatham's in rear—between Stone's River and the Triune Road), but Hardee, with McCown's and Cleburne's divisions (10,459 effectives), marched westward to extend the Confederate line beyond the Triune Road. Hardee placed McCown's three brigades (4,414 men) in front and Cleburne's four brigades five hundred yards behind in a second line. The only infantry units which Bragg left on the Confederate right, east of the river, were Breckinridge's division and Jackson's brigade (7,698 effectives). To protect the army's exposed flanks, Bragg ordered Wharton's cavalry brigade (1,950 effectives) to the left and Pegram's (about 500 effectives) to the right.[30] Bragg placed three batteries of artillery in reserve

[29] Brent Diary, December 30, 1862; OR, XX (pt. 1), 663–64; Dyer, *Wheeler*, pp. 81–84.

[30] OR, XX (pt. 1), 663–64, 686, 773; Brent Diary, December 30, 1862; Colonel T. B. Roy to Breckinridge, December 30, 1862 (copy), Wheeler Collection; Roy to Breckinridge [December 31, 1862?], 9:20 A.M., Thomas Benton Roy Collection, Chicago Historical Society. Confederate strength has been compiled from printed information found in OR, XX (pt. 1), 676–81, 693, 780, 852, 855, 875, 900; and from unpublished reports in the Palmer Collection of Bragg Papers. My esti-

and assigned each of the other twenty-two to a brigade.[31]

Bragg's tactical plan called for the execution of a right wheel. Four fifths of the army (all but Breckinridge's command) would pivot on Polk's extreme right flank, swing around to the northeast, force the enemy back beyond the Nashville Pike, and cut his line of retreat. "In making this movement," read Bragg's order, "the general desires that your attack shall be vigorous and persistent. In so doing, keep up the touch of elbows to the right, in order that the line may be unbroken. The movement of the second line will correspond with that of the first." [32]

---

mate of the number of Confederate effectives present at Murfreesboro is slightly higher than Livermore's (*Numbers and Losses*, p. 97). Bragg's infantry was divided into two corps, five divisions, twenty brigades, eighty-eight regiments, and ten battalions. (Kenneth P. Williams, *Lincoln Finds a General*, IV, 263, claimed Bragg's infantry consisted of 102 regiments. Williams undoubtedly counted some battalions as regiments and the nine consolidated regiments twice.) Infantry brigades, which were composed of from three to six regiments, averaged about 1,600 effectives. A few regiments mustered over five hundred effectives, but many took less than two hundred men into battle. The Seventeenth Tennessee, with 598 effectives, carried more men into action than any other regiment; the Fifth Mississippi, with only 170 effectives, carried fewer than any other regiment. The average fighting strength of the infantry regiments was about 320 men. The largest battalion mustered three hundred effectives; the smallest, fifty. Average strength of battalions was probably about one hundred men. Bragg's cavalry was divided into four brigades, eighteen regiments, four battalions, and two companies.

[31] Printed reports do not indicate how many pieces of artillery the Confederates had at Murfreesboro. Bragg merely reported thirty Union guns captured and three Confederate guns lost. An unpublished report in the Palmer Collection of Bragg Papers, which shows 129 guns in the Army of Tennessee's possession on April 30, 1863, suggests that Bragg had slightly more than one hundred pieces of artillery at Murfreesboro, a small number compared with the 247 guns Lee had at Gettysburg. Most of Bragg's guns were smoothbore Napoleons and howitzers. In April 1863 only thirty-two of the army's 129 guns were rifled. A battery was composed of from four to six guns pulled by horses and manned by from forty-five to one hundred men.

[32] *OR*, XX (pt. 1), 664; (pt. 2), 469.

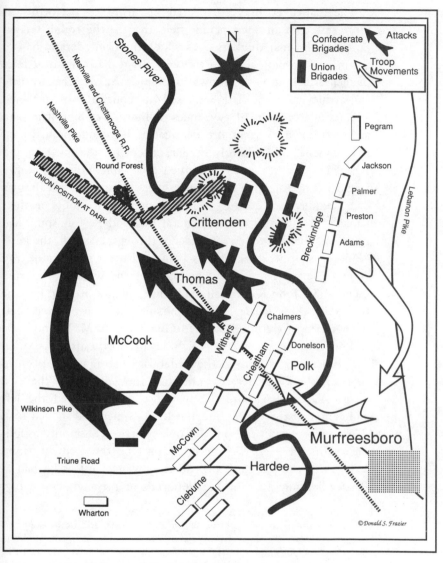

BATTLE OF MURFREESBORO, December 31, 1862

The maneuver Bragg expected his army to perform was more suited to an open parade field than to the rough terrain dotted with cedar thickets over which the Confederates had to advance. At Shiloh and at Perryville Bragg had seen neat lines of men attacking with elbows touching torn to pieces by rifle and artillery fire; he had witnessed the confusion of sustained assaults over a front of two miles or more. Yet his battle plan at Murfreesboro was almost identical with the one he had used at Perryville and strikingly similar, except for the pivoting and wheeling, to the tactics employed at Shiloh. Officers simply found it impossible to keep their lines "unbroken," as Bragg's order required, or even to maintain contact with units on their flanks. "[M]y line," wrote General Bushrod R. Johnson, "had been somewhat broken in passing through a small thicket." "Finding myself alone at this point, with no support on my right or left, I halted my command in the woods," reported General St. John R. Liddell. "The lines of my brigade became broken in the eagerness of the pursuit, the men of each regiment mixing together," recalled General S. A. M. Wood.[33]

The Confederate attack, which began shortly after 6 A.M. on December 31,[34] surprised the Federals. Rosecrans had planned to assail the Confederate right that same day with the two corps (Crittenden's and Thomas's) which occupied the left and center of the Union line, but Bragg's men had moved first. Their initial assault fell on McCook's corps, whose only assignment for the day had been to protect the Federal right. Wharton, who led the Confederate advance just as he had at Perryville, quickly captured hundreds of prisoners and a bat-

33 *Ibid.* (pt. 1), 875, 857, 898.

34 Bragg stated that the action began about 7 A.M. and he insisted that McCown caused the delay by his failure "to execute during the night an order for a slight change in the line of his division . . . which had to be done the next morning." *OR,* XX (pt. 1), 664. McCown later denied this charge (*ibid.,* 917–26), but apparently he did cause some delay (see Hardee's and McCown's initial reports, *ibid.,* 774, 912). Even so, the attack probably began nearer six than seven (see *ibid.,* 919, 921, 923–24).

tery. As the Confederate cavalrymen swept toward the Wilkinson Road, Hardee's infantrymen crashed through the first enemy camps. Outflanked and overwhelmed, McCook's brigades retreated. "The enemy several times attempted to make a stand," reported Hardee, "but were each time forced back. Our troops were vigorously pressing forward. . . . The cannonade was fierce, but could not check our advance. After a stubborn combat the enemy were broken, and fled to the cedar brakes between the Nashville and Wilkinson turnpikes." [35]

But the Confederate drive gradually lost momentum. McCown, contrary to orders, continued northward for a time instead of swinging east, and soon he became separated from Withers's division on his right. This forced Hardee to move Cleburne's division up to fill the interval and reduced the Confederate assault force on the extreme left to a single unsupported line. By 7 A.M., when the first of Withers's brigades went into action, some of the Federals had rallied and taken strong positions in broken ground. Two spirited charges failed to dislodge these Union troops, who continually mauled Cleburne's flank with an enfilading artillery fire. "The battle at this point was bloody," noted Hardee, who sent word to Bragg that Cleburne's flank was exposed because Cheatham had failed to move forward. Bragg ordered Cheatham to advance immediately and soon his brigades were in action. Once committed, Cheatham's men fought as bravely as any other unit, but the Federals now contested every inch of the ground. "General Cheatham's division advanced," recalled Union General Philip H. Sheridan, who commanded one of McCook's divisions. "The contest then became terrible. The enemy made three attacks, and were three times repulsed, the artillery range of the respective batteries being not over 200 yards." [36]

[35] *OR*, XX (pt. 1), 184, 192–93, 773–75.

[36] *Ibid.*, 774–76, 664, 349. Most of Bragg's critics have either denied that Cheatham was slow moving forward on the morning of December

Thousands of men on both sides were slaughtered as the Confederates drove toward the Nashville Pike and the Federal army struggled to keep from being bent back upon itself and destroyed. Just as at Shiloh and at Perryville, the defenders suffered relatively fewer casualties, except in those units which were outflanked or surrounded. But often the Federals attacked to relieve exposed regiments or brigades or to slow the Confederate advance, and it is significant that half of the most battered Union regiments incurred their highest casualties when they attacked or counterattacked. For example, the Fifteenth Indiana lost 130 of its 440 men in a single bayonet charge, and the Thirty-fourth Illinois and the Thirty-ninth Indiana each sustained 50 per cent casualties in a counterattack. In still another attempt to check the Confederates a brigade of regulars charged into a dense cedar grove and lost five hundred men in about twenty minutes. The Sixteenth and Eighteenth U. S. Infantry regiments, which formed the center of this assault group, lost 456 men from a combined total of 910.[37]

Confederate losses were even more exceptional. Of the eighty-eight Confederate regiments present at Murfreesboro,

31 or they have ignored the charge, but there is evidence that he was tardy and that his delay cost the Confederates time and casualties. "General Cheatham's left did not move forward at the same moment as my right," reported Cleburne (*ibid.*, 844), "and . . . a gap was soon left between us." Cheatham himself admitted (*ibid.*, 706–7) that it was after 8 A.M. before he ordered Colonel A. J. Vaughan, who commanded Smith's brigade, to "take position on General Cleburne's right." Hardee told him, Bragg wrote Samuel Cooper (April 9, 1863, Palmer Collection of Bragg Papers), "Cheatham was drunk, and unfitted for duty during the heavy engagement on 31st December." Later, Bragg claimed, he mentioned this charge to Polk, who allegedly "replied . . . that he regretted to say he had received the same information, and added that he had spoken or written to Genl Cheatham on the subject." "Having never received any denial from Genl Cheatham or Genl Polk," wrote Bragg, "I have taken the charge as confessed." A private (Watkins, "*Co. Aytch*," pp. 93, 95) claimed that many officers were so drunk during the battle that they were unable to distinguish Confederate from Federal units.

37 *OR*, XX (pt. 1), 495–96, 305–6, 314–15, 319–21, 325–26, 394–95, 401–3.

twenty-three suffered over 40 per cent casualties. Moreover, 40 per cent of the infantry regimental commanders were killed or wounded, and in several regiments every field officer was lost. Eight of the twenty Confederate infantry brigades which fought at Murfreesboro sustained more than 35 per cent casualties, and 25 per cent of the infantry brigade commanders were killed or wounded.[38]

CONFEDERATE ATTACK ON BEATTY'S BRIGADE
Library of Congress

Reckless assaults accounted for most Confederate casualties. The First Louisiana charged across an open field. "Our loss was very severe at this place," wrote Captain Taylor Beatty,

[38] *Ibid.*, 676–81, 693, 758, 780, 852, 855, 875, 900; unpublished reports in the Palmer Collection of Bragg Papers.

who assumed command when "Col. [J. A.] Jaquess . . . deserted his regiment & colors." The regiment lost seven of its twenty-one officers and nearly a hundred of its 231 men. Attacks made by other units were just as costly. Colonel J. J. Scales, commander of the Thirtieth Mississippi, was ordered to charge several Federal batteries. Five hundred yards of open ground "lay between us and those . . . batteries," wrote Scales. "As we entered [this field] a large body of [Union] infantry in addition to the Batteries on my flanks and front rained their leaden hail upon us. Men fell around on every side like autumn leaves and every foot of soil over which we passed seemed dyed with the life blood of some one or more of [my] gallant [men]. . . . Still no one faltered," recalled Scales, "but the whole line advanced boldly and swiftly to within seventy-five yds. of the battery when the storm of death increased in such fury that the regt. as if by instinct fell to the ground." This single charge cost the Thirtieth Mississippi half of its four hundred men. A young soldier in the Twenty-fourth Alabama recalled how his regiment made three desperate attacks and that each time thirty or forty of his comrades fell. The commander of the Twenty-sixth Alabama reported the Federal fire so heavy that thirty-eight of his men defected during the first assault.[39]

By 10 A.M. the Confederate wheeling movement had reached the strongly defended Union center. Here, in the Round Forest, where the Federal line formed an acute angle, Rosecrans had concentrated every available brigade and battery. The first Confederate unit to strike this formidable position was General James R. Chalmers's brigade of Mississippians, which charged across an open field toward the Round

[39] Taylor Beatty Diary, January 1, 1863; Beatty's report, Palmer Collection of Bragg Papers; Scales's report, ibid.; Charles T. Jones, Jr., "Five Confederates: The Sons of Bolling Hall in the Civil War," Alabama Historical Quarterly, XXIV (1962), 167; Lieutenant Colonel N. N. Clements's report, Palmer Collection of Bragg Papers.

Forest.[40] The Mississippians were hopelessly outnumbered and outgunned; half the men in the Forty-fourth Mississippi Regiment went into battle armed only with sticks, and most of the Ninth Mississippi's rifles were still too wet from the previous night's rain to fire. Before the men reached the woods, Chalmers was wounded and his brigade became disorganized.[41]

As the Mississippians faltered, General Daniel S. Donelson's brigade of Tennesseeans came up. No unit on either side fought any harder than this brigade; it dashed itself to bits against the Union center. One of Donelson's regiments lost half its officers and 68 per cent of its men; another lost 42 per cent of its officers and over half its men. The Eighth and the Sixteenth Tennessee regiments spent several hours and 513 of their combined total of 821 men in brave but unsuccessful efforts to break the Federal line.[42]

Reports which reached Bragg indicated the confusion at the front as well as the intensity of the battle. Shortly after 10 A.M. he realized that the Confederate assault had lost much of its

[40] Reports vary on exactly when Chalmers attacked. Polk said 10 A.M. (OR, XX [pt. 1], 689); Withers said 11 A.M. (ibid., 756). Apparently Chalmers made no report, but Colonel T. W. White, who took command of the brigade after Chalmers fell, stated that the charge began about eleven (White's report, Palmer Collection of Bragg Papers). A regimental commander, however, reported that he received orders to attack about ten (Lieutenant Colonel B. F. Johns's report, ibid.).

[41] Reports of Major J. O. Thompson, Forty-fourth (Blythe's) Mississippi Infantry, and Lieutenant Colonel T. H. Lyman, Ninth Mississippi Infantry, Palmer Collection of Bragg Papers. Thompson reported: "During the night of Friday [December] 26 all guns in the hands of Blythe's Regiment were taken from them and distributed among the regiments of Chalmers's Brigade. The Sunday morning following we were furnished with refuse guns that had been turned over to the Brigade ordnance officer. Many of these guns were worthless. . . . Even of these poor arms there was not a sufficiency and after every exertion on my part to procure arms, one half of the Regt. moved out with no other resemblance to a gun that such sticks as they could gather."

[42] OR, XX (pt. 1), 710–12, 714–18, 543–46.

early drive. He had learned that several units were out of ammunition; others were intermingled and disorganized, and nearly everyone who had been in action and was still alive was either wounded or exhausted. If the Federals were to be crushed Bragg decided he must use Breckinridge's troops.[43]

How to get these fresh brigades into action was Bragg's problem. About 10 A.M., in response to Hardee's appeal for reinforcements, Bragg had asked Breckinridge for two brigades. Instead of reinforcements, Breckinridge sent back the following dispatch at 10:10 A.M.: "The enemy are undoubtedly advancing upon me. The Lebanon road is unprotected, and I have no troops to fill out my line to it." At almost the same time Pegram, whose cavalry was screening Breckinridge's right flank, notified Bragg that "a pretty strong infantry force" was crossing the river in his front. Upon receipt of this information from Breckinridge and Pegram, Bragg countermanded his order for reinforcements, and directed Breckinridge to attack immediately any enemy force east of the river. Major William Clare, Bragg's assistant inspector general who carried the order, reached Breckinridge's position about 10:30 A.M., but Breckinridge refused to advance. Clare returned to Bragg's headquarters only to be sent back to "tell Maj Gen Breckinridge that unless he was certain the enemy were upon him to go ahead." Breckinridge replied that "he could be certain of nothing." A few moments later Colonel J. Stoddard Johnston rode up and repeated Bragg's order to advance. Despite the urging of these two messengers, Breckinridge did not move until 11:30 A.M. At that time he wrote Bragg: "I am obeying your order, but . . . if I advance my whole line farther forward . . . it will take me clear away from the Lebanon road, and expose my right . . . to a heavy force of the enemy. . . ." After he had moved forward only half a mile, Breckinridge wrote again at 12:50 P.M.: "It is not certain

43 Brent Diary, December 31, 1862; Johnston Diary, December 31, 1862; OR, XX (pt. 1), 665–66.

the enemy is advancing upon me. . . ." [44] Three critical hours had passed without any reinforcements being sent west of the river.

Breckinridge and Pegram were responsible for this needless delay. Their "unfortunate misapprehensions" that a large Federal force was advancing upon them, wrote Bragg, "with held from active operations three fine brigades until the enemy had succeeded in checking our progress, had re-established his lines, and had collected many of his broken battalions." Two Federal divisions had in fact started across the river toward Breckinridge earlier that morning, but they had been withdrawn to reinforce the Union right shortly after 8 A.M. Only a brigade was left to guard the river fords. In his report, which contained some inaccurate statements and only a partial account of what actually happened, Breckinridge tried to make Pegram the only culprit. "From my front," Breckinridge wrote, "information came to me from Pegram's cavalry . . . that the enemy . . . were moving on my position in line of battle. This proved to be incorrect, and it is to be regretted that sufficient care was not taken by the authors of the report to discriminate rumor from fact. About 10:30 A.M.," continued Breckinridge, "I received, through Col. J. Stoddard Johnston, a suggestion from the general commanding to move against the enemy instead of awaiting his attack. I find that Colonel Johnston regarded it as an order, but, as I moved at once, it is not material." [45] At once, it will be recalled, was an hour later.

By the time Breckinridge finally realized that he faced only

[44] *OR*, XX (pt. 1), 788, 789; Pegram to Bragg, December 31, 1862, 10 A.M., Palmer Collection of Bragg Papers; Clare to Bragg, June 2, 1863, *ibid.*

[45] *OR*, XX (pt. 1), 666, 192–93, 782–83. Pegram's report has not been found. William Polk (*Leonidas Polk*, II, 193) blamed Breckinridge's delay on "the absence of Morgan's cavalry, which had so recently been sent into Kentucky. Its presence would have given sufficient cavalry force to make clear the situation and thus relieve Breckinridge."

an imaginary threat, Bragg had again changed his plans. He directed Breckinridge to bring four brigades across the river to suppport Polk instead of Hardee, whose progress had been checked. When these brigades arrived, Bragg ordered Polk to crush the Union center by throwing "all the force he could collect" against the Round Forest. Bragg believed that this assault, even if it failed, would force Rosecrans to withdraw enough men from the Union right to enable Hardee to occupy the Nashville Road.[46]

Bragg could not have picked a worse spot to make his major attack, and Polk compounded the error by sending his reinforcements into battle piecemeal. Sometime between 1:30 and 2:00 P.M. Jackson's and Adams's brigades arrived from the Confederate right. They were sent forward, one after the other, across a field thick with bodies where Chalmers's and Donelson's men had failed to crack the Union defense. Jackson made two furious assaults; both aborted, he explained, "for the want of support from others, and the smallness of my own numbers." In an hour of combat Jackson lost more than a third of his men, including all of his regimental commanders. One of his regiments, the Eighth Mississippi, lost 133 of its 282 men. Though Adams made what one Federal called "the most daring, courageous, and best-executed attack . . . on our

[46] There is some question about the wording of Bragg's order, which has not been found. Probably it was oral and carried by a staff officer. Breckinridge remembered receiving two separate orders, the first about 1 P.M. He reported (*OR*, XX [pt. 1], 783): "We had marched about half a mile when I received . . . an order . . . to send at least one brigade to the support of . . . Polk . . . and, as I recollect, two, if I could spare them. I immediately sent Adams and Jackson. . . ." Soon, Breckinridge recalled, "I received an order . . . to leave Hanson . . . and with the remainder of my command to report to . . . Polk. The brigades of Preston and Palmer were immediately moved . . . and the order of the general executed with great rapidity." Seemingly Bragg forgot how many brigades he ordered Breckinridge to bring west of the river. Bragg wrote in his report (*ibid.*, 666): ". . . Breckinridge was ordered to leave two brigades . . . and with the balance of the force to cross to the left and report to . . . Polk." Despite his lapse of memory, it is certain that Bragg requested four brigades. See *ibid.*, 690.

line," he had no more success than Jackson. Adams was wounded and his brigade, caught in a cross fire, retreated. One of his units, the Thirteenth and Twentieth Consolidated Louisiana Infantry, which entered the fight with 620 men, lost 187 on the afternoon of December 31.[47]

Just as Adams and Jackson retreated, Breckinridge arrived opposite the Round Forest with Preston's and Palmer's brigades. While these fresh troops aligned for battle, Breckinridge rode over to see if Jackson's and Adams's men could make another assault. He found them too "much cut up." When Preston and Palmer had formed their battlelines, Breckinridge led them in a series of advances which achieved little. He decided, after Preston's brigade had lost 155 men, that it was futile to continue the action. The Federals, Breckinridge reported, were "strongly posted in two lines of battle, supported by numerous batteries. One of [the enemy's] . . . lines had the protection of the railroad cut, forming an excellent breastwork. We had no artillery, the nature of the ground forbidding its use. It was deemed reckless to [continue the] attack with the force present." [48]

Action continued sporadically along the front until dark, but the Confederates could not muster another vigorous charge. To Hardee's final appeal for reinforcements sometime after 4 P.M., Bragg replied that he had no men to send. Only Hanson's brigade was fresh and it could not be called west of the river without endangering the Confederate right flank. Without support, Hardee refused to order another assault. "The enemy," he wrote, "lay beyond the range of our guns, securely sheltered behind the strong defense of the railroad embankment, with wide open fields intervening, which were swept by their superior artillery. It would have been folly, not valor, to assail them in this position. I gave the order . . . to bivouac for the night." [49]

[47] OR, XX (pt. 1), 838–39, 841–42, 795–99: Alexander F. Stevenson, The Battle of Stone's River (Boston, 1884), p. 113.
[48] OR, XX (pt. 1), 783–84.   [49] Ibid., 777.

After ten hours of combat both armies were crippled, and many men were so exhausted that they slept despite rain, cold, and the screams of the wounded. Bragg seems to have been as tired as his men. He went to bed without inspecting his lines after sending a wire to Richmond announcing that Rosecrans had been driven "from every position except his extreme left." Years later General Liddell, whose brigade occupied a position on the extreme Confederate left, insisted that a wonderful chance to crush the enemy was lost on the night of December 31. "In the evening," he wrote, "Hardee came along and I took the opportunity to call his attention to the fact that we were in command of the Rail Road and Nashville Turnpike and by bringing up all reserves and driving Rosecrans towards Murfreesboro by attacking him in rear I had no doubt that success would be with us. From some cause Hardee would not listen to me saying that 'he was disgusted.' " Liddell claimed that he never forgave himself "for not going to see Bragg . . . and persuading him if possible to come and look for himself; but there were several obstacles to my leaving my brigade then. . . . The truth is I ought to have gone since no one else would do it even if I had been arrested for it." "It struck me that Bragg did not know whom to trust," continued Liddell. "He was not popular with his generals and hence I feared that zealous cooperation on their part was wanting. If he had caused even one or two of us to be shot I firmly believe the balance would have done better." Though parts of Liddell's story sound plausible, neither his nor any other officer's report suggested that the Confederates commanded the railroad or the Nashville Turnpike. Equally important, Bragg had no reserves to "bring up" and use against the Federal army's rear.[50]

Some writers believed that Bragg would have crushed

[50] Liddell, "Liddell's Record of the Civil War," Liddell Papers. In his report (OR, XX [pt. 1], 858–59) Liddell only noted that his brigade was near the Nashville Turnpike when ordered to halt for the night.

Rosecrans on December 31 if Davis had left Stevenson's division at Murfreesboro instead of sending it to Mississippi just before the battle. In 1864 General Alexander P. Stewart lamented to Bragg: "If instead of taking ten thousand away from you in Dec. 62, [the government] . . . could have added that number, or even let the ten thousand remain, how different would be our situation now." And the respected historian Bruce Catton concluded that the Confederates "almost certainly would have won decisively if Stevenson's missing division had been there to help." [51]

But such views are based upon the questionable assumption that Bragg would have used Stevenson's division effectively—held it in reserve until just the right time and then committed it against the weakest point in the Federal line. It seems doubtful that Bragg would have employed Stevenson's division any differently than he did the units at his disposal. The absence of Stevenson's division did not in itself deprive Bragg of a reserve; he could have withheld a division from Polk's corps until the Union retreat revealed the most appropriate point to strike. But Bragg kept no reserves ready to exploit a breakthrough; Breckinridge's brigades, which Bragg used as reinforcements, arrived at the front too late to be effective and then were used in the wrong place, against the strongest rather than the weakest Federal position. The outcome probably would have been the same if Bragg had had Stevenson's men and used them as part of the initial assault force or even as a reserve to be fed into action in driblets as were Breckinridge's brigades.

The truth is that Bragg's tactical plan lacked that subtlety and flexibility so necessary for success; it had within itself all the elements of failure. First, the perfectly aligned wheeling movement of men touching elbows which Bragg expected his

[51] Stewart to Bragg, March 19, 1864, Palmer Collection of Bragg Papers; Catton, *Never Call Retreat*, p. 43. See also Jones, *A Rebel War Clerk's Diary*, I, 232.

army to perform would have been impossible in the broken country around Murfreesboro even if the enemy had not fought back. Second, he assigned the important left flank position, where the battle opened, to McCown, whom Bragg considered his worst division commander. To this man Bragg entrusted the vital responsibility of cutting the Federals off from their base at Nashville by slashing through to the railroad and to the Nashville Pike. Third, Bragg's plan was defective because, unless the Union army collapsed at the first onslaught, it would be pushed back into a tighter and stronger defensive position as the battle continued, while Confederate forces would gradually lose momentum, become disorganized, and grow weaker. Like a snowball, the Federals would pick up strength from the debris of battle if they retreated in good order. But the Confederates would inevitably unwind like a ball of string as they advanced.

Bragg's chance for victory was further reduced by the failure of Breckinridge to respond quickly to orders and by the way his troops were used. He sent his men west of the river in "detachments of two brigades each," reported General Polk; "the first arrived nearly two hours after Donelson's attack, the other about an hour after the first." "Unfortunately," continued Polk, "the opportune moment for putting in these detachments had passed. Could they have been thrown upon the enemy's left immediately following Chalmers's and Donelson's assault in quick succession, the extraordinary strength of [the enemy's] . . . position would have availed him nothing." On the other hand, Polk probably should have waited until all four brigades had arrived before launching another assault, instead of sending them forward singly or two at a time. Adams thought that breaking the Union line in his front "was more than any brigade could accomplish, and full work for a division, well directed." [52]

[52] *OR*, XX (pt. 1), 690, 794. Colonel G. C. Kniffin, a Union staff officer, wrote ("The Battle of Stone's River," *Battles and Leaders*, III,

If Polk sent too few men to do too much, Bragg must also share the blame. His headquarters were nearby and he should have prevented a piecemeal attack if he did not approve. Yet a careful student of the battle doubts that the assault failed because it was delivered in fragments.. "Actually," wrote Kenneth P. Williams, "there seems to have been room for no more than a two-brigade front, and how close one assault can follow another must always be a matter of dispute. A long interval favors the defender, but a short one can cause the second assault to become disorganized by men from the one that has failed." [53]

What seems clear is that Bragg used Breckinridge's men at the wrong place. "If . . . a fresh division could have replaced Cleburne's exhausted troops," wrote Hardee, "the route of Rosecrans's army would have been complete." But Bragg claimed that by the time Breckinridge's brigades crossed the river "it was too late to send this force to . . . Hardee's support." [54] To reach Hardee, Breckinridge's troops would have had to follow a circuitous route around the rear of the entire army. Besides, such a move would have exhausted the men, involved an even longer delay than in fact occurred, and left the Confederate right flank exposed. Probably Bragg could have made the most effective use of Breckinridge's men by sending them across the river against the Union left. Such a movement would have protected the Confederate right and formed a pincer in conjunction with Hardee's advance.

At dawn on January 1 Confederate skirmishers went forward all along the line, but no serious effort was made to turn either of the Union flanks. Polk's men occupied the Round Forest, which they had fought so hard to take the day

---

626): "The error made by General Polk in making an attack with the two brigades that first arrived upon the field, instead of waiting the arrival of General Breckinridge with the remaining brigades, was so palpable as to render an excuse for failure necessary."

[53] Williams, *Lincoln Finds a General*, IV, 273.
[54] *OR*, XX (pt. 1), 777, 666.

before and the Federals had abandoned during the night in order to shorten their line. Breckinridge recrossed the river with Palmer's brigade to strengthen the Confederate right, and Bragg sent cavalry to harass the enemy's rear. "Nothing of consequence," noted a member of Bragg's staff. "Reported retreat of the enemy unconfirmed. Wheeler and Wharton operating with cavalry on enemy's trains with success. Occasional firing with artillery on our lines." [55]

On January 2 Bragg again sent skirmishers forward at daylight. They reported no change in the enemy's position, yet cavalrymen, just back from the Federal rear, insisted that Rosecrans planned to withdraw. Bragg ordered Wharton and Pegram to guard Breckinridge's right flank while Wheeler returned to the Union rear. He must remain behind the lines, Bragg told him, "until he could definitely report whether any retrograde movement was being made." [56]

About noon, before Bragg heard from Wheeler, reconnaissance by staff officers revealed that Rosecrans was not withdrawing. A Union division had quietly crossed Stone's River and was occupying a position on the east bank "from which . . . Polk's line was both commanded and enfiladed," recalled Bragg. "The dislodgment of this force or the withdrawal of Polk's line was an evident necessity." [57]

Bragg decided to attack. He called Breckinridge to his headquarters and ordered him to drive the Federals back across the river. For this work, Bragg allotted Breckinridge his own division of 6,000 men (four infantry brigades and four artillery batteries), ten Napoleon guns under the command of Captain Felix H. Robertson of Withers's division, and Wharton's and Pegram's 2,000 cavalrymen. To divert Union

---

[55] *Ibid.*, 667, 691, 784; Wheeler to Bragg, January 1, 1863, 1:30 P.M., Palmer Collection of Bragg Papers; Wharton to Polk, January 1, 1863, 1:30 P.M., *ibid.*; Wharton to Polk, January 1, 1863, 6 P.M., *ibid.*; Pegram to Bragg, January 1, 1863, *ibid.*; J. Stoddard Johnston Diary, January 1, 1863.

[56] *OR*, XX (pt. 1), 667.

[57] Brent Diary, January 2, 1863; *OR*, XX (pt. 1), 667–68.

attention from the assault, Bragg opened an artillery barrage
along Polk's front at 3:30 P.M.[58]

About thirty minutes later Breckinridge's men advanced in
two lines. "Instantly the troops moved forward at a quick step
and in admirable order," reported Breckinridge. "The front line
had bayonets fixed, with orders to deliver one volley, and then
use the bayonet." The best brief account of what happened
was written by Bragg's acting chief of staff that night. "The
Division moved beautifully across an open field to the work,"
Colonel Brent noted in his diary. "A murderous fire was
opened upon them. The enemy had concentrated a large force
there & had combined a concentric fire from his Artillery
upon it. Our troops nevertheless, marched up bravely & drove
the enemy from the hill. The left of the Division improvi-
dently crossed the River contrary to orders: It was driven
back in confusion. In [the] meantime the enemy in large force
assailed the right of the Division, & it was compelled to retire.
The [Confederate] Cavalry [men] on the right were ordered to
cooperate, but they were mere spectators. It was a terrible
affair, altho short." An hour and twenty minutes of combat
had gained the Confederates nothing but casualties.[59]

Historians have justly condemned Bragg for ordering Breckinridge's abortive attack. Apparently what he had seen at
Shiloh, at Perryville, and on December 31 at Murfreesboro had
taught Bragg nothing; he still expected bayonet assaults to rout
even the most strongly posted enemy. The distinguished
scholar Kenneth P. Williams believed that the concentration
of fifty-eight Union guns and their strategic location doomed
Breckinridge's assault from the outset. Perhaps so, but the
counterattack by Union infantry on Breckinridge's exposed
right flank hastened the Confederate retreat.[60]

[58] OR, XX (pt. 1), 667–68. Breckinridge incorrectly claimed (ibid.,
785) that his division numbered only 4,500 effectives. See ibid., 678–79,
789.
[59] Ibid., 786; Brent Diary, January 2, 1863.
[60] Williams, Lincoln Finds a General, IV, 278, 281; OR, XX (pt. 1),
808, 812; Brent Diary, January 2, 1863.

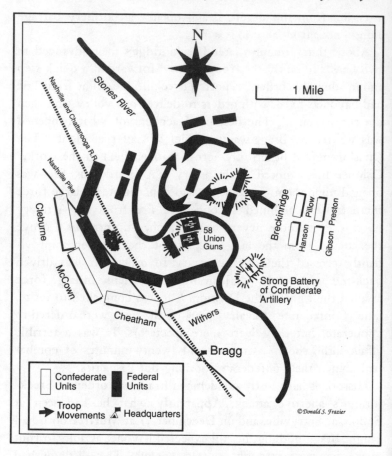

BATTLE OF MURFREESBORO, January 2, 1863

Others besides Bragg contributed to the Confederate failure on January 2. Wharton and Pegram were primarily responsible for their cavalrymen's inaction, but Breckinridge failed to establish proper communication with them. Just before the infantry advanced, General Gideon Pillow, a recent arrival whom Bragg had assigned to command Palmer's brigade, asked Breckinridge if there was support on the right. Informed that

Wharton and Pegram were there, Pillow then asked if any communication had been made with them. When Breckinridge admitted that he had not sent or received a message from either cavalry commander, Pillow said it was "not only proper, but important to communicate with them prior to the movement." Yet Breckinridge ordered his infantry forward without any assurance from the cavalrymen themselves that they would cooperate.[61]

Breckinridge also misused his artillery. According to Captain Robertson, Bragg instructed the artillerists to move forward only after the infantry had taken the enemy position, but Breckinridge planned to advance the batteries between two lines of infantry. Robertson explained that such an arrangement of forces was likely to cause misdirection of fire and confusion, and every gun might be lost if the attack failed. "General Breckinridge, thinking differently, however, formed his batteries and advanced them simultaneously with his infantry," wrote Robertson. "Colonel Brent . . . was present on this occasion and heard the conversation." Just as Robertson feared, the Confederate gunners were unable to find a clear field of fire. Federal shells wrecked a number of exposed guns, and at least three were captured when Breckinridge's infantry retreated. Robertson formed a line with seven Napoleon guns to cover the withdrawal. His claim, that if his artillery had not checked them "the enemy would have gone into Murfreesboro easily that evening," may have been an exaggeration, but unquestionably his stand, made almost entirely without infantry support, discouraged the Federal counterattackers.[62]

Bragg, who criticized the way Breckinridge had delivered his attack, also charged that Breckinridge's division did not fight as well as it should have. Breckenridge replied that "the

[61] George W. Brent to Bragg, March 15, 1863, Palmer Collection of Bragg Papers; OR, XX (pt. 1), 786.
[62] OR, XX (pt. 1), 759, 761. See also the reports of various Union officers. Ibid., 294, 430, 437, 440, 543.

failure of my troops to hold the position which they carried
. . . was due to no fault of theirs or mine, but to the fact that
we were commanded to do an impossible thing." He claimed
that "1,700 heroic spirits stretched upon that bloody field
. . . attested our efforts to obey the order." But if the number
of casualties sustained is any indication of effort, Breckinridge's argument is weak. Unit reports show that Breckinridge
exaggerated his losses by 368 men. All of his brigades lost
fewer than 30 per cent of their men (two of the four fewer
than 20 per cent), and six of his fifteen regiments lost fewer
than 20 per cent of their effectives. Compared with losses
sustained by other units on December 31, Breckinridge's
casualties on January 2 were small. Hanson's Kentucky brigade, which had not engaged in the earlier fighting, lost only
19 per cent of its men. The fact that two of Hanson's regiments (the Fourth and Sixth Kentucky) were among those
suffering the fewest casualties at both Murfreesboro and
Chickamauga suggests the possibility that these men fought
reluctantly.[63]

When Bragg learned of "the disorderly retreat being made
by General Breckinridge's division," he sent reinforcements.
Anderson's brigade crossed the river about dark and deployed
to support Robertson's guns. By daylight the Confederate
right was again stable; Breckinridge had assembled his scattered units, and Hardee had arrived from the left with
Cleburne's division to assume command.[64]

But the Confederate position was now precarious. Soldiers
who had fought and waited in the rain and cold for five days
without sufficient rest were losing their morale; straggling had

[63] *Ibid.*, 668, 791. The Fourth Kentucky lost 12 per cent of its effective
strength at Murfreesboro, and 21 per cent at Chickamauga. The Sixth
Kentucky lost 17 per cent of its effective strength at Murfreesboro, and
11 per cent at Chickamauga.

[64] *OR*, XX (pt. 1), 668. Breckinridge reported (*ibid.*, 787) that his
division retreated "without the slightest appearance of panic" and "reformed behind Robertson's battery." A letter from Anderson to

increased significantly. About 2 A.M. on January 3 Bragg was awakened and handed a note from Withers and Cheatham which advised him to retreat. "You have but three brigades [65] that are at all reliable," they informed him. At the bottom of their dispatch Polk had added: ". . . I very greatly fear the consequences of another engagement at this place. . . . We could now, perhaps, get off with some safety and some credit, if the affair is well managed. Should we fail in the meditated attack [by the enemy today], the consequences might be very disastrous." After glancing at the message, Bragg told Polk's courier: "Say to the general we shall maintain our position at every hazard." [66]

Before noon, however, Bragg changed his mind. Stone's River, which had risen rapidly after several days of heavy rain, might soon become unfordable and thus isolate half the army. Furthermore, Bragg had just seen captured documents which indicated that the Federal force numbered 70,000 men,[67] far more than he had guessed, and Wheeler reported enemy reinforcements arriving from Nashville. About 10 A.M. Bragg called Polk and Hardee to headquarters for consultation. Both advised him to retreat, and he agreed to do so.[68]

Withers's assistant adjutant general, however, indicated that Breckinridge's units were still disorganized at 10:45 P.M. See J. Patton Anderson to Major D. E. Huger, January 2, 1863, 10:45 P.M. (copy), Palmer Collection of Bragg Papers. See also Colonel David Urquhart's statement, June 12, 1863, *ibid.*

[65] Later Withers and Cheatham claimed they meant three divisions. See *OR*, XX (pt. 1), 702.

[66] *Ibid.*, 700-1. After receiving Bragg's reply, Polk wrote Hardee: "I think the decision of the general unwise, and, am compelled to add, in a high degree."

[67] Rosecrans had 81,000 men under his command, but only about 44,000 actually engaged in battle at Murfreesboro. See *OR*, XX (pt. 1), 201.

[68] *Ibid.*, 669, 682; Wheeler to Bragg, January 3, 1862, Palmer Collection of Bragg Papers. Wheeler's report was correct; an infantry brigade and 303 wagons loaded with food reached Rosecrans's lines at 5 A.M., on January 3. See Williams, *Lincoln Finds a General*, IV, 281.

The Confederate retreat from Murfreesboro, which began at 11 P.M. on January 3 in a drenching rain, was made without mishap. Supply trains led the way south, followed by the infantry. A cavalry screen protected the movements. The enemy did not pursue, but nearly two thousand badly wounded Confederates and their medical attendants were left behind.[69]

After the war General Liddell recalled a conversation he had with Bragg just before the retreat. "His manner it seemed to me was thoughtful and hesitating and he finally gave me to understand that the troops were exhausted . . . and that to withdraw . . . was necessary," remembered Liddell, who insisted his men could still fight. "Everything depends upon your success here," Liddell told Bragg, "and if you will throw your army between Rosecrans and Nashville you will cut off reinforcements . . . and then I would fight him to the last." Bragg answered: "Genl. I know that you will fight it out but others will not." To which Liddell replied: "Give the order Genl., and every man will obey you." A few minutes passed before Bragg spoke again. Then he said: "No it has now become a matter of imperative necessity to withdraw and . . . it must be done at once." [70]

Just as at Perryville, Bragg seemed to change under stress from a bold and aggressive attacker to a hesitant and cautious retreater. He had, of course, sound reasons for withdrawing from Murfreesboro. His principal subordinates advised him to retreat. He had lost nearly 30 per cent of his men [71] in the

[69] Brent Diary, January 3, 1863; *OR*, XX (pt. 1), 669.
[70] Liddell, "Liddell's Record of the Civil War," Liddell Papers.
[71] Approximate Confederate losses were: 1,274 killed; 7,969 wounded; and 1,071 captured or missing. Federal losses were: 1,730 killed; 7,802 wounded; and 3,717 captured or missing. See *OR*, XX (pt. 1), 215, 676–81, 693, 758, 780, 852, 855, 875, 900, and unpublished reports in the Palmer Collection of Bragg Papers. Conflicting reports make it impossible to give the exact number of Confederate casualties. My estimate, particularly of the number captured or missing, differs from that of both

recent battles; if forced to fight again without some rest, his army might disintegrate. But his decision to retreat allowed his enemies to charge that once again Bragg had lost his nerve.

Livermore (*Numbers and Losses,* p. 97) and Williams (*Lincoln Finds a General,* IV, 284, 540), because I believe they counted the wounded left at Murfreesboro twice.

CHAPTER XVI

Send some one to relieve me

JANUARY 4–APRIL 10, 1863

THE MURFREESBORO campaign and its aftermath destroyed Bragg's usefulness as a field commander. For several days after the battle he was uncertain where to halt his retreat. At first he selected the Elk River, some fifty miles south of Murfreesboro, but on January 7, when it became clear that the Federals were not pursuing, Bragg changed his mind. He ordered a defense line established along Duck River, about thirty miles from Murfreesboro. "The policy, of holding as much of Tennessee as we can, is good," concluded Colonel Brent. "It is unfortunate that on leaving Murfreesboro, the line of the Duck had not been determined on. The movement so far to the rear, has had a bad effect on the troops & the public mind." [1]

As Brent predicted, the retreat set off an avalanche of criticism. "General Bragg has certainly retreated . . . from his victory at Murfreesboro, as he did last fall from his victory at Perryville," sneered an editor. "I wish you all could get rid of Bragg—everybody seems to hate him so," complained General Cheatham's sister. Cheatham himself insisted he would never go into battle again under Bragg. [2] "Bragg is said to have lost the confidence of his command completely," noted a government official. "It is quite manifest that there are deep quarrels in that army, and that Bragg is cordially hated by a large

[1] Brent Diary, January 7–8, 1863.

[2] Richmond *Examiner*, January 6, 1863; Martha Cheatham to Benjamin F. Cheatham, March 30 [1863], Cheatham Papers; Joseph E. Johnston to Jefferson Davis, February 3, 1863, Joseph E. Johnston Papers, Duke University.

number of his officers."[3] General McCown, who had denounced the Confederacy as "a *damned* stinking cotton
oligarchy . . . gotten up for the benefit of [Tennessee's
Governor] Isham G. Harris and Jeff Davis and their damned
corrupt cliques," said he was going to quit the army and raise
potatoes on his four-acre farm in East Tennessee unless the
government removed Bragg.[4] And a soldier, incorrectly
informed that Mrs. Bragg had died, wrote: ". . . I assure you,
had it of been him instead of her, there would have been
rejoicing in the Southern Army as far as privates are concerned. No one man, that ever lived, I don't believe ever had as
much hatred expressed against him, as Bragg."[5]

Yet Colonel Brent observed: ". . . dissatisfaction [with
Bragg] in Polk's Corps, does not appear so marked & decided
as in Hardee's. It is surmised by some that the great 'hue & cry'
was raised by Breckinridge, who by some means seduced
Hardee to participate therein." According to one report,
Breckinridge was so embittered by Bragg's criticism of his
conduct at Murfreesboro that he almost resigned his commission and challenged Bragg to a duel.[6]

Goaded by such denunciation, Bragg decided to ask his
subordinates what they really thought of his military ability.
On January 10, 1863, he read to his staff an article from the
Chattanooga *Rebel* which charged that he "had lost the confidence of his Army—that a change was necessary & that the
retrograde movement from Murfreesboro was against the
advice of his general officers." Bragg, who asked his staff to

[3] Younger, ed., *Kean Diary*, pp. 38, 42.

[4] McCown was also "severe in his censure of Genl Withers for a card
he had published in Mobile papers in defense of Genl Bragg, and of
Genl Cheatham who . . . 'said one thing among the officers behind Genl
Bragg's back, and wrote him a totally different thing.'" See Gideon J.
Pillow to Major William Clare, March 9, 1863, Palmer Collection of
Bragg Papers.

[5] C. William Fackler to His Sister, March 26 [1863] (typescript), C.
William Fackler Papers, Duke University.

[6] Brent Diary, January 12, 1863; Gordon, *Reminiscences*, p. 193.

consider these charges, added that "if he had lost the confidence of his Army . . . he would retire." The staff met, compared opinions, and concluded "that under existing circumstances the general interests required that Gen Bragg should ask to be relieved." [7]

Bragg gave the impression that he thought so too, because that same day he wrote Senator C. C. Clay: ". . . it has become with me a serious question as to whether it would not be better for the President to send some one to relieve me." But actually Bragg wanted sympathy and understanding rather than relief from command. He felt persecuted, desperately in need of support and encouragement. "Understand me, my dear sir, I am asking for nothing in this great struggle of ours but justice," he wrote Senator Thomas Jenkins Semmes. "Washington was assailed as a traitor and swindler. Wellington suffered as much. . . . And even Christ was crucified. . . ." Bragg had begun to view himself as a martyr. He admitted to General John K. Jackson: "With so little support, my aching head rebels against the heart, and cries for relief—still I shall die in the traces." [8]

On January 11, the day after his staff conference, Bragg wrote to his corps and division commanders asking for their candid opinion of his military ability and their admission that they had recommended retreating from Murfreesboro. His staff advised him not to send the letter. He did strike out those portions which asked specifically for an expression of confidence in him, but his letter "was still broad," noted Colonel Brent, "& tended to open up controversy, which ought to be avoided." In part it read: "Finding myself assailed in private and public, by the press . . . by officers and citizens, for the

[7] Brent Diary, January 10, 1863.
[8] Bragg to Clay, January 10, 1863, Clement Claiborne Clay Papers, Duke University; Bragg to Semmes [January] 13, 1863, Thomas Jenkins Semmes Papers, Duke University; Bragg to Jackson, January 24, 1863 (microfilm copy), Jackson-McKinne Papers, Southern Historical Collection, University of North Carolina.

movement from Murfreesboro, which was resisted by me for some time after advised by my corps and division commanders [to withdraw] . . . it becomes necessary for me to save my fair name, if I cannot stop the deluge of abuse, which will destroy my usefulness and demoralize the army." Bragg's staff believed he should have ended his letter after asking his generals to acquit him of the charge that he had insisted upon retreat against their advice. Instead he had continued: "I desire that you will consult your subordinate commanders and be candid with me. . . . I shall retire without a regret if I find I have lost the good opinion of my generals, upon whom I have ever relied as upon a foundation of rock." [9]

Bragg thus gave his enemies an unexpected opportunity. While many of his staunchest supporters were absent,[10] he encouraged an official expression of discontent from certain officers whom his tactlessness had already alienated and whose bitterness had damaged his prestige. Jefferson Davis believed Bragg meant what he said: "No one more readily than General Bragg would surrender a desirable position to promote the public interest, and I have not feared any hesitation on his part, if he should find that he could better serve his country by a change of position." But when the President heard about Bragg's letter, he wrote: "Why General Bragg should have selected that tribunal, and have invited its judgment upon him, is to me unexplained." [11]

What neither the President nor Bragg apparently understood was that the strain of command had become too great; Bragg had lost confidence in himself. He could not even withhold his letter until more of his friends returned to duty. Of course, his action indicates that he no longer knew who his

[9] Brent Diary, January 11, 1863; OR, XX (pt. 1), 699.
[10] At this time six of Bragg's strongest partisans among the generals were on leave because of sickness or wounds: Jones M. Withers, Daniel W. Adams, James R. Chalmers, Marcus J. Wright, Edward C. Walthall, and Zachary C. Deas.
[11] OR, XXIII (pt. 2), 640–41, 613.

friends were if, in fact, he had ever known. Bragg now needed the immediate assurance that his generals trusted and sustained him. In a sense, his letter was a pathetic plea for love and understanding.

But the replies Bragg received gave him no comfort. Hardee and his subordinates admitted that they had advised retreat, but they also expressed their lack of confidence in Bragg. Cleburne wrote: "I have consulted with my brigade commanders . . . and they unite with me in personal regard for yourself, in a high appreciation of your patriotism and gallantry, and in a conviction of your great capacity for organization, but at the same time they see, with regret . . . that you do not possess the confidence of the army in other respects in that degree necessary to secure success." Breckinridge wrote that his brigade commanders "request me to say that while they entertain the highest respect for your patriotism, it is their opinion that you do not possess the confidence of the army to an extent which will enable you to be useful as its commander. In this opinion I feel bound to state that I concur." [12]

Though Polk believed Bragg's letter called for answers to two questions, some of his subordinates disagreed, and he refused to reply until its purpose was clarified. Bragg, given this opportunity to reconsider what he had written, said he had asked only one question—had his generals advised retreat? —and that his letter "had been grossly and intentionally misrepresented . . . for my injury." The purpose of his letter, he now insisted, merely "was to relieve my mind of all doubt," and the "paragraph relating to my supersedure was only an expression of the feeling with which I should receive your replies, should they prove I had been misled in my construction of your opinion and advice." [13]

Bragg's answer prevented Polk from saying more than that he and his division commanders had advocated retreating from

[12] *Ibid.*, XX (pt. 1), 682–84. [13] *Ibid.*, 701–2.

Murfreesboro, but it did not prevent Davis from ordering General Joseph E. Johnston to Tullahoma to investigate the situation. Davis wrote: ". . . though my confidence in General Bragg is unshaken, it cannot be doubted that if he is distrusted by his officers and troops, a disaster may result which, but for that cause, would have been avoided. You will, I trust, be able, by conversation with General Bragg and others of his command, to decide what the best interests of the service require, and to give me the advice which I need at this juncture. As that army is a part of your command, no order will be necessary to give you authority there. . . ." [14]

Johnston, who was on an inspection tour of his department when Davis's order reached him, went directly to Tullahoma. "Genl Joseph E. Johnston arrived at this place today," a soldier noted on January 27. "His presence will no doubt put fresh zeal into the troops. He is regarded as one of the great chieftains of the age." After Johnston had consulted various people, he concluded that there were no just grounds for Bragg's removal. "I am very glad . . . that your confidence in General Bragg is unshaken," Johnston wrote Davis on February 3. "My own is confirmed by his recent operations, which in my opinion evince great vigor & skill. It would be very unfortunate to remove him at this juncture, when he has just earned if not won the gratitude of the country." Johnston admitted that Governor Isham G. Harris, "with whom the general officers converse more freely, probably, than with their military superiors, thinks that they want confidence in their commander—but that it is due to the Kentucky campaign & thinks that it is declining. He thinks that it is not such an evil as would result from the removal of Genl Bragg." [15] Obviously, the generals had not been as frank with Johnston as they had with Bragg.

[14] *Ibid.*, XXIII (pt. 2), 613–14.

[15] D. Coleman Diary, January 27, 1863, Southern Historical Collection, University of North Carolina; Johnston to Davis, February 3, 1863, Johnston Papers, Duke University.

In another letter to the President on February 12 Johnston
again praised Bragg and requested that he be kept in command
of the Army of Tennessee. "My object has been to ascertain if
the confidence of the troops in the ability of the army to beat
the enemy is at all impaired," said Johnston. "I find no indication that it is. . . . While this feeling exists, and you regard
General Bragg as brave and skillful, the fact that some or all of
the general officers . . . think that you might give them a
commander with fewer defects, cannot, I think, greatly
diminish his value. To me it seems that the operations of this
army . . . have been conducted admirably. I can find no
record of more effective fighting in modern battles than that
of this army in December, evincing skill in the commander
and courage in the troops. . . ." Johnston concluded his
strong vindication of Bragg with an ultimatum: "I have been
told by . . . Polk and Hardee that they have advised you to
remove General Bragg and place me in command of this army.
I am sure that you will agree with me that the part I have
borne in this investigation would render it inconsistent with
my personal honor to occupy that position. I believe, however,
that the interests of the service require that General Bragg
should not be removed." [16]

Johnston was not alone; other generals still supported Bragg.
"I have noticed . . . in the [Chattanooga] Rebel that you
have applied to be relieved," General Jackson wrote Bragg on
January 14. "Will you pardon the expression of a hope from
one, who has gladly served under you from the breaking out
of hostilities, that this is not so. You may be assailed—who is
not? You may feel wounded at the ingratitude of some of your
countrymen—who does not? But you owe it to your country
not to yield to your enemies in your rear any sooner than you
would surrender to those in front." Three days later Jackson
wrote again: "You may with confidence rely upon all the
support that I can bring to your aid, and I am sure you may

16 OR, XXIII (pt. 2), 632–33.

with equal confidence place your trust in one officer of your staff—Col. J. P. Jones. It will afford me great pleasure, General, to be of service to you at any time and in any way, publicly or privately, personally or officially." Generals Wheeler, Withers, and Chalmers also expressed their confidence in Bragg. Indeed, Withers defended his commander in a letter to a newspaper. Another assurance of support came from General Preston Smith, who wrote that he and General Donelson were sorry Bragg was being assailed "by the vicious & ignorant for doing his duty to his country." [17]

Bragg received further support from some officers below the rank of general [18] and from some soldiers. Among the encouraging letters sent to him by enlisted men was one from a wounded private. "Enclosed you will please find a copy of a communication written by myself to the 'Atlanta Intelligencer,'" wrote Wilbur F. Johnson. "I enclose it . . . to assure you that *one* of your *old Pensacola soldiers* . . . will not fail, as long as it is in his power, to see justice done to his Genl. . . ." A wounded junior officer wrote his brother: "Rumor says that Beauregard is to be . . . placed in immediate command of the Army. . . . Yet I do not want Bragg to be taken away. . . . Let Beauregard supervise and Bragg execute and discipline. Bragg is one of the greatest of our leaders and though the present generation will not do him justice, *Time* the great rectifier, and History will." [19]

[17] Jackson to Bragg, January 14, 17, 1863, Palmer Collection of Bragg Papers; Wheeler to Bragg, January 23, 1863, *ibid.*; Bragg to Benjamin S. Ewell, February 6, 1863, *ibid.*; Gideon J. Pillow to William Clare, March 9, 1863, *ibid.*; Withers to Editor, *Mobile Advertiser and Register*, January 18, 1863; Smith to Bragg, January 17, 1863, Palmer Collection of Bragg Papers.

[18] See Major M. H. Wright to Bragg, February 14, 1863, Palmer Collection of Bragg Papers; Colonel Henry Maury to Bragg, February 23, 1863, *ibid.*; Surgeon J. C. Nott to Bragg, January 31, March 1, 1863, *ibid.*; Major John J. Walker to Bragg, May 19, 1863, *ibid.*

[19] Johnson to Bragg, March 3, 1863, Palmer Collection of Bragg Papers; E. John Ellis to His Brother, July 10, 1863, E. John, Thomas

A number of civilians also defended Bragg. One even asked General Leonidas Polk to help. "Now, as I frankly admit that I have wronged a noble warrior who has risked everything in the cause of his country, property, life, honor," wrote John M. Huger, "I call upon you to lend me assistance in wiping out an impression from the public mind unjust as it is injurious to Genl Bragg. . . . Write me then, my dear General, such a statement in reference to Murfreesboro, as may, under the authority of your name, roll back the wave of popular error . . . which now dims the bright shield of your brother warrior." [20] Several members of Congress remained Bragg partisans.[21] "In my humble judgment," wrote Congressman Francis S. Lyon, "you have won a title to the respect and gratitude of the entire people of the Confederate States, and as a citizen I have to acknowledge my part of the obligation so justly due from every one who feels an interest in the existing struggle between liberty and despotism. It is the fate of leading men in times of revolution and excitement to encounter occasionally abuse and misrepresentation—but these things are only temporary, and truth & justice will prevail in the end." A former Congressman announced: ". . . I abide in confidence that you will shed new luster on the recent glory of our arms." And from Mobile a physician assured Bragg: "You have some firm friends in this place who being satisfied with your course will sustain you as you will finally be sustained by all who are honest in their opinions formed after mature deliberation." "All of our Generals have been subjects of these inevitable vituperations . . . all have received the accursed abuse of

C. W. Ellis and Family Papers. At this time Ellis was recovering from a wound he had received at Murfreesboro. See Fannie A. Beers, *Memoirs* (Philadelpia, 1889), p. 90.

20 Huger to Polk, February 15, 1863 (microfilm copy), Leonidas Polk Papers, Southern Historical Collection, University of North Carolina.

21 See James L. Pugh to Bragg, March 5, 1863, Palmer Collection of Bragg Papers; James Phelan to Bragg, March 6, 1863, *ibid.*; Thomas J. Semmes to Bragg, March 6, 1863, *ibid.*

political tricksters and the would be great men of the Confederacy," insisted another citizen. "Rest assured . . . that if the war were closed today no name would stand higher, no character would shine brighter on the page of history than that of Braxton Bragg." "I think your true happiness & best policy are to be found in cultivating peace with your Generals & the public," advised John Forsyth. "If the Government . . . gives you anything like a fair chance, I feel confident that you will triumph over . . . your enemies & fully vindicate the opinion & justify the expectations of your friends." A lady sent Bragg a heartening message, and another wrote in her diary: "When the history of this war is impartially written, it is my deliberate opinion, that to *Bragg* will be awarded the praise of *having done more with his men and means, than any other Gen. of the War, with equal resources.*" 22

Such expressions of support temporarily restored Bragg's self-confidence.23 "I will advise with you," Bragg claimed Johnston told him, "but will not give an order or assume one particle of direction, as you have proven yourself the ablest commander in the service, and with less means have accomplished more than any of us." 24 To his old West Point instructor, Benjamin S. Ewell, now on Johnston's staff, Bragg wrote: "I am very happy to say that all seems to be subsiding into quiet satisfaction. And the only dissatisfaction that ever existed was fomented by a few disappointed Generals who supposed they could cover their own tracks and rise on my downfall. They have failed. Mainly owing to the discrimination and just conception of your noble chief, who saw at a

22 Lyon to Bragg, January 12, 1863, Palmer Collection of Bragg Papers; Robert H. Smith to Bragg, May 7, 1863, *ibid.;* Dr. Andrew J. Foard to Bragg, January 31, 1863, *ibid.;* Jenkes Campbell to Bragg, March 1, 1863, *ibid.;* Forsyth to Bragg, June 15, 1863, *ibid.;* Mrs. H. Withers Huger to Bragg, February 4, 1863, *ibid.;* Sarah Ridley Trimble, ed., "Behind the Lines in Middle Tennessee, 1863–1865: The Journal of Bettie Ridley Blackmore," *Tennessee Historical Quarterly,* XII (1953), 54.
23 Brent Diary, January 24–February 2, 1863.
24 Bragg to William W. Mackall, February 14, 1863, Mackall Papers.

glance the whole bearing. An expression of regret, now almost universal, reaches me constantly—but I pay no heed & pursue the even turn of my way." [25] Either Bragg was unaware of his unpopularity, which is difficult to believe, or he simply deceived himself into believing only what he wanted to hear. Whatever the case, it seems clear that at this point Bragg was no longer able to view his position realistically; he was too disoriented for further field command.

He believed all was well, but his position was still quite precarious. On February 19 the President wrote Johnston: "It is not given to all men of ability to excite enthusiasm and win affection of their troops, and it is only the few who are thus endowed who can overcome the distrust, and alienation of their principal officers." Davis, despite his own confidence in Bragg, wanted to replace him as commander of the Army of Tennessee. Only Johnston stood in the way. "You limit the selection of a new man," complained Davis, "and, in terms very embarrassing to me, object to being yourself the immediate commander." "The removal of General Bragg would only affect you in so far as it deprived you of his services, and might restrain your freedom of movement by requiring more of your attention to that army. Therefore, I do not think that your personal honor is involved, as you could have nothing to gain by the removal of General Bragg." But Davis promised not to urge any course upon Johnston which would wound his "sensibility or views of professional propriety." [26]

For a few weeks Davis kept his promise, though Secretary of War James A. Seddon, probably with the President's knowledge, exerted considerable pressure on Johnston to change his mind. On March 3 Seddon, who favored Bragg's removal, wrote Johnston: "In your generous appreciation of a

[25] Bragg to Ewell, February 27, 1863, Benjamin S. Ewell Papers, Henry E. Huntington Library.
[26] OR, XXIII (pt. 2), 640–41.

brother officer, who very possibly may have been harshly judged, you certainly do not realize the popular dissatisfaction at Bragg's commanding, nor the distrust and discontent unfortunately pervading all ranks of the army toward him." Seddon suggested that, even if Johnston was unwilling to sanction Bragg's recall, he could establish his departmental headquarters at Tullahoma and personally direct the operation of the Army of Tennessee. This, argued Seddon, would allow Johnston to keep "Bragg (as I understand, admirably qualified to be) an organizer and administrator under you." [27]

Johnston refused to be swayed by either the President's or the Secretary of War's appeals; he clung instead to the curiously ambivalent attitude he had expressed privately to his friend Senator Louis T. Wigfall. Johnston dearly wanted to command an army, but he believed it would be unjust to replace Bragg. On February 14 Johnston had written Wigfall: "Each of the . . . departments assigned to me has its general & as there is no room for two, & I can't remove him appointed by the prest. for the precise place, nothing but the part of inspector general is left to me. I wrote to the president on the subject, trying to explain that I am virtually laid on the shelf with the responsibility of command but he has not replied, perhaps because he has no better place for me. I should much prefer the *command* of fifty men. . . ."

On March 4 Johnston had explained his objections to the command assigned him and why he opposed the removal of Bragg:

. . . I can not ask or desire the place of either of the department commanders (nominally) under me [Johnson wrote]. In relation to Bragg—I think you under rate him. We agree as to his Kentucky operations. I think that he has commanded extremely well in Middle Tennessee—that he has exhibited great energy & discre-

tion in his operations in that district & has done the enemy more
harm than any body else has done with the same force in the same
time—against such a force. Nobody seems to consider that the
expeditions & successes of Wheeler, Forrest & Morgan were under
his orders—or that the falling back of Grant in Mississippi was
brought about by Forrest's operations directed by him [Bragg] for
the purpose, on the first intelligence that Genl. Pemberton wanted
help. At Murfreesboro he fought double numbers & the enemy's
loss was equal to about 70 percent of his force engaged [Johnston
is mistaken here]. In the great European battles of modern times
there was no destruction equal to it, in proportion to the destroying force. Thinking that great injustice has been done to him by
the country—that is to say by the press & Congress—I should
regret very much to see him removed. Since the battle at Murfreesboro he has brought up his army to its former strength—indeed
to a greater. This could have been done by nobody else. Observing
his course since the beginning of December, I have not been able
to discover any serious fault in his course.

. . .

I agree with you fully, that it would not do for me to be placed in
command of the Army of Tennessee. . . . If there were not other
objections, the great injustice to him [Bragg] would be a sufficient
one. But there is another still to my being assigned to that army—
that on learning that there was some feeling against Genl. Bragg
in his army, the president directed me . . . to go to Tullahoma &
ascertain & report the state of things. Now to remove the officer
& put me in his place, & upon my investigations & report, would
not look well, & would certainly expose me, injure me. The
president's idea that I am to take command of these armies suc-
cessively, at my pleasure, would be a very mischievous one in
practice. It is virtually having two generals for one army. If I
were to go to Mississippi now, it is probable that I should find
dispositions & a plan of operations different from those I would
make. I could not carry them out so well as Genl. Pemberton. If
I attempted to change them to suit my own ideas the enemy might
interrupt me—& Pemberton, when again left in command, would
naturally go back to his own system. The other part of the Prest's

plan, connecting the armies . . . for combined operations under me, is not practicable, from the great distance between them.[28]

Davis, of course, did not see the situation through Johnston's eyes. He failed to understand Johnston's objections to the command arrangement in the western theatre. When Johnston ignored what the President considered Seddon's sound suggestion to use Bragg as an organizer and administrator,[29] Davis lost his patience. He ordered Johnston to assume active command of the Army of Tennessee and to send Bragg to Richmond. Bragg's official report of the Murfreesboro campaign, which had just arrived in Richmond, may have influenced the President. Bragg's criticism of Breckinridge, Cheatham, and McCown had "raised a storm in Congress," a friend informed General Polk. "The Tennesseeans could stand his pitching into McCown, but not Cheatham. General |Senator| Henry says however that Genl Bragg will not be removed. Others . . . speak with equal confidence of his being retired at an early day and say that is the object of his being ordered to Richmond at this time. . . . I venture to predict his certain removal. His Report has done the work. . . ."[30]

But Johnston simply refused to carry out the President's order. Elise Bragg, who had just arrived in Tennessee, was "at the point of death" in Winchester. "On account of Mrs. Bragg's critical condition, I shall not now give the order [for Bragg's removal from command]," explained Johnston on March 19. But he also added: "Should the enemy advance, General Bragg will be indispensable here." Bragg spent most of

[28] Johnston to Wigfall, February 14, March 4, 1863, Louis T. Wigfall Family Papers, University of Texas.

[29] An arrangement similar to the one Seddon suggested to Johnston worked admirably in the Union Army of the Potomac later in the war.

[30] OR, XXIII (pt. 2), 674; William Dudley Gale to Leonidas Polk, March 27, 1863 (microfilm copy), Polk Papers, University of North Carolina.

a month with Elise, and by the time she had recovered her health Johnston was bedridden. On April 10 he wrote Davis: "I . . . am not now able to serve in the field. General Bragg is therefore necessary here." [31]

Confronted with such obstinacy, Davis relented; probably he feared that if he insisted upon Bragg's removal Johnston might resign. Davis had no great affection for Johnston, but he preferred him to Beauregard, the only other full general available and therefore Johnston's logical successor as western commander. To anyone who disliked Beauregard as much as the President did,[32] maintenance of the status quo, despite the general dissatisfaction with Bragg, must have seemed less objectionable than the alternative.

Johnston's support and a combination of circumstances kept Bragg in command in early 1863, but less than a year later nearly everybody in the Confederacy knew that it had been a mistake. In March 1864 Senator Wigfall informed Johnston that his refusal to sanction Bragg's removal had given Davis the chance to blame him for Bragg's later failures. Johnston's friends, wrote Wigfall, "did regret that you had not simply published the order for Bragg to report to Richmond 'for conference' & left it to him & the War Department to decide how long he should remain with his sick wife." [33]

Even at the time, in the winter and early spring of 1863, many people realized that Bragg was no longer fit for command. A soldier remembered that Bragg's staff, "witnessing his severe and persistent mental and physical labors, were . . . fearful that he would not take nutriment enough to sustain

[31] OR, XXIII (pt. 2), 708, 745; Brent Diary, March 16–April 14, 1863; Joseph E. Johnston, "Jefferson Davis and the Mississippi Campaign," Battles and Leaders, III, 476, 477. Elise Bragg had typhoid fever.

[32] Davis's dislike of Beauregard was evident to contemporaries (see Thomas Bragg Diary, passim), and has been confirmed by historians (see Williams, Beauregard, passim).

[33] Wigfall to Johnston, March 18, 1864, Joseph E. Johnston Papers, Huntington Library.

life. They often forced this fear upon his attention by sending his meals to him and urging him to eat while at his desk." He seemed sick and despondent. "He was mentally and physically an old, wornout man, unfit to actively manage an army in the field," recalled a regimental commander. Bragg admitted that he had been suffering from a siege of boils which culminated in "a general break-down." He claimed he had recovered, but Hardee considered him too feeble "either to examine and determine his line of battle or to take command on the field." English Colonel James Fremantle, who saw Bragg in the spring of 1863, also noticed how weak he looked. "This officer is in appearance the least prepossessing of the Confederate generals," wrote Fremantle. "He is very thin. He stoops, and has a sickly, cadaverous, haggard appearance . . . but his eyes are bright and piercing." [34]

This sick man, who had lost touch with reality, had already marched far toward disgrace and condemnation. In a few weeks he would be maneuvered out of Tennessee by the Federals. In eight months his career as a trusted field commander would be over. And before the war ended he would become the most denounced general in the Confederacy.

He had failed as a field commander for a number of reasons. After the war Beauregard called Bragg "a good subordinate," but "inferior" as an army commander. "He had not the 'feu sacré' as Napoleon calls it." Another officer was more blunt. "Bragg had none of the instincts and elements of a great soldier," concluded Colonel John H. Savage.[35] Perhaps such an

[34] Stout, "Reminiscences," Palmer Collection of Bragg Papers; Savage, *Life of John H. Savage*, p. 137; Polk, *Leonidas Polk*, II, 222; Lord, ed., *Fremantle Diary*, p. 115. Another soldier commented on Bragg's eyes: "I saw Gen. Bragg yesterday for the first time. He is tall and thin, quite gray, face long and somewhat narrow, nose slightly aquiline. The most remarkable feature is the eye, which is dark-gray and as strong and unflinching as a hawk's." Unsigned letter, Richmond *Sentinel*, April 29, 1863.

[35] Beauregard to Mrs. S. A. Dorsey, June 23, 1869, Beauregard Papers, Duke University; Savage, *Life of John H. Savage*, p. 137.

evaluation is too harsh. Bragg was courageous, and at times imaginative, resourceful, and bold. But he was never patient, either with his men or with the enemy, and he lacked that imperturbability and resolution so necessary in field commanders. Handicapped by poor health, he had no real taste for combat. And he was not lucky. Nor did he have the ability to inspire confidence in his subordinates. Notoriously inept at getting along with people he disliked, he simply could not win the loyalty of his chief lieutenants. He lacked what has been called the common touch. By training and by preference a regular army man, contemptuous of volunteers and a democratic military establishment, he was unsuited to lead an army composed overwhelmingly of individualistic citizen-soldiers. A mediocre tactician, he seemed unaware of the technological changes that had outdated pre-war assault tactics and strengthened the advantages of defensive combat.

Despite all these shortcomings, Bragg might have been more successful if he had learned from his own mistakes. Some of his contemporaries grew as soldiers as the war progressed, but Bragg was no better as a combat leader in 1863 than he had been in 1862. He had not developed that flexibility, the ability to modify his tactics to meet a new situation, which all students of the art of war consider indispensable in a great soldier. Bragg had perfected neither an efficient intelligence system nor a capable staff to assess information and to make plans. At times he had moved rapidly and deceived the enemy, but he had demonstrated little understanding of the economy of war. Repeatedly he had wasted men in rash attacks when he could have accomplished much more by skillful defenses at a fraction of the cost to the Confederacy. He had contributed significantly to that purposeless attrition—the numerous frontal assaults—which ultimately destroyed the South's armies. As for security, he obviously had not heeded Frederick the Great's advice: "Never deceive yourself, but picture skillfully all the measures that the enemy will take to oppose your plans, in order never to be caught by surprise. Then, having foreseen everything in advance, you will already have remedies prepared for any eventuality." [36]

Though Bragg had little talent for field command, he had characteristics which the Confederates needed desperately but used inadequately. Intelligent, diligent, and patriotic, Bragg by all accounts was an excellent organizer and disciplinarian. He "possessed qualifications such as, rightly directed, would have made him as great in the Confederate army as Moltke in the Prussian," asserted Colonel J. Stoddard Johnston. Higher ranking officers also thought that the President should have appointed Bragg inspector general or chief of staff of the Confederate armies. In February 1863 Beauregard wrote his friend William P. Miles: ". . . with Bragg in [Adjutant and Inspector General Samuel] Cooper's place . . . all would go right." And in March 1863 General Leonidas Polk asked Davis to transfer Bragg "to another field, where his peculiar talent— that of organization and discipline—could find a more ample scope. For that kind of service he has, undoubtedly, peculiar talent," admitted Polk. "His tastes and natural inclination fit him for it. . . . The application of that talent is not always easy or agreeable where it exists, yet there are few armies which would not be benefited by it. . . . My opinion is that the general could be of service to all the armies of the Confederacy, if placed in the proper position. Such a position would be that of . . . Inspector-General." "The whole family of idlers, drones, and shirks, of high or low degree, far and near, would feel his searching hand, and be made to take their places and do their duty." [37]

One of the great ironies of Confederate military history is that Jefferson Davis, who prided himself so on his knowledge

[36] Jay Luvaas, ed., *Frederick the Great on the Art of War* (New York, 1966), p. 334.

[37] Quoted in Johnston, *Life of A. S. Johnston*, p. 546; OR, LIII, 307; XXIII (pt. 2), 729–30.

392 CHAPTER XVI JANUARY 4–APRIL 10, 1863

of the capabilities of those former regular army officers who fought for the South, failed early in the war to assign Bragg to a position where his talents could be used best. Instead, the President had placed and retained Bragg in a post—as commander of the Confederacy's second most important army—where he made a major contribution to Confederate defeat.

SELECTED BIBLIOGRAPHY

Only items cited in the previous pages are included in this bibliography. It does not include numerous manuscript collections, periodicals, and books which I have searched, but from which I have not quoted.

Manuscripts and Scrapbooks

Application Papers of West Point Cadets, 1814–1866, National Archives, Washington, D.C.

Army Papers, Missouri Historical Society, St. Louis.

Ayers, Alexander M., Papers (typed copy), Centenary College of Louisiana.

Barringer, Daniel Moreau, Papers, Southern Historical Collection, University of North Carolina, Chapel Hill.

Beatty, Charlotte, Diary, *ibid.*

Beatty, Taylor, Diary, *ibid.*

Beauregard, Pierre Gustave Toutant, Papers, Duke University.

Boyd, David F., Family Papers, Walter L. Fleming Collection, Louisiana State University, Baton Rouge.

Bragg, Braxton, Court-Martial, April 2, 1844, National Archives.

—— Court of Inquiry, January 15, 1845, *ibid.*

—— Papers, Duke University.

—— Papers, Henry E. Huntington Library, San Marino, California.

—— Papers, Rosenberg Library, Galveston, Texas.

—— Papers, Samuel Richey Confederate Collection, Miami University, Oxford, Ohio.

—— Papers, Southern Historical Collection, University of North Carolina.

—— Papers, United States Military Academy.

—— Papers, William K. Bixby Collection, Missouri Historical Society.

—— Papers, William P. Palmer Collection, Western Reserve Historical Society, Cleveland.

Bragg, Mrs. Braxton, Papers, University of Texas, Austin.

Bragg, Eliza Brooks, Papers, Chicago Historical Society.

Bragg, John, Papers, Southern Historical Collection, University of North Carolina.

Bragg, Thomas, Diary, *ibid.*

Buckner, Simon B., Papers, Henry E. Huntington Library.

Buie, John, Papers, Duke University.

Butler, Anna E., Papers, Butler Family Papers (G), Louisiana State University.

Butler, Edward George Washington, Papers, Duke University.

Butler, Thomas, and Family Papers, Butler Family Papers (C), (F), (H), Louisiana State University.

Butler, Thomas W., Papers, *ibid.*

Cheatham, Benjamin Franklin, Papers, Tennessee State Library, Nashville.

Clay, Clement C., Papers, Duke University.

Coleman, D., Diary, Southern Historical Collection, University of North Carolina.

Confederate Civil War Papers, Missouri Historical Society.

Confederate Records, War Department Collection, National Archives.

Confederate Scrapbook, Alabama Department of Archives, Montgomery.

Davis, Jefferson, Papers, Louisiana Historical Association Collection, Tulane University.

Doub, William Clark, Papers, Duke University.

Duncan, James, Papers, United States Military Academy.

Edmondston, Mrs. Katharine Ann Devereux, Diary, North Carolina State Department of Archives and History, Raleigh.

Eighth Census of the United States, 1860, Louisiana (microfilm copy), Louisiana State University.

Eldridge, James W., Papers, Henry E. Huntington Library.

Ellis, E. John, Thomas C. W., and Family, Papers, Louisiana State University.

Ellis, E. John, Thomas C. W., and Family, Papers (B), *ibid.*

Ewell, Benjamin S., Papers, Henry E. Huntington Library.

Fackler, C. William, Papers, Duke University.

Fifth Census of the United States, 1830, North Carolina, National Archives.

Fourth Census of the United States, 1820, North Carolina, *ibid.*
Fraser, William, Papers, United States Military Academy.
French, Samuel G., Papers, *ibid.*
Fox, Gustavus V., Papers, New York Historical Society.
Governors' Papers, Mississippi Department of Archives, Jackson.
Grant, Ulysses Simpson, Papers, Chicago Historical Society.
Gray, R. M., Papers, Southern Historical Collection, University of North Carolina.
Hammond, James H., Papers, Library of Congress, Washington, D.C.
Hardee, William Joseph, Papers, *ibid.*
Harris, David Bullock, Papers, Duke University.
Hemphill, William R., J. C., and R. R., Papers, *ibid.*
Heth-Seldon Papers, University of Virginia.
Jackson-McKinne Papers (microfilm copy), Southern Historical Collection, University of North Carolina.
Johnston, Albert Sidney and William Preston, Papers, Mrs. Mason Barret Collection, Tulane University.
Johnston, Joseph E., Papers, Duke University.
—— Papers, Henry E. Huntington Library.
Johnston, J. Stoddard, Diary, Filson Club, Louisville, Kentucky.
—— Military Papers, *ibid.*
Jones, Charles Colcock, Papers, Duke University.
Kirkpatrick Scrapbook, Alabama Department of Archives.
Lafourche Parish Conveyance Book No. 3, Lafourche Parish Court House, Thibodaux, Louisiana.
Letters Received and Sent, Adjutant General's Office, Old Army Section, War Records Branch, National Archives.
Library Book Circulation Records, 1826–1841, United States Military Academy.
Liddell, Moses, St. John R., and Family, Papers, Louisiana State University.
Lovell, Mansfield, Papers, Henry E. Huntington Library.
Mackall, William W., Papers, Southern Historical Collection, University of North Carolina.
Magee, John Euclid, Diary, Duke University.
Maury, Richard L., Papers, *ibid.*
McLaws, Lafayette, Papers, *ibid.*
Mexican War Records Group 94, Adjutant General's Office, Old Army Section, War Records Branch, National Archives.
Miscellaneous Personal Papers, Library of Congress.

Moore, Thomas Overton, Papers, Chicago Historical Society.
—— Papers, Louisiana State University.
Mordecai, Pattie, Papers, North Carolina State Department of Archives and History.
Outlaw, David, Papers, Southern Historical Collection, University of North Carolina.
Overton Scrapbook, Alabama Department of Archives.
Parker, Nathan, Diary (photostatic copy), University of Kentucky.
Pierce, Franklin, Papers, Library of Congress.
Polk, Leonidas, Papers, ibid.
—— Papers (microfilm copy), Southern Historical Collection, University of North Carolina.
Polk, William H., Papers, North Carolina Department of Archives and History.
Post Orders, 1833–1837, United States Military Academy.
Pugh, Richard L., Papers, Louisiana State University.
Randolph, George Wythe, Papers, Chicago Historical Society.
Randolph, William B., Papers, Library of Congress.
Roy, Thomas Benton, Papers, Chicago Historical Society.
Ruggles, Daniel, Papers, Duke University.
Seddon, James A., Papers, ibid.
Semmes, Thomas Jenkins, Papers, ibid.
Sherman, William T., Papers, Library of Congress.
Smith, Edmund Kirby, Papers, Duke University.
Solomons, M. J., Scrapbook, ibid.
Stevens, Isaac Ingalls, Papers, University of Washington, Seattle.
Stuart, George Hay, Papers, Library of Congress.
Taylor, Richard, Papers, Urquhart Collection, Tulane University.
Taylor, Zachary, Papers, Library of Congress.
Terry, William, and Family Papers, Louisiana State University.
Thomas, George H., Papers (microfilm copy), New York Public Library.
Walker, Leroy Pope, Papers, Chicago Historical Society.
Walker, William Henry Talbot, Papers, Duke University.
Walthall, William T., Papers, Mississippi Department of Archives.
Warren County Marriage Bonds, North Carolina State Department of Archives and History.
Weaver, William, Papers, Duke University.
Wheeler, Joseph, Papers, Chicago Historical Society.
Wigfall, Louis T., and Family Papers, University of Texas.

Newspapers

Corinth (Mississippi) *Missouri Army Argus*
Greensboro *Alabama Beacon*
Mobile *Daily Tribune*
Mobile *Advertiser and Register* [title varies]
Morning Courier & New York Inquirer
New Orleans *Crescent*
New Orleans *Daily Picayune*
New Orleans *Weekly Delta*
New York *Daily Plebeian*
New York Herald
New York *Spirit of the Times*
Philadelphia North American and U. S. Gazette
Richmond *Daily Dispatch*
Richmond *Daily Whig*
Richmond Enquirer
Richmond *Examiner*
Richmond *Sentinel*
Washington *National Intelligencer*
Wetumpka [Alabama] *Daily State Guard*

Printed Primary Sources

Adams, John Q. *Memoirs of John Quincy Adams . . . Portions of His Diary from 1795 to 1848.* Edited by Charles Francis Adams. 12 vols. Philadelphia, 1874–1877.
Anderson, Robert. *An Artillery Officer in the Mexican War, 1846–7: Letters of Robert Anderson, Captain, 3rd Artillery, U.S.A.* New York, 1911.
[Ballentine, George]. *Autobiography of an English Soldier in the United States Army, Comprising Observations and Adventures in the States and Mexico.* New York, 1854.
Barbour, Philip N. *Journals of . . . Brevet Major Philip Norbourne Barbour. . . .* Edited by Rhoda van Bibber Tanner Doubleday. New York, 1936.
Beers, Fannie A. *Memories. . . .* Philadelphia, 1889.
Blackmore, Bettie Ridley. "Behind the Lines in Middle Tennessee, 1863–1865: The Journal of Bettie Ridley Blackmore." Edited by Sarah Ridley Trimble. *Tennessee Historical Quarterly*, XII (1953), 48–80.

Booth, Andrew B., compiler. *Records of Louisiana Confederate Soldiers and Louisiana Confederate Commands.* 2 vols. New Orleans, 1920.

Bragg, Braxton. "Notes on Our Army," *Southern Literary Messenger*, X (1844), 86–88, 155–57, 246–51, 283–87, 372–77, 750–53.
——— "Notes on Our Army," *Southern Literary Messenger*, XI (1845), 39–47, 104–9.
——— "Our Army Again," *Southern Literary Messenger*, X (1844), 510–12.

Browning, Orville H. *The Diary of Orville Hickman Browning.* Edited by Theodore Calvin Pease and James G. Randall. 2 vols. Springfield, 1925.

Buck, Irving A. *Cleburne and His Command.* Edited by Thomas Robson Hay. Jackson, Tenn., 1959.

Butler, Pierce. *The Unhurried Years: Memoirs of the Old Natchez Region.* Baton Rouge, 1948.

Chesnut, Mary Boykin. *A Diary from Dixie.* Edited by Ben Ames Williams. Boston, 1961.

Confederate Veteran, IV (1896); VIII (1900); XIX (1911); XXI (1913); XXVI (1918); XL (1932).

Congressional Globe, 28 Cong., 1 sess. (1844).

Daly, Maria Lydig. *Diary of a Union Lady.* Edited by Harold E. Hammond. New York, 1962.

Davis, Jefferson. *Jefferson Davis, Constitutionalist: His Letters, Papers and Speeches.* Edited by Dunbar Rowland. 10 vols. Jackson, Miss., 1923.

Delafield, Richard. *Report on the Art of War in Europe in 1854, 1855, and 1856.* (*Senate Executive Document*, 36 Cong., 1 sess., No. 59.) Washington, 1860.

Dickins, Asbury, and John W. Forney, eds. *American State Papers.* 38 vols. Washington, 1832–1861.

du Pont, Henry A. "West Point in the Fifties: The Letters of Henry A. du Pont." Edited by Stephen E. Ambrose. *Civil War History*, X (1964), 291–308.

Eighth Annual Reunion of the Association of the Graduates of the United States Military Academy . . . 1877. New York, 1877.

Frederick the Great. *Frederick the Great on the Art of War.* Edited by Jay Luvaas. New York, 1966.

Fremantle, Arthur J. L. *The Fremantle Diary. . . .* Edited by Walter Lord. Boston, 1954.

French, Samuel G. *Two Wars: An Autobiography.* Nashville, 1901.

The General Taylor Almanac, for the Year of our Lord 1848. . . . Philadelphia, 1848.

[Giddings, Luther]. *Sketches of the Campaign in Northern Mexico in Eighteen Hundred Forty-Six and Seven.* New York, 1853.

Gordon, John B. *Reminiscences of the Civil War.* New York, 1904.

Grant, Ulysses S. *Personal Memoirs of U. S. Grant.* 2 vols. New York, 1885.

Greene, Evarts B., ed. "Letters to Gustav Koerner, 1837–1863," *Transactions of the Illinois State Historical Society, 1907,* 222–46. Springfield, 1908.

Gregg, Josiah. *Diary & Letters of Josiah Gregg: Excursions in Mexico & California, 1847–1850.* Edited by Maurice G. Fulton. Norman, 1944.

[Hammond, Marcellus C. M.]. "Battle of Buena Vista," *Southern Quarterly Review,* new series, III (1851), 175–79.

Henry, William S. *Campaign Sketches of the War with Mexico.* New York, 1847.

Heth, Henry. "The Memoirs of Henry Heth." Edited by James L. Morrison, Jr. *Civil War History,* VIII (1962), 5–24.

Hitchcock, Ethan Allen. *Fifty Years in Camp and Field: Diary of . . . Ethan Allen Hitchcock.* . . . Edited by W. A. Croffut. New York, 1909.

Hone, Philip. *The Diary of Philip Hone, 1828–1851.* Edited by Allan Nevins. 2 vols. New York, 1927.

House Document, 29 Cong., 2 sess., No. 4.

House Executive Document, 28 Cong., 1 sess., No. 211; 30 Cong., 1 sess., No. 60; 35 Cong., 2 sess., No. 93.

Johnson, Robert U., and Clarence C. Buel, eds. *Battles and Leaders of the Civil War.* 4 vols. New York, 1956.

Johnston, Joseph E. *Narrative of Military Operations.* Bloomington, 1959.

Jomini, Antoine Henri. *Summary of the Art of War.* Translated by G. H. Mendell and W. P. Craighill. Philadelphia, 1879.

Jones, John B. *A Rebel War Clerk's Diary at the Confederate States Capital.* 2 vols. Philadelphia, 1866.

Jordan, Thomas. "Recollections of General Beauregard's Service in West Tennessee in the Spring of 1862," *Southern Historical Society Papers,* VIII (1880), 404–17.

Kean, Robert G. H. *Inside the Confederate Government: The Diary of Robert Garlick Hill Kean.* Edited by Edward Younger. New York, 1957.

Kenly, John R. *Memoirs of a Maryland Volunteer.* . . . Philadelphia, 1873.

Keyes, Erasmus D. *Fifty Years' Observation of Men and Events Civil and Military.* New York, 1884.

Lincoln, Abraham. *The Collected Works of Abraham Lincoln.* Edited by Roy P. Basler. 8 vols. New Brunswick, 1953.

Logan, John A. *The Volunteer Soldier of America.* Chicago, 1887.

Mahan, Dennis H. *An Elementary Treatise on Advanced-Guard.* . . . New Orleans, 1861.

—— *An Elementary Treatise on Advanced-Guard.* . . . New York, 1864.

Mangum, Willie P. *The Papers of Willie Person Mangum.* Edited by Henry Thomas Shanks. 5 vols. Raleigh, 1950–1956.

Maury, Dabney Herndon. *Recollections of a Virginian in the Mexican, Indian, and Civil Wars.* New York, 1894.

McCall, George A. *Letters From the Frontiers.* . . . Philadelphia, 1868.

McPherson, Elizabeth Gregory, ed. "Unpublished Letters from North Carolinians to Van Buren," *North Carolina Historical Review,* XV (1938), 53–81.

Meade, George. *The Life and Letters of George Gordon Meade.* 2 vols. New York, 1913.

Mentor. "To the Commanding General of the Army," *Military and Naval Magazine of the United States,* IV (1834), 179–85.

Minor, Benjamin B. "Editor's Table," *Southern Literary Messenger,* X (1844), 387–88.

Napoleon. *Commentaires de Napoleon Premier.* 6 vols. Paris, 1867.

—— *The Mind of Napoleon: A Selection from His Written and Spoken Words.* Edited by J. Christopher Herold. New York, 1955.

"Notes on the Army of the United States," *Military and Naval Magazine of the United States,* I (1833), 104–8.

Niles' National Register, sixth series, XXIII (1847), 88–89.

Official Records of the Union and Confederate Navies in the War of the Rebellion. 30 vols. Washington, 1894–1927.

Official Register of the Officers and Cadets of the U. S. Military Academy. . . . *1834–37.* New York, 1834–37.

Patrick, Robert. *Reluctant Rebel: The Secret Diary of Robert Patrick, 1861–1865.* Edited by F. Jay Taylor. Baton Rouge, 1959.

Pender, William Dorsey. *The General to His Lady: The Civil*

War Letters of William Dorsey Pender to Fanny Pender. Edited by William W. Hassler. Chapel Hill, 1965.

Polk, James K. *The Diary of James K. Polk.* Edited by Milo M. Quaife. 4 vols. Chicago, 1910.

"Recollections of Cadet Life," *Army and Navy Journal,* XXXIX (June 14, 1902), 1027–28.

Register of the Officers and Cadets of the U. S. Military Academy, 1833. New York, 1833.

Reid, Samuel C., Jr. *The Scouting Expeditions of McCollouch's Texas Rangers. . . .* Philadelphia, 1848.

Richardson, James D., ed. *A Compilation of the Messages and Papers of the Presidents, 1789–1910.* 11 vols. New York, 1911.

Russell, William Howard. *My Diary North and South.* Boston, 1863.

Sandburg, Carl, ed. *Lincoln Collector.* New York, 1949.

Savage, John H. *The Life of John H. Savage, Citizen, Soldier, Lawyer, Congressman.* Nashville, 1903.

Scott, Winfield. *Infantry Tactics.* New York, 1861.

Senate Executive Document, 30 Cong., 1 sess., No. 1.

Sherman, William T. *General Sherman as a College President. . . .* Edited by Walter L. Fleming. Cleveland, 1912.

—— *Memoirs of General William T. Sherman.* 2 vols. in one. Bloomington, 1957.

—— "Old Shady, With a Moral," *North American Review,* CXLVII (1888), 361–68.

Society of the Army of the Cumberland, Fifth Re-Union, Detroit, 1871. Cincinnati, 1872.

Stout, L. H. *Reminiscences of General Braxton Bragg.* Hattiesburg, Mississippi, 1942.

Sykes, E. T. "Walthall's Brigade . . . ," *Mississippi Historical Society, Publications,* centenary series, I (1916), 477–623.

[Talcott, George]. "Reply to 'A Subaltern,'" *Southern Literary Messenger,* X (1844), 509–10.

Taylor, Richard. *Destruction and Reconstruction: Personal Experiences of the Late War.* New York, 1900.

Thorp, Margaret Newbold. "A 'Yankee Teacher' in North Carolina." Edited by Richard L. Morton. *North Carolina Historical Review,* XXX (1953), 564–82.

War of the Rebellion: A Compilation of the Official Records of the Union and Confederate Armies. 128 vols. Washington, 1880–1901.

Watkins, Sam R. "*Co. Aytch,*" *Maury Grays First Tennessee Regiment, or a Side Show of the Big Show.* Jackson, Tennessee, 1952.
Watson, William. *Life in the Confederate Army.* . . . London, 1887.
Wilcox, Cadmus Marcellus. *History of the Mexican War.* Edited by Mary Rachel Wilcox. Washington, 1892.

Secondary Sources

Ambrose, Stephen A. *Duty, Honor, Country: A History of West Point.* Baltimore, 1966.
Bancroft, Hubert Howe. *History of Mexico.* 6 vols. San Francisco, 1883–1888.
Barbee, David R. "The Line of Blood—Lincoln and the Coming of the War," *Tennessee Historical Quarterly,* XVI (1957), 3–54.
Bearss, Edwin C. "Civil War Operations in and Around Pensacola," *Florida Historical Quarterly,* XXXVI (1957), 125–65.
Birkhimer, William E. *Historical Sketch of the Organization, Administration, Material and Tactics of the Artillery, United States Army.* Washington, 1884.
Bishop, Charles W. F. "Civil War Field Artillery in the West, 1862–1863," M. A. Thesis, University of British Columbia, 1967.
Black, Robert C. III. *The Railroads of the Confederacy.* Chapel Hill, 1952.
Brackett, Albert. *History of the United States Cavalry . . . to June, 1863.* New York, 1865.
Bridges, Hal. *Lee's Maverick General: Daniel Harvey Hill.* New York, 1961.
Bryan, Thomas Conn, ed. "General William J. Hardee and Confederate Publication Rights," *Journal of Southern History,* XII (1946), 264–66.
Carleton, James Henry. *The Battle of Buena Vista.* New York, 1848.
Catton, Bruce. *The Centennial History of the Civil War (The Coming Fury, Terrible Swift Sword,* and *Never Call Retreat).* 3 vols. New York, 1961–1965.
—— *Grant Moves South.* Boston, 1960.
—— *U. S. Grant and the American Military Tradition.* Boston, 1954.
The Centennial of the United States Military Academy at West Point . . . 1802–1902. 2 vols. Washington, 1904.

Cleves, Freeman. *Rock of Chickamauga: The Life of General George H. Thomas.* Norman, 1948.

Connelly, Thomas Lawrence. *Army of the Heartland: The Army of Tennessee, 1861–1862.* Baton Rouge, 1967.

Coulter, E. Merton. *The Civil War and Readjustment in Kentucky.* Chapel Hill, 1926.

Cullum, George W. *Biographical Register of the Officers and Graduates of the U. S. Military Academy.* . . . 2 vols. New York, 1868.

Current, Richard W. "The Confederates and the First Shot," *Civil War History,* VII (1961), 357–69.

—— *Lincoln and the First Shot.* Philadelphia, 1963.

Donald, David. *Lincoln Reconsidered: Essays on the Civil War Era.* New York, 1956.

——, ed. *Divided We Fought: A Pictorial History of the War, 1861–1865.* New York, 1952.

——, ed. *Why the North Won the Civil War.* Baton Rouge, 1960.

Dowdey, Clifford. *The Land They Fought For: The Story of the South as the Confederacy, 1832–65.* New York, 1955.

Dyer, Brainerd. *Zachary Taylor.* Baton Rouge, 1946.

Dyer, John P. *"Fightin' Joe" Wheeler.* Baton Rouge, 1941.

Earle, Edward Meade, ed. *Makers of Modern Strategy: Military Thought from Machiavelli to Hitler.* Princeton, 1944.

Falk, Stanley L. "The Warrenton Female Academy of Jacob Mordecai, 1809–1818," *North Carolina Historical Review,* XXXV (1958), 281–98.

Forman, Sidney. *West Point: A History of the United States Military Academy.* New York, 1950.

Freeman, Douglas Southall. *R. E. Lee: A Biography.* 4 vols. New York, 1934.

Gardner, Charles Kitchell. *A Dictionary of All Officers . . . in the Army of the United States.* . . . New York, 1860.

Govan, Gilbert E., and James W. Livingood. *A Different Valor: The Story of General Joseph E. Johnston, C.S.A.* Indianapolis, 1956.

Gow, June I. "The Johnston and Brent Diaries: A Problem of Authorship," *Civil War History,* XIV (1968), 46–50.

Hagerman, Edward. "From Jomini to Dennis Hart Mahan: The Evolution of Trench Warfare and the American Civil War," *Civil War History,* XIII (1967), 197–220.

Hamilton, Holman. *Zachary Taylor, Soldier of the Republic.* Indianapolis, 1941.

Hartje, Robert G. *Van Dorn: The Life and Times of a Confederate General.* Nashville, 1967.

Hay, Thomas Robson. "Braxton Bragg and the Southern Confederacy," *Georgia Historical Quarterly,* IX (1925), 267–316.

Henry, Robert S. *The Story of the Mexican War.* Indianapolis, 1950.

Hill, Louise Biles. *Joseph E. Brown and the Confederacy.* Chapel Hill, 1939.

Holland, Cecil Fletcher. *Morgan and His Raiders.* New York, 1943.

Hoogenboom, Ari. "Gustavus Fox and the Relief of Fort Sumter," *Civil War History,* IX (1963), 383–98.

Horn, Stanley F. *The Army of Tennessee.* Norman, Okla., 1953.

Howard, Michael, ed. *The Theory and Practice of War: Essays Presented to Captain B. H. Liddell Hart.* London, 1965.

Hughes, Nathaniel Cheairs, Jr. *General William J. Hardee, Old Reliable.* Baton Rouge, 1965.

Johnson, Guion Griffis. *Ante-Bellum North Carolina: A Social History.* Chapel Hill, 1937.

Johnson, Ludwell H. "Fort Sumter and Confederate Diplomacy," *Journal of Southern History,* XXVI (1960), 441–77.

Johnston, William Preston. *The Life of Albert Sidney Johnston.* New York, 1878.

Jones, Archer. *Confederate Strategy from Shiloh to Vicksburg.* Baton Rouge, 1961.

—— "Jomini and Napoleon as Civil War Mentors." Paper read at the Thirty-first Annual Meeting of the Southern Historical Association, November 18, 1965.

Jones, Charles T., Jr. "Five Sons of Bolling Hall in the Civil War," *Alabama Historical Quarterly,* XXIV (1962), 133–221.

Lamers, William M. *The Edge of Glory: A Biography of General William S. Rosecrans, U.S.A.* New York, 1961.

Lewis, Lloyd. *Captain Sam Grant.* Boston, 1950.

—— *Sherman: Fighting Prophet.* New York, 1932.

Livermore, Thomas L. *Numbers and Losses in the Civil War.* Bloomington, 1957.

Louisiana Historical Records Survey. *Inventory of the Parish Archives of Louisiana, No. 29, Lafourche Parish (Thibodaux).* Baton Rouge, 1942.

McWhiney, Grady. "Braxton Bragg at Shiloh," *Tennessee Historical Quarterly*, XII (1962), 19–30.

—— "The Confederacy's First Shot," *Civil War History*, XIV (1968), 5–14.

—— "Controversy in Kentucky: Braxton Bragg's Campaign of 1862," *Civil War History*, VI (1960), 5–42.

—— "Who Whipped Whom? Confederate Defeat Reexamined." *Civil War History*, XI (1965), 5–26.

——, ed. *Grant, Lee, Lincoln and the Radicals: Essays on Civil War Leadership*. Evanston, 1964.

Montgomery, Lizzie Wilson. *Sketches of Old Warrenton, North Carolina*. Raleigh, 1924.

Nevins, Allan. *Ordeal of the Union*. 2 vols. New York, 1947.

—— *The War for the Union*. 2 vols. to date. New York, 1959——.

Nichols, Edward J. *Toward Gettysburg: A Biography of General John F. Reynolds*. University Park, 1958.

—— *Zach Taylor's Little Army*. New York, 1963.

Nichols, Roy F. *Franklin Pierce: Young Hickory of the Granite Hills*. Philadelphia, 1931.

Owen, Thomas M. *History of Alabama and Dictionary of Alabama Biography*. 4 vols. Chicago, 1921.

Parks, Joseph H. *General Edmund Kirby Smith, C.S.A.* Baton Rouge, 1954.

—— *General Leonidas Polk, C.S.A.: The Fighting Bishop*. Baton Rouge, 1962.

Peele, W. J., ed. *Lives of Distinguished North Carolinians*. Raleigh, 1898.

Polk, William M. *Leonidas Polk: Bishop and General*. 2 vols. New York, 1915.

Potter, David M. *Lincoln and His Party in the Secession Crisis*. New Haven, 1942.

Powell, William H. *List of Officers of the Army of the United States from 1779 to 1900*. New York, 1900.

Quimby, Robert S. *The Background of Napoleonic Warfare*. New York, 1957.

Ramsdell, Charles W. "Lincoln and Fort Sumter," *Journal of Southern History*, III (1937), 259–88.

Randall, James G. *Lincoln the President: Springfield to Gettysburg*. 2 vols. New York, 1945.

—— "When War Came in 1861," *Abraham Lincoln Quarterly*, I (1940), 3–42.

Robinson, Fayette. *An Account of the Organization of the Army of the United States.* 2 vols. Philadelphia, 1848.

Roland, Charles P. *Albert Sidney Johnston: Soldier of Three Republics.* Austin, 1964.

—— "Albert Sidney Johnston and the Loss of Forts Henry and Donelson," *Journal of Southern History,* XXIII (1957), 45–69.

—— "Albert Sidney Johnston and the Shiloh Campaign," *Civil War History,* IV (1958), 355–82.

—— *Louisiana Sugar Plantations during the American Civil War.* Leiden, 1957.

Roman, Alfred. *The Military Operations of General Beauregard in the War Between the States, 1861–1865.* 2 vols. New York, 1884.

Seitz, Don Carlos. *Braxton Bragg, General of the Confederacy.* Columbia, 1924.

Silver, James W. *Edmund Pendleton Gaines: Frontier General.* Baton Rouge, 1949.

Singletary, Otis. *The Mexican War.* Chicago, 1960.

Sitterson, J. Carlyle. *Sugar Country: The Cane Sugar Industry in the South, 1753–1950.* Lexington, 1953.

Smith, Justin H. *The War With Mexico.* 2 vols. New York, 1919.

Sprague, John T. *The Origins, Progress, and Conclusion of the Florida War.* New York, 1848.

Stampp, Kenneth M. *And the War Came: The North and the Secession Crisis, 1860–1861.* Baton Rouge, 1950.

—— "Lincoln and the Strategy of Defense in the Crisis of 1861," *Journal of Southern History,* XI (1945), 297–323.

Stevens, Hazard. *The Life of Isaac Ingalls Stevens.* 2 vols. Boston, 1900.

Stevenson, Alexander F. *The Battle of Stone's River.* Boston, 1884.

Stewart, George R. *John Phoenix, Esq., . . . A Life of Captain George H. Derby, U.S.A.* New York, 1937.

Stickles, Arndt M. *Simon Bolivar Buckner, Borderland Knight.* Chapel Hill, 1940.

Strode, Hudson, *Jefferson Davis.* 3 vols. New York, 1955–1964.

Swanberg, W. A. *First Blood: The Story of Fort Sumter.* New York, 1957.

Thorpe, T. B. *Our Army at Monterey.* Philadelphia, 1847.

Tilley, John S. *Lincoln Takes Command.* Chapel Hill, 1941.

Vandiver, Frank E. *Rebel Brass: The Confederate Command System.* Baton Rouge, 1956.

7

Warner, Ezra J. *Generals in Gray: Lives of Confederate Commanders.* Baton Rouge, 1959.

Weigley, Russel F. *Towards an American Army: Military Thought from Washington to Marshall.* New York, 1962.

Wellman, Manly Wade. *The County of Warren, North Carolina, 1586–1917.* Chapel Hill, 1959.

White, Leonard D. *The Jacksonians: A Study in Administrative History, 1829–1861.* New York, 1954.

Whittington, G. P. "Thomas O. Moore: Governor of Louisiana, 1860–1864," *Louisiana Historical Quarterly,* XIII (1930), 5–36.

Wiley, Bell Irvin. *The Life of Johnny Reb.* Indianapolis, 1943.

—— *The Road to Appomattox.* Memphis, 1956.

Williams, Kenneth P. *Lincoln Finds a General: A Military Study of the Civil War.* 5 vols. New York, 1949–1959.

Williams, T. Harry. *Americans at War: The Development of the American Military System.* New York, 1962.

—— *P. G. T. Beauregard: Napoleon in Gray.* Baton Rouge, 1955.

Wooster, Ralph A. "Confederate Success at Perryville," *Register of the Kentucky Historical Society,* LIX (1961), 318–23.

Adams, Daniel W., 360, 361
Adams, Henry A., 166; quoted, 160
Adams, John Quincy: quoted, 41
Alexandria, Louisiana: state military school at, 147
Allen, Henry W.: quoted, 235, 238
Allen, Robert, 98
Anderson, J. Patton, 193, 221, 277, 302, 370; quoted, 306
Anderson, Richard H., 192, 193, 194
Army of Tennessee: commanded by Bragg, 344, 380; Johnston ordered to assume command, 387
Army organization: reforms proposed by Bragg, 36 ff., 106 ff., 132; brevet ranks, 54; Bragg appointed chief of staff, 213 ff., 224; lack of overall supervision and coordination in Confederate armies, 213, 281; Bragg's changes in, as prototypes for Union and Confederate armies, 274-75, 277
Artillery, horse-drawn, 54, 63

Barbour, Philip, 63
Bardstown, Kentucky: Bragg's arrival at, 293, 294; response to presence of Confederates, 295-96
Barringer, Daniel M., 105
Baton Rouge arsenal: surrenders to Bragg, 151
Bayonet attacks, 231, 232, 251, 252
Bayou Lafourche, 141
Beard, William K.: quoted, 310
Beatty, John C., 113
Beatty, Taylor, 222, 271; quoted, 234, 355-56
Beauregard, P. G. T., 16, 22, 178, 199; resentment toward Bragg, 153; attacks Fort Sumter, 171; commands southern defense line, 204; ill health and fears, 205; army reorganized by, 216 ff.; responsibility for faults in Pittsburg Landing marching plans, 221; hesitancy before battle of Shiloh, 226-27; battle plans for Shiloh, 229 ff.; withdrawal order at Shiloh, 243 ff.; attacks Halleck's army, 256; Davis's dislike of, 388; quoted, 391
Bells, plantation, 205
Benjamin, Judah P., 158
Benton, Thomas Hart, 47, 105
Berard, Claudius, 11
Bethel Station, Tennessee, 208, 210

410   INDEX

Bivouac (Bragg's estate), 141
Black, James A., 39
Bliss, W. W. S., 91
Blockade, Union, 178, 189
Boggs, William R., 182
"Bonnie Blue Flag, The" (Macarthy), 183
Bourdett, Sarah ("the Great Western"), 58
Bowling Green, Kentucky: Buell's army at, 285; impossibility of Confederate siege of, 289 ff.
Bragg, Alexander, 4
Bragg, Braxton, *early life:* birth, 1; student days, 4; at West Point, 10 ff., 23, 24; appointed second lieutenant, 26; susceptibility to disease, 27, 28, 93-94, 178 ff.; eccentricities and abilities, 28; problems of rank, 28; disputes with Jones, 30 ff.; dilemma of commander vs. quartermaster, 33; reputation as sectionalist, 34, 35; army reforms proposed by, 36 ff.; arrest and court-martial, 41 ff.; quarrel with Gates, 48; demands court of inquiry, 49
Mexican War: joins Taylor's army in New Orleans, 52; drilling of artillerymen, 56; made brevet captain, 61; march to Monterey, 64; failure to learn lesson of Monterey, 72; commands Company C artillery, 74-75; supports Taylor against Scott, 77; at Saltillo and Buena Vista, 79 ff.; credits Taylor with victory, 86; contempt for volun-teers, 87 ff.; failure to learn lesson of Buena Vista, 89; "grape" incident, 90 ff.; attempts to discredit Scott, 95; attempted assassination, 97-98; devotion to welfare of soldiers, 98; made brevet lieutenant colonel, 99
interwar years: returns to U.S. as hero, 101 ff.; concern over sectionalism, 105 ff.; urges army reform, 106 ff., 132 ff.; as member of Gaines's staff, 107; meets Elise Ellis, 111; proposes, 114; marriage, 118; assigned to Jefferson Barracks, 121; assigned to Fort Gibson, 136; assigned to Fort Washita, 137; resigns commission, 139; purchases sugar plantation, 141; views on slavery, 142 ff.; interest in public affairs, 144 ff.; supports state military college, 147; disturbed by secession movement, 149
secession and Civil War: appointed to state military board, 150; accepts surrender of Baton Rouge arsenal, 151; appointed major general in Louisiana army, 152; appointed general in Confederate Army, 154; prohibits sale of liquor to soldiers, 161; problems at Fort Pickens, 162 ff.; reply to Davis on taking of Fort Pickens, 169; ordered to send troops to Virginia, 176; disciplinary methods at Fort Pickens, 178 ff.; tributes from

soldiers and civilians, 185-86; promoted to major general with command of Alabama and western Florida, 190; inspection tour of Mobile and Montgomery, 195; advises Davis on military strategy, 199; arrival at Jackson, Tennessee, 204 ff.; made chief of staff and corps commander, 213 ff., 224; commander of Second Corps after Beauregard's army reorganization, 216
battle of Shiloh: hesitancy before battle, 226-27; criticism of battle plans, 229 ff.; denies request for artillery support, 239; tactical mistakes, 240 ff.; analyzes causes of failure, 250-51; unawareness of his own errors, 251
into Tennessee and Kentucky: appointed general, 253; praise and criticism, 253 ff.; popularity declines, 258 ff., 264; replaces Beauregard as army commander, 260; plans for invasion, 267 ff.; relations with E. K. Smith, 272 ff.; reorganizes army, 274-75, 277; orders court-martial of generals, 278; becomes his own chief of staff, 279; orders army northward, 281; abandons Munfordville, 288; achievements at time of leaving Munfordville, 292; unable to prevent Buell's arrival in Louisville, 294; encourages enlistment of Kentuckians, 296 ff.; problems of establishing defense line in

Kentucky, 299; censured for evacuation of Frankfort, 308
battle of Perryville: arrival at Perryville, 312 ff.; significance of battle, 319 ff.; decides to abandon Kentucky, 321; widespread bitterness toward, 323 ff.; arrival in Richmond, 325; retains support of many officers, 330-31; ability for high field command questioned, 333 ff.
battle of Murfreesboro: plans for movement into Middle Tennessee, 337 ff.; use of cavalry, 341n; reorganizes army, 343; tactical errors, 348 ff., 363 ff.; orders and counterorders, 358 ff., 371; continued belief in bayonet assaults, 367; denounced for failure, 374 ff.; requests opinions of corps and division commanders, 376; expressions of confidence in, 379 ff.; inability to view situation realistically, 384; retains command, 388; indications of mental and physical breakdown, 388; reasons for failure as field commander, 389 ff.
Bragg, Dunbar, 4
Bragg, Elise (Mrs. Braxton Bragg), 108 ff.; visits Pensacola, 187; criticism of Johnston and Beauregard, 207; influence on military decisions of husband, 217; urges army to advance, 267-68; criticizes Bragg's failure in Kentucky, 324-25; illness, 387

Bragg, John, 4, 5, 13, 47, 130, 134, 136
Bragg, Margaret Crosland, 2
Bragg, Thomas, 2, 5
Bragg, Thomas, Jr., 4, 152; quoted, 192, 200
Bragg, William, 4
Bragg family, 1 ff.
Bratt, John, 16
Breckinridge, John C., 217, 221, 241, 295, 349; at battle of Murfreesboro, 358, 359, 360, 361, 364 ff., 368 ff.; lack of confidence in Bragg, 378
Brent, George William, 280, 342; quoted, 298, 314, 322, 323, 367, 375
Brooks, Phillips, 109
Brown, Harvey, 171, 174
Brown, Jacob, 60
Brown, John Calvin, 318
Brown, Joseph E., 162
Browning, Orville H., 159
Bruce, E. M.: quoted, 207-8n
Bryantsville, Kentucky, 321 ff.
Buchanan, James, 157, 158
Buckner, Simon B., 277, 297, 313, 342
Buell, Don Carlos, 204; arrival at Shiloh, 246, 251; movement of army toward Chattanooga, 266; arrives at Louisville, 289; strategy of, misunderstood by Bragg, 300 ff., 305; four-column march from Louisville, 303 ff.
Buena Vista, Mexico: battle of, 79 ff., 89
Buford, Abraham, 280n
Buie, John: quoted, 265, 284-85
Burke, Martin, 34

Burnett, Henry C., 326, 332
Butler, Thomas, 188; quoted, 181
Butler, William O., 69, 96

Camp Rensselaer, 7 ff.
Carroll, William H., 217, 262, 278
Carthage, Tennessee, 283
Cass, Lewis, 106
Catton, Bruce: quoted, 363
Cave City, Kentucky, 285
Chalmers, James R., 182, 193, 221, 241-42, 285; at battle of Murfreesboro, 356-57, 360; confidence in Bragg, 381
Chamberlain, S. E., 91
Charleston, South Carolina, 105
Chattanooga, Tennessee: Buell's army moves toward, 266; Bragg plans Tennessee invasion from, 267 ff.; marital law ordered by Bragg, 277; Bragg's staff changes at, 279
Cheatham, Benjamin F., 241, 262, 276-77, 281, 314 ff., 353; quoted, 71
Chesnut, Mary Boykin, 259
Chickamauga, battle of: casualties, 370
Church, Samuel R., 98
Churchill, William H., 48
Citizen soldiers: American tradition of, 20
Clare, William, 358
Clark, Charles, 237
Clark, John B., 326, 332
Clay, Clement C., 326, 376
Clay, Henry, 107
Cleburne, Patrick R., 277, 293, 343; at battle of Murfrees-

boro, 349, 353; lack of confidence in Bragg, 378

Clinton, James G., 39

Communications, combat, 233, 236, 282

Concentration of forces: Bragg's strategy of, 295, 300

Confederate armies: administrative deficiencies, 215 ff.; election of officers, 262, 264; office of chief of staff, 279n; multi-army offensive, 281; casualties at battle of Murfreesboro, 354 ff.; need for efficient inspector general, 391

Confederate War Department, 162, 165

Conrad, Charles M., 129-30

Conscription Act, 254, 262, 297

Cooper, Samuel, 139

Corinth, Mississippi: disorder and confusion in, 211 ff.; Confederate retreat from, 257

Corpus Christi, Texas, 53, 54, 58

Cox, Jacob D.: quoted, 232

Crittenden, George B., 217, 262, 278

Crittenden, John J., 217

Crittenden, Thomas L., 303, 305, 346

Crosland, J. H., 2

Crosland, Margaret, see Bragg, Margaret Crosland

Cumberland Gap, 272, 273, 274, 283, 293, 322, 335

Curry, Jabez L. M., 263; quoted, 253-54

Daily Dispatch (newspaper): cited, 325

Danville, Kentucky, 298

Davies, Charles, 11

Davis, Jefferson, 83, 85, 135, 154, 158; letters to Bragg, 167-68, 282; defensive-offensive strategy, 200 ff.; confidence in Johnston, 207 ff.; appointment of officers for political reasons, 278; favorable attitude toward Bragg, 326 ff.; failure to give Bragg unified command, 334; denies promotion to officers recommended by Bragg, 344; orders part of Army of Tennessee to Mississippi, 345; partial responsibility for defeat at Murfreesboro, 363; orders investigation of Bragg's relationship to officers, 379; orders Johnston to assume command of Army of Tennessee, 387; dislike of Beauregard, 388; failure to assign men to proper positions, 391-92; quoted, 200, 377

Defensive tactics, 348

DeRussy, R. E., 6

Doctor's Creek, Perryville, 313 ff.

Donelson, Daniel S., 316, 317, 343, 344, 357, 360

Dubroca, E. M., 238

Duck River: Confederate line established along, 374

Duels: at West Point, 10

Dumont, Ebenezer, 304, 305

Duncan, James, 35, 38, 53, 61, 107, 117, 120

Duncan, Johnson K., 342

du Pont, Henry A.: quoted, 232-33

Dyer, Alexander B., 15, 23, 26

Early, Jubal A., 9, 12, 16, 26
Eighteenth U.S. Infantry regiment, 354
Eighth Mississippi regiment, 360
Eighth Tennessee regiment, 357
Elementary Treatise on Advanced Guard, . . . An (Mahan), 16-17
Ellis, E. John: quoted, 322-23
Ellis, Eliza Brooks (Elise), *see* Bragg, Elise (Mrs. Braxton Bragg)
Ellis, Mary Jane Towson, 108
Ellis, Mary Seraphine (Puss), 123
Ellis, Richard Gaillard, 108
Ellis, Towson, 183, 184; quoted, 145
Evergreen Plantation, 108
Ewell, Benjamin S., 383
Ewing, Thomas: quoted, 93

Fabian policy, 204, 267
Fifteenth Indiana regiment, 354
First Louisiana regiment, 355-56
Florida: Seminole war in, 26 ff.
"Flying artillery," 54, 62
Foote, Henry S.: quoted, 324
Forrest, Nathan Bedford, 247, 280n, 340
Forsyth, John, 332; quoted, 284, 383
Fort Barrancas, Pensacola, Florida, 157
Fort Bragg, California, 101
Fort Bragg, North Carolina, 101
Fort Brown, *see* Fort Texas
Fort Donelson: captured by Grant, 198, 277
Fort Gibson, 136

Fort Henry: captured by Grant, 198
Fort McRee, Pensacola, Florida, 157, 196
Fort Morgan, Mobile Bay, 195
Fort Pickens, Pensacola, Florida, 155, 157; plans for defense and attack of, 165 ff., 174 ff.; secondary importance of, 177; Confederate hospital at, 183-84; clash between Federals and Confederates, 192 ff.; Federal attack, 196
Fort Pillow, 212
Fort Sumter, Charleston, South Carolina, 155; Confederate attack on, 170-71
Fort Teneria, Mexico, 69
Fort Texas, 59, 60, 61
Fort Washita, 137
Forty-fourth Mississippi regiment, 357
Fourth Kentucky regiment, 370
Frankfort, Kentucky: Confederates retire to, 300; Bragg arrives at, 301; Federal advance on, 305; Confederate abandonment of, 307
Fraser, J. H.: quoted, 185-86
Fremantle, A. J. L., 275; quoted, 389

Gaines, Edmund Pendleton, 36, 44, 107
Gardner, Franklin, 342
Garner, George G., 182
Gates, William, 26, 34, 48
Gibson, Randall L., 221, 237 ff., 240
Giddings, Luther: quoted, 64
Gilbert, Charles C., 303, 305

Gladden, Adley H., 212, 221, 241
Glasgow, Kentucky, 283
Goode, F. S., 145
Graham, G. Mason, 148
Grand Junction ammunition depot, 206
Grant, Ulysses S., 204; Forts Henry and Donelson captured by, 198; at Pittsburg Landing, 219; at Shiloh, 228; retreat from Mississippi, 341; quoted, 23, 33
"Great Western, the," see Bourdett, Sarah
Green, Charles Plummer, 14
Gunnison, John, 16

Hall, John, 6
Halleck, Henry W., 16n, 21, 255
Hammett, William H., 39
Hammond, Marcellus C. M., 15, 91
Hardee, William J., 16n, 21, 216, 219, 233, 262, 263, 276; requests reinforcements from Bragg, 309-10; offers advice to Bragg, 311; criticism of Bragg's campaign, 320n; at battle of Murfreesboro, 347, 349, 353, 358, 361; lack of confidence in Bragg, 378; quoted 215, 251, 365
Harris, Isham G., 283, 379
Harrodsburg, Kentucky, 307 ff., 320
Hawes, James M., 262, 278
Hawes, Richard, 297, 298, 307, 332
Hawkins, M. T., 6
Henry, G. A.: quoted, 324

Henry, William S.: quoted, 56, 63
Hill, D. H., 35, 53
Hindman, Thomas, 237
Hitchcock, Ethan Allen: quoted, 56, 91
Hodge, B. L., 239
Holmes, Theophilus H., 155-56, 339
Hone, Philip: quoted, 104
Hooker, Joseph, 9, 16; quoted, 10 24
Horn, Stanley F.: quoted, 288-89, 290, 291
Hornets' Nest, 236, 237, 240, 241, 242
Hospitals, Confederate, 183-84
Houston, George S., 74
Huger, John M.: quoted, 382
Hunt, Henry J., 344n; quoted, 171-72
Hurlbut, Stephen A., 210, 236

Immigrants: as army recruits, 30
Infantry firearms, 231 ff.
Infantry tactics, 62

Jackson, John K., 182, 193, 221, 274, 329, 347, 349; at battle of Murfreesboro, 360, 361; confidence in Bragg, 380-81; quoted, 331
Jackson, Tennessee, 204 ff.
Jaquess, J. A., 356
Jefferson Barracks, Missouri, 121, 122, 128
Jesup, Thomas S., 44
Johnson, Bushrod R.: quoted, 352
Johnson, George W., 297n
Johnson, Wilbur F.: quoted, 381

Johnston, Albert Sidney, 199, 204, 211; criticisms of, 207 ff.; decision to attack Grant, 218; plans for Shiloh, 227 ff.; death, 240

Johnston, J. Stoddard: quoted, 260, 272, 289, 307-8, 314, 333, 358, 359, 391

Johnston, Joseph E., 178, 327; assigned command in Tennessee, 338 ff.; investigates Bragg's relationship with officers, 379; endorsement of Bragg, 380; reluctance to supersede Bragg, 384 ff.; ordered to assume command of Army of Tennessee, 387; quoted, 385-87

Johnston, William Preston, 263, 298; quoted, 265-66

Jomini, Antoine Henri, 20, 231; quoted, 21

Jones, Charles: quoted, 235

Jones, J. P., 381

Jones, John: quoted, 201

Jones, Robert T., 15, 23

Jones, Roger, 28; quoted, 29

Jones, Samuel, 197, 277, 342

Jones, Thomas W., 182

Jordan, Thomas, 218, 279, 280n, 342; quoted, 214

Judd, Henry B., 49-50

Kentucky: Confederate belief in secession of, 273-74; Union forces in, 292; Bragg's apprehensions about invasion of, 294 ff.; lack of enthusiasm for Confederate cause, 295 ff.; rival state governments, 297 ff.; defense problems of Confederates in, 299; Bragg's decision to leave, 321; hostility toward Confederates, 320n, 332 ff.

Ketchum, William H., 249

Keyes, Erasmus D., 34, 46

Kilburn, Charles L., 79, 94

King, William R., 135

Lane, Joseph, 131

Lay, John F., 275n

Lebanon Pike, 346, 358

Lee, Robert E., 178, 275, 280n, 281, 335

Lexington, Kentucky: E. K. Smith's plans to march to, 273, 292

Liddell, St. John R., 9, 10, 146-47, 318; quoted, 352, 362, 372

Lincoln, Abraham, 149, 159-60

Lockett, Samuel H., 239

Longstreet, James, 22

Louisiana: political affairs in, 146; secedes from Union, 151

Louisville, Kentucky: Buell's arrival at, 289, 294

Louisville and Nashville Railroad, 341

Love, Mary F., 123

Lovell, Mansfield, 191, 260; quoted, 153

Lyman, T. H., 357n

Lyon, Francis S.: quoted, 331, 382

Macarthy, Harry, 183

McCall, George A., 59

McClellan, George B., 21

McCook, Alexander M., 304, 305, 346, 352, 353

McCown, John P., 262, 267, 268, 277; at battle of Murfreesboro,

347, 349, 352n, 353, 364; quoted, 375
McCulloch, Ben, 197
McIntosh, James S., 58
Mackall, William W., 9, 342
McKee, William R., 79
Magee, John, 270-71
Mahan, Dennis H., 16 ff., 231; quoted, 17, 18, 19, 20
Mallory, Stephen R., 157
Manassas, Virginia: battle of (1861), 189, 201
Maney, George, 316
Mangum, Willie P., 105; quoted, 2, 5
Manigault, Arthur M., 344
Marching campaign: through Tennessee and Kentucky, 282 ff., 288; effective strength of Confederate army, 291
Marshall, Humphrey, 131, 293
Matamoros, Mexico, 59, 63
Maury, John H.: quoted, 265
Maxey, Samuel B.: 277, 342
Meade, George G.: quoted, 56
Memphis & Chattanooga Railroad, 266
Mexican War: preparations for, 52 ff.; siege of Fort Texas, 60 ff.; value of light batteries demonstrated in, 62; alternative strategies proposed by Taylor and Scott, 76 ff.
Mexico City: Scott's victory at, 99
Mickey's house, 219, 222, 223
Military college: at Alexandria, 147
Military theory: Mahan's influence on, 16 ff.; offensive vs. defensive concepts, 20, 200,

231, 348; staff reforms proposed by Bragg, 36 ff.; introduction of light batteries in Mexican War, 62 ff.; lesson of Buena Vista, 89; Bragg advises Davis on strategy, 199; technological changes underestimated by Confederate generals, 227, 231, 232; significance of Shiloh, 228, 251-52
Minie bullet ("ball"), 232
Minor, Benjamin B., 45
Mobile and Ohio Railroad, 208
Monterey, Mexico: battle of, 64 ff., 71-72
Moore, Thomas O., 146; quoted, 149
Mordecai, Jacob, 2
Morgan, John H., 273, 341
Munfordville, Kentucky: Union garrison surrenders, 285-86; abandoned by Bragg, 288
Murfreesboro, battle of: estimates of Confederate strength, 349-50n; Bragg's tactical plans, 350 ff., 363 ff.; casualties, 354 ff., 370, 372n; pause during night, 362; Confederate skirmishing renewed, 365 ff.; Union forces at, 371; Confederate retreat, 371, 372-73
Murfreesboro, Tennessee, 346 ff.
Musket, smoothbore, 231, 232
Myers, Abraham C., 48

Napoleon I: military concepts, 20, 231; quoted, 20-21
Nashville, Tennessee, 341, 346
Nashville & Chattanooga Railroad, 347
Nashville Pike, 347, 350, 354, 360

New Orleans Daily Delta (newspaper): "grape" incident reported in, 90
New York Herald (newspaper): cited, 92
Ninth Mississippi regiment, 357
"Notes on Our Army" (Bragg), 35
Nott, J. C.: quoted, 342

O'Bannon, L. W., 182, 280, 342
Oladowski, Hypolite, 163, 182
Orr, James L., 326, 332
Otey, James H., 117
Outlaw, David: quoted, 3, 102

Palo Alto, Texas: Taylor's victory at, 61
Pea Ridge, Arkansas, 213
Pegram, John: at battle of Murfreesboro, 349, 358, 359, 368
Pemberton, John C., 9, 12, 23, 339
Pender, William Dorsey, 163
Perryville, battle of, 310 ff., 319, 348, 352
Phelan, James, 326; quoted, 331
Pierce, Franklin, 134, 135
Pillow, Gideon, 368
Pittsburg Landing, Tennessee, 208 ff., 219, 221 ff., 255
Plundering: by Confederate troops, 216, 258
Poinsett, Joel R., 28
Point Isabel: depot established at, 58
Polk, James K., 47, 53, 77
Polk, Leonidas, 205, 210, 214n, 216, 221, 262, 263, 275, 298, 312; disregards Bragg's orders, 300 ff., 306, 307; misinforms

Bragg about Federals, 308-9; at battle of Perryville, 318; criticism of Bragg's campaign, 320n; reports to Davis, 326-27; military shortcomings, 328-29n; at battle of Murfreesboro, 347, 349 ff., 360, 364 ff., 378-79; quoted, 246, 391
Pond, Preston, Jr., 221
Pope, John, 96, 256
Prentiss, Benjamin M., 236, 242
Price, Sterling, 268, 281, 321
Professionalism, dogma of, 20, 22, 205
Pugh, I. C., 241
Pugh, James L., 202; quoted, 329, 331

Railroads: Pensacola-Mobile line completed, 196; disorganized conditions in Confederacy, 216; troop movements dependent on, 261, 268; Bragg's strategic use of, 271
Randolph, George W., 338, 339
Rebel (newspaper): cited, 375
Recruitment, army, 29-30
Resaca de la Palma: Taylor's victory at, 61
Reynolds, John F., 35, 53
Richmond, Virginia: Confederate government transferred to, 177
Richmond Enquirer (newspaper): cited, 177
Richmond Whig (newspaper): cited, 325
Ridgley, S. G., 42, 61, 74
Rifles: improvements in, 232
Ringgold, Samuel, 53, 61, 74

Rio Grande: Fort Texas established on, 59
Robertson, Felix H., 366; quoted, 369
Roland, Charles P., 142*n*
Root, Elihu, 38
Rosecrans, William S.: at battle of Murfreesboro, 344 ff., 356
Round Forest, 356, 360, 361, 365
Rousseau, Lovell H.: quoted, 97
Ruggles, Daniel, 192, 206, 210, 212, 220, 244
Russell, William H.: quoted, 176

Saltillo, Mexico, 79
Sandel, John, 118
Savage, John H.: quoted, 389
Scales, J. J., 356
Scheibert, Justus: quoted, 234
Scott, Winfield, 8, 48; Bragg's attempts to discredit, 36 ff., 95; dispute with Taylor, 76 ff.; quoted, 32
Secession, 149
Sectionalism: evidence of, after Mexican War, 105 ff.
Seddon, James A., 338, 384
Sedgwick, John, 9, 23
Seminole Indians in Florida, 26 ff.
Semmes, Thomas Jenkins, 376
Seven Days' Battle, 275
Seward, William H., 159
Shaw, William T., 241
Shelbyville, Kentucky: Confederate abandonment of, 300
Sheridan, Philip H.: quoted, 353
Sherman, John, 148
Sherman, Thomas W., 74
Sherman, William Tecumseh (Cump), 30, 35, 50, 147 ff.;

Union commander in Tennessee, 209 ff.; at Shiloh, 228; quoted, 22, 150, 152, 153
Shields, James, 131
Shiloh, battle of: a strategic surprise, 228; progress of, 229 ff., 247 ff., Confederate tactics, 234, 348, 352; Confederate defeat, 249
Shorter, John Gill, 253
Shover, William H., 79, 94
Sill, Joshua W., 304, 305
Simms, William E., 332
Sitterson, J. Carlyle, 142*n*
Sixteenth Tennessee regiment, 357
Sixteenth U.S. Infantry regiment, 354
Sixth Kentucky regiment, 370
Slaughter, James E., 182, 279, 280*n*, 342
Slavery, 142
Smith, Edmund Kirby, 266; relations with Bragg, 272 ff.; in Kentucky, 281, 295; decision to march to Lexington, 292; failure to join Bragg in Bardstown, 293, 294; reports to Davis, 326-27; at battle of Murfreesboro, 347
Smith, Gustavus W., 153
Smith, Preston, 277, 293, 312, 381; quoted, 329
Smith, Robert H., 202
Southern Literary Messenger (periodical), 35 ff., 45 ff.
Southern Quarterly Review (periodical), 53
Sparta, Tennessee, 282-83
Spence, Philip B.: quoted, 265
Stanley, W. A.: quoted, 234-35

420 INDEX

Stark, W. E., 178
Stevens, Isaac I.: quoted, 12
Stevenson, Carter L., 293, 363
Stewart, Alexander P., 316; quoted, 363
Stewart, Joseph, 49
Stone's River, 347, 349, 366
Sturgis, Samuel D., 63n
"Subaltern, A," see Bragg, Braxton
Sumner, Charles, 144

Taylor, Richard, 145, 182, 278, 279
Taylor, Zachary, 51, 55, 106; military ability, 54, 56; strategy and tactics at Monterey, 65 ff., 72; disagreements with Scott and Polk, 76 ff.; strategy and tactics at Buena Vista, 89; "grape" incident, 90 ff.; quoted, 77
Tennessee: critical situation in, 204 ff.; plans for invasion of, 267 ff.; see also Army of Tennessee
Tennessee, East: Confederates return to, 323
Tennessee, Middle: plans for invasion of, 272 ff.; plans for advance to Nashville, 337
Tennessee and Ohio Railroad, 206
Tennessee River, 199
Texas: threatened by Mexican invasion, 52 ff.
Textbooks: in West Point curriculum, 11
Thibodaux, Louisiana, 108
Third Artillery regiment, 26
Thirteenth and Twentieth Con-
solidated Louisiana Infantry, 361
Thirtieth Mississippi regiment, 356
Thirty-fourth Illinois regiment, 354
Thirty-ninth Indiana regiment, 354
Thomas, Francis J., 94
Thomas, George H., 31, 35, 53, 94, 107, 346
Thompson, J. O.: quoted, 357n
Thornton, Seth, 59, 63
Toombs, Robert, 132, 201
Towson, Nathaniel, 109
Trans-Mississippi Department, 197-98
Trapier, James H., 262, 278
Triune Road, 347, 349
Tupelo, Mississippi: Confederate army retreats to, 258 ff.
Turner, Daniel, 6
Twenty-fourth Alabama regiment, 356
Twenty-sixth Alabama regiment, 356
Twiggs, David E., 54, 56, 106
Tyler, John, 43

United States Military Academy, see West Point
Urquhart, David: quoted, 214, 259, 310-11

Van Dorn, Earl, 198, 212, 213, 218, 256, 266, 269, 281, 295; defeat at Corinth, 321, 323; destroys Union supplies, 341
Vera Cruz, Mexico, 76
Vicksburg, Mississippi, 266
Virginia: secession of, 177

Vogdes, Israel, 160, 166
Volunteer troops: Bragg's opinion of, 87 ff.; in Confederate army, 162 ff., 192, 194; resentment against Bragg, 254

Walker, H. W., 182
Walker, Leroy Pope, 197
Walker, Lucius M., 262, 278
Walker, William H. T., 9; quoted, 22, 188-89
Wallace, Lew, 228
Wallace, W. H. L., 236
Walter, H. W.: quoted, 282-83
Warfare, offensive, 19, 20
Warrenton, North Carolina, 1 ff., 102
Warrenton Female Academy, 2
Warrenton Male Academy, 3, 4
Washington, John M., 103
Watkins, Sam R.: quoted, 218, 265
Watson, William: quoted, 255
Watts, Thomas H., 264n
Weigley, Russell F., 17n
West Point: academic inadequacies, 6; severity of discipline, 7 ff.; curriculum and methods of instruction, 10 ff., 232
Wharton, John A., 275n, 313, 316, 349, 352, 368
Wheeler, Joseph, 275n, 348-49, 381; quoted, 185, 286-88
Whistler, William, 56
Wigfall, Louis T., 215n, 326, 332, 385; quoted, 388
Wilcox, Cadmus M.: quoted, 56-57
Wilder, John T., 285-86
Williams, Kenneth P., 367; quoted, 292, 294n, 365
Withers, Jones M., 195, 197, 210, 221, 241, 244, 276-77, 353, 381; quoted, 203
Wood, Sterling A. M., 302, 318; quoted, 352
Woodbridge, Francis, 15
Wool, John E., 49, 79, 86-87, 96-97
Worth, William J., 54, 56, 69-70

Yancey, William L., 264n, 326
Yandell, D. W.: quoted, 275, 324

Grady McWhiney is Lyndon Baines Johnson Professor of American History, Texas Christian University. He received his B.S. from Centenary College of Louisiana, his M.A. from Louisiana State University, and his Ph.D. from Columbia University. He is author of *Southerners and Other Americans*, *Cracker Culture: Celtic Ways in the Old South*, co-author of *Attack and Die: Civil War Military Tactics and the Southern Heritage* (with Perry D. Jamieson), general editor of *Primary Sources of American History*, editor of *Grant, Lee, Lincoln and the Radicals: Essays on Civil War Leadership*, *Reconstruction and the Freedmen*, and co-editor of *To Mexico with Taylor and Scott, 1845–1847* (with Sue B. McWhiney), *Historical Vistas: Reading in United States History* (with Robert Wiebe), and *Robert E. Lee's Dispatches to Jefferson Davis, 1862–1865* (with Douglas S. Freeman).